Stitch by Stitch

Volume 5

TORSTAR BOOKS
NEW YORK · TORONTO

Stitch by Stitch

TORSTAR BOOKS INC.
300 E.42ND STREET
NEW YORK, NY 10017

Knitting and crochet abbreviations

approx=approximately
beg=begin(ning)
ch=chain(s)
cm=centimeter(s)
cont=continue(ing)
dc=double crochet
dec=decreas(e)(ing)
dtr=double triple
foll=follow(ing)
g=gram(s)
grp=group(s)
dc=half double crochet
in=inch(es)
inc=increas(e)(ing)
K=knit
oz=ounce(s)
P=purl
patt=pattern
psso=pass slipped stitch over
rem=remain(ing)
rep=repeat
RS=right side
sc=single crochet
sl=slip
sl st=slip stitch
sp=space(s)
st(s)=stitch(es)
tbl=through back of loop(s)
tog=together
tr=triple crochet
WS=wrong side
wyib=with yarn in back
wyif=with yarn in front
yd=yard(s)
yo=yarn over

A guide to the pattern sizes

		10	12	14	16	18	20
Bust	in	32½	34	36	38	40	42
	cm	83	87	92	97	102	107
Waist	in	25	26½	28	30	32	34
	cm	64	67	71	76	81	87
Hips	in	34½	36	38	40	42	44
	cm	88	92	97	102	107	112

Library of Congress Cataloging in Publication Data
Main entry under title:

Stitch by stitch.

Includes index.
1. Needlework. I. Torstar Books (Firm)
TT705.S74 1984 746.4 84-111
ISBN 0-920269-00-1 (set)

98765432

Printed in Belgium

ISBN 0–920269–05–2 (Volume 5)

Step-by-Step Crochet Course

Step-by-Step Knitting Course

Contents

Crochet/COURSE 19

*Making shell patterns
*Simple shell pattern
*Open shell pattern
*Stitch Wise: shell trellis pattern
*Pattern for a sleeveless jacket

Making shell patterns

Shell patterns are among the most popular crochet stitches, and fortunately, there is an amazing variety of them from which to choose. One advantage of shell patterns is that they look good whether worked in a fine crochet cotton or in a thicker knitting yarn.
The basic principle of shell patterns—working three or more stitches into one stitch—can be used in many ways. If the stitches are all the same kind, the shell produced will be a simple fan shape. Alternatively, by working a series of different stitches which gradually increase and decrease in height—for example, from a single crochet through to a triple and back to a single crochet—you can make a dome-shaped shell. For an open effect you can work one chain between each stitch. Whatever types of stitches are used, the pattern will usually call for an uneven number of stitches to be worked in each shell.
Here we give you step-by-step directions for two different patterns. Once you have practiced them you will find the shell stitch featured in the sleeveless jacket simple to work. On page 7 we introduce Stitch Wise, an occasional feature containing various stitch patterns.

Simple shell pattern

This pattern is a perfect example of double and single crochets used alternately on each row to produce an all-over shell pattern. It is worked over a multiple of 6 chains with 2 extra for the turning chain. Our sample uses a knitting worsted yarn and a size G (4.50mm) hook and is worked on a foundation of 26 chains.

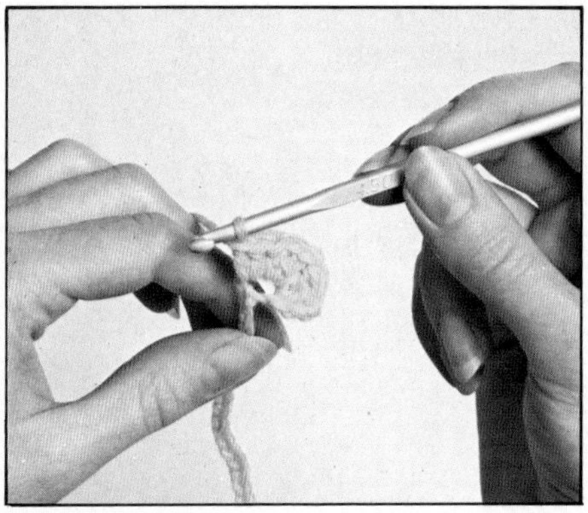

1 Make the first shell by working 3 doubles, 1 chain and 3 doubles all into the 5th chain from the hook. The first 4 chains will count as the first single crochet and 2 chains.

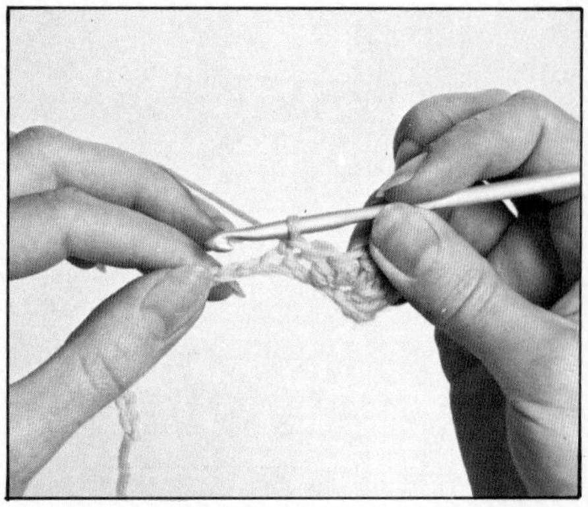

2 Skip the next 2 chains and work 1 single crochet into the following chain.

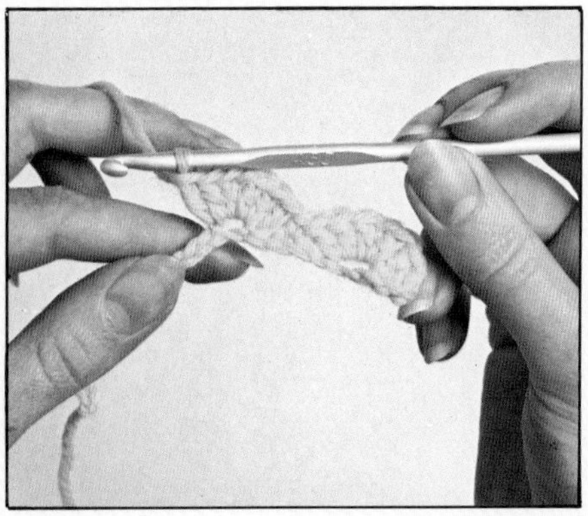

3 Skip the next 2 chains. Now work another shell in the same way as before into the next chain.

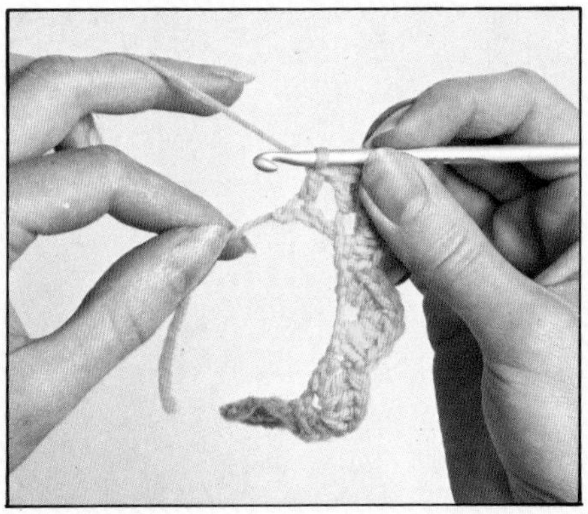

4 Continue to repeat steps 2 and 3 all the way along the chain until only 3 chains remain unworked. Skip the next 2 chains and work 1 double into the last chain.

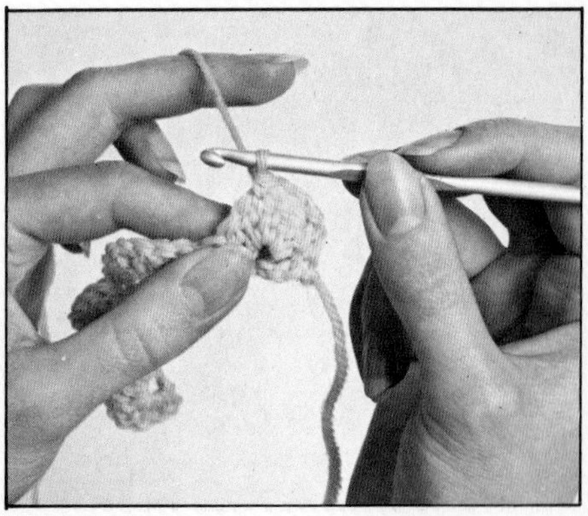

5 Turn and work 3 chains as the first double. Now work 1 single crochet into the center chain between the doubles in the first shell.

Fred Mancini

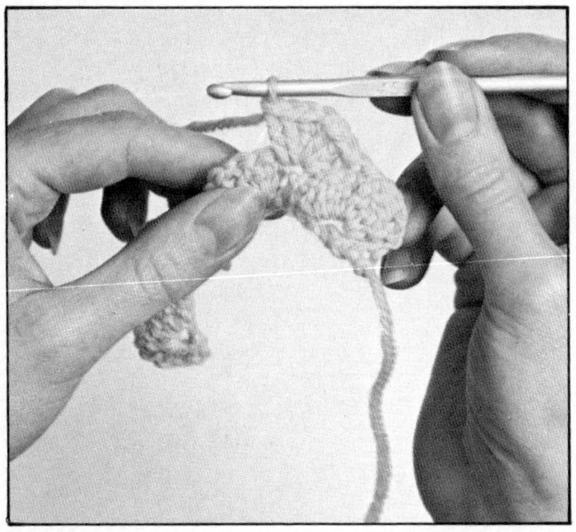

6 Now work 1 shell in the same way as before into the single crochet between the first and 2nd shells.

7 Continue to work 1 single crochet into the middle of each shell and 1 shell into each single crochet between the shells in the previous row until 1 shell remains unworked.

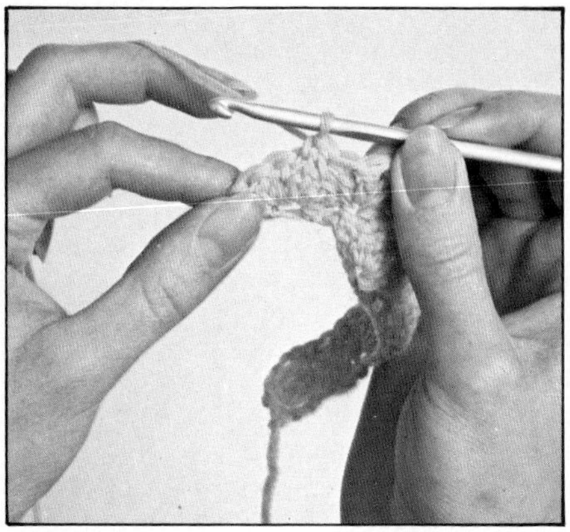

8 Now work 1 single crochet into the center of the last shell.

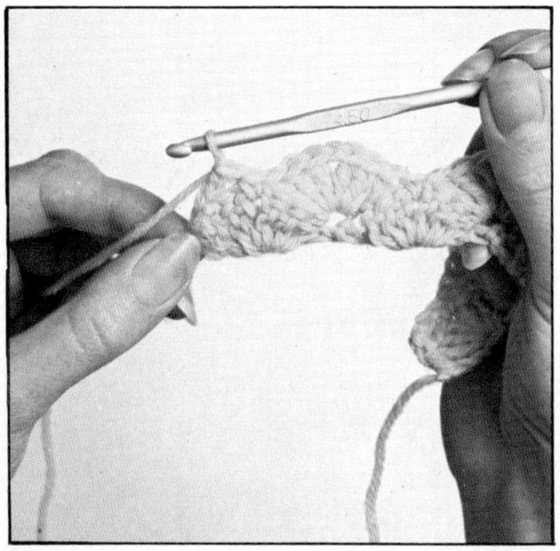

9 Work 1 double into the turning chain of the previous row to complete the 2nd row.

10 Turn and work 2 chains to count as the first single crochet. Now work 1 shell into the first single crochet of the previous row.

11 Now work 1 single crochet into the center of the next shell.

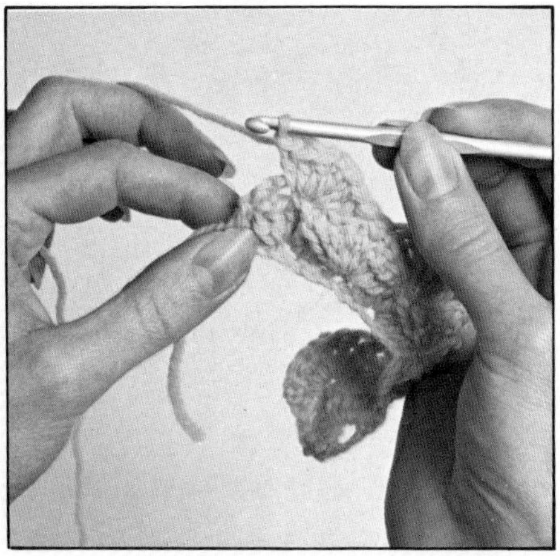

12 Continue to work across the row as before, working 1 shell into each single crochet and 1 single crochet into each shell until only the turning chain remains unworked in the previous row.

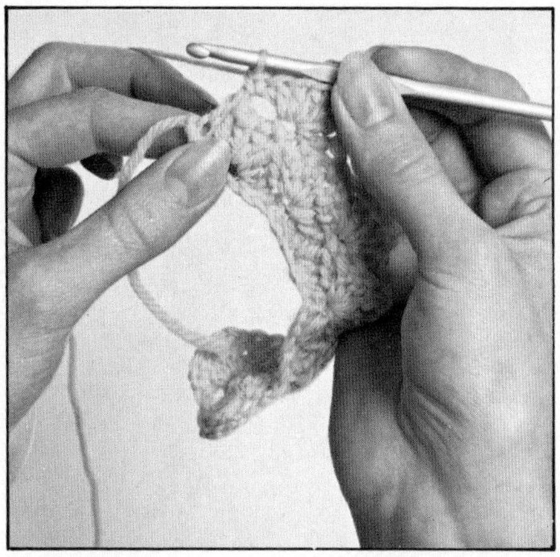

13 Now work 1 single crochet into the turning chain to complete 3rd row.

14 Continue to alternate the shell on each row in same way, beginning each subsequent row with either 2 chains for a single crochet or 3 chains for a double to keep the pattern correct.

continued

Open shell pattern

This very simple pattern produces a pretty, open effect which is particularly effective when worked in crochet cotton. Our sample is based on 31 chains and worked in a sport yarn with a size F (4.00mm) hook. If you wish to make the sample larger or smaller, use any multiple of 4 chains plus 3 extra for the turning chain.

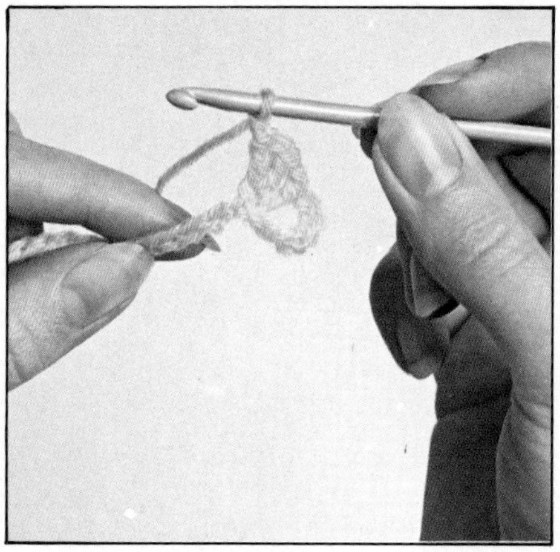

1 Make the first shell by working (1 double and 1 chain) 3 times, all into the 7th chain from the hook.

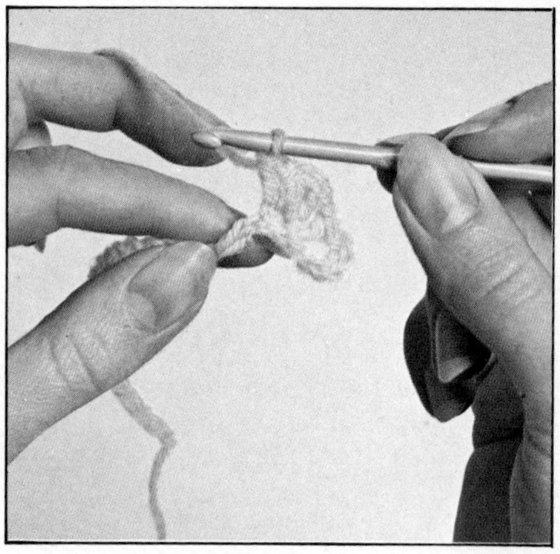

2 Now work 1 more double into the same chain so that there are 4 doubles with 1 chain between each in the completed shell.

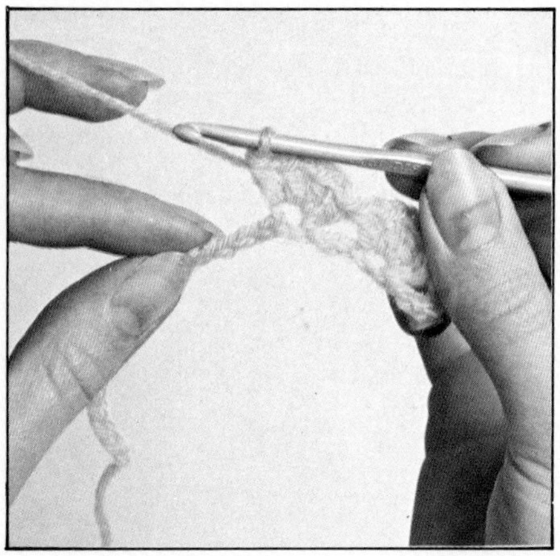

3 Skip the next 3 chains and work another shell in exactly the same way into the next chain. The center of the shell is the 2nd 1-chain space.

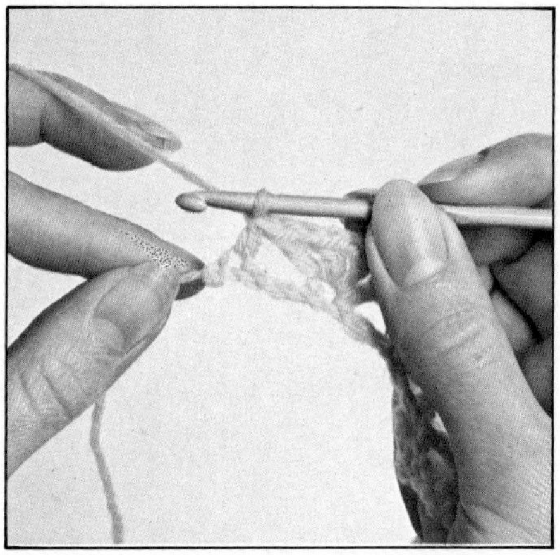

4 Repeat step 3 all along the chain until 4 chains remain unworked. Skip the next 3 chains and work 1 double into the last chain to complete the first row.

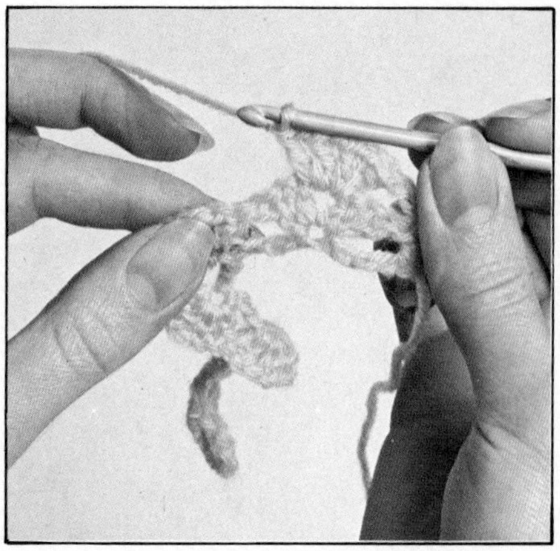

5 Turn and work 3 chains to count as the first double. Work 1 shell in the same way as before into the center 1-chain space of the first shell in the previous row.

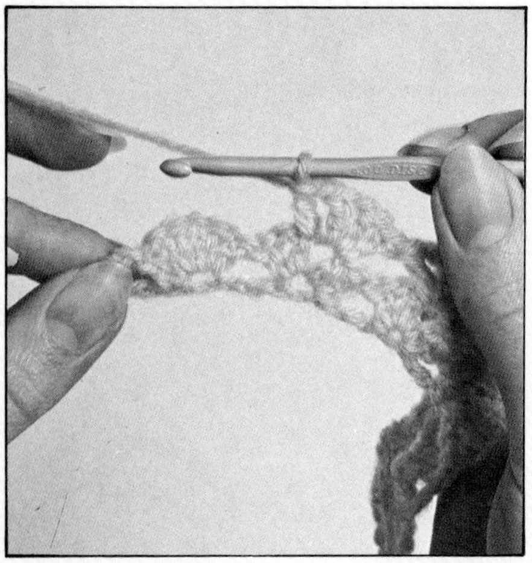

6 Work 1 shell into the center of each shell in the same way all along the row until the last shell only remains unworked.

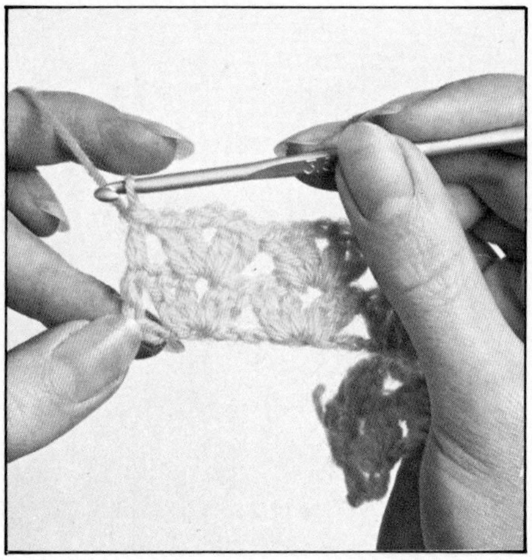

7 Work 1 shell into the last shell. Now work 1 double into the turning chain to complete the 2nd row.

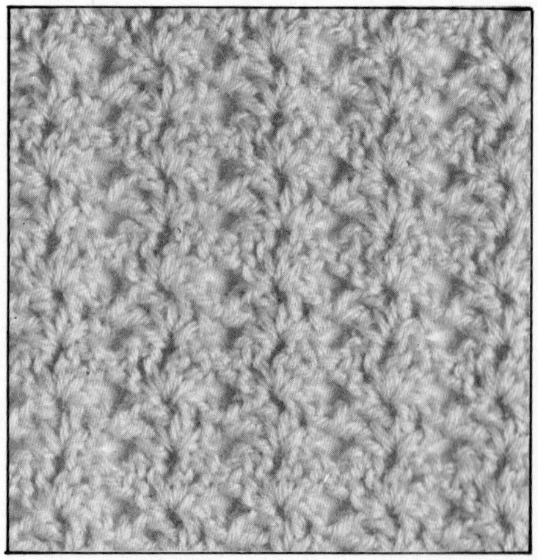

8 Continue to work each row in the same way, repeating steps 5-7 each time.

Fred Mancini

Stitch Wise

Shell trellis pattern

This classic pattern, in which the shells are worked in vertical lines with chain bars between each, has many variations. Our version combines doubles, single crochets and chain spaces to make a very pretty pattern, which looks good worked in either a fine or thick yarn. The basic method for working shell patterns has been covered in this course. Make a sample of this stitch for future reference.

Make 32 chains.

Base row 1sc into 8th ch from hook, *3ch, skip next 2ch, 1sc into next ch, 2ch, skip next 2ch, 1dc into next ch, 2ch, skip next 2ch, 1sc into next ch, rep from * to last 6ch, 3ch, skip next 2ch, 1sc into next ch, 2ch, skip next 2ch, 1 double into last ch. Turn. 9ch sp.

1st row 2ch, skip first 2ch sp, * work (2dc, 1ch, 2dc, 1ch, 2dc) all into next 3ch sp—called 1 shell—; 1 ch, 1 sc into next dc in previous row, 1ch, rep from * to last 3ch sp, 1 shell into this sp, skip next 2ch, 1sc into next chain. Turn.

2nd row 5ch, * work 1sc into space between first 2 pairs of doubles in first shell, 3ch, 1sc into space between next 2 pairs of doubles in same shell, 2ch, 1dc into next sc in previous row, 2ch, rep from * to last shell, 1sc into space between first 2 pairs of doubles in last shell, 3ch, 1sc into space between next 2 pairs of doubles in same shell, 2ch, 1dc into turning chain. Turn. These last 2 rows form patt and are repeated throughout.

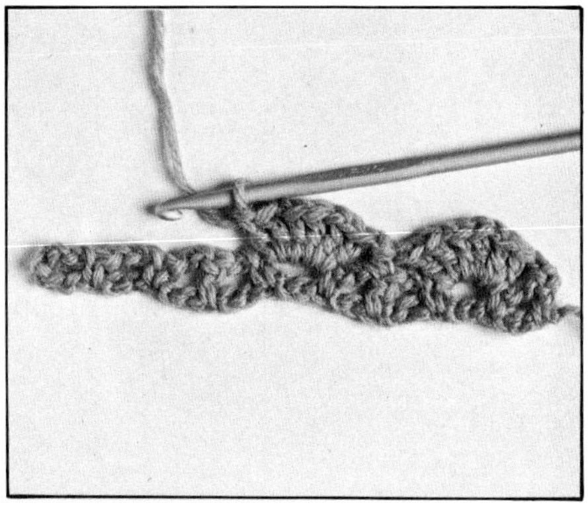

A shell worked into the 3 chain space made in the base row.

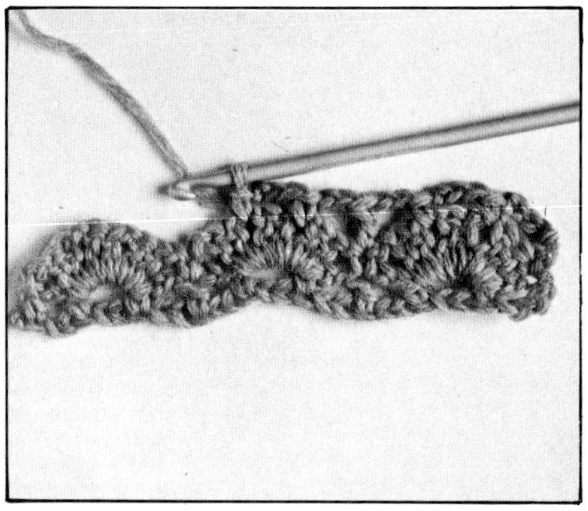

A single crochet worked into each side of the shell to form the base for the shell in the next row.

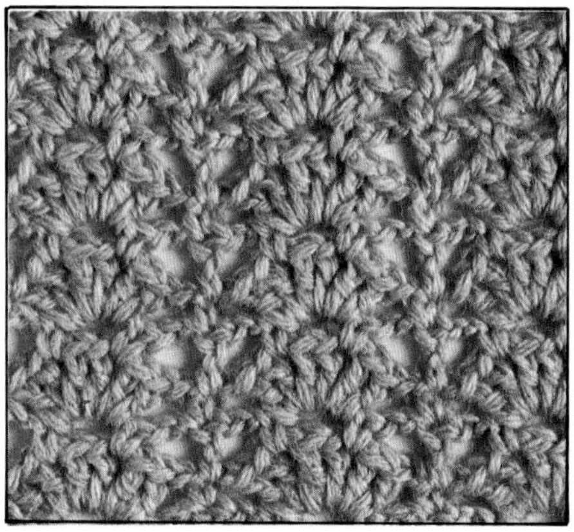

Several rows of the completed pattern.

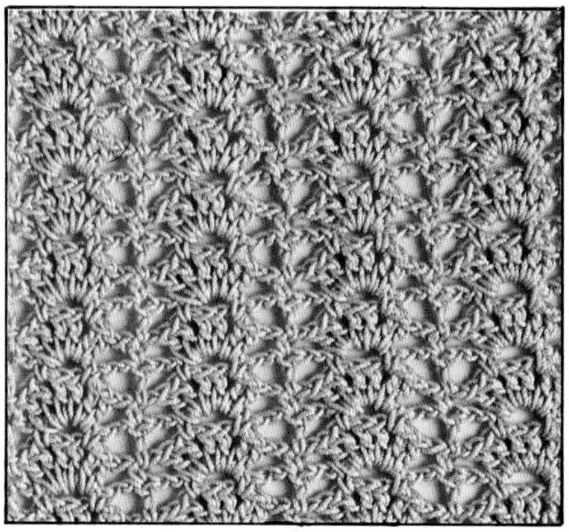

The versatility of crochet—the same stitch worked in a fine crochet cotton.

Long and lacy

This attractive sleeveless jacket can be worn in many ways. This version—worked in a shell stitch using a soft mohair yarn—is shown here belted over a blouse, but it looks just as good worn loose with a sweater and skirt.

Sizes

To fit 34[36:38]in (87[92:97]cm) bust.
Length 32in (81cm).

Note Directions for larger sizes are in brackets []. Where there is only one set of figures it applies to all sizes.

Materials

20[22:22]oz (550[600:600]g) of a medium weight mohair yarn
Size H (5.50mm) crochet hook

Gauge

1 patt repeat measures $2\frac{1}{4}$in (6cm) in width and 2 patt repeats measure $2\frac{1}{4}$in (6cm) in depth.

Left front

* * Using size H (5.50mm) hook chain 33[35:38].

Base row 1sc into 3rd ch from hook, 1sc into each ch to end. Turn. 32[34:37] sc.

Next row 2ch to count as first sc, 1sc into each sc to end, working last sc into the turning ch. Turn.

Rep last row 3 times more. * *

Commence patt.

The patt rows for each size are given separately. Follow appropriate directions for size that you are making.

1st size only

1st row (RS) 3ch to count as first dc, *skip next 3sc, 7dc all into next sc—shell formed, skip next 3sc, 1dc into each of next 2sc, rep from * twice more, skip next 3sc, 4dc into last sc—half shell formed. Turn.

2nd row 5ch to count as first sc and 3ch, *1dc into each of next 2 single dc, 3ch, 1sc into center dc of next shell, 3ch, rep from * twice more, 1 dc into last dc. Turn.

3rd row 3ch, *1 shell into next sc at center of previous shell, 1dc into each of next 2dc, rep from * twice more, 4dc into 2nd of the 5ch. Turn.

The 2nd and 3rd rows form patt for the 1st size.

2nd size only

1st row (RS) 3ch to count as first dc, 1dc into each of next 2sc, *skip next 3sc, 7dc all into next sc—shell formed, skip next 3sc, 1dc into each of next 2sc, rep from * twice more, skip next 3sc, 4dc into last sc—half shell formed. Turn.

2nd row 5ch to count as first sc and 3ch, *1dc into each of next 2 single dc, 3ch, 1sc into center of next shell, 3ch, rep

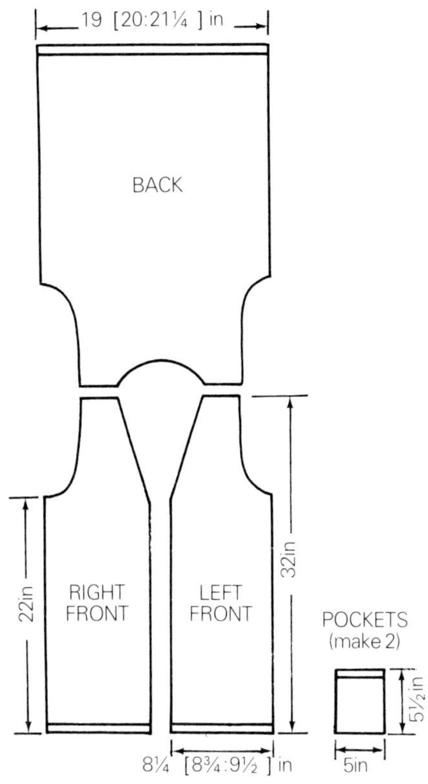

from * twice more, 1dc into each of last 3dc. Turn.
3rd row 3ch, 1dc into each of next 2dc, *1 shell into sc at center of previous shell, 1dc into each of next 2dc, rep from * twice more, 4dc into 2nd of the 5ch. Turn.
The 2nd and 3rd rows form patt for the 2nd size.
3rd size only
1st row (RS) 3ch to count as first dc, 3dc into first sc, skip next 3sc, 1dc into each of next 2sc, *skip next 3sc, 7dc all into next sc—shell formed, skip next 3sc, 1dc into each of next 2sc, rep from * twice more, skip next 3sc, 4dc into last sc—half shell formed. Turn.
2nd row 5ch to count as first sc and 3ch, *1dc into each of next 2 single dc, 3ch, 1sc into center dc of next shell, 3ch, rep from * twice more, 1dc into each of next 2 single dc, 3ch, 1sc into last dc. Turn.
3rd row 3ch, 3dc into first sc, *1dc into each of next 2dc, 1 shell into sc at center of previous shell, rep from * twice more, 1dc into each of next 2dc, 4dc into 2nd of the 5ch. Turn.
The 2nd and 3rd rows form patt for the 3rd size.
All sizes
Cont in patt until work measures 22in (56cm) from beg, ending with a 3rd patt row.
Shape armhole
Next row Patt to last 9sts (including turning ch), turn and leave these sts unworked.
Shape neck
1st row Patt to within last 4ch, work 2dc into ch, now work 2dc tog.
2nd row 2ch to count as first st, 1dc into each of next 2dc, work in patt to end of row. Turn.
3rd row Patt to within last 2sts, work 2dc tog. Turn.
Cont to dec one st at neck edge on every other row in the same way until 16[18:21] sts rem.
Next row 4ch, 1sc into center dc of next shell, patt to end. Turn.
Next row Patt to within last sc, 4dc into last sc, 1dc into each of next 2ch. Turn. 16sts.
Rep these 2 rows until armhole measures 10in (25cm) from beg. Fasten off.

Right front
Work as given for left front from * * to * *
Commence patt.
1st size only
1st row (RS) 3ch to count as first dc, 3dc into first st, skip next 3sc, *1dc into each of next 2sc, skip next 3sc, 1 shell into next sc, skip next 3sc, rep from * twice more, 1dc into last dc. Turn.
This sets patt for the 1st size.
2nd size only
1st row (RS) 3ch to count as first dc, 3dc into first st, skip next 3sc, *1dc into each of next 2sc, skip next 3sc, 1 shell into next sc, skip next 3sc, rep from * twice more, 1dc into each of last 3sc. Turn.
This sets patt for 2nd size.
3rd size only
1st row (RS) 3ch to count as first dc, 3dc into first st, skip next 3sc, *1 dc into each of next 2sc, skip next 3sc, 1 shell into next sc, skip next 3sc, rep from * twice more, 1dc into each of next 3sc, skip next 3sc, 4dc into last sc. Turn.
This sets patt for 3rd size.
All sizes
Cont in patt as set until work measures same as left front to armhole, ending with a 3rd patt row. Fasten off and turn work.
Shape armhole
Next row Skip first 9sts. Rejoin yarn to next st, 2ch, patt to end. Turn.
Complete as given for left front, reversing neck shaping.

Back
Using size H (5.50mm) hook chain 73[77:83]. Work base row as given for left front. 72[76:82] sts. Work 4 rows in sc.
Commence patt.
1st size only
1st row (RS) 3ch to count as first dc, *skip next 3sc, 1 shell into next sc, skip next 3sc, 1dc into each of next 2sc, rep from * to within last 8sc, skip next 3sc, 1 shell into next sc, skip next 3sc, 1dc into last sc. Turn.
This sets patt for the 1st size.
2nd size only
1st row (RS) 3ch to count as first dc, 1dc into each of next 2sc, *skip next 3sc, 1 shell into next sc, skip next 3sc, 1dc into each of next 2sc, rep from * to within last sc, 1dc into last sc. Turn.
This sets patt for the 2nd size.
3rd size only
1st row (RS) 3ch to count as first dc, 3dc into first sc, skip next 3sc, 1dc into each of next 2sc, *skip next 3sc, 1 shell into next sc, skip next 3sc, 1dc into each of next 2sc, rep from * to within last 4sc, skip next 3sc, 4dc into last sc. Turn.
This sets patt for the 3rd size.
All sizes
Cont in patt as set until work measures same as left front to armholes, ending with a 3rd patt row. Fasten off and turn work.
Shape armholes
Next row Skip first 9sts, rejoin yarn to next st, work 2ch, patt to within last 9sts, turn and leave these 9sts unworked.
Cont in patt until armholes measure same as left front, ending with a 3rd patt row. Fasten off.

Pockets (make 2)
Using size H (5.50mm) hook chain 21.
Base row 4dc into 3rd ch from hook, skip next 3ch, 1dc into each of next 2ch, skip next 3ch, 1 shell into next ch, skip next 3ch, 1dc into each of next 2ch, skip next 3ch, 4dc into last ch. Turn.
Work 6 rows in patt as set.
Next row Work 1sc into each st to end, dec 4sts evenly across the row. Turn.
Work 4 more rows in sc. Fasten off.

To finish
Do not press. Join shoulder seams together.
Front border
With RS of right front facing and beg at lower edge, work a row of sc up right front to shoulder, working 1sc into each row end of border and 2sc into each patt row end. Work 1sc into each st across back of neck and now work in sc down left front as before. Turn and work 4 rows in sc. Fasten off.
Armhole borders (alike)
Beg at side edge and work a row of sc around armhole edge, working 1sc into each st at underarm and 2sc into each patt row end.
1st row 1ch, now work 1sc into each of next 3sts, (work next 2sc tog) 3 times, now work 1sc into each sc until 10sts rem, (work 2sc tog) 3 times, 1sc into each of next 3sts, 1sc into turning ch. Turn.
2nd row 1ch, 1sc into each st to end. Turn.
3rd row 1ch, 1sc into each of next 3sts, (work 2sc tog) 4 times, 1sc into each st until 11sts rem unworked, (work 2sc tog) 4 times, 1sc into each of next 2sts, 1sc into turning ch. Turn.
4th row As 2nd row. Fasten off.
Join the side seams and sew the pockets to the fronts.

John Hutchinson

Crochet/COURSE 20

- *An introduction to Aran-style crochet
- *Uneven berry stitch
- *Lattice stitch
- *Pattern for an Aran-style afghan

An introduction to Aran-style crochet

"Aran" is a term which is rightly associated with knitting, rather than crochet. It refers to the intricate and highly textured knitting stitches that originated on the Aran Islands of Inishmore, Inisheer and Inishmaan, which lie off the west coast of Ireland. Although crochet cannot duplicate exactly the appearance of Aran knitting, it can create patterns that resemble some of the Aran stitches, such as seed (or moss) stitch, berry stitch and many others. This Aran-style crochet has its own appeal, and devotees of crochet appreciate its relative simplicity, compared to knitting, as well as its pleasing appearance.

The following step-by-step directions are intended to help you work two of the more complicated stitches used to make the afghan featured at the end of this course.

Uneven berry stitch

This simple, but effective, stitch is worked by drawing the yarn several times through the same stitch, then working all the loops off the hook to make a bobble or "berry." The size of the bobble depends on the number of times the yarn is drawn through the stitch (and also, of course, on the thickness of the yarn). Practice making the bobbles with a bulky or Aran-type yarn and a size I (6.00mm) hook. Make 20 chains and start the sample by working 18 single crochets into the chain so that there are 19 stitches in all, including the turning chain.

1 Begin the first row of the pattern with 1 chain. This will be the WS of the work. Skip the first single crochet. Now wind the yarn over the hook and insert it into the next single crochet.

2 Wind the yarn over the hook and draw it through the stitch, pulling up the yarn so that the loop is quite loose.

3 Wind the yarn over the hook and draw it through the first loop on the hook. 3 loops now remain on the hook.

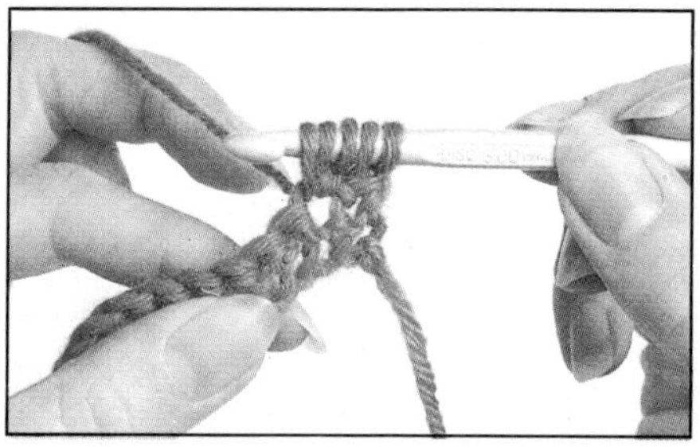

4 Wind the yarn over the hook and insert it once more into the same stitch as before. Repeat step 2 once more. 5 loops on the hook.

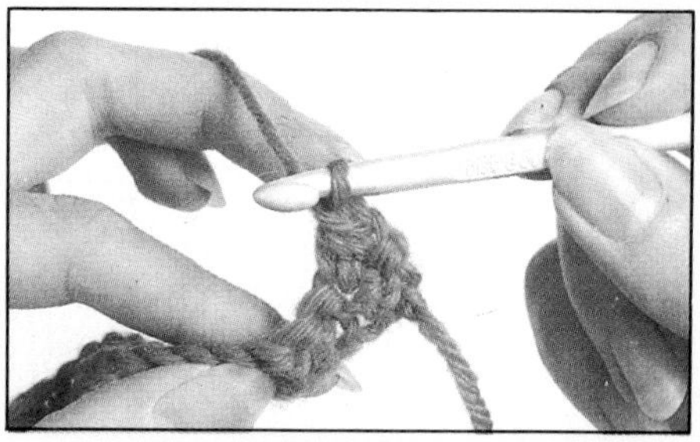

5 Wind the yarn over the hook and draw it through the first 4 loops—2 loops remain. Now draw yarn in same way through last 2 loops to form bobble.

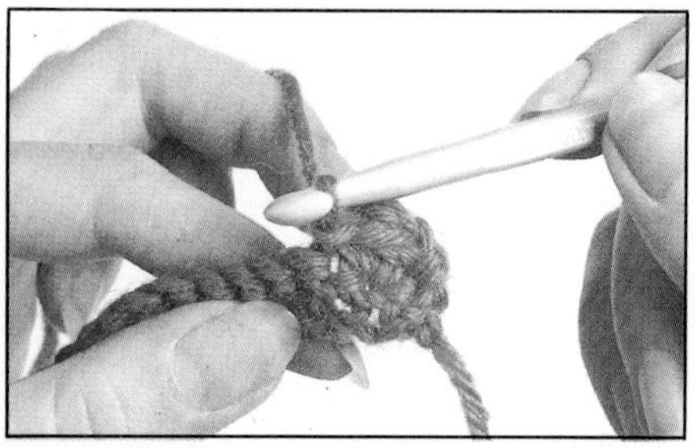

6 Work 1 slip stitch into the next single crochet to hold the bobble in place.

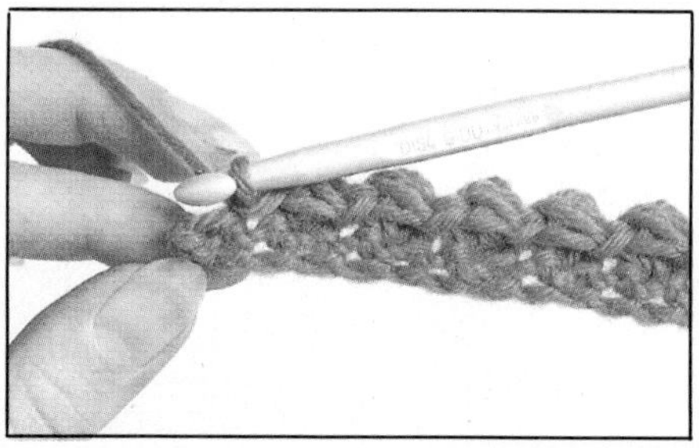

7 Work 1 bobble into next stitch, then 1 slip stitch into the next stitch, alternately until 2 stitches remain.

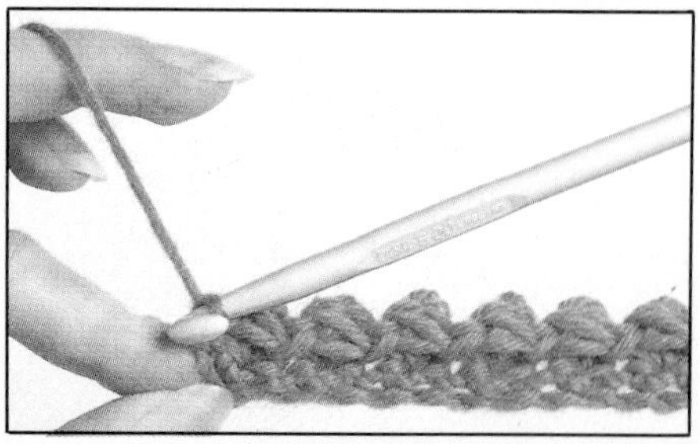

8 Work 1 bobble into the next stitch and then 1 single crochet into the turning chain to complete the first row.

Fred Mancini

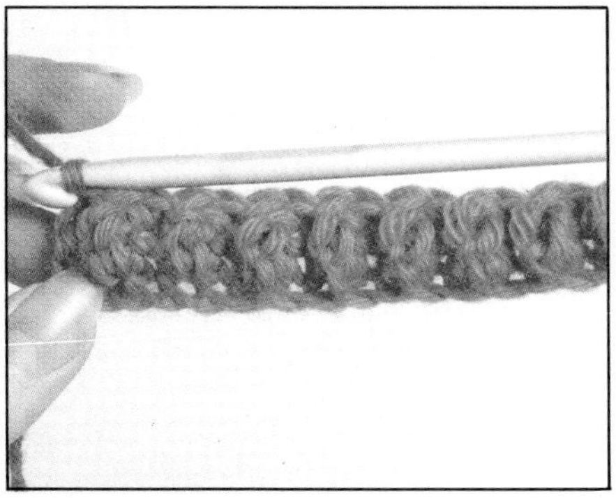

9 Turn. The 2nd row is worked on the RS of the work. Make 1 chain and skip the first single crochet. Now work a slip stitch into the top of each bobble and 1 single crochet into each slip stitch across the row Work the last single crochet into the turning chain.

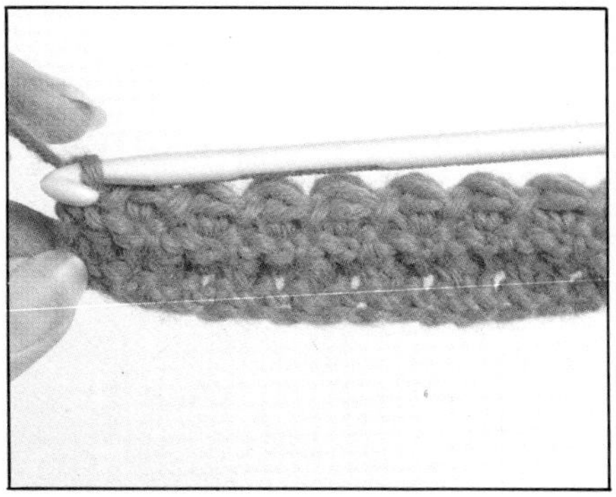

10 The 3rd row is worked like the first, but to alter the position of the bobbles, you must work 1 slip stitch into each slip stitch and 1 bobble into each single crochet of the previous row.

11 The bobbles are alternated in the same way each time. You work a slip stitch into each berry and a single crochet into each slip stitch on RS rows and a bobble into each single crochet and a slip stitch into each slip stitch on WS rows. Alter the row ends accordingly to keep the pattern correct.

Lattice stitch

This highly textured stitch with a lattice or honeycomb effect is achieved by working triples onto the front of the fabric, working around the stem of the stitch rather than into the top of the stitches in the normal way. It is important to place the hook correctly, but once you have mastered this technique you will find the pattern quite simple to work. The step-by-step directions show you exactly how this is done.

To work the sample make 22 chains using a bulky or Aran-type yarn, and work 20 doubles into this chain, including the turning chain.

1 Begin to work the pattern on the front of these doubles. Wind yarn twice over the hook and insert hook into base of the 3rd double, working from right to left so that your hook passes through the stitch.

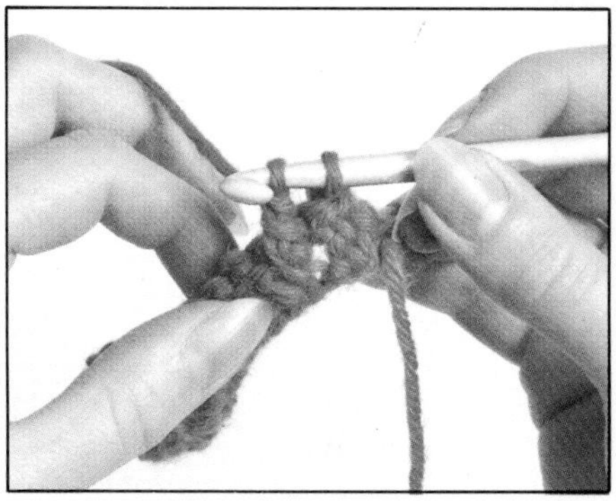

2 Yarn over hook and draw a loop of yarn through the stitch to give 4 loops on hook. Now wind yarn over hook and draw it through first 2 loops. Repeat this action once more through second 2 loops. This makes 1 open triple, leaving 2 loops on hook.

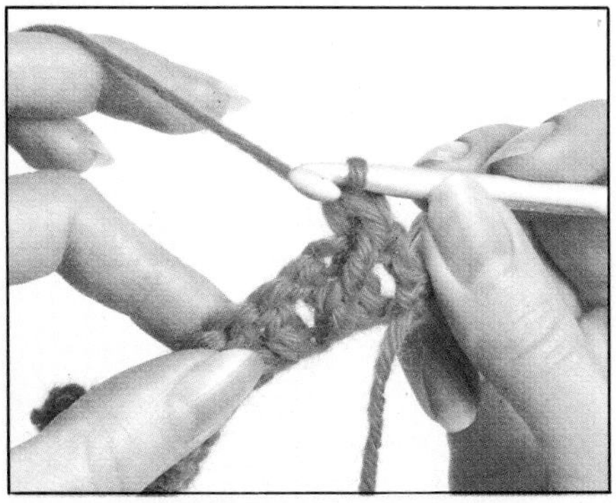

3 Insert the hook into top of the first double of the row and draw through a loop—3 loops on hook. Now wind yarn over the hook and draw it through these 3 loops. This closes the first open triple.

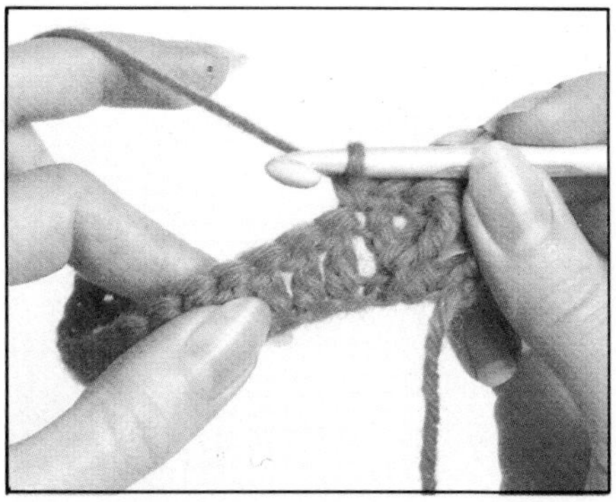

4 Work 1 single crochet into each of the next 2 stitches. The first of these stitches should be worked into the stitch behind the triple.

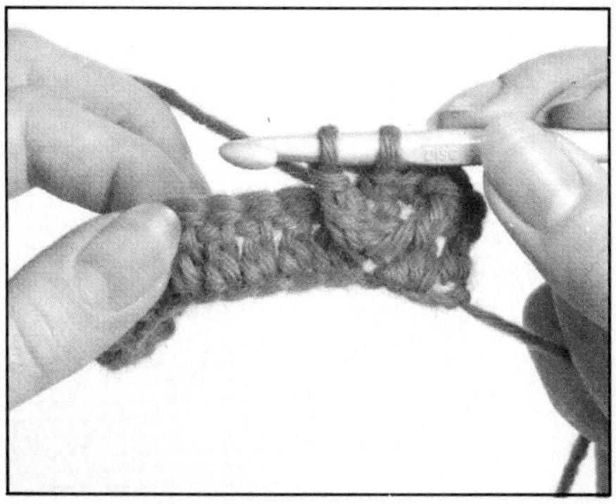

5 Now work an open triple as before into the same stitch as the last open triple, so that you make a V-shape on the front of the fabric.

continued

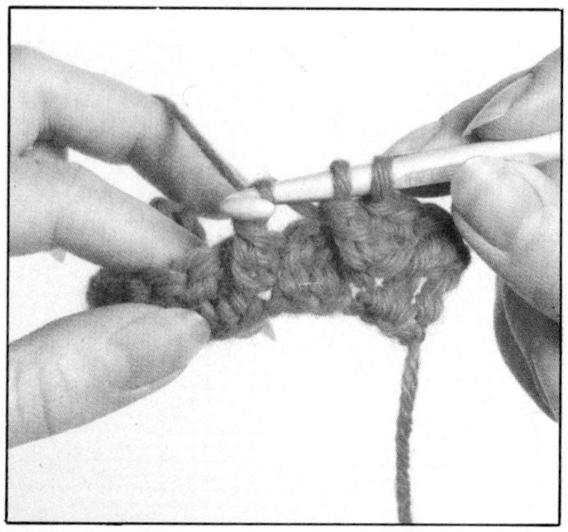

6 Skip the next 2 doubles and work another open triple into the base of the next stitch in the same way as before. 3 loops on hook.

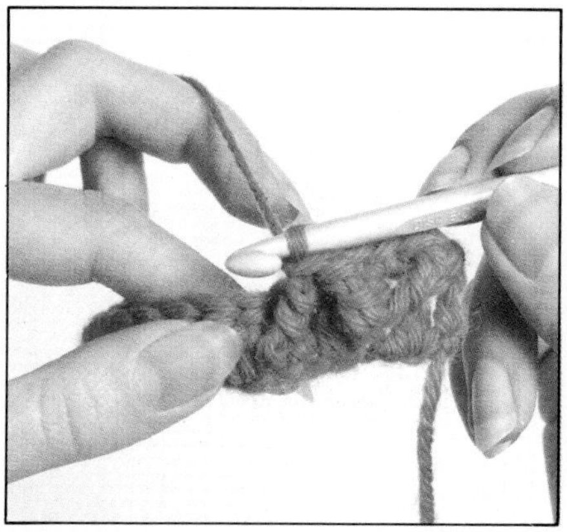

7 Now insert the hook into the first stitch after the last single crochet worked and pull the yarn through. Wind the yarn over the hook and draw it through all 4 loops on the hook. This will be called close 2 triples.

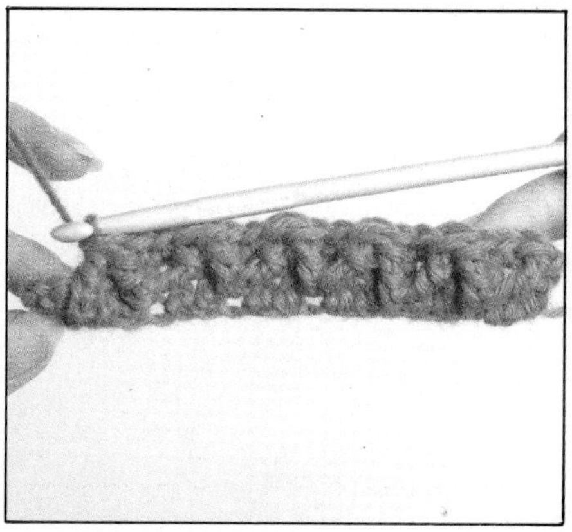

8 Repeat steps 4 to 7 four more times, so that you have worked 11 triples in all on the front of the fabric.

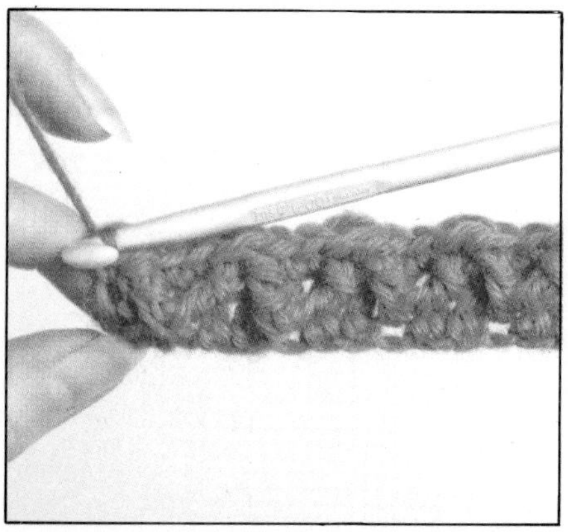

9 Repeat steps 4 and 5 once more. Now insert the hook into the next double crochet and draw a loop through. Now draw yarn through all 3 loops on hook. Work 1 single crochet into the turning chain to complete first row.

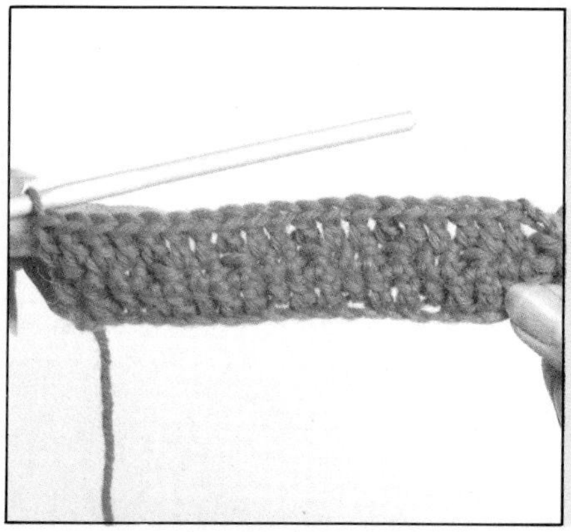

10 Turn. Make 3 chains. Now work 1 double into each stitch to end of row. You should have 20 stitches in all.

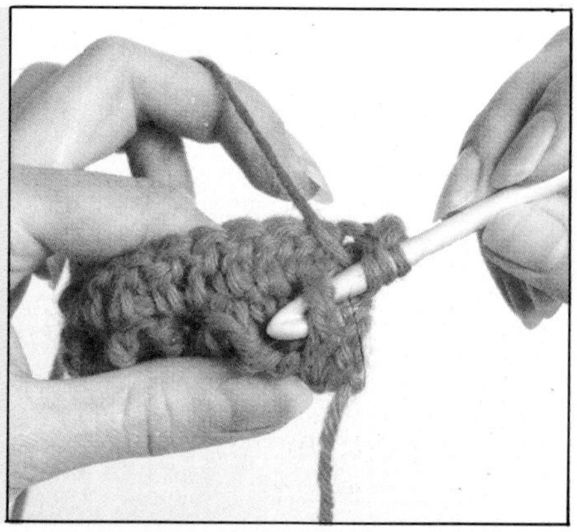

11 Turn. Make 1 chain. Skip first stitch and work 1 single crochet into next stitch. Wind yarn twice over hook and insert it from right to left around the back of the first triple 2 rows below.

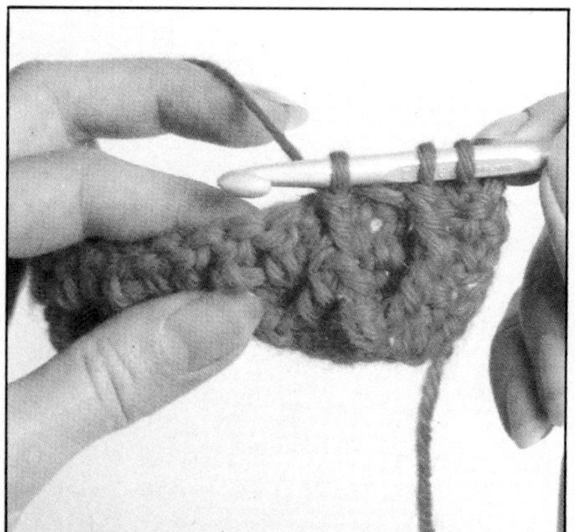

12 Complete the open triple as before. Now work another open triple, inserting the hook from right to left behind next group of 2 triples where they meet at the top.

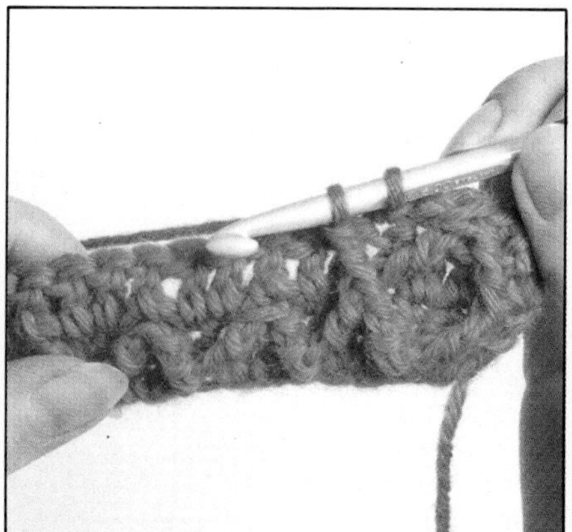

13 Repeat step 7 once more to close these 2 stitches. Repeat step 4 once more. Work an open triple around same group as last triple to make the first V-shape of this row.

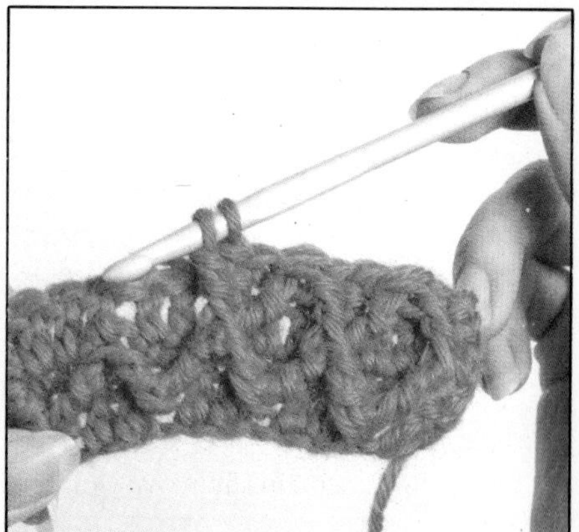

14 Work 1 open triple group around next group. Repeat step 7, then step 4 once more. Work an open triple around same group as last triple for next V.

Fred Mancini

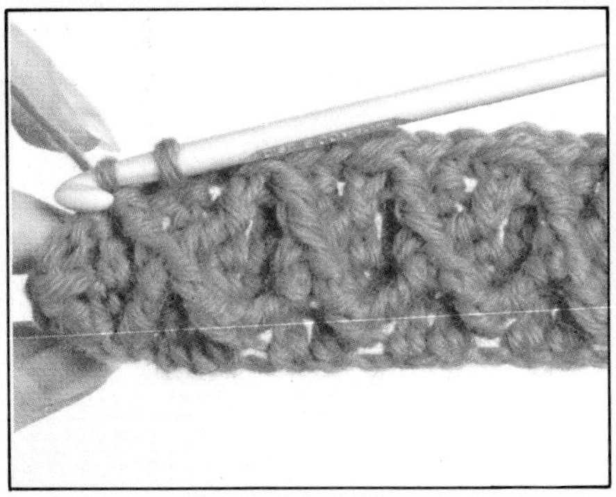

15 Continue to work across the row in this way until you have worked 2 open triples around last group and only the single triple in the previous row remains unworked.

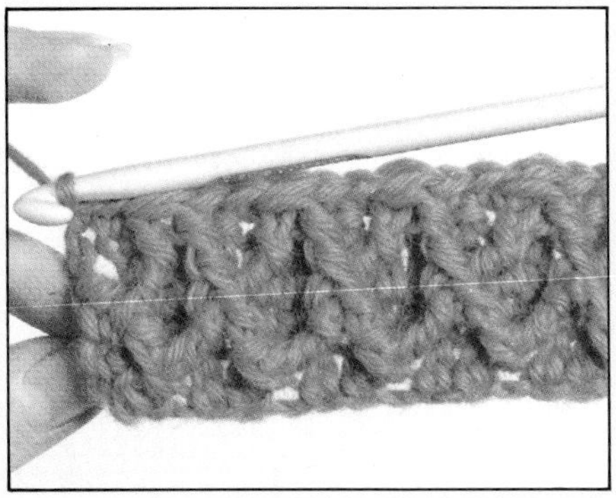

16 Work an open triple around the last remaining triple. Now repeat step 7 to close these 2 stitches, and work 1 single crochet into each of the last 2 stitches to complete the row.

Fred Mancini

17 This completed sample shows several rows of this stitch, worked so that you can see the full effect of working triples in this way.

Aran-style afghan

The enduring appeal of Aran patterns worked here in crochet will make this afghan a treasured family heirloom. Four different stitches are used to make the squares, and the completed squares are then joined together to form the finished afghan.

Size
56 x 75in (143 x 191cm) approximately.

Note This afghan is made up of four different patterned squares. For easy reference we have given them each a letter—A, B, C and D.

Materials
94oz (2650g) of a knitting worsted yarn
Sizes I and K (6.00 and 7.00mm) hooks

Gauge
A, 4 patt repeats to $2\frac{1}{4}$in (6cm) in width worked on size K (7.00mm) hook
B, 3 patt repeats to 2in (5cm) in width worked on size K (7.00mm) hook
C, 8 sc to $2\frac{1}{4}$in (6cm) in width worked on size I (6.00mm) hook
D, 2 patt repeats to 2in (5cm) in width worked on size I (6.00mm) hook

A (worked in even seed stitch, see page 19)
Using size K (7.00mm) hook make 31 ch fairly loosely.
Base row (RS) Sl st into 3rd ch from hook, * 1 hdc into next ch, sl st into next ch, rep from * to end. Turn.
Patt row 2ch to count as first hdc, skip first sl st, * sl st into next hdc, 1 hdc into next sl st, rep from * to within turning ch, sl st into 2nd of first 2ch. Turn.
Rep patt row until work measures 9in (23cm) from beg. Fasten off.
Make 11 more squares in the same way.

B (worked in uneven berry stitch)
Using size K (7.00mm) hook make 30ch fairly loosely.
Base row (RS) 1sc into 3rd ch from hook, then work 1sc into each ch to end. Turn.
1st row 1 ch, skip first sc, *yo, insert hook into next sc and draw a loop through loosely, yo and draw through one loop on hook (3 loops on hook), yo, insert hook into same sc and draw a loop through loosely (5 loops on hook), yo and draw through 4 loops on hook, yo and draw through rem 2 loops on hook—called B1, sl st into next sc, rep from * to last 2 sts, B1 into next sc, 1sc into 2nd of first 2ch. Turn.
2nd row 1 ch, skip first sc, *sl st into next B1, 1sc into next sl st, rep from * to within last 2 sts, sl st into next B1, 1sc into first ch. Turn.
3rd row 1 ch, skip first sc, *sl st into next sl st, B1 into next sc, rep from * to within last 2 sts, sl st into next sl st, 1sc into first ch. Turn.
4th row 1 ch, skip first sc, *1sc into next sl st, sl st into next B1, rep from * to within last 2 sts, 1sc into next sl st, 1sc into first ch. Turn.
5th row 1 ch, skip first sc, *B1 into next sc, sl st into next sl st, rep from * to within last 2 sts, B1 into next sc, 1sc into first ch. Turn.
The 2nd to 5th rows form the patt.
Cont in patt until work measures 9in (23cm) from beg; end with 2nd or 4th row. Fasten off.
Make 11 more squares in same way.

C (worked in ribbing st)
Using size I (6.00mm) hook make 32ch fairly loosely.
Base row (WS) 1sc into 3rd ch from hook, 1sc into each ch to end. Turn.
Patt row 1ch to count as first sc, skip first sc, 1sc into each sc to end, placing the hook into the horizontal loop under the normal ch loop of the sc, 1sc into turning ch, turn.
Rep the patt row until work measures 9in (23cm) from beg. Fasten off.
Make 11 more squares in same way.

D (worked in lattice stitch)
Using size I (6.00mm) hook make 29ch fairly loosely.
Base row (WS) 1dc into 3rd ch from hook, 1dc into each ch to end, turn.
1st row Working patt on front of the fabric work (yo) twice, insert hook into base of 3rd dc on base row from right to left, yo and draw a loop through, (yo and draw through 2 loops on hook) twice—called 1 open tr—, insert hook into top of first dc, yo and draw a loop through, yo and draw through all 3 loops on hook—called close 1 tr—, 1 sc in each of next 2dc, * 1 open tr into base of same dc as before, skip next 2dc, 1 open tr in base of next dc, insert hook into top of dc after last sc worked, yo and draw a loop through, yo and draw through all 4 loops on hook—called close 2tr—, 1sc into each of next 2dc, rep from * to within last dc, 1 open tr into base of same dc as before, close 1 tr in last dc. Turn.
2nd row 2 ch for first dc, skip first sc, 1dc into each sc to end. Turn. 28dc.
3rd row 1 ch for first sc, skip first dc, 1sc into next dc, inserting hook from right to

Gary Warren

left under first tr 2 rows below, work 1 open tr, then work 1 open tr under next grp of 2tr, close 2tr, 1sc in each of next 2dc, * 1 open tr under same grp of 2tr as before, 1 open tr under next grp of 2tr, close 2tr, 1sc into each of next 2dc, rep from * to within last 2dc, 1 open tr, under same grp of 2tr as before, 1 open tr under last tr, close 2tr, 1sc into last dc. Turn.
4th row As 2nd patt row.
5th row 1 open tr under first grp of 2tr, close 1tr working into first dc, 1sc into each of next 2dc, * 1 open tr under same grp of 2tr as before, 1 open tr under next grp of 2tr, close 2tr, 1sc into each of next 2dc, rep from * to within last dc, 1 open tr under same grp of 2tr as before, 1 open tr into last dc, close 2 tr. Turn.
The 2nd to 5th rows form the patt.
Cont to rep these rows until work measures 9in (23cm) from beg; end with a 5th row. Fasten off.
Make 11 more squares in same way.

To finish
Join the squares tog with a flat seam on the WS of the work, following the diagram.

Border
With RS facing and using size K (7.00mm) hook join yarn to one corner and make 1ch to count as first sc, work an uneven number of sc evenly along each edge with 3sc into first 3 corners and 2sc into last corner; join with sl st to first ch. Turn. Work in uneven seed st as foll:
1st round Sl st into center sc at first corner, 1 ch to count as first sc, * (sl st into next sc, 1hdc into next sc) to center sc at next corner, 3sc into center sc, rep from * all around edge; end with a sl st into first sl st, 2sc into same sc as sl st, sl st into first ch to complete round. Turn.
2nd round Sl st into center sc at first corner, 1ch for first sc, * (1hdc into next sc, sl st into sl st, 1hdc into next hdc, sl st into next sl st), to 3sc at next corner, 1hdc into next sc, 3sc into next sc, rep from * all around edge; end last rep with 1hdc into first sl st, 2sc into same sc as sl st, sl st into first ch to complete round. Turn.
3rd round Sl st into center sc at first corner, 1ch, * (1hdc into next sc, sl st into next hdc, 1hdc into next sl st, sl st into next hdc) to 3sc at next corner, 1hdc into next sc, 3sc into next sc, rep from * all around edge; end last rep with 1hdc into first sl st, 2sc into same sc as sl st, sl st into first ch to complete round. Turn.
4th round Sl st into center sc at first corner, 1ch, * (sl st into next sc, 1hdc into next hdc, sl st into next sl st, 1hdc into next hdc) to 3sc at next corner sl st into next sc, 3sc into next sc, rep from * all around edge; end last rep with sl st into first sl st, 2sc into same sc as sl st, sl st into first ch to complete round. Turn.
5th round Sl st into center sc at first corner, 1 ch, * (sl st into next sc, 1hdc into next sl st, sl st into next hdc, 1hdc into next sl st) to 3sc at next corner, sl st into next sc, 3sc into next sc, rep from * all around edge; end last rep with sl st into first sl st, 2sc into same sc as sl st, sl st to first ch to complete round. Turn. Rep 2nd, 3rd and 4th rounds once more. Fasten off.
Press work lightly on WS with a warm iron and a damp cloth, taking care not to flatten pattern.

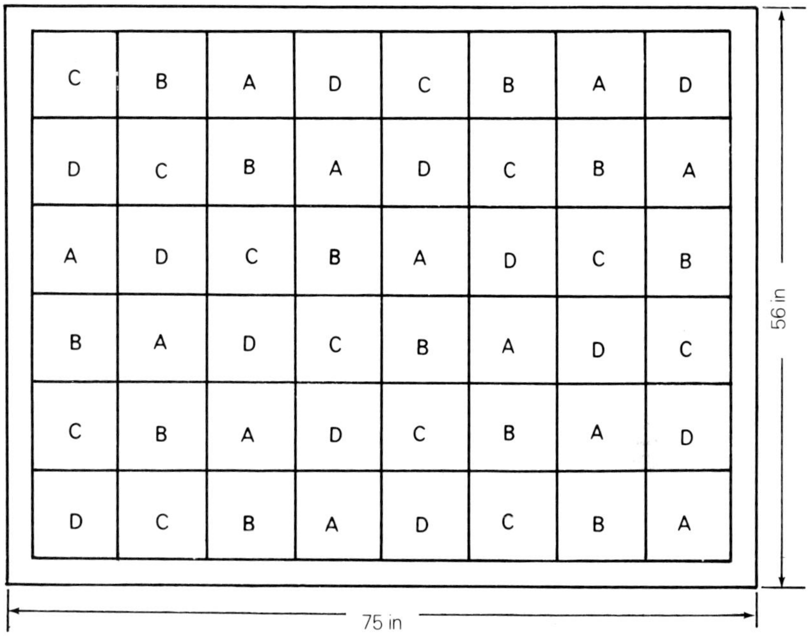

John Hutchinson

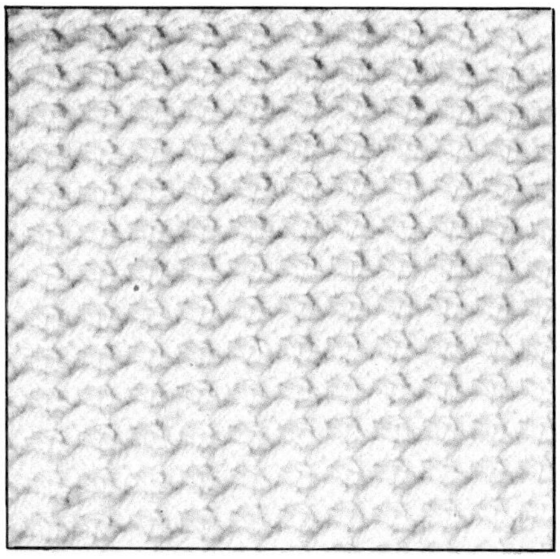
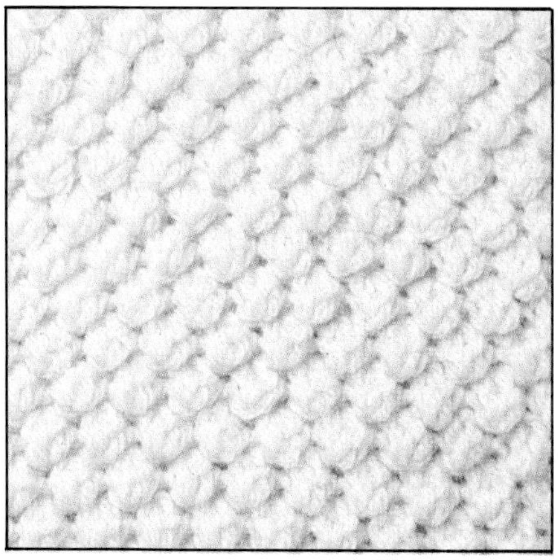
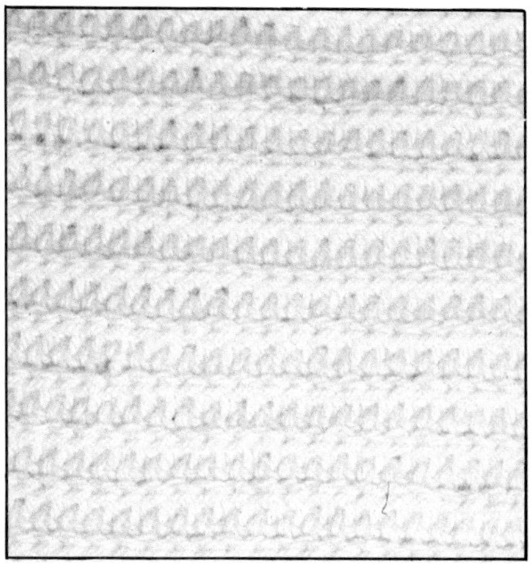
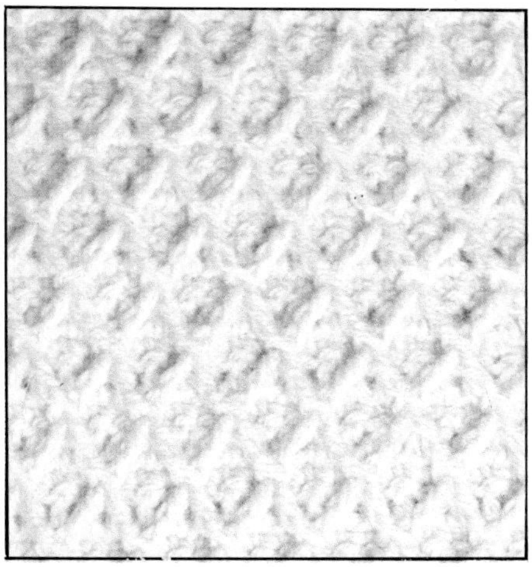

Crochet/COURSE 21

*More about Aran-style crochet
*Simple zig-zag pattern
*Mock cable panel
*Stitch Wise: more Aran patterns
*Pattern for a child's sweater

More about Aran-style crochet

In the previous course we showed you how to work some of the background stitches which can be used in crochet to produce Aran-type fabrics. Here we concentrate on how to work cables and zig-zag patterns by working around the stem of certain stitches to produce a raised effect. Single crochet, half doubles or crochet seed stitch are the best stitches to use for the background, since they make a firm, even fabric. Double and triple fabrics tend to be too open and therefore the motifs will not stand out so effectively against them. Once you have practiced our samples, you will find it quite easy to experiment with the basic working method. For example, simply by varying the number of rows worked before crossing a cable each time, you can alter its appearance considerably. Similarly, by working three or four stitches together in the zig-zag pattern, rather than separating the stitches each time, you will produce a very different effect.

Simple zig-zag pattern

This pattern shows you how raised doubles can be made to slant alternately from right to left to produce a zig-zag effect. You can vary the pattern, either by working two or more raised stitches side by side for a more solid effect, or by working a stitch between each raised double as shown here.
To make this sample use a bulky or Aran-type yarn and a size H (5.50mm) hook. Make 24 chains and work 23 single crochets into the chain (including the turning chain).

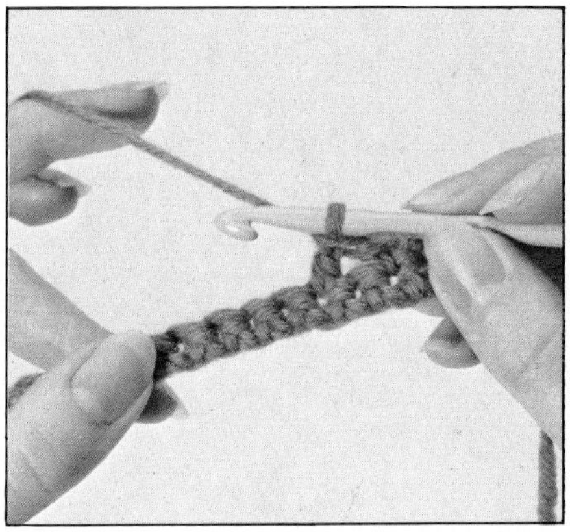

1 Begin the next row with 1 chain. Skip the first single crochet and work 1 single crochet into the next stitch. Skip the next single crochet and work 1 double into the next stitch.

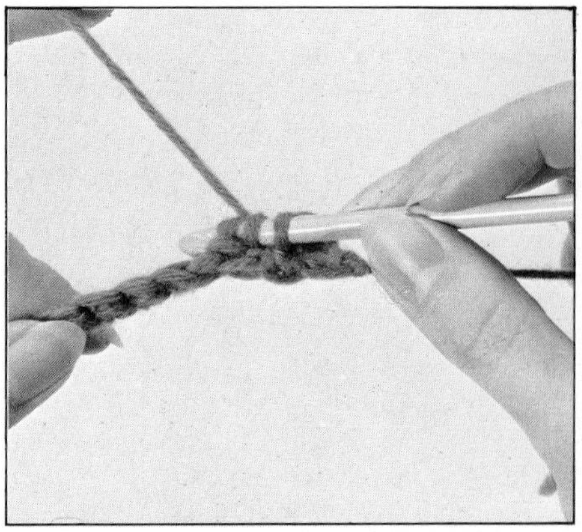

2 Keep the hook at the back of the work so that it is behind the double just made. Wind the yarn over the hook and insert it from front to back through the stitch just skipped.

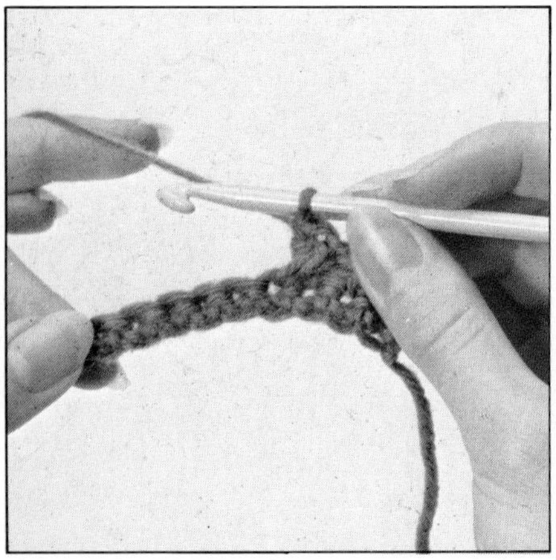

3 Now complete this double in the usual way. These 2 doubles have been crossed at the back of the work.

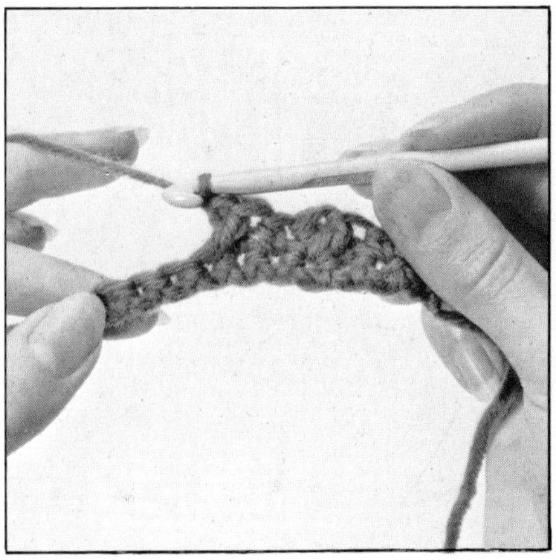

4 Work 1 single crochet into the next stitch and then cross the next 2 stitches at the back in the same way as before. This completes the first group of crossed doubles.

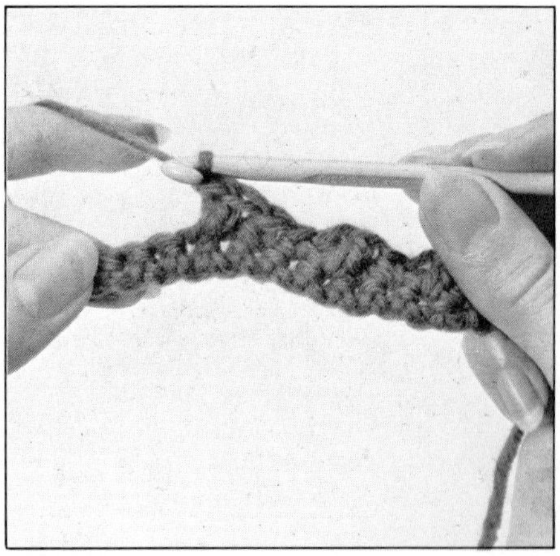

5 Work 1 single crochet into each of the next 2 single crochets. Now cross the next 2 doubles at the back of the work as before.

Mike Berend

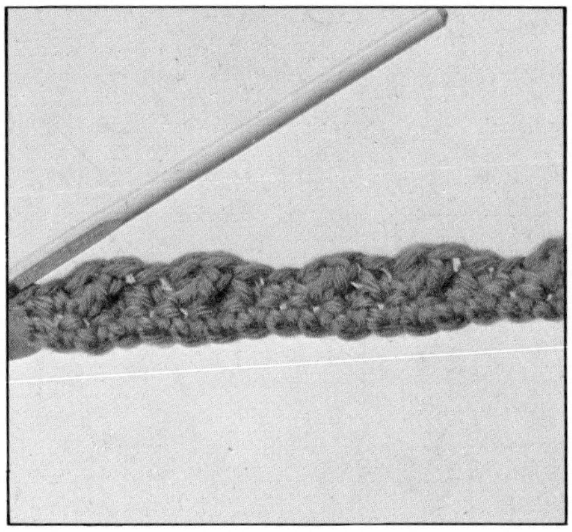

6 Continue to repeat steps 4 and 5 all the way across row, ending with step 4. Work 1 single crochet into the next stitch, then 1 single crochet into the turning chain. There should be 3 groups of 2 crossed doubles in all.

7 Turn. Make 1 chain. Skip the first stitch and work 1 single crochet into the next stitch. Skip next double. Work 1 double into next double. Keep the hook at the front of the work. Wind yarn over hook and insert it from right to left around stem of skipped raised double.

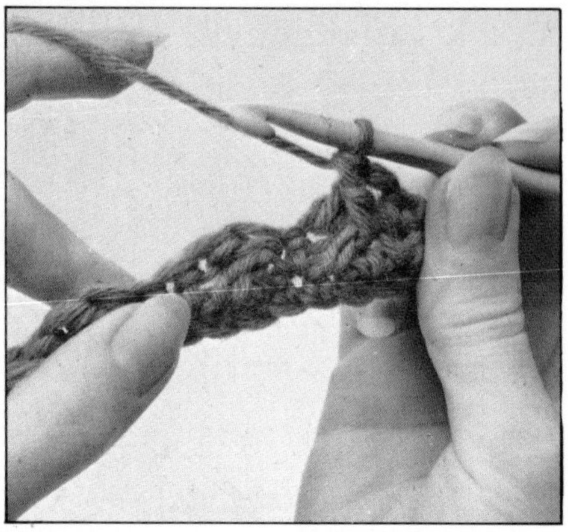

8 Complete this double in the usual way. These 2 doubles have now been crossed at the front (RS) of the fabric. Work crossed doubles at front in the same way each time.

9 Work 1 single crochet into the next single crochet. Now cross the next 2 doubles at front (RS) of fabric as before.

10 Continue to work across the row in this way, with 1 single crochet worked into each single crochet and 2 doubles crossed at the front each time. Work last single crochet into the turning chain.

11 Turn. Now work 1 chain and first 2 stitches as in step 7. Keep hook at back (RS) of work. Wind yarn over hook and place hook around stem of skipped raised double on RS of work from right to left.

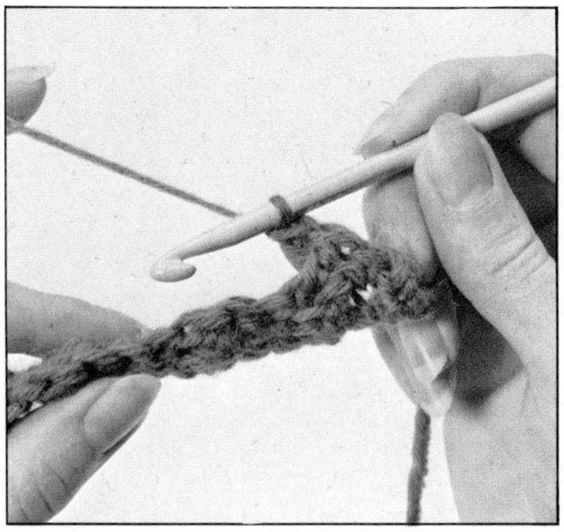

12 Wind yarn over hook and complete the double in the normal way. This crosses the 2 doubles at back and slants them to the right on RS of fabric.

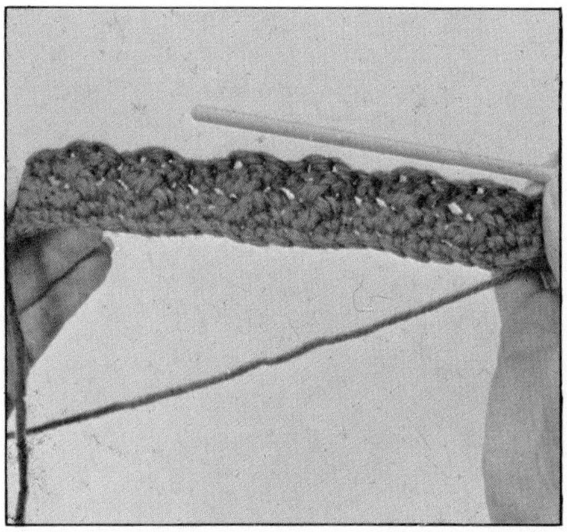

13 Continue to work 1 single crochet into each single crochet and cross two doubles at back (RS) of work each time. Work last single crochet into turning chain. Here we show you the completed row on the RS.

Mike Berend

14 Each row is worked alternately to make the pattern, so that the doubles are crossed at the front when the RS is facing and at the back when the WS is facing.

Mock cable panel

Here we show you how to work a cable on a half double background. We use the same basic principle of working around the stem of the stitches in the row below to produce a raised effect. By using triples to cross the stitches you can achieve a cable effect, and you can vary the appearance of the cables simply by working fewer or more rows between each cross-over row.

To make this sample, first make 14 chains and work 13 half doubles into the chain. We have used a size H (5.50mm) hook and Aran-type yarn.

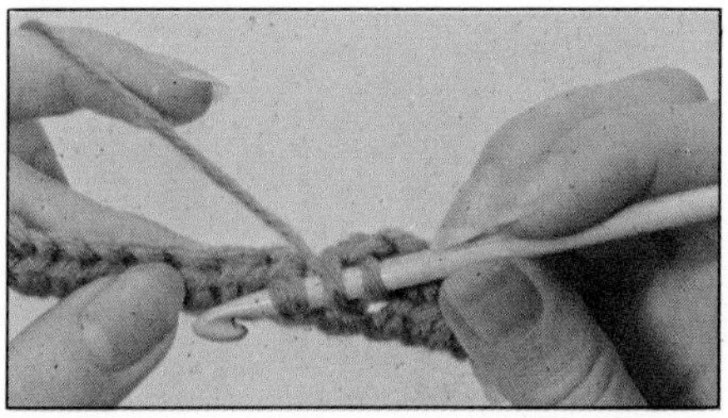

1 Turn. Make 2 chains. Now work 1 half double into each of next 3 stitches. Begin each cable row in the same way. Now wind the yarn over the hook and insert it around the stem of the next stitch from right to left.

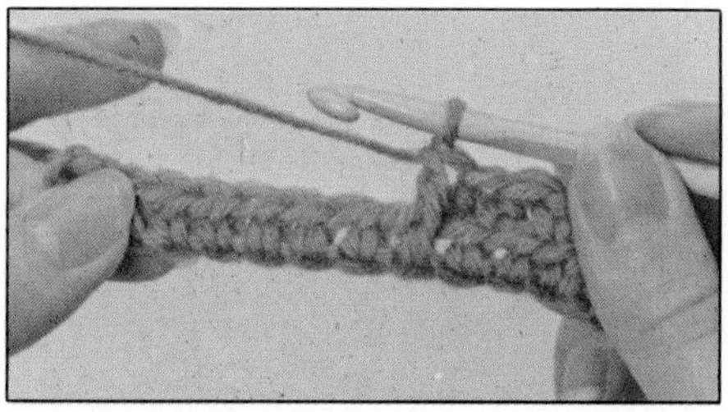

2 Now complete 1 double in the usual way. This completes the first raised double. Work each raised double in the same way.

3 Work another raised double around the stem of the next stitch. Now work 1 half double into the next half double. This stitch is in the center of the cable and separates the raised stitches.

4 Work 1 raised double around the stem of each of the next 2 stitches. Now work 1 half double into each stitch to the end of the row (4 in all). Complete each cable row in this way.

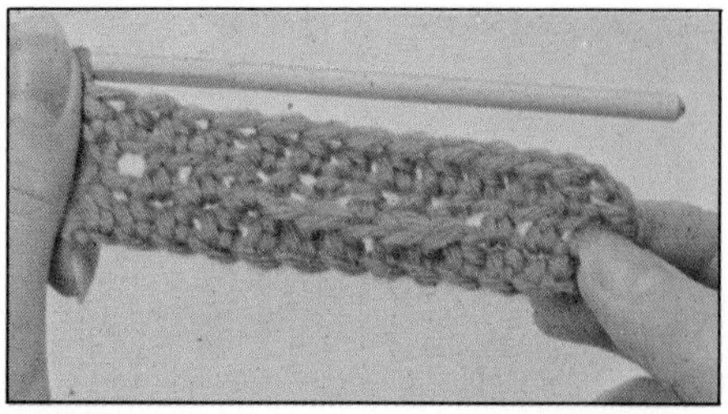

5 Begin the 2nd pattern row with 1 chain. Skip the first stitch and work 1 half double into each stitch to the end so that there are 13 stitches. Work each alternate row in the same way.

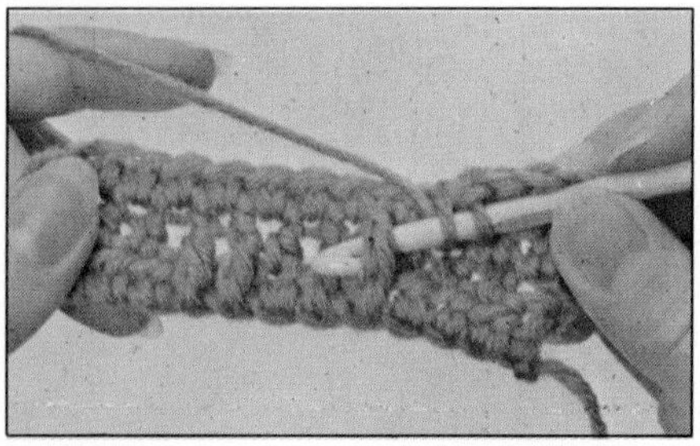

6 Turn and begin cable row as before. Now wind the yarn over the hook and insert it from right to left around the raised double worked in the previous cable row.

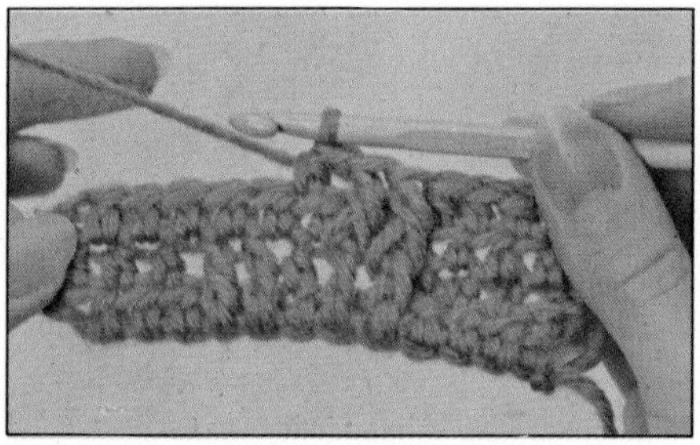

7 Complete the double as before extending the yarn slightly to avoid distorting the fabric. Work another raised double around the next raised double in the previous cable row. Now work 1 half double into the next (center) half double.

8 Work 1 raised double around each of the next 2 raised doubles in the previous cable row. This completes the cable section for this row. Complete the row as before.

Mike Berend

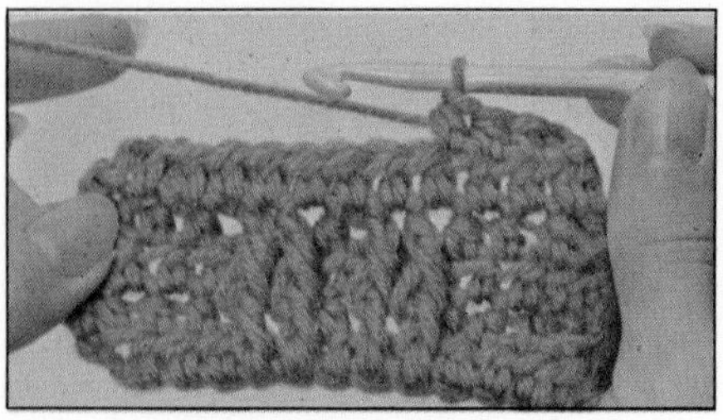

9 Turn and repeat step 5 once more. Now turn and work 4 half doubles as before for the beginning of the next row.

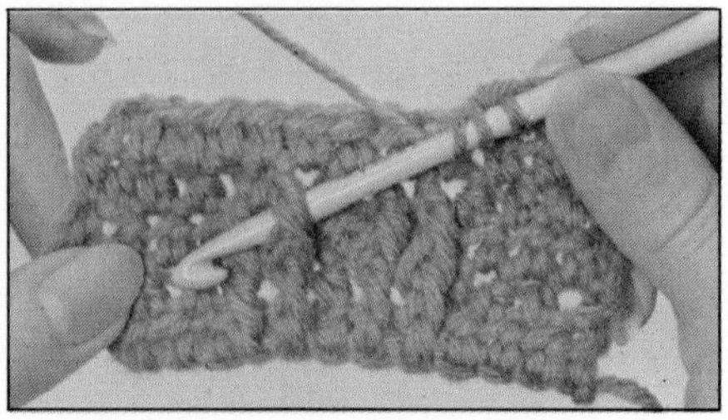

10 Skip the next 2 raised doubles in the previous row and the center half double. Wind yarn twice over hook and insert hook from right to left around next raised double.

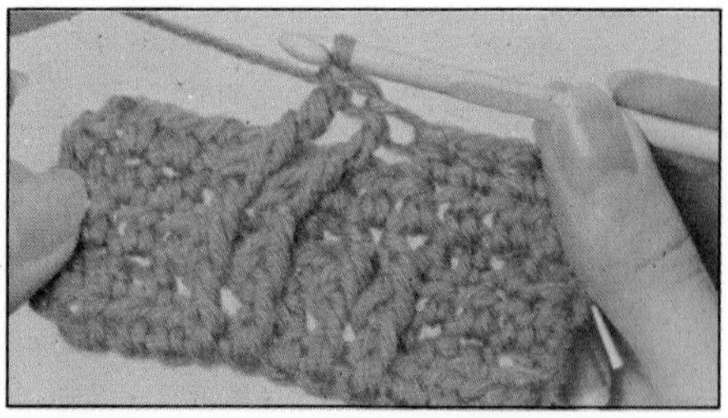

11 Complete 1 triple in the normal way. Work another raised triple around the next raised double in the previous row. These 2 stitches now slant to the right.

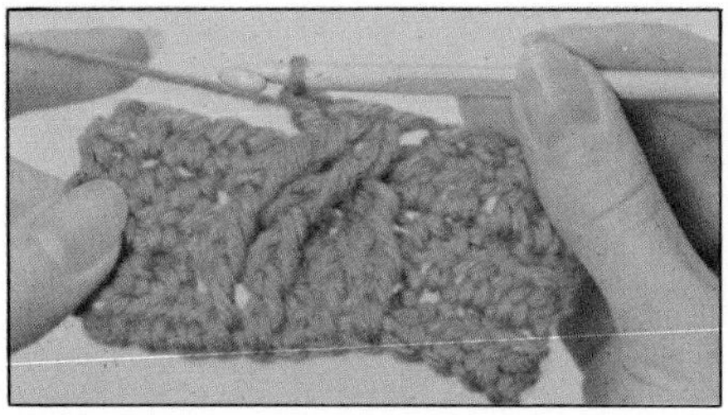

Mike Berend

12 Hold the hook behind these 2 stitches and work 1 half double into the skipped (center) half double. Still keeping the hook behind the 2 triples, work 1 triple around the first of the skipped raised doubles.

13 Work another triple in the same way around the 2nd of skipped raised doubles. These 2 stitches slant from right to left behind first 2 triples.

14 Complete the row as before. Work the next cable twist by repeating steps 5 to 8 twice. Now repeat steps 9 to 13 once more. You have thus worked 5 rows in all before crossing the raised doubles again.

Stitch Wise

Even seed stitch

Make a length of chain which has a multiple of 2 stitches.
1st row Skip first ch, sl st into next ch, *1hdc into next ch, sl st into next ch, rep from * to end. Turn.
2nd row 1 ch, skip first st, *1hdc into next st, sl st into next st, rep from * to end of row, working last sl st into turning chain. Turn. The 2nd row forms the patt. Repeat it each time.

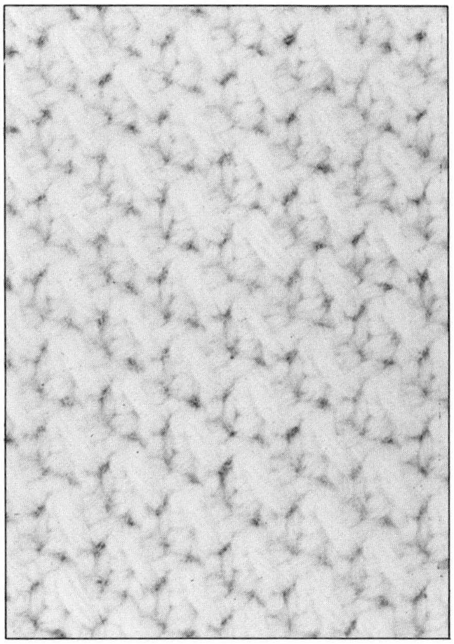

Uneven seed stitch

Make a length of chain which has a multiple of 2 stitches.
Work the 1st and 2nd rows in exactly the same way as given for even seed stitch.
3rd row 2ch to count as first hdc, skip first st, sl st into next st, *1hdc into next st, sl st into next st, rep from * to end of row, working last hdc into turning chain. Turn.
4th row As 3rd.
5th row As 2nd row.
6th row As 2nd row.
The 3rd to 6th rows form the pattern and are repeated throughout.

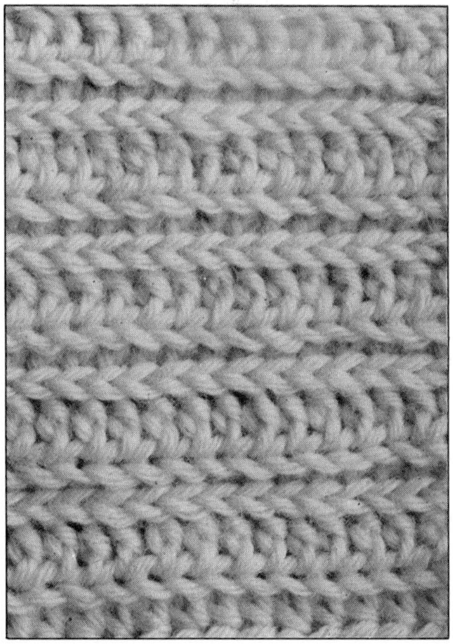

Aran rib stitch

Make a length of chain with a multiple of 2 plus 1 extra chain.
1st row (RS of fabric) Work 1hdc into 3rd ch from hook, 1hdc into each ch to end. Turn.
2nd row 2ch, skip first st, *work 1hdc into horizontal loop (below two horizontal loops at top of stitch) at front of next hdc, rep from * to end, working last hdc into turning chain. Turn.
3rd row 2ch, skip first st, *work 1hdc into back loop of top two horizontal loops of next st, rep from * to end, working last hdc into turning chain. Turn. 2nd and 3rd rows form patt and are repeated throughout.
This stitch gives the appearance of ribbing, although the WS is flat.

Artful Aran

The intriguing textures of Aran-style crochet are used here to make a smart sweater for a child. The round neckline goes easily over a shirt and the saddle shoulders add style.

Sizes

To fit 26[28:30]in (66[71:76]cm) chest.
Length, 17[18:19½]in (43[46:50]cm).
Sleeve seam, 13[14¼:15¼]in (33[36:39] cm).

Note Directions for larger sizes are in brackets [ ]; where there is only one set of figures it applies to all sizes.

Materials

12[14:15]oz (340[380:420]g) of a knitting worsted; or 11[12:14]oz (300[340:380]g) of a knitting worsted and 2oz (40g) in a contrasting color
Sizes E and F (3.50 and 4.00mm) hooks

Gauge

18 sts and 18 rows to 4in (10cm) in seed st on size F (4.00mm) hook.

Front and back (alike)

Using size E (3.50mm) hook chain 9[10:11] for side edge of waistband.
Base row 1sc into 3rd ch from hook, 1sc into each ch to end. Turn.
Ribbing row 1ch, 1sc into back loop only of each sc to end. Turn. Rep ribbing row 57[67:73] times more. This completes ribbing for waistband. Do not turn but work along one long edge.
Next row 2ch to count as first sc, then 1sc into each row end to end. Turn. 59[69:75] sc. Change to size F (4.00mm) hook.
Next row (WS) 2ch to count as first hdc, *sl st into next sc, 1hdc into next sc, rep from * to end, finishing sl st into turning ch. Turn. Beg seed st patt.
Patt row 2ch, *sl st into next hdc, 1hdc into next sl st, rep from * to end, finishing sl st into turning ch. Turn. This row forms the patt. Cont until work measures 15½[16½:18]in (39[42:46]cm); end with WS row. Fasten off.

Sleeves

Using size E (3.50mm) hook make 8ch for side edge of cuff and work in ribbing as for front until 29[33:39] rows in all have been worked, then work 1sc into each row end along one long side. Turn. 29[33:39] sts. Change to size F (4.00mm) hook.
1st row 2ch, (sl st into next sc, 1hdc into next sc) 3[4:4] times, 1sc into next sc, (skip next sc, 1dc into next sc, keeping hook at back of work, work 1dc into last sc skipped, so forming 2 crossed dc, 1sc into next sc) 1[1:2] times, (yo, insert hook into next sc, yo and draw a loop through, yo and draw through one loop on hook, yo, insert hook into same sc, yo and draw a loop through so having 5 loops on hook, yo and draw through first 4 loops on hook, yo and draw through rem 2 loops, called bobble 1, or B1, sl st into next sc) 3 times, B1, (1sc into next sc, cross 2dc) 1[1:2] times, 1sc into next sc, sl st into next sc, (1hdc into next sc, sl st into next sc) 3[4:4] times. Turn.
2nd row 2ch, seed st 6[8:8], 1sc into next sc, (skip next dc, 1dc into next dc, keeping hook at front of work, work 1dc around dc that was skipped, called cross 2dc front, or Cr2F, 1sc into next sc) 1[1:2] times, (1sc into B1, 1 sc into next sl st) 3 times, 1sc into B1, (1sc into next sc, Cr2F) 1[1:2] times, 1sc into next sc, seed st to end. Turn.
3rd row 2ch, seed st 6[8:8], 1sc into next sc, (skip next dc, 1dc into next dc, keeping hook at back of work, work 1dc around dc that was skipped, called cross 2dc back, or Cr2B, 1sc into next sc) 1[1:2] times, sl st into next sc, (B1 into next sc, sl st into next sc) 3 times, (1sc into next sc, Cr2B) 1[1:2] times, 1sc into next sc, seed st to end. Turn.
4th row 2ch, seed st 6[8:8], 1sc into next sc, (Cr2F, 1sc into next sc) 1[1:2] times, 1sc into next sl st, (1sc into next B1, 1 sc into next sl st) 3 times, (1 sc into next sc, Cr2F) 1[1:2] times, 1sc into next sc, seed st to end. Turn.
5th row 2ch, seed st 6[8:8], 1sc into next sc, (Cr2B, 1sc into next sc) 1[1:2] times, B1 into next sc, (sl st into next sc, B1 into next sc) 3 times, 1sc into next sc, (Cr2B, 1sc into next sc) 1[1:2] times, seed st to end. Turn. The 2nd to 5th rows form patt.
Cont in this pattern, inc one st at each end of 2nd and every foll 6th row by working 2sts into first and last sts, working extra sts into seed st, until there are 47[51:57] sts. Cont without shaping until sleeve measures 13[14¼:15¼]in (33[36:39]cm) from beg; end with WS row. Cut off yarn. With RS facing rejoin yarn to first sc at beg of panel, cont across panel sts only for 4[4¼:4¾]in (10[11:12]cm) for saddle shoulder extension; end with WS row. Fasten off.

Neckband

Using size E (3.50mm) hook make 8ch and rib as for front for 14¼[15¼:16½]in (36[39:42]cm). Fasten off.

To finish

Press or block according to yarn used. Sew saddle extensions to shoulder seams on front and back, then sew top of sleeves to sides of back and front. Join side and sleeve seams. Join short ends of neckband, then sew neckband to neck. Press seams lightly.

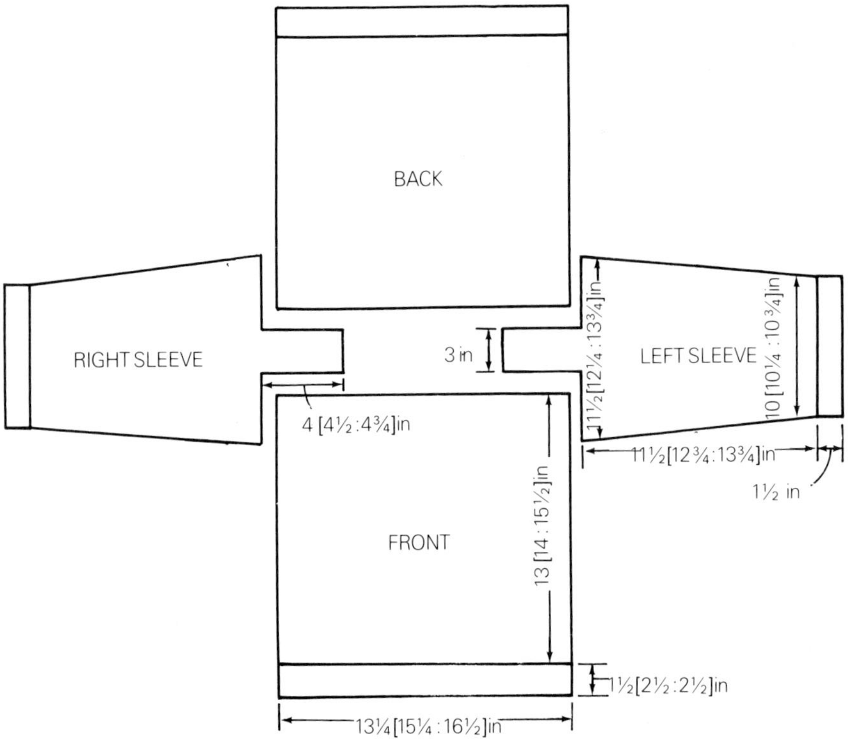

John Hutchinson

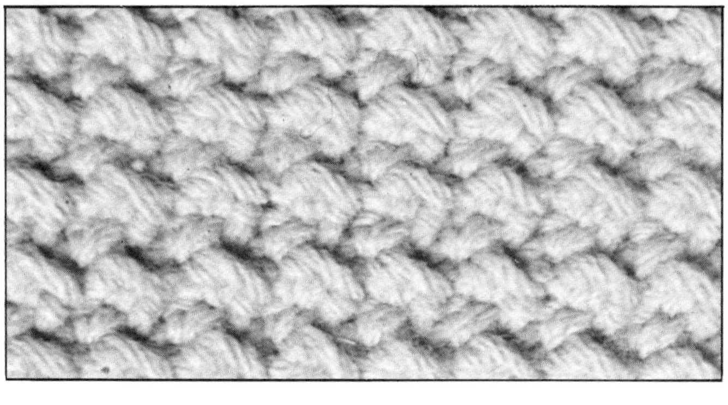

Steve Bicknell

Crochet/COURSE 22

*Working large lace patterns
*Scallop shells
*Japanese fan stitch
*Stitch Wise: more lace patterns
*Pattern for a lacy shawl

Working large lace patterns

There are several ways of making lace—with a needle or bobbins, for example—but crocheted lace is probably the easiest method, since all you need is a crochet hook, some yarn and the ability to work all the basic crochet stitches that you have learned so far. The variety of patterns available is enormous, but basically they are all made in the same way: by building up groups of crochet stitches to form different shapes or motifs, such as shells or pyramids, and joining these with chain bars or single stitches. Don't be put off by the fact that some of these patterns appear complicated. They are much easier than they look, and as long as you follow the directions carefully you will succeed in making a beautiful fabric. The type of lace fabric you make will, of course, depend on the thickness of yarn and the size of hook you use, but you will find that most of the patterns look equally good in a fine or a thick yarn.

Scallop shells

By working a simple pattern like the one shown here, you will begin to understand how large lace patterns are created. The basic principle is very similar however intricate the stitch might be, and thus, practicing something quite simple like this scallop shell pattern will enable you to progress to a more complicated pattern without difficulty. To work this sample, first make 31 chains.

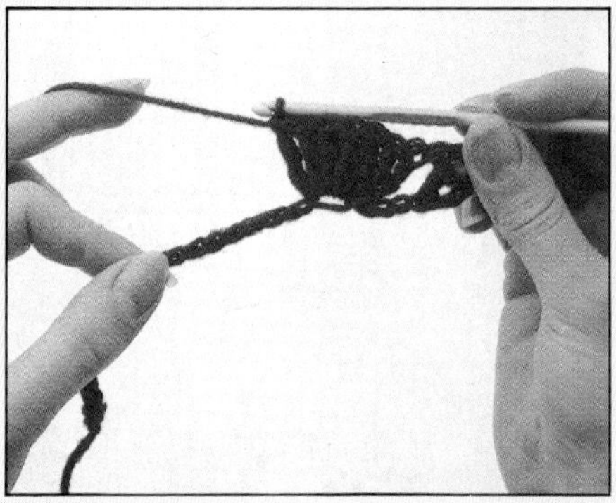

1 Work 1 triple into 6th chain from hook. Skip next 3 chains and work 7 triples into next chain for first shell. The chains are left unworked at each side of the shell or motif to create a space so that the motif can fan outward and the fabric lies flat.

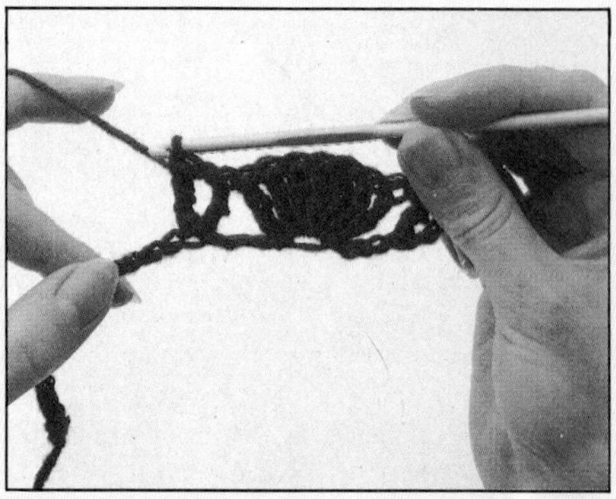

2 Skip next 3 chains. Now work 1 triple, 1 chain and 1 triple all into next chain. This "V" group acts as a link between the shells. Lengths of chain and single stitches can also be used for this purpose, but you must still leave a space at each side of the group.

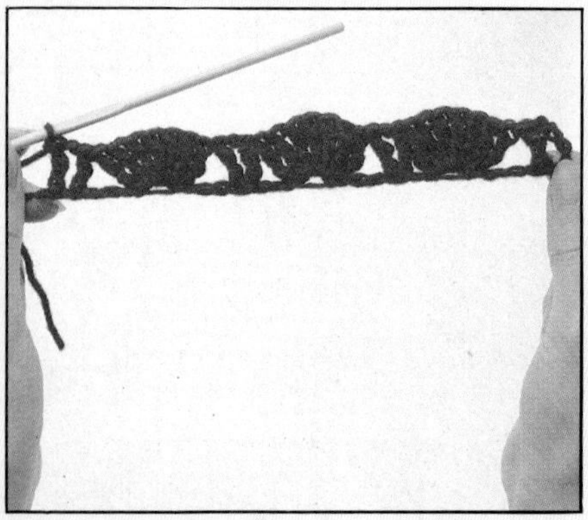

3 Work a shell and a V group alternately across the row in the same way. Make the last V group by working 1 triple into the 2nd to last chain, 1 chain and the final triple into the last chain. Most patterns will tell you exactly how to work the beginning and end of each row in order to maintain the continuity of the pattern.

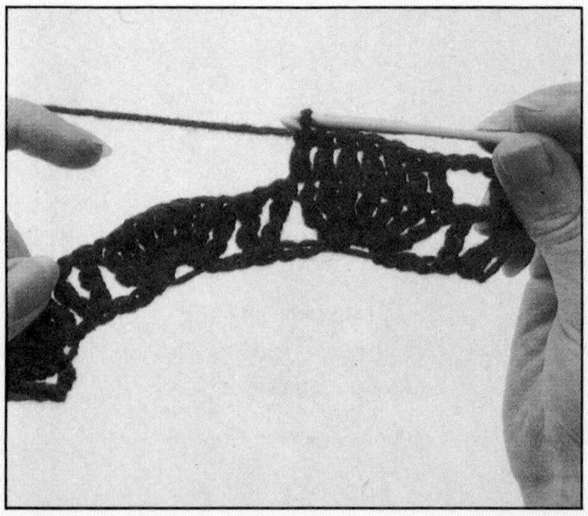

4 Begin next row with 3 chains. Now work 1 double into the first chain space. Work 3 chains, then 1 double into each stitch in the first shell. Thus you begin to build up and enlarge the original shape. One chain is sometimes worked between these doubles to fan the motif outward even further.

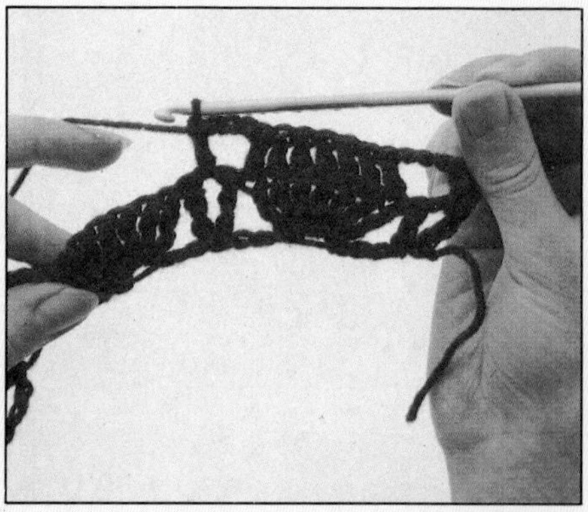

5 Make another 3 chains. Now work 1 double into the center of the next V group. The 3 chains and double now form the link between the motifs in place of the V group, at the same time maintaining the open effect.

Paul Williams

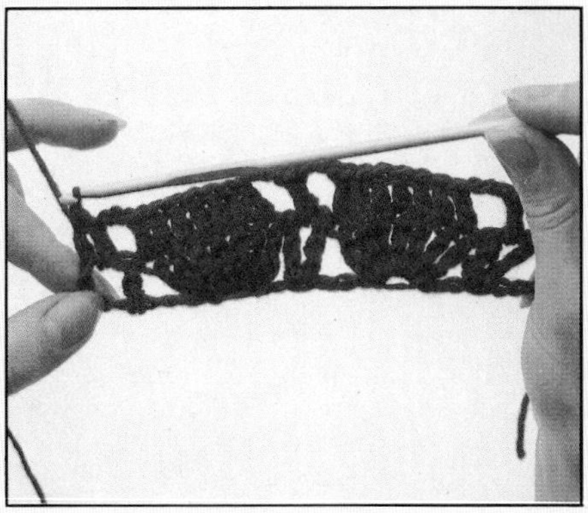

6 Continue to work into each shell and V group across the row, working 3 chains at each side. Finish the row with 1 double into last space and 1 double into turning chain. The last double acts as the edge stitch.

7 The next row is worked in the same way as the first, except that the motifs are alternated by working a shell into each of the single doubles between the shells, and a V group into the center stitch of each shell. To keep the pattern correct work 3 triples at the beginning and end of the row to act as a half shell, since the full shell would be too wide.

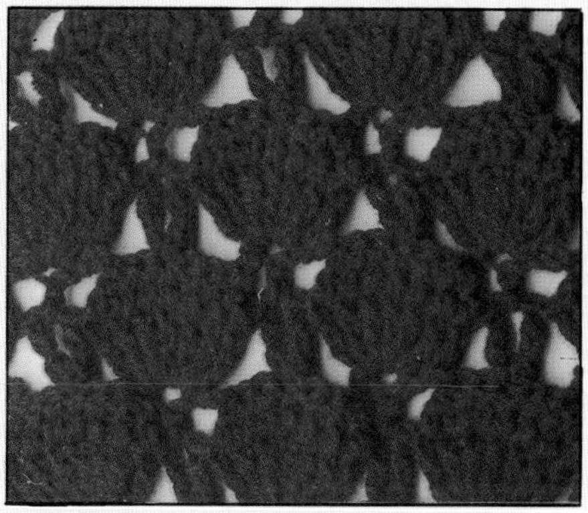

8 As the pattern develops the shells and V groups are alternated so that they are positioned diagonally from one another. On other patterns more rows are required to build up the basic shape, and more chains are used, creating a really open lace fabric.

Japanese fan stitch

The soft fan shape of the shells in this pattern is achieved by working longer doubles than normal into one stitch. The resulting shell is much softer and thicker than it would normally be, creating a pretty, warm pattern, ideal for a cozy shawl.

The pattern is worked over a multiple of 14 chains plus 1. To make our sample work 30 chains (1 extra for the turning chain). Work 1 single crochet into 3rd chain and then 1 single crochet into each chain to end, so that there are 29 stitches in all. To make the sample wider, add 14 extra chains for each pattern repeat.

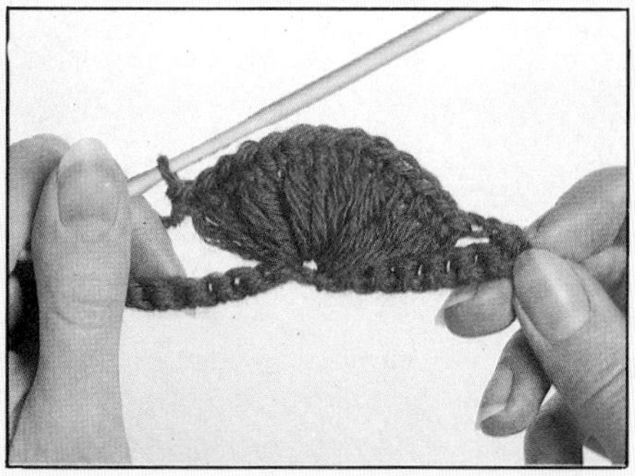

1 Turn and make 2 chains to count as first stitch. Skip next 6 stitches (7 including edge stitch). Now work 13 doubles into next stitch, drawing yarn out to about $\frac{1}{2}$in (1.2cm) each time you work a double, to make a long stitch. These 13 doubles form the first shell.

2 Skip next 6 stitches and work a single crochet into next stitch. Now skip next 6 stitches and work another shell into next stitch in same way as before. Skip next 6 stitches and work a single crochet into top of turning chain to complete first row.

3 Now turn and work 4 chains. Work a long double as before into first (edge) stitch. Now make 5 chains and work a single crochet into 7th (center) double of next shell. Make 5 chains and work 2 long doubles into next single crochet between the shells.

4 Repeat these actions to complete the 2nd row, working 5 chains then a single crochet into the center of the next shell; 5 chains and then 2 long doubles into top of the turning chain.

5 To continue pattern turn and make 2 chains. Now work a shell as before into single crochet worked in center of each shell in previous row and a single crochet between doubles worked in previous row, working last single crochet into top of turning chain. Continue to alternate 2nd and 3rd rows.

Paul Williams

Stitch Wise

Two lace patterns

Try working one or both of these two lace stitches. The first pattern, Window panes, makes use of square blocks of doubles and chain bars to create an unusual lace effect, which would be ideal for a bed-spread, worked in a fairly thick crochet cotton. The second, Shell and chain pattern, uses the more conventional method of working shell shapes and inter-locking chains to produce an openwork lace fabric which could be worked in a fine crochet cotton or thicker crochet yarn.

Window panes

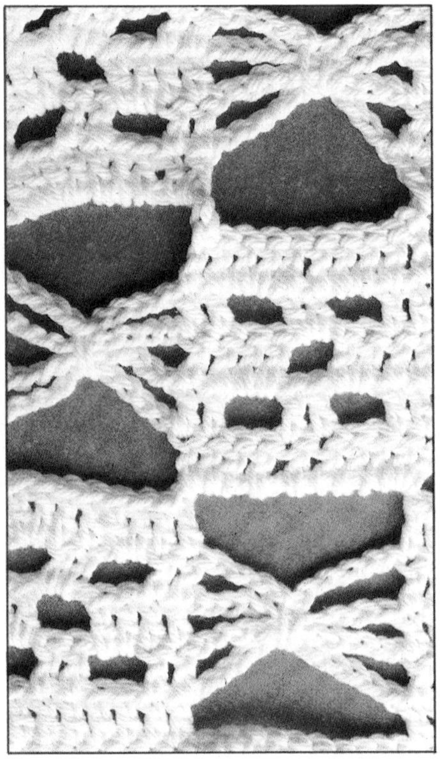

This pattern is worked over a multiple of 10 chains plus 1 extra turning chain. We give directions for working 3 blocks of pattern across the row. When using the pattern for a crochet fabric you will need to work extra stitches at each side to form a firm edge.
Make 31 chains; work 29 single crochet into chain to make 30 stitches.

Base row 3ch, skip first st, 1dc into each of next 9sc, 10ch, skip 10sc, 1dc into each sc to end, working last dc into turning chain. Turn.
1st row 3ch, skip first st, 1dc into next st, *2ch, skip 2 sts, 1dc into each of next 2 sts, *, rep from * to * once more, 10ch, 1dc into each of next 2 sts, rep from * to * twice more, working last dc into turning chain. Turn.
2nd row 3ch, skip first st, 1dc into next st, *2dc into next 2ch sp, 2ch, skip next 2 sts, 2dc into next 2ch sp, 1 dc into each of next 2 sts*, 10ch, 1 dc into each of next 2dc, rep from * to * once more, working last dc into turning chain. Turn.
3rd row 3ch, skip first st, 1dc into next st, * 2ch, skip 2 sts, 2dc into next 2ch sp, 2ch, skip 2 sts, 1dc into each of next 2dc * 4ch, insert hook under first 10 chain loop from front to back, work 1sc around all 3 loops at center to draw them tog—called 1sc around ch; 4ch, 1dc into each of next 2dc, rep from * to * once more, working last dc into turning chain. Turn.
4th row 3ch, skip first st, *1dc into each dc and 2dc into each 2ch sp*, 10ch, rep from * to * once more, working last dc into turning chain. Turn.
5th row 3ch to count as first dc, 10ch, 10dc into next 10ch loop, 10ch, 1dc into turning chain. Turn.
6th row 3ch to count as first dc, 10ch, 1dc into each of next 2dc, *2ch, skip 2 sts, 1dc into each of next 2 sts, rep from * once more, 10ch, 1dc into 3rd of first 3ch. Turn.
7th row 3ch to count as first dc, 10ch, 1dc into each of next 2dc, 2dc into 2ch sp, 2ch, skip 2 sts, 2dc into 2ch sp, 1dc into each of next 2dc, 10ch, 1dc into 3rd of first 3ch. Turn.
8th row 3ch to count as first dc, *4ch, 1sc around ch, 4ch*, 1dc into each of next 2dc, 2ch, skip 2 sts, 2dc into next 2ch sp, 2ch, skip 2 sts, 1dc into each of next 2 sts, rep from * to * once more, 1 dc into 3rd of first 3ch. Turn.
9th row 3ch to count as first dc, 10ch, 1dc into each dc and 2dc into each 2ch sp, 10ch, 1dc into 3rd of first 3ch. Turn.
10th row 3ch, 9dc into 10ch loop, 10ch, 9dc into 10ch loop, 1dc into 3rd of first 3ch. Turn. (10dc in each lattice section as before.)
Rows 1 to 10 form patt and are rep throughout so that position of squares is reversed each time. To work more squares across, rep lattice and chain sections alternately as many times as required, only working the turning chain at side edge.

Shell and chain pattern

This pattern is worked over a number of chains divisible by 10, plus 1 chain and 5 extra turning chains.

Base row (RS) 1dc into 6th ch from hook, *3ch, skip 3ch, 1sc into each of next 3ch, 3ch, skip 3ch, (1dc, 3ch, 1dc) all into next ch, rep from * ending last rep (1dc, 2ch, 1 dc) all worked into last ch. Turn.
1st row 3ch, skip first dc, 3dc into first 2ch sp, *3ch, 1sc into 2nd of next 3sc, 3ch, 7dc into next 3ch sp between dc, rep from * to end, ending by working 3dc (half shell) instead of 7dc into last sp between dc and turning chain and last dc into top of turning ch. Turn.
2nd row 1ch, skip first st, 1sc into each of next 3dc, *5ch, 1sc into each of next 7dc, rep from * to last half shell, 5ch, 1sc into each of next 3dc, 1sc into 3rd of first 3ch. Turn.
3rd row 1ch, skip first sc, 1sc into next sc, *3ch, (1dc, 3ch, 1dc) all into 3rd of next 5ch, 3ch, skip first 2sc of next shell, 1sc into each of next 3sc, rep from * ending last rep, skip next 2sc, 1sc into

next sc, 1sc into first ch. Turn.
4th row 1ch to count as first sc, *3ch, now work 7dc into next 3ch sp between dc, 3ch, 1sc into 2nd of next 3sc at center of shell, rep from * to end, working last sc into first ch of previous row. Turn.
5th row 1ch to count as first sc, 2ch, * 1sc into each of next 7dc of shell, 5ch, rep from * to last shell, 1sc into each of the 7dc in last shell, 2ch, 1sc into first ch of previous row. Turn.
6th row 3ch to count as first dc, 2ch, 1dc into first st at edge of work, *3ch, skip 2sc, 1sc into each of next 3sc at center of shell, 3ch, (1dc, 3ch, 1dc) all into 3rd of next 5ch, rep from * to end, ending last rep by working (1dc, 2ch, 1dc) all into first ch of previous row. Turn.
The first to 6th rows form the pattern and are repeated throughout.

Lacy luxury

A delicate lace pattern and a soft fine yarn make this pretty evening wrap. Wear it in the daytime, too, when you want a bit of extra warmth.

Size
Length when hanging, 35½in (90cm) excluding fringe.

Materials
9oz (240g) of a sport yarn
Size E (3.50mm) crochet hook

Gauge
1 patt rep measures 2¼in (5.5cm) in width and 2½in (6cm) in depth.

To make
Make 244 ch very loosely.
Base row 3dc into 4th ch from hook, *skip next 3ch, 1sc into next ch, skip next 3ch, 7dc all into next ch, rep from * to end, but finish last rep 4dc into last ch instead of 7dc. Turn.
1st row 4ch, skip first dc, *1dc into next dc, 1ch, rep from * to end, finishing 1dc into turning ch. Turn.
2nd row 1ch, 1sc into first sp, 3ch, 1sc into next sp, 3ch, *skip next dc, 1sc into next dc, 1ch, 1sc into next dc, 3ch, skip next sp, (1sc into next sp, 3ch) 4 times, rep from * to within last 6 sps, skip next dc, 1sc into next dc, 1ch, 1sc into next dc, 3ch, skip next sp, 1 sc into next sp, 3ch, 1sc into last sp. Turn.
3rd row Sl st into first 3-ch, 3ch, 1sc into next 3-ch sp, *2ch, (1sc into next 3-ch sp, 3ch) 4 times, 1sc into next 3-ch sp, rep from * to end, finishing 2ch, 1sc into next 3-ch sp, 3ch, 1sc into last 3-ch sp. Turn.
4th row Sl st into first 3-ch sp, *3ch, 1sc into next 3-ch sp, rep from * to end. Turn.
5th row *5ch, skip next 3-ch sp, (1sc into next 3-ch sp, 3ch) twice, 1sc into next 3-ch sp, rep from * to end, finishing 5ch, skip last 3-ch sp, 1sc into sl st. Turn.
6th row *7ch, 1sc into next 3-ch sp, 3ch, 1sc into next 3-ch sp, rep from * to end, finishing 7ch, 1sc into the last sc of the 4th row. Turn.
7th row Sl st over the 7ch and into 3-ch sp, 3ch, 3dc into same sp, *2ch, 1sc into 4th of 7ch, 2ch, 7dc into 3-ch sp, rep from * to end, but finish last rep 4dc into last 3-ch sp instead of 7dc. Turn.
Rep rows 1 to 7 to form shawl, ending with a 6th row. Fasten off.

To finish
Using four 12in (30cm) lengths of yarn together, knot fringe evenly along two side edges. Trim ends. Do not block.

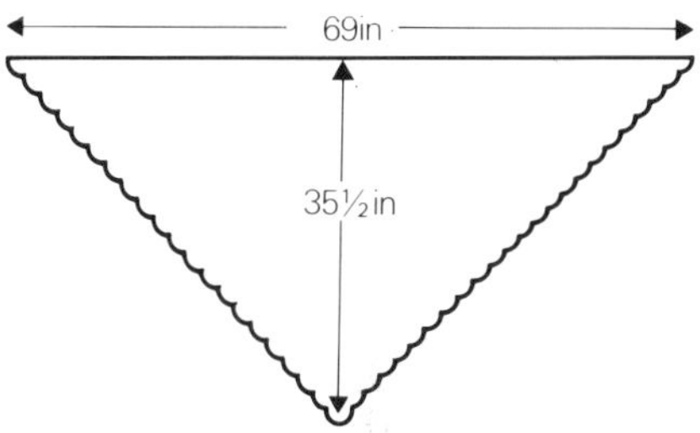

Brian Mayor

Gary Warren

Shoestring

Ollie Owl

This delightful furry mascot is easily made from two wooly pompoms.

Di Lewis

Materials

1oz (25g) of mustard bouclé yarn
2oz (50g) of dark brown bouclé yarn
Piece of beige felt 8×6in (20×15cm)
One orange pipe cleaner
Two $\frac{5}{8}$in (1.5cm) goggle eyes with back loops
Thick cardboard
Black nylon bristles from an old hairbrush
Matching thread
Tracing paper for pattern

1 From thick cardboard cut one 4in (10cm)-diameter circle. From the center cut out a $2\frac{1}{4}$in (6cm)-diameter circle, leaving a $\frac{3}{4}$in (2cm)-wide ring.
2 From thick cardboard cut one $2\frac{3}{4}$in (7cm)-diameter circle. From the center cut out a $1\frac{1}{2}$in (4cm)-diameter circle, leaving a $\frac{5}{8}$in (1.5cm)-wide ring.
3 Using the dark brown yarn, wind it around and around the larger ring, bringing the yarn through the center and over the edge, until the ring is three-quarters covered.
4 Cover the remaining quarter of the ring with mustard yarn. Remember, the more yarn you pull through the ring, the thicker the pompom.
5 Cut the yarn loops around the outer edge of the covered ring. Before removing the cardboard ring, securely tie a piece of brown yarn around the center and cut off the ends. Remove the cardboard ring. This forms the owl's body.
6 Repeat steps 3 to 5 on the smaller cardboard ring to make a pompom for the owl's head.
7 Sew the head securely to the body with thread, with the mustard-colored parts matching on one side. Trim pompoms to make an evenly rounded shape.
8 Take a small bundle of bristles and wind a thread tightly around one end to hold them together. Sew a bundle of bristles to one side of the top of the head for tufts. Repeat to make a second tuft on the opposite side of the head.
9 Sew the back loop of each eye firmly in place on the mustard-colored part of the head.
10 Bend the pipe cleaner in half and then in half again for the beak. Sew the beak firmly in place and bend gently to shape if necessary.
11 Trace the wing pattern and cut out four wings from felt. Place wings together in pairs. Pin, baste and topstitch all around. Sew wings in place.

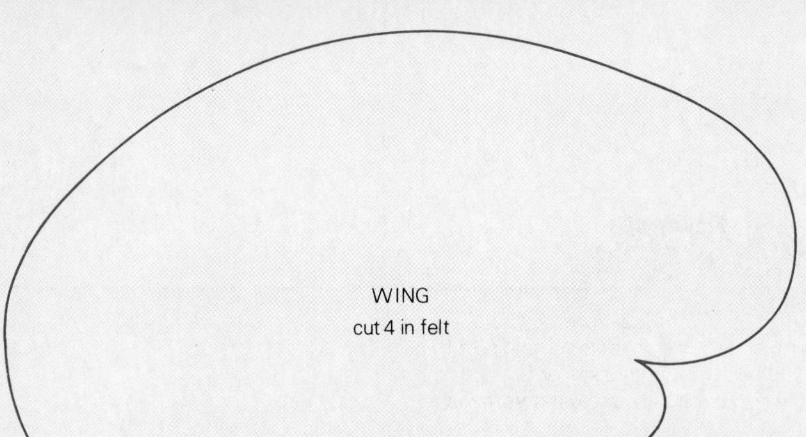

John Hutchinson

* Working cluster or bobble stitches
* Making a simple cluster group
* Raised bobbles
* Pineapple stitch
* Stitch Wise: more cluster patterns
* Pattern for a pullover

Working cluster or bobble stitches

Cluster stitches—or bobble stitches as they are sometimes called—can be grouped together to form diamond or square shapes on a plain background, or incorporated into square, flat motifs, or used as an allover pattern to produce a really bulky crochet fabric. There are various ways of making these stitches. The preferred method depends largely on the type of stitch being used for the background and on the kind of texture desired. A few single stitches, grouped together and interspersed with other stitches, will produce a softly textured fabric. Other techniques will form large bobbles that stand out against the fabric, giving it a highly embossed appearance.

All kinds of cluster stitches are made in essentially the same way: by working a number of loops or stitches into the same place and then gathering them together with a chain to complete the group. In a pattern containing cluster stitches, the directions will specify the particular method of working the clusters for that garment.

Making a simple cluster group

This is a simple stitch to work; all you do is draw a number of loops through one stitch in the previous row, then draw the yarn through all the loops, gathering them together. The width of each cluster will tend to make a row of these stitches wider than the rest of the fabric. If you are working bands of clusters in a plain fabric, you should insert a row of single crochet between each two cluster rows to control the extra fullness and maintain the shape of the fabric.

1 Work at least 2 doubles at the beginning of the row where the cluster is to be made. This will be the RS of the fabric. Wind the yarn over the hook and insert the hook into the next stitch. Draw through a length of yarn, pulling it up to approximately $\frac{1}{2}$in (1.5cm), or so it is the same height as the previous stitch. There are now 3 loops on the hook.

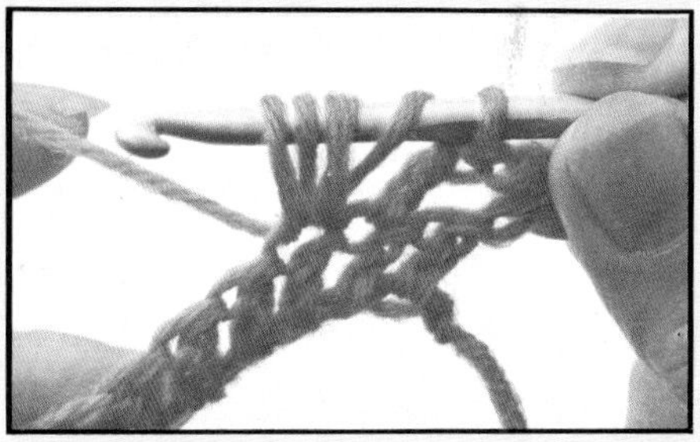

2 Wind the yarn over the hook and insert it into the same stitch as before. Now draw up another loop so that it is the same height as the first loop. There are now 5 loops on the hook.

3 Repeat step 2 twice more, so that there are now 9 loops on the hook. The number of times you repeat this step will depend on the size of bobble or cluster you wish to make.

4 Now wind the yarn over the hook and draw it through all the loops on the hook to complete the cluster. Make 1 chain to hold the stitches firmly together.

Paul Williams

5 Work at least 1 double between each cluster all the way across row and 2 doubles after last group to keep edge straight. This sample shows several rows worked with 1 single crochet row between each cluster row. Work a single crochet into each double and into the top of each cluster on the single crochet rows to maintain the number of stitches.

Raised bobbles

The following method produces firm, raised bobbles made of doubles worked against a background of single crochet. You can work these bobbles to make an allover pattern or group them into diamond or square shapes on a plain background. You will need to work at least 2 rows in single crochet before making the bobbles.

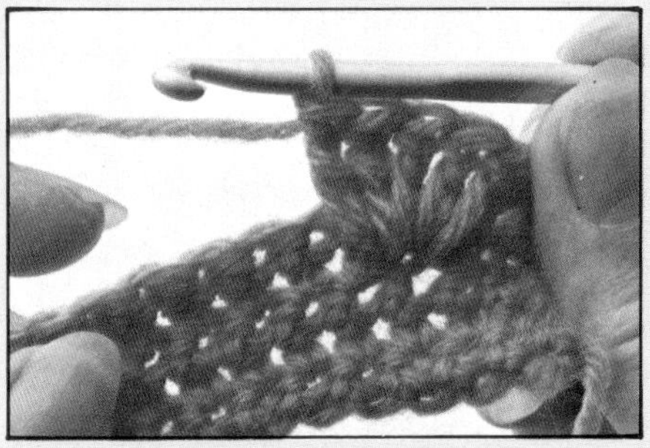

1 Work at least 2 single crochets at the beginning of the row. Now work 5 doubles into the next stitch in the row below (placing the hook into the center of the stitch), drawing the yarn up each time to the same height as the stitches in the row being worked.

2 Remove the hook from the working loop and insert it under the two horizontal loops of the first of these 5 doubles. Take care not to pull the working loop back through the last stitch when withdrawing the hook.

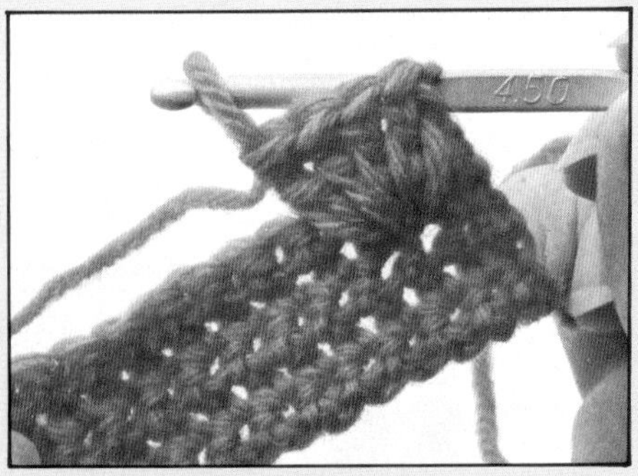

3 Now insert the hook once more into the working loop, so that the first double and last double of the group are both on the hook at the same time and the hook passes behind the 5 doubles.

4 Draw the working loop through the first of these loops to complete the bobble. Make 1 chain to hold the stitches just worked firmly together.

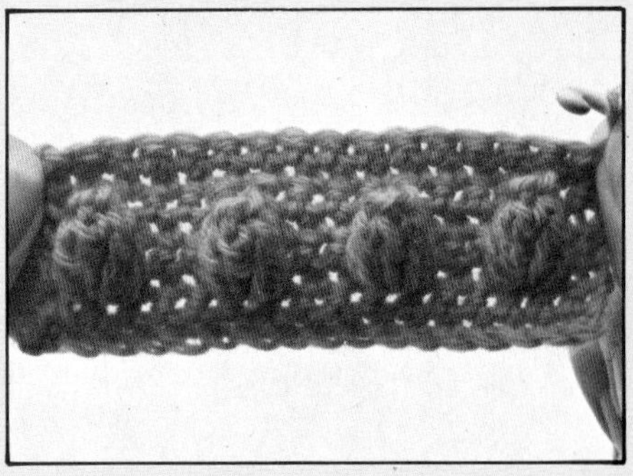

5 Continue to work bobbles across the row; skip the next stitch (the stitch skipped in this row when 5 doubles were worked into the row below) then work 1 single crochet into each of the next 3 stitches before making the next bobble in the same way as before. Finish the row by working at least 1 or 2 single crochets after the last bobble.

Pineapple stitch

This is a classic crochet cluster stitch in which loops are drawn through the vertical strand at the side of each group to make a horizontal rather than a vertical cluster. Pineapple stitch makes an ideal edging for a jacket or cardigan.
You will need to work at least one row in single or double crochet before working the cluster row, and you must have an even number of stitches on which to work it.

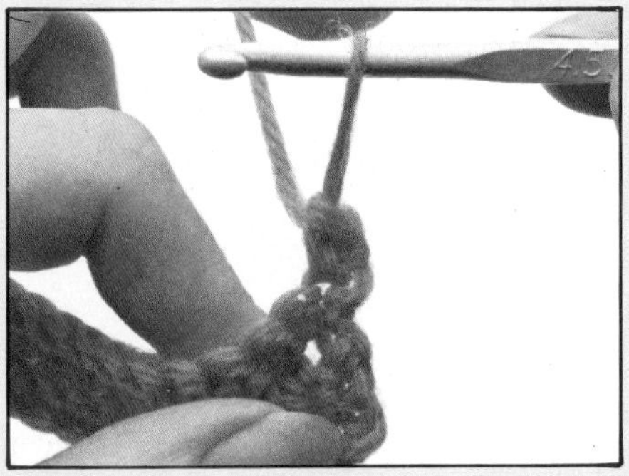

1 Work 2 chains at the beginning of the cluster row to keep the edge straight. Work a single crochet into the first (edge) stitch and then 1 chain. Now draw this chain (working loop) out loosely so it's about ½in (1.5cm) long.

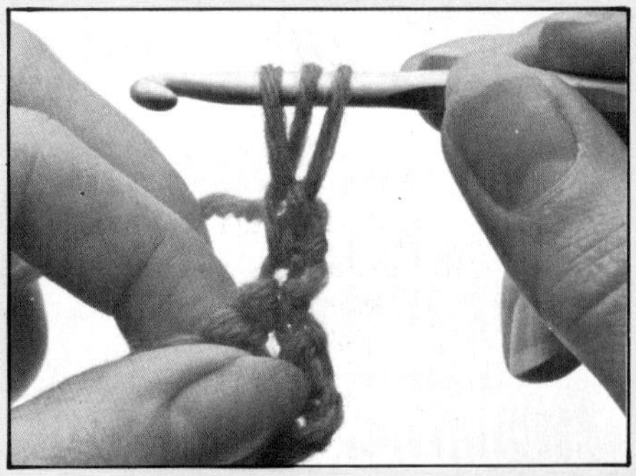

2 Wind the yarn over hook and insert the hook from front to back into the vertical loop at the side of the last stitch. Now draw through a loop loosely, extending it to the same height as before (3 loops on hook).

Paul Williams

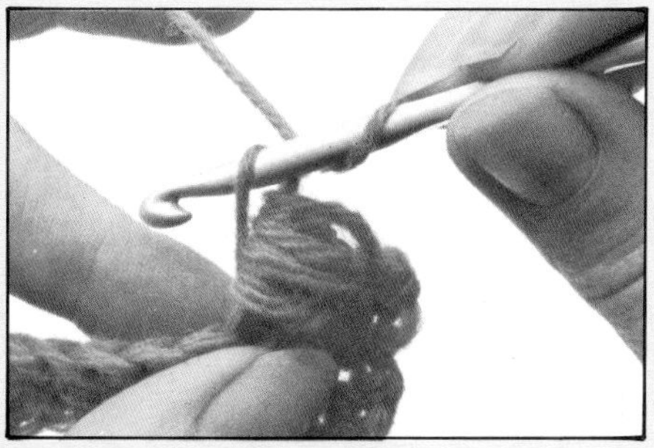

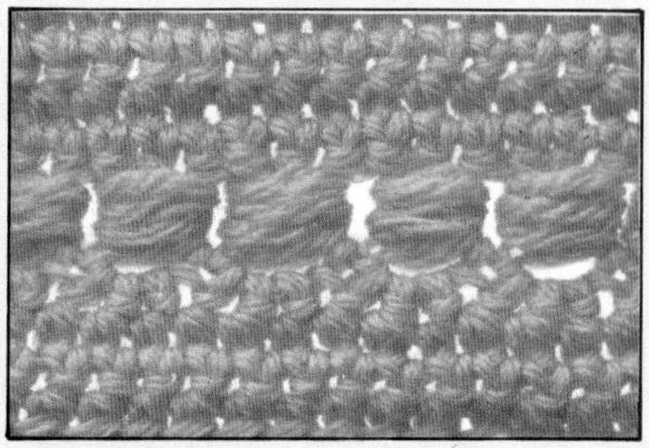

3 Repeat step 2 three times more (9 loops on hook). Pull each loop through loosely to prevent the cluster from becoming distorted. Skip next 2 single crochets. Insert hook into next stitch; wind yarn over hook and draw it through this stitch and all loops on hook to complete first cluster.

4 To make the next cluster make 2 chains, drawing 2nd chain out to $\frac{1}{2}$in (1.5cm) as before. Wind the yarn over hook and insert it from front to back into vertical loop at side of the last cluster made when first chain was worked after last cluster.

5 Complete this cluster as before. Make each cluster in same way, inserting hook each time into vertical loop at side of last cluster worked. Finish row with 1 chain and 1 double into turning chain. For next row, work 3 single crochets under top 2 loops of each cluster and 1 single crochet at each end.

Stitch Wise

Cluster stitch motif

Cluster groups worked in rounds have been used to make this highly textured square motif. You can make it in a fine or bulky yarn either using one color, or changing the color of the yarn at the end of each round for an effect that is really colorful.

Make 6ch and join into a circle with a slip stitch.

1st round 2ch to count as first sc, work 1sc into circle. Join with a sl st to 2nd of first 2ch. 16sc.

2nd round 4ch to count as first cluster and 1 ch sp, *yo and insert hook into next st, yo and draw through a loop, yo and draw through all 3 loops, called Cl1, 1 ch, rep from * to end of round. Join last ch to 3rd of first 4ch with sl st. 16 clusters.

3rd round Sl st into first ch sp, 3ch, (yo and insert hook into same sp, yo and draw through a loop) twice, yo and draw through all loops on hook, 2ch, * (yo and insert hook into next 1 ch sp, yo and draw through a loop) 3 times, yo and draw through all loops on hook, called Cl3, 2ch, rep from * to end of round. Sl st into 3rd of first 3ch.

4th round Sl st into first 2ch sp, 3ch to count as first dc, 1dc into same sp, (2dc into next 2ch sp, 1ch) twice, 1ch (Cl3, 2ch, Cl3) into next 2ch sp, called corner group, 1ch, *(2dc into next 2ch sp, 1ch) 3 times, 1 corner group into next 2ch sp, rep from * to end of round, working last corner group into sp before first 3ch in previous round and joining last ch to 3rd of first 3ch with sl st. Fasten off.

Allover cluster pattern

Several loops are worked into one stitch in the row below to create this bulky cluster pattern. It may be substituted for the raised bobbles opposite. Make a number of chains divisible by 4 plus 1, with 1 extra for turning chain.

1st row (RS) 1sc into 3rd ch from hook, 1sc into each ch to end. Turn.

2nd row 1ch to count as first sc, skip first sc, 1sc into each sc to end, working last sc into turning chain. Turn.

3rd row 1 ch, skip first sc, 1sc into next sc, * (yo, insert hook into st in row below next sc, yo and draw a loop through, extending it to the height of row being worked) 5 times, yo and draw a loop through all loops on hook, 1 ch, called Cl1, 1 sc into next sc, rep from * to end. 1 sc into turning chain. Turn.

4th row 1 ch, skip first sc, 1sc into next sc, *1sc into top of next cluster, 1 sc into sc between clusters, rep from * to last cluster, 1 sc into top of last cluster, 1 sc into next sc, 1 sc into turning chain. Turn.

5th row 1 ch, skip first sc, *Cl1 into next st in row below next sc, 1 sc into next sc, rep from * to last 2 sc, Cl1 into next st in row below next st, 1 sc into turning chain. Turn.

6th row 1 ch, *1sc into top of cluster, 1 sc into next sc between clusters, rep from * to last cluster, 1 sc into top of last cluster, 1 sc into turning chain. Turn.

3rd to 6th rows form pattern.

Kim Sayer

Kim Sayer

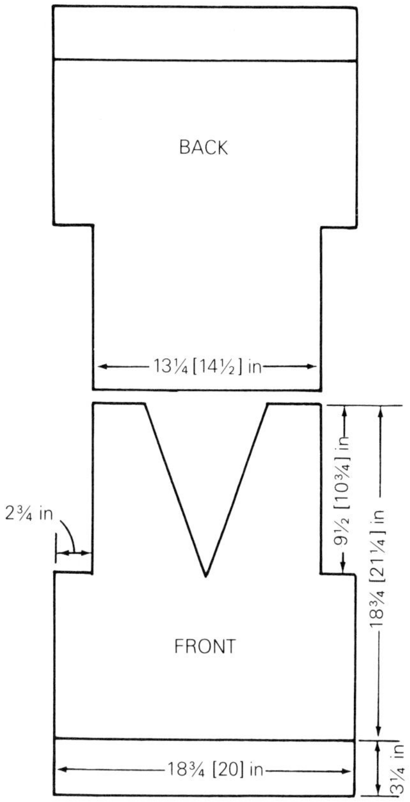

John Hutchinson

Soft clusters

This classic pullover made in a mohair-type yarn has bands of cluster stitches.

Sizes
To fit 32/34[36/38]in (82/87[92/97]cm) bust.
Length, 22[24½]in (56[62]cm).

Note Directions for larger size are in brackets [ ]; where there is only one set of figures it applies to both sizes.

Materials
9[11]oz (250[300]g) of a lightweight mohair
Sizes G and H (4.50 and 5.50mm) hooks

Gauge
6 clusters and 10 rows to 4in (10cm) in patt on size H (5.50mm) hook.

Back
**Using size G (4.50mm) hook chain 13 for side edge of waistband.
Base row 1sc into 3rd ch from hook, 1sc into each ch to end. Turn.
Next row 2ch to count as first sc, skip first st, *1sc into back loop only of next st, rep from * to end, working last st into back loop of turning ch. Turn. 12sc.
Rep last row 54[58] times more. This completes the ribbing for waistband.
Do not turn but cont to work down long side edge of ribbing. Change to size H (5.50mm) hook. Working into row ends, work 59[63] sc evenly along this edge. Turn.
Next row 2ch to count as first sc, 1sc into each sc to end. Turn. 59[63] sc.
Beg patt.
1st row 4ch to count as first dc and 1ch, skip next sc, yo, insert hook into next sc, yo and draw a loop through, (yo, insert hook into same sc, yo and draw a loop through) 3 times, yo and draw through all loops on hook, called Cl1, *1ch, skip next sc, 1 cluster into next sc, 1ch, skip next sc, rep from * to end, finishing 1ch, skip next sc, 1dc into turning ch. Turn. 28[30] clusters.
2nd row 2ch, *1sc into next ch, 1sc into top of next cluster, rep from * to end, finishing 1sc into each of next 2ch. Turn. 59[63] sc.
3rd row 2ch, 1sc into each sc to end. Turn.
These 3 rows form patt. Cont in patt until back measures 12½[13¾]in (32[35]cm) from beg; end with 3rd patt row.**

Shape armholes
Next row Sl st over first 9sc, 4ch, *skip next sc, Cl1 into next sc, 1ch, rep from * until 20[22] clusters in all have been worked, 1ch, skip next sc, 1dc into next sc, turn and leave rem sts unworked.
Cont in patt as set, working 43[47] sts in each sc row, until back measures 9½[10¾]in (24[27]cm) from beg of armhole; end with 2nd patt row.

Shape shoulders
1st row Sl st over first 8sts, patt to within last 7sts, turn.
2nd row Patt to end. Turn.
3rd row Sl st over first 7sts, patt to within last 6sts. Fasten off.

Front
Work as for back from ** to **

Shape armholes and divide for neck
Next row Sl st over first 9sc; cont in patt until 10[11] clusters in all have been worked, turn and leave rem sts.
1st row Patt to end. Turn. 21[23] sc.
2nd row Patt to within last 3sc, work next 2sc tog to dec one st, 1sc into last sc. Turn. 20[22] sc.
3rd row 3ch, Cl1 into next sc, patt to end. Turn. 9[10] clusters.
4th row Patt to end. Turn.
5th row 2ch, dec one sc, patt to end. Turn.
6th row Patt to end. Turn.
Rep these 6 rows until 6 clusters rem, ending with a cluster row.

Shape shoulders
Next row Work 7[8]sc. Fasten off.
Return to rem sts. With RS of work facing, skip next sc, rejoin yarn to next st, Cl1, cont in patt until 10[11] clusters have been worked in all, 1ch, skip next sc, 1dc into next sc, turn and leave rem sts for armhole. Complete to match first side reversing shaping.

To finish
Join shoulder seams. Do not press.
Neck border
With RS of left front facing and using size G (4.50mm) hook, rejoin yarn to neck edge and work 33[37]sc down left front neck, skip center st, 33[37]sc up right front neck and 16[17]dc across back neck. Join with sl st to first sc. 82[91]sc. Working into back loop only, work 3 rounds in sc, dec 2sts at center on each round by working 3sc tog at point of V on every round. Fasten off.
Armhole borders (alike)
Join side seams. With RS of work facing join yarn to underarm and using size G (4.50mm) hook work 1sc into each st along underarm, then work in sc around armhole working 2sc into each cluster row end and 1sc for every 2sc row ends, then work 1sc into each st along underarm. Join with sl st to first sc. Working into back loop only, work 1 round in sc, sl st into first sc.
Next round Work 7sc, now work 2sc tog to dec one st, work 1sc into each sc all around armhole to within last 10sc, work next 2sc tog, work to end, sl st into first sc.
Next round 1sc into each of first 6sc, work next 2sc tog, 1sc into each sc to within last 9sc, work next 2sc tog, 1sc into each sc to end. Fasten off.

Knitting/COURSE 19

*Shaping a V-neck
*Making a traditional neckband using a pair of needles
*Making a cross-over neckband
*Pattern for two V-neck sweaters

Shaping a V-neck

When you make a garment with a V-neck you must divide the front of the work in the center and shape each side of the neck separately. The depth of the V may vary according to taste, but generally it is level with, or slightly lower than, the armhole shaping. Some patterns include precise directions for both sides of the neck while others give you directions for one side, then tell you to complete the second side to match the first; if this is the case, make sure you work the shaping at the correct edge.

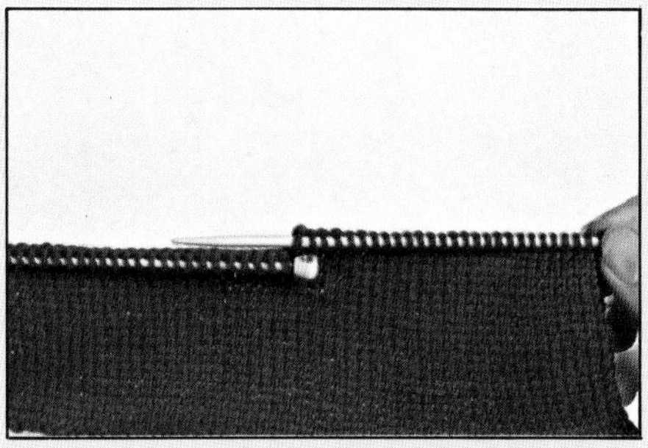

1 The neck shaping begins in the center of the front. On the right side row, work half the total number of stitches; leave the remainder of the row on a spare needle.

2 Turn and continue on first set of stitches for left side. In our sample there are 27 stitches, 15 of which are required for the shoulder shaping; so 12 stitches must be decreased. The frequency of decreasing depends on the row stitch gauge of the fabric.

3 When you have decreased to the necessary number of stitches for the shoulder you may have to work a small amount without shaping to reach the required armhole depth.

4 End at the armhole (outer) edge before beginning the shoulder shaping. Work the shoulder shaping as instructed in the pattern. The left side of the neck is complete here.

5 Return to the stitches left on a spare needle for the right side of the neck. Transfer the stitches onto a working needle; the point of the needle should be at the center front.

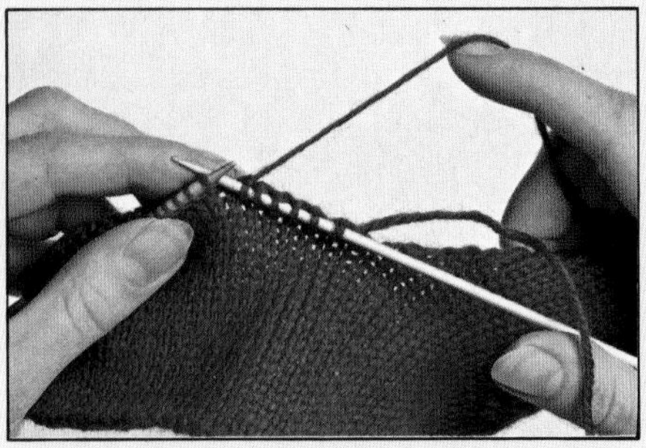

6 With the right side of the work facing, rejoin the yarn at the center front and knit to the end of the row.

7 Complete the second side of the neck to match the first. Take care to work the neck shaping at the correct edge; don't confuse the neck and armhole shapings and work them the wrong way around.

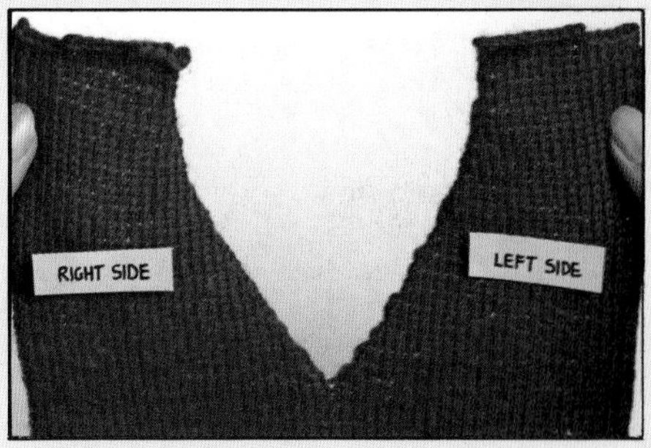

8 This is the completed front with the V-neck: it still requires some form of neckband to finish. The labels denote the right and left sides of the neck when the garment is worn.

Fred Mancini

Making a traditional neckband using a pair of needles

A ribbed neckband, worked directly onto the V-neck using picked-up stitches, neatens the edges of the neckline so that it fits correctly without gaping. The easiest method of working the neckband is with a pair of needles. By leaving open one shoulder seam—usually the left—you can knit the entire neckband backward and forward in rows. Afterward you must join the row ends of the neckband in line with the open shoulder. Stitches decreased at each side of the V-point at the center front neck help to maintain the neck shape. Often the decreases are at each side of a central stitch to give the effect of diagonal lines of ribbing converging on a central point. The center front stitch is repeated up through the neckband to form a vertical knit ribbing.

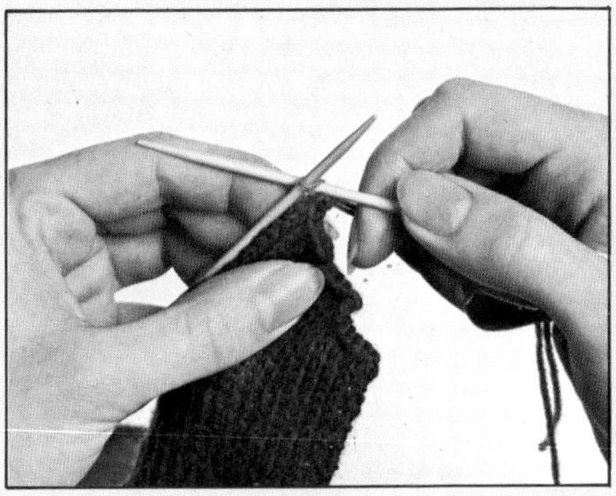

1 Join the right shoulder seam in the usual way. Take a pair of needles (generally two sizes smaller than those used for the main fabric) and the yarn for the neckband; with the right side of the work facing you, start picking up stitches at the left front shoulder.

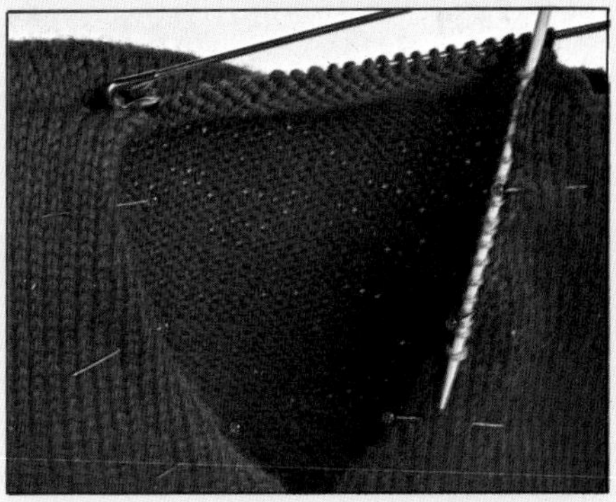

2 Some patterns tell you how many stitches to pick up in each section of the neck; others merely state the total number. When there is only a total number, divide each side of the neck into smaller, equal sections and pick up approximately the same number of stitches within each section. Generally you must pick up about two stitches to every three rows.

3 Pick up an odd number of stitches down the left side of the neck until you reach the point of V. Tie a marker loop of contrasting-colored yarn on right-hand needle. Pick up a stitch from the point of V; insert left-hand needle from front to back under horizontal loop of yarn lying between stitches at center front and pick it up and knit.

4 Tie another marker loop onto the right-hand needle after the center front stitch: these markers enclose the center front stitch and are slipped on every row. Continue up to the right shoulder, picking up the same number of stitches as on the other side of the neck.

5 Slip the back neck stitches from the holder onto the left-hand needle. In some cases, back neck stitches are previously bound off. In this case you would pick up and knit the necessary number of stitches across the bound-off edge.

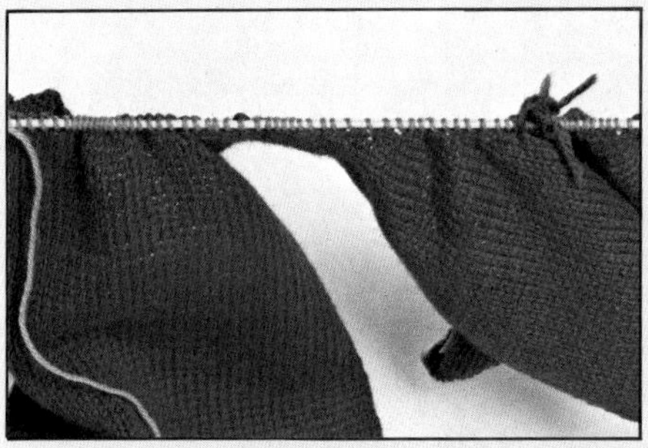

6 Knit across the back neck stitches from the needle, finishing at the open left shoulder. All the neck stitches are now on one needle. Notice that the neckline appears very distorted at this stage, having been put on one straight needle.

7 The wrong side of the work is now facing for the first (WS) row. Work in K1, P1 ribbing as directed to within two stitches of first marker; knit next two stitches together. Slip first marker; purl center stitch. Slip second marker. Knit next two stitches together. Rib to end.

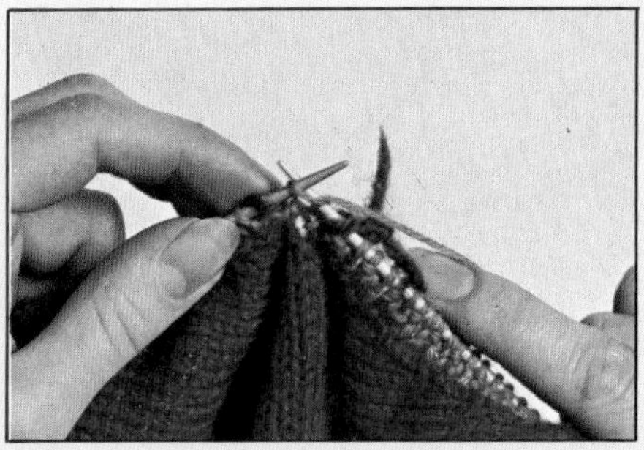

8 Work the second row on the right side of the fabric. There is no decrease on this row. Instead, work in ribbing as set, remembering to slip the markers as before. Here the center front stitch is always knitted on a right-side row and purled on a wrong-side row. *continued*

9 Repeat the last 2 rows for the depth you require; generally a neckband is about $1\frac{1}{4}$ to $1\frac{1}{2}$in (3 to 4cm) deep on an adult's garment. Finish with a wrong-side row.

10 Bind off in ribbing to give a flexible edge. Concentrate on keeping an even tension throughout, so that the ribs lie smoothly without slanting to the right or to the left. This takes a little practice. In some patterns you may have to decrease at each side of the center front stitch before binding off the resulting single stitch. Discard the markers.

11 This is the finished neckband with a knit rib running up the center front neck and neat decreases at each side of it. Complete the neckline by joining the left shoulder and neckband seams.

Making a cross-over neckband

A cross-over neckband is a classic variation of the traditional type; it is worked in a similar ribbing, but overlaps at the center front. This is an easy style to work, as it requires no shaping. Again, you can leave an open shoulder and use a pair of needles for working the band in rows. Pick up stitches down one side of the front neck and complete this side first; then use stitches from the other side of the front neck, plus the back neck stitches, to make another similar band. Afterward, overlap the neckband row end at the center front and neatly sew them down.

1 Join the right shoulder seam in the usual way. Follow steps 1 and 2 of making a traditional neckband until you have picked up the required number of stitches down the left side of the neck.

2 Work in rows of K1, P1 ribbing on the left side of the neck until the band is the required depth. Bind off in ribbing.

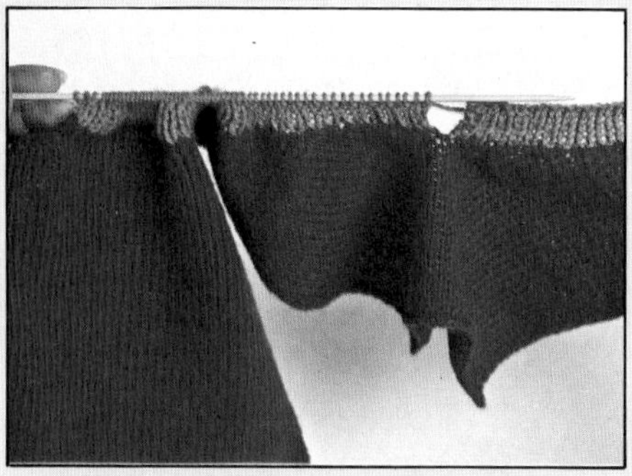

3 With the right side of the work facing you, begin at the center front neck and work along the right side of the neck to the shoulder. Pick up the same number of stitches as before, then slip back neck stitches on to the left-hand needle and knit across them.

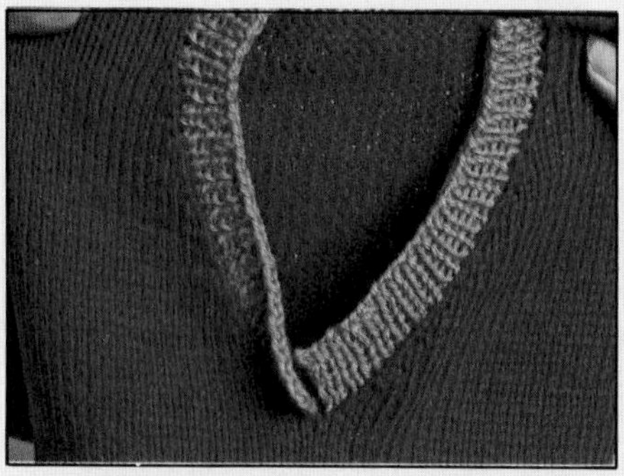

4 Continue in K1, P1 ribbing on these stitches: work same number of rows as for other side of neck. Bind off in ribbing.

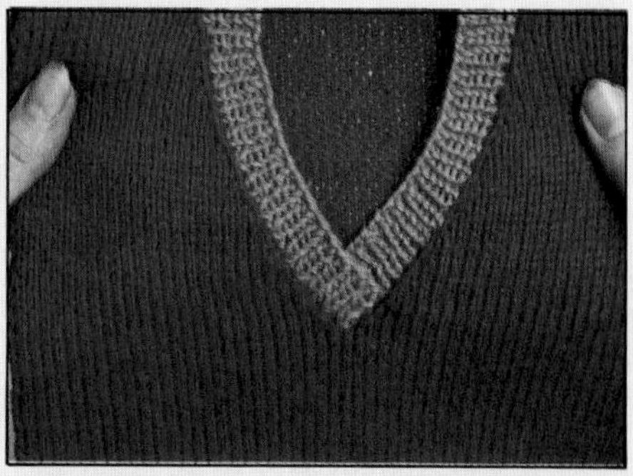

5 Finish the cross-over at the center front neck as follows: lap the right neckband over the left. Secure the left edge first by slip stitching the ends of rows of the neckband along the ridge of picked up stitches on the wrong side of the work. On the right side, neatly sew down the ends of rows from the right neckband in the same way.

Fred Mancini

Winter Classics

A must for your winter wardrobe, these classic styles have been updated by using a fashionable bouclé yarn with interesting combinations of color and texture.

Sizes
To fit 32[34:36:38]in (83[87:92:97]cm) bust.
Length, $22\frac{3}{4}$ [23:$23\frac{1}{2}$:24]in (58 [59:60:61]cm).
Sleeve seam, 17 [$17\frac{1}{2}$:18:$18\frac{1}{2}$]in (43 [44:46:47]cm).

Note Directions for larger sizes are in brackets [ ]; where there is only one set of figures it applies to all sizes.

Materials
Sleeveless sweater: 7 [9:9:9]oz (200 [250:250:250]g) of a medium weight bouclé yarn in main color, 3oz (75g) of a knitting worsted in contrasting color
Sweater with sleeves: $12\frac{1}{2}$ [$12\frac{1}{2}$:14:14]oz (350 [350:400:400]g) of a medium weight bouclé yarn in main color, 2 [2:3:3]oz

Kim Sayer

(50 [50:75:75]g) of a knitting worsted in a contrasting color
1 pair each Nos. 5 and 7 (4 and 5mm) knitting needles

Gauge
16 sts and 24 rows to 4in (10cm) in reverse stockinette st.

Sleeveless sweater

Back
Using No. 5 (4mm) needles and knitting worsted, cast on 68 [72:76:80] sts. Work in K1, P1 ribbing for 3½in (8cm). Change to No. 7 (5mm) needles and bouclé yarn. Beg with a P row, cont in reverse stockinette st until back measures 14½ [14½:15:15]in (37 [37:38:38]cm); end with K row.

Shape armholes
Bind off 8 sts at beg of next 2 rows. 52 [56:60:64] sts. Cont without shaping until armholes measure 8¼ [8½:8½:9]in (21 [22:22:23]cm); end with K row.

Shape shoulders
Bind off 8 [9:10:10] sts at beg of next 4 rows. Leave rem sts on a holder.

Front
Work as for back until 13½[13¾:13¾:14]in (34[35:35:35.5]cm) have been completed from beg; end with K row

Divide for neck
Next row P34 [36:38:40] sts, turn and leave rem sts on spare needle. Complete left side of neck first. Dec one st at neck edge on next and every foll 4th row until 31 [33:35:37] sts rem; end with K row.

Shape armholes
Bind off 8 sts at beg of next row. 23 [25:27:29] sts. Keeping armhole edge straight, cont to shape front edge on every 4th row until 16[18:20:22] sts rem. Cont straight until armhole measures 8¼[8½:8½:9]in (21 [22:22:23]cm) from beg, ending at armhole edge.

Shape shoulder
Bind off 8 [9:10:10] sts at beg of next row. Work 1 row. Bind off. With RS facing, join yarn to inner end of sts on spare needle and complete to match first side, reversing shapings.

Neckband
Join right shoulder seam. Using No. 5 (4mm) needles, knitting worsted and with RS of work facing, pick up and K 41 [43:45:47] sts along left front neck. Tie a loop of contrasting-colored yarn to act as a marker on right-hand needle, pick up and K one loop from center front neck, add another marker loop, pick up and K 41 [43:45:47] sts along right front neck, then K the back neck sts from holder. 103 [107:111:119] sts.
1st row (WS) K1, (P1, K1) to within 2 sts of 1st marker, K2 tog, sl first marker, P center front st, sl 2nd marker, K2 tog, K1, (P1, K1) to end.
2nd row Keep ribs as set; work to end. Rep these 2 rows 3 times; work first row again. Bind off loosely in ribbing.

Armhole borders
Join left shoulder and neckband seam. Using No. 5 (4mm) needles, knitting worsted and with RS of work facing, pick up and K 82 [82:84:84] sts along straight edge of armhole, omitting bound-off sts. Work K1, P1 ribbing for 2in (5cm), ending with a WS row. Bind off loosely in ribbing.

To finish
Join side seams. Join short edges of armhole borders to bound-off sts at underarm.

Sweater with sleeves

Front and back as sleeveless sweater.

Sleeves
Using No. 5 (4mm) needles and knitting worsted, cast on 36 [38:40:42] sts. Work K1, P1 ribbing for 3½in (8cm). Change to No. 7 (5mm) needles and bouclé yarn. Beg with a P row, cont in reverse stockinette st, inc one st at each end of next and every foll 5th row until there are 64 [66:68:68] sts. Cont without shaping until sleeve measures 17 [17½:18:18½]in (43 [44:46:47]cm) from beg. Bind off.

Neckband
Join right shoulder seam. Using No. 5 (4mm) needles, knitting worsted and with RS of work facing pick up and K 42 [44:46:48] sts along left front neck. Work K1, P1 ribbing for 1½in (4cm). Bind off loosely in ribbing.
Using No. 5 (4mm) needles, knitting worsted and RS facing, pick up and K 42 [44:46:48] sts along right front neck; K the back neck sts from holder. 62 [64:66:72] sts. Rib K1, P1 for 1½in (4cm). Bind off in ribbing.

To finish
Join left shoulder and neckband. Join sides. Join sleeves; leave 2in (5cm) open at top. Set in sleeves; sew open ends to bound-off sts at underarm. Sew on short ends of neckband, right on top.

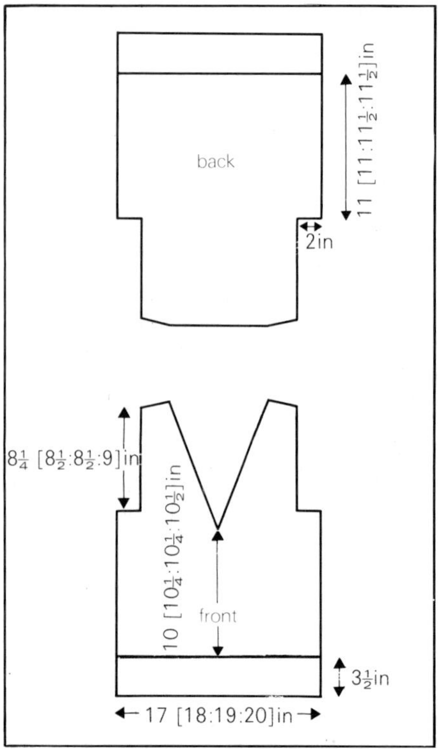

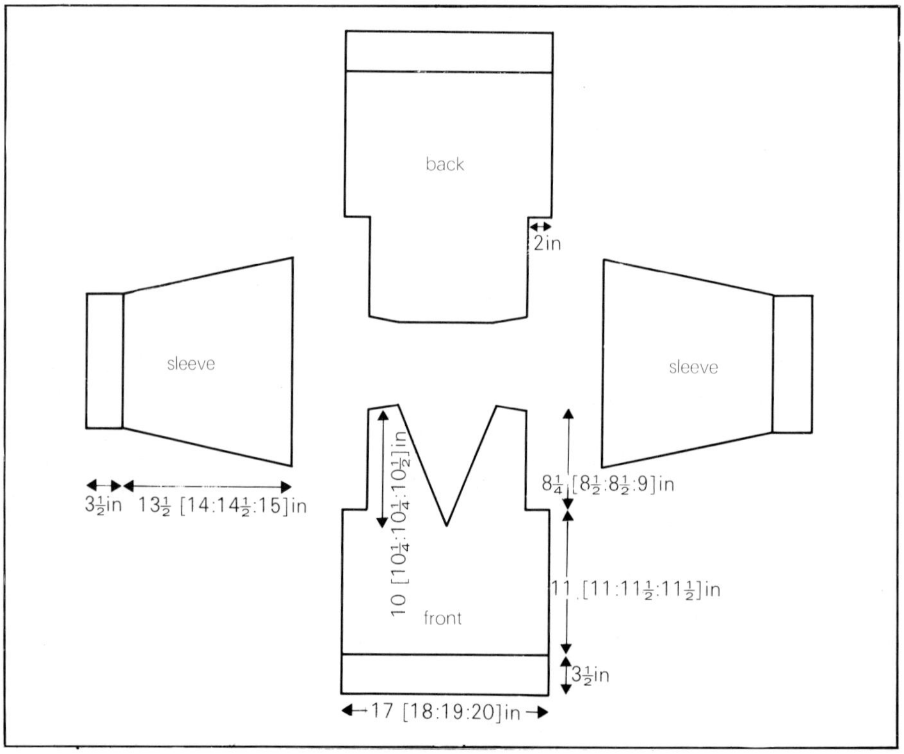

Brian Mayor

*Sewn-in hem
*Knitted-in hem
*Eyelet holes
*Picot hem
*Pattern for a girl's top and skirt

Sewn-in hem

The lower edges of skirts, dresses, coats and jackets often benefit from having extra weight—such as that provided by a hem—to help them hang properly.
There are two main ways of turning up a horizontal hem worked in one with the main fabric. In one method you turn up the hem after the garment is complete and then stitch it in place. In the other method you knit the cast-on edge into the fabric, so forming the hem as you knit the garment.
For a particularly neat appearance a pattern will sometimes instruct you to use one size smaller needles to work the underside of the hem and then change to the larger needle size after the row that marks the hemline.

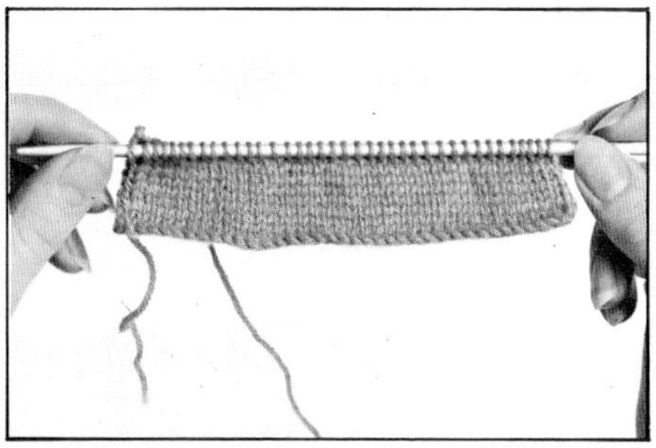

1 Cast on the required number of stitches using the two-needle method. Beginning with a knit row, work an odd number of rows—here it is nine—in stockinette stitch to give the necessary depth for the underside of the hem.

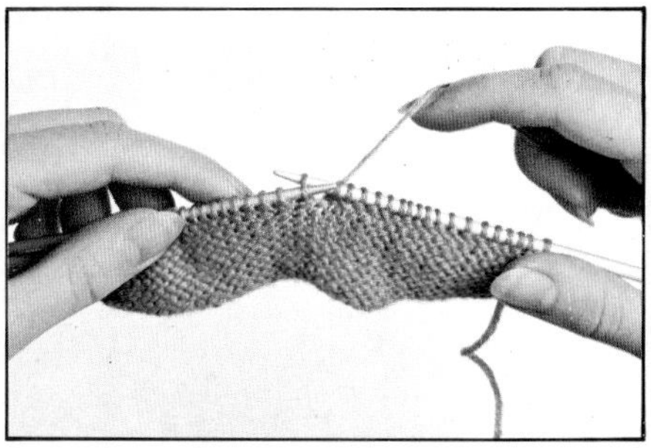

2 Instead of purling the next row, knit each stitch through the back of the loop.

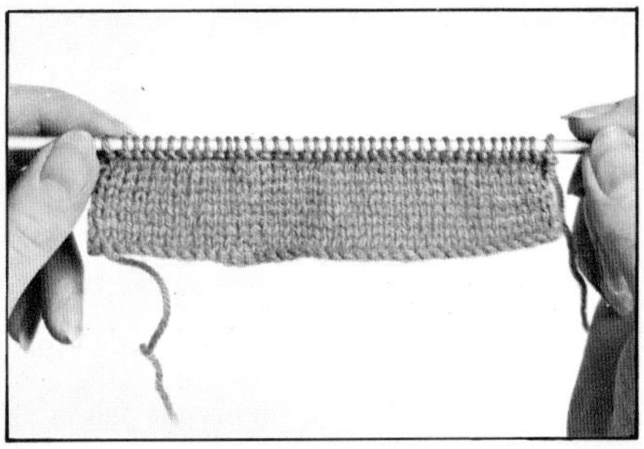

3 This makes a garter stitch-type ridge on the right side of the knitting to mark the foldline (or lower edge) of the hem.

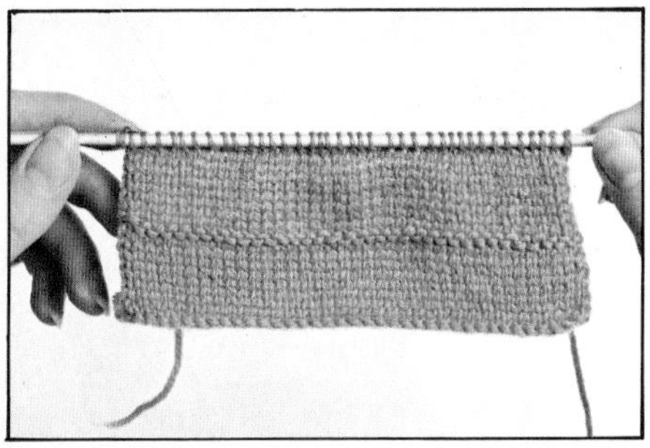

4 Beginning with a knit row, continue working stockinette stitch for the depth stated in the pattern. You need at least one more row than the number worked on underside of hem.

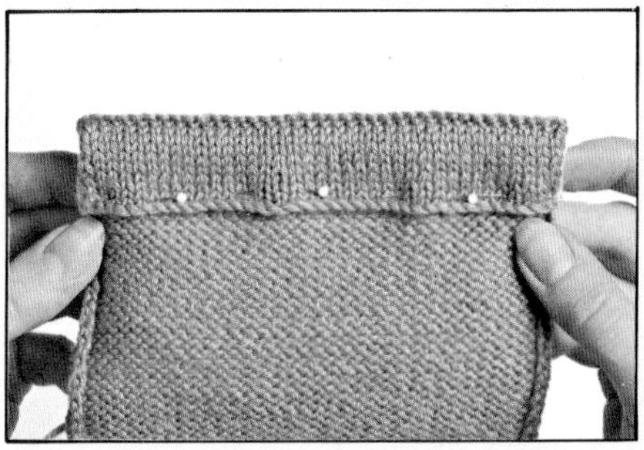

5 After the garment is complete, turn the hem to the wrong side at the foldline: pin in position keeping the cast-on edge straight in line with a row of knitting.

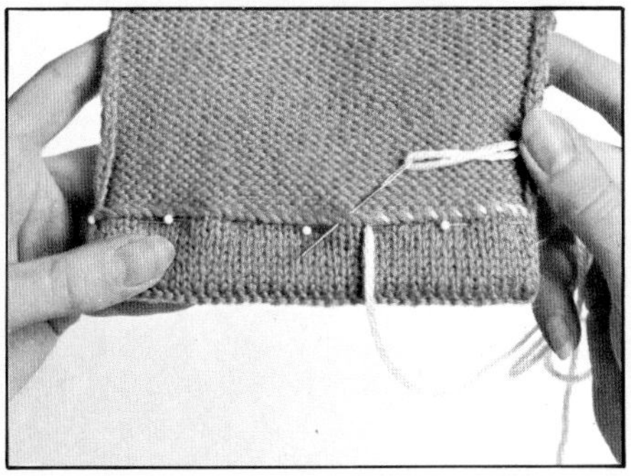

6 Using matching yarn (here it is in a contrasting color for clarity), slip stitch the hem in position.

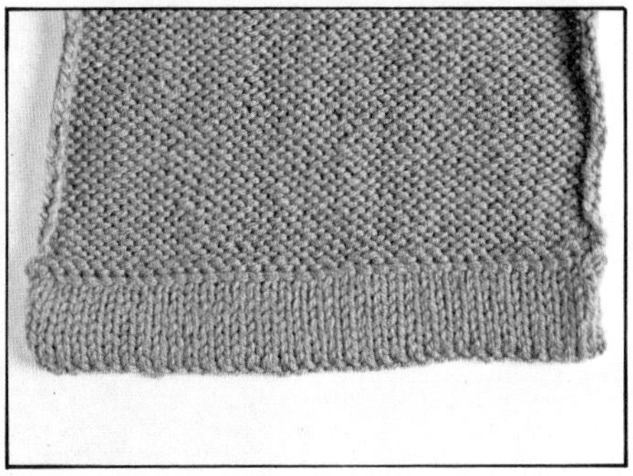

7 The picture shows the finished hem on the wrong side of the work. Note that the stitching is practically invisible.

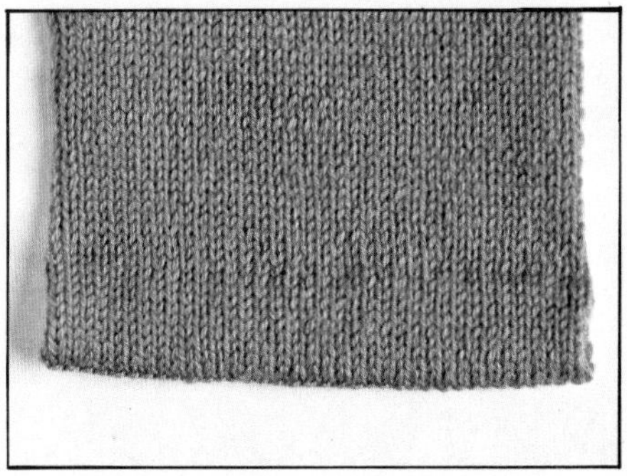

8 Here is the finished hem on the right side of the work; it has a slightly scalloped appearance where the hem is folded back.

Fred Mancini

Knitted-in hem

This is the other popular way of making a hem. It appears similar to the sewn-in hem on the right side of the work, but the hem is knitted into the fabric instead of being stitched. Use an extra needle to pick up loops from the cast-on edge. Pick up the same number of stitches as you are working and then knit the two sets together so that you automatically knit the edge of the hem into the fabric. At a later stage, when you join the side seams of the fabric, sew through both thicknesses of the hem.

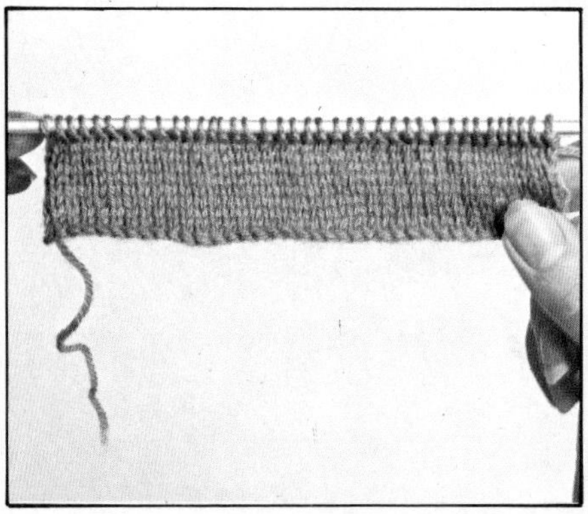

1 Cast on the required number of stitches using the two-needle method. Work as given for sewn-in hem until you have completed step 2.

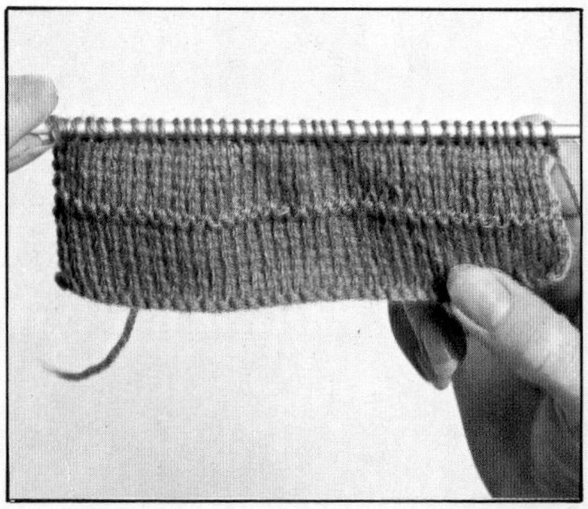

2 Beginning with a knit row, continue in stockinette stitch. Work one row less than for underside of hem—here it is eight—so ending with a purl row.

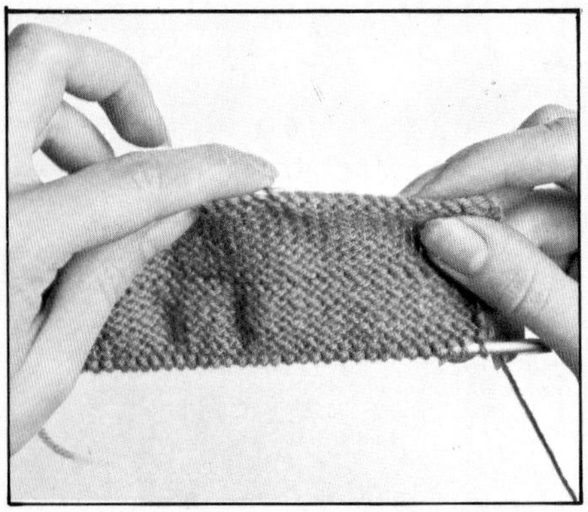

3 Take a spare needle the same size as the pair you are using. With the wrong side of the work facing and cast-on edge at the top, work from left to right and use the spare needle to pick up loops from the cast-on edge. Slip the needle from front to back through each loop. Check that you have the same number of stitches as you cast on originally.

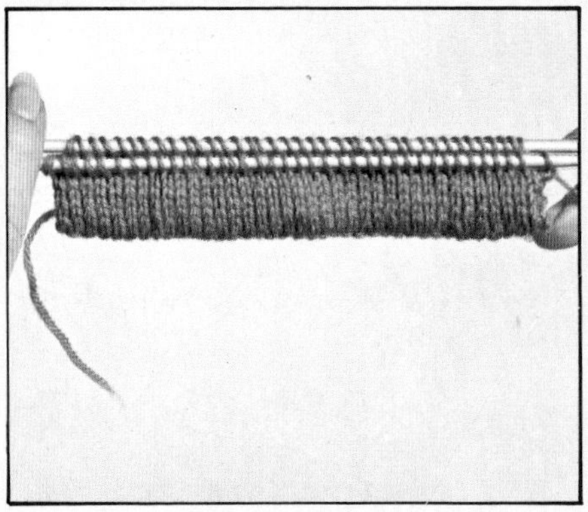

4 Fold the work in half so that the two stitches are level, with both needle points facing in the same direction. The needle holding the loops from the cast-on edge is at the back and the foldline is at the lower edge.

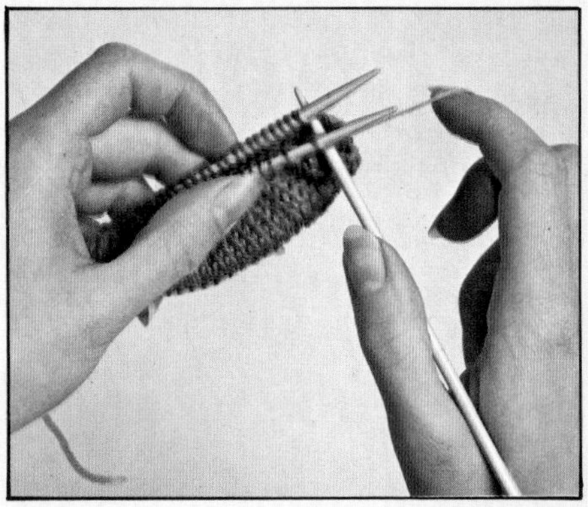

5 Insert right-hand needle knitwise through the first stitch on needle at the front of the work. Push needle-point further and insert it knitwise through the first stitch on the needle at the back of the work. Knit both stitches simultaneously so that there is one stitch on the right-hand needle.

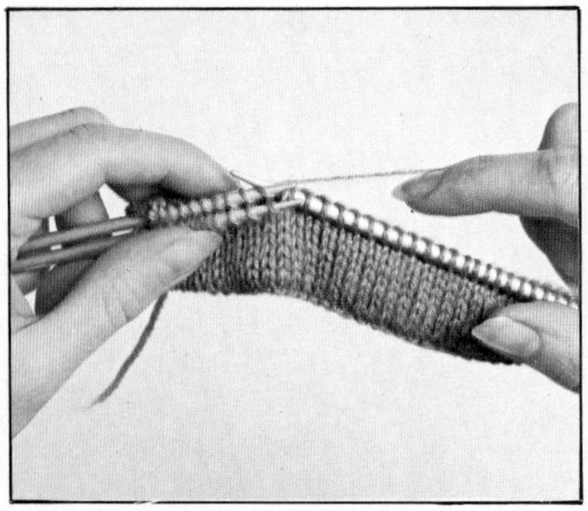

6 Continue knitting across the row, taking one stitch from the front needle and one from the back (cast-on loops) each time.

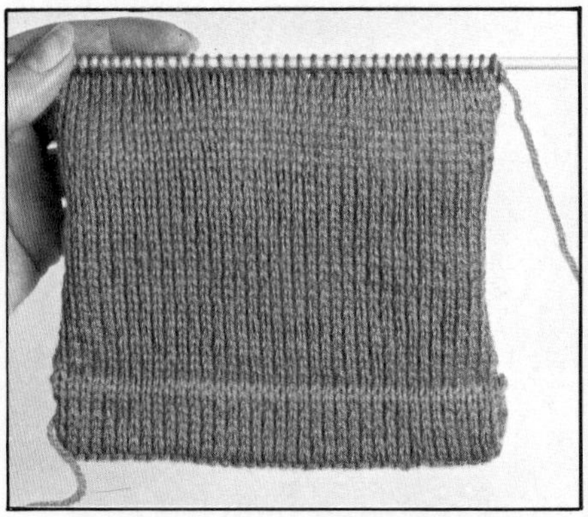

7 Beginning with a purl row continue in stockinette stitch or pattern as directed.

8 The photograph shows the finished hem on the wrong and right sides of the work. The wrong side is particularly neat where the edge of the hem is knitted into the fabric. The right side appears similar to a sewn-in hem.

Eyelet holes

An eyelet is a hole made in the fabric by a technique known as "decorative increasing"; this type of increasing is the basis of many lace patterns which require a decorative eyelet—you can see how they could be used on the girl's top and skirt, page 41.

Apart from being attractive, eyelets have other, more functional purposes. Thread a drawstring in and out of the holes, then draw it up to gather the fabric for a simple, yet stylish method of shaping the fabric and fastening the garment at the same time.

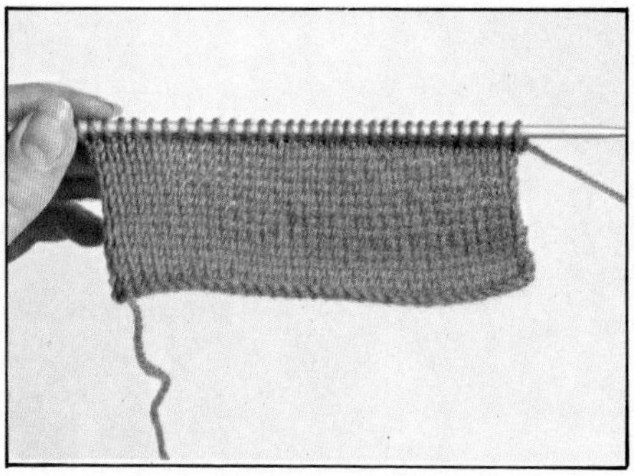

1 Work a stockinette stitch fabric on an odd number of stitches as the basis for the eyelet holes. Start to work the eyelet holes with the right side of the fabric facing you.

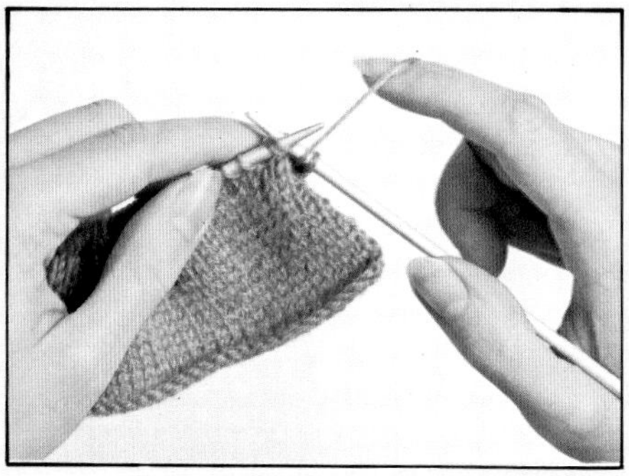

2 Knit the first two stitches together. Bring yarn forward to the front of the work between the two needles, then back over the needle to knit the next two stitches together—which is abbreviated as "yo." This makes an extra loop on the right-hand needle, thereby replacing the stitch that you will have lost by decreasing.

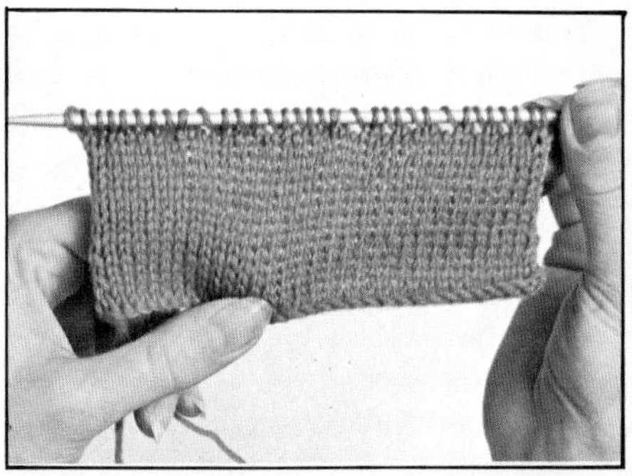

3 Continue in this way, bringing the yarn forward, then over the needle and knitting two stitches together, until you reach the last stitch; bring the yarn forward and knit this in the usual way, which increase one stitch to balance the decrease at the start of the row.

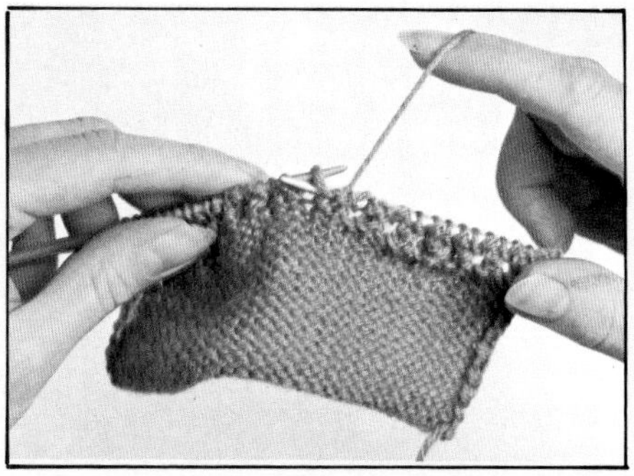

4 Beginning with a purl row, continue in stockinette stitch. The stitches made by taking the yarn over needle in the previous row are merely long loose strands; when you purl them the hole appears in the fabric.

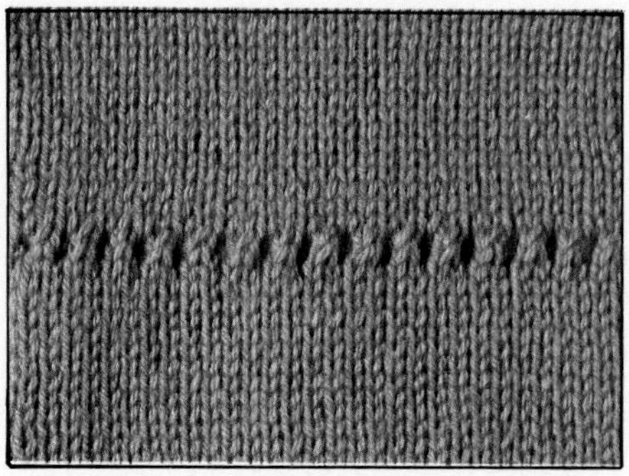

5 This shows the finished effect of the eyelet holes on the right side of the work. In some patterns—such as the top and skirt in this course—the holes are spaced farther apart and a drawstring is threaded through the holes to gather up the fabric.

Picot hem

This variation of a stockinette stitch hem can either be knitted in or sewn at a later stage. A row of eyelet holes marks the foldline; when the hem is folded in half, the eyelets form a dainty, pointed—or picot—edging.

Picots are small loops of yarn with a twisted appearance that often decorate lacy edgings: babies' garments often feature picot hems as the loops are particularly effective worked in the more delicate yarns and patterns.

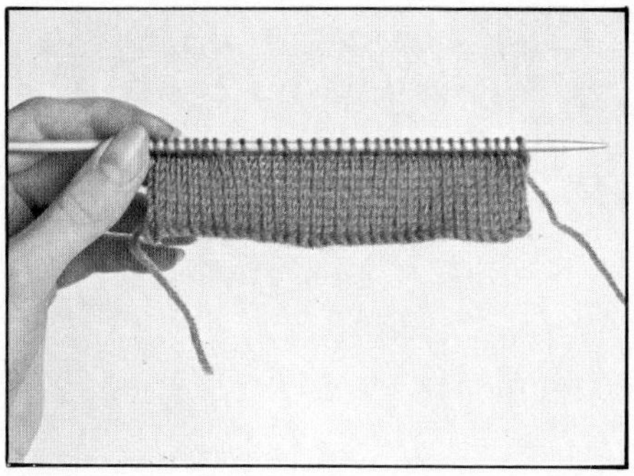

1 Cast on an odd number of stitches using the two-needle method. Beginning with a knit row, work an even number of rows—here it is 10—in stockinette stitch, ending with a purl row.

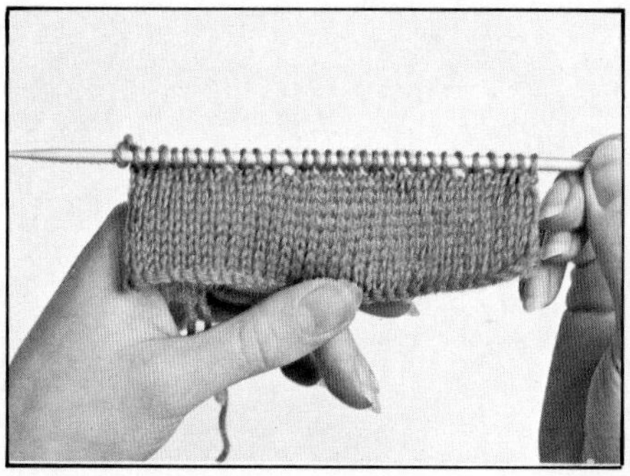

2 Work eyelet holes in the next row as described in steps 2 and 3 of "Eyelet holes."

Fred Mancini

continued

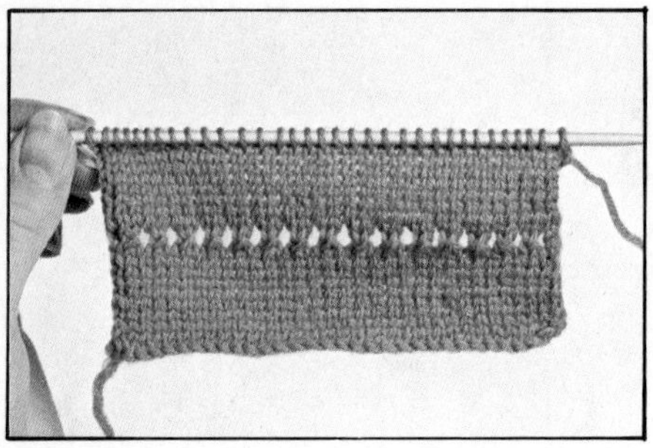

3 Beginning with a purl row, work one row less—here there are nine rows—than in underside of hem, so ending with a purl row.

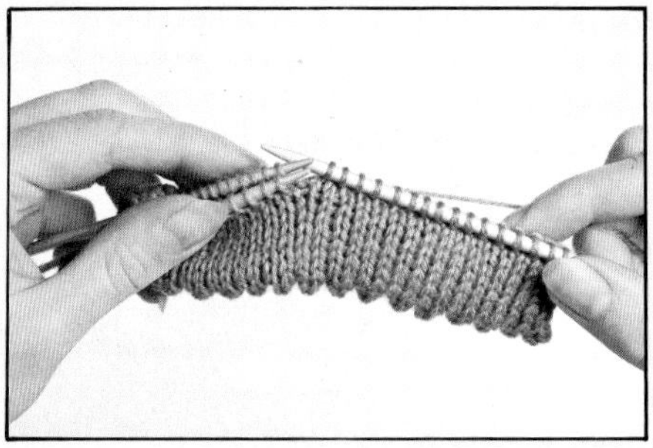

4 Knit in the hem as given for steps 4, 5 and 6 of "Knitted-in hem." Fold hem in half at eyelet-hole row. Or, if you prefer, continue knitting, and sew up the hem afterward.

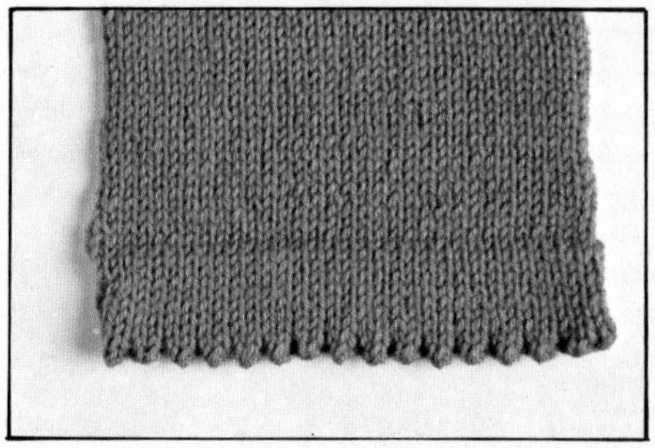

5 The photograph above shows the finished effect of the hem on the right side of the work. The eyelet-hole row folds in half to give the serrated effect of picot points.

Fred Mancini

Pretty as a picture

This pretty skirt and top can be worn together or separately. They are based on a simple rectangular shape and have a dainty picot edging. Both are gathered with a twisted cord.

Sizes

Top to fit, 26[28:30]in (66[71:76]cm) chest.

Length of top to underarm, 10¼[11¼: 12½]in (26[29:32]cm).

Skirt length, 18[19½:21]in (46[50: 54]cm).

Note Directions for larger sizes are in brackets [ ]; where there is only one set of figures it applies to all sizes.

Materials

Top 4[5:5]oz (100[120:140]g) of a variegated sport yarn

Skirt 9[9:10]oz (240[240:260]g) of a variegated sport yarn

1 pair of No. 3 (3¼mm) knitting needles

Gauge

28 sts and 36 rows to 4in (10cm) in stockinette st.

Top (back and front alike)

Using No. 3 (3¼mm) needles and two-needle method, cast on 129[137:145]sts.

** Beg with a K row, work 10 rows stockinette st.

Picot row *K2tog, yo, rep from * to last st, K1.

Beg with a P row, work 9 rows stockinette st.

Hem row Fold work in half with cast on edge behind work and K tog one st from needle with one st from cast-on edge, rep to end of row. This completes hem.

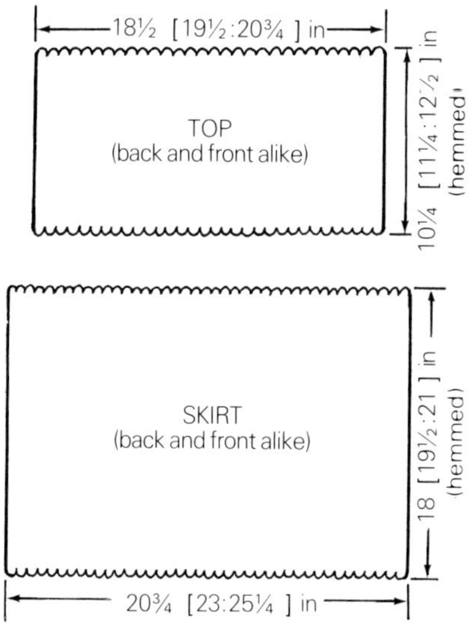

John Hutchinson

Beg with P row, work 15 rows in stockinette st.

Commence patt.

1st row K4, *yo, K2tog, K6, rep from * to last 5sts, yo, K2tog, K3.

2nd-6th rows Beg with a P row, work in stockinette st.

7th row K8, *yo, K2tog, K6, rep from * to last st, K1.

8th-12th rows Beg with a P row, work in stockinette st.

13th row As first row. **

Cont in stockinette st until work measures 10[11:12¼]in (25[28:31]cm) from hem; end with P row.

Eyelet-hole row K4, *yo, K2tog, K6, rep from * to last 5sts, yo, K2tog, K3. Work 3 rows stockinette st.

Picot row *K2tog, yo, rep from * to last st, K1.

Work 3 rows in stockinette st.

Eyelet-hole row K4, *yo, K2tog, K6, rep from * to last 5sts, yo, K2tog, K3.

Work 3 rows stockinette st. Bind off.

To finish

Block according to yarn used, pressing lightly. Join side seams. Fold top hem in half at picot row; slip stitch. Press seams. Using 4 strands of yarn together make a twisted cord 47in (120cm) long and thread through eyelet holes in top hem. Using 4 strands of yarn make 8 cords 27in (70cm) long, thread one cord through 2 eyelet holes on front and another cord through corresponding 2 eyelet holes on back to form shoulder strap. Make other shoulder strap in the same way.

Skirt (back and front alike)

Using No. 3 (3¼mm) needles and two-needle method, cast on 145[161:177] sts and work as for smock from ** to **.

Cont in stockinette st until work measures 17¾[19¼:20¾]in (45[49:53]cm) from hem; end with P row.

Next row K4, *bind off 2, K until there are 6 sts on right-hand needle after bound-off group, rep from * to last 5 sts, bind off 2, K to end.

Next row P to end, casting on 2 sts over each 2 bound off.

Work 10 rows stockinette st.

Picot row *K2tog, yo, rep from * to last st, K1.

Beg with a P row, work 9 rows stockinette st. Bind off.

To finish

Press as for top. Join side seams. Fold top hem in half at picot row and slip stitch in position. Press seams. Using 4 strands of yarn make a twisted cord 55in (140cm) long and thread through holes at waist.

*Making an inserted horizontal pocket
*Making an inserted vertical pocket
*Pattern for a woman's jacket

Making an inserted horizontal pocket

Many garments feature pockets for decorative and practical purposes. Inserted pockets consist of a knitted lining (this is often in stockinette stitch regardless of the main fabric) inserted behind an opening made in the main fabric; the open edge is finished at a later stage. Besides being functional, these pockets are also fairly inconspicuous. Details of working methods are included in pattern directions, but you can adapt a basic design to include pockets if you like. First, decide on the size and position of the pocket. An inserted horizontal pocket is normally placed just above the waistband of a cardigan. Calculate the position of the opening so that the lining lies clear of any ribbing beneath it or any border or edge to the side of it.

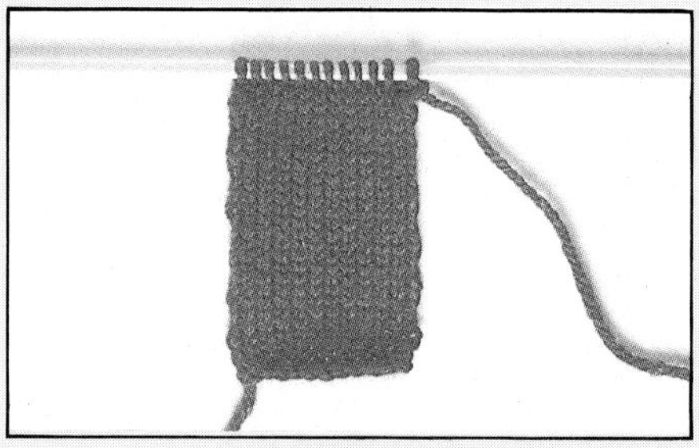

1 First make the pocket lining. Using the same size needles and yarn as those used for the main fabric, cast on the required number of stitches. Here the lining is a different color from the main fabric for the sake of clarity. Work the necessary depth in stockinette stitch, ending with a purl row. Cut off the yarn and then slip these stitches onto a spare needle. Put the lining aside for the time being.

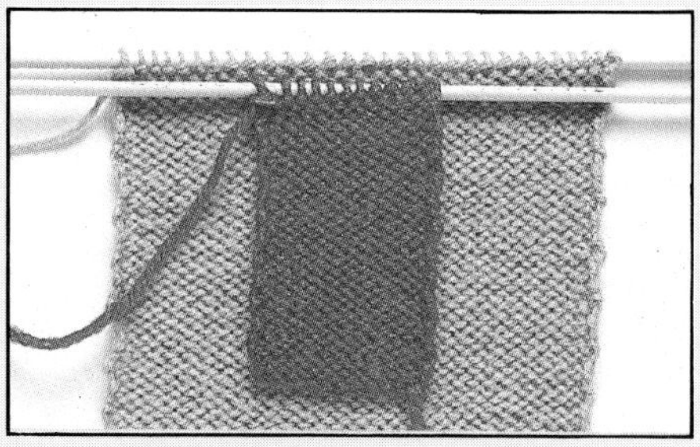

2 Work on the main fabric as instructed in the pattern. You need enough depth above any hem or waistband for the lining to fit in. Continue until you reach the position for the opening of the pocket, ending with a purl row.

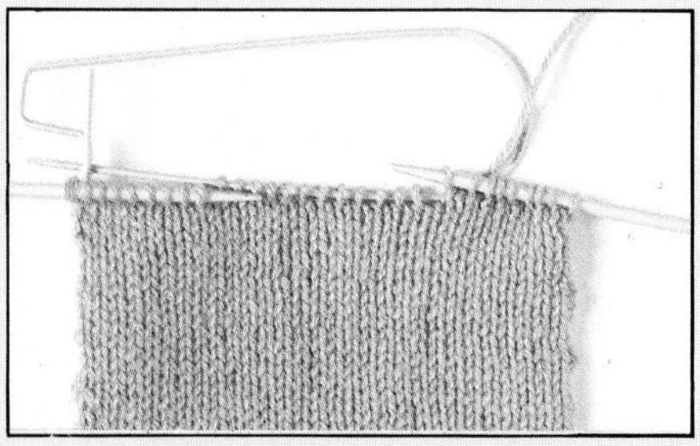

3 On the next row—usually known as the "pocket row"—knit to the position of the opening. Slip the next group of stitches onto a holder. These must correspond to those in the lining.

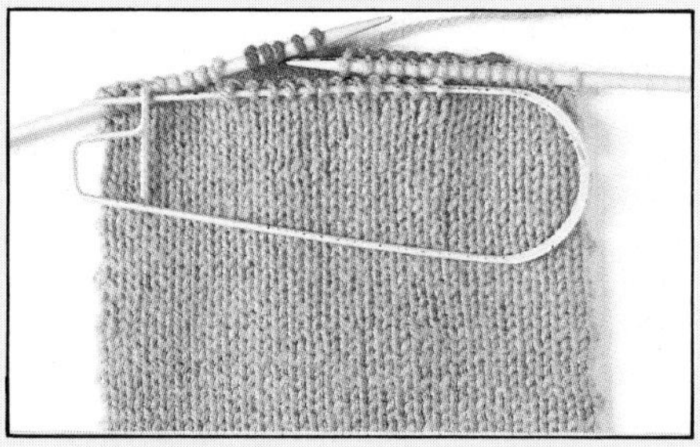

4 Replace stitches on holder with those of lining. Slip lining stitches onto left-hand needle so that RS of lining is against WS of main fabric. Knit across lining stitches.

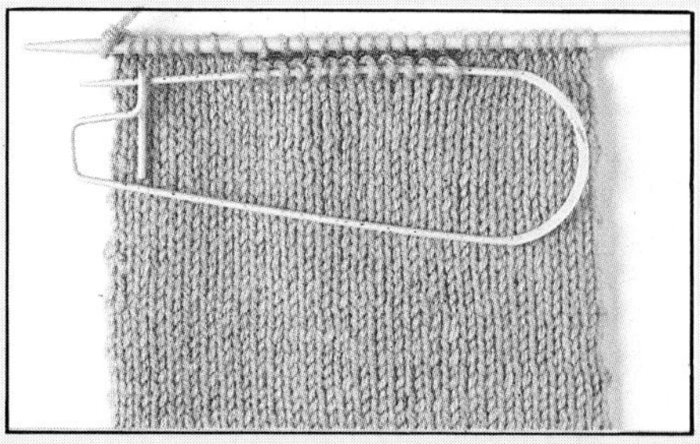

5 After all the lining stitches have been knitted onto the right-hand needle, continue knitting the stitches of the main fabric until you reach the end of the row.

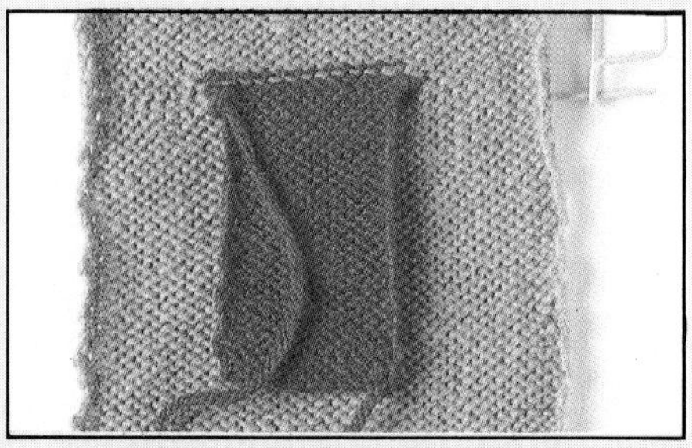

6 The pocket is now inserted. Beginning with a wrong-side row, continue with the main fabric, following the pattern directions.

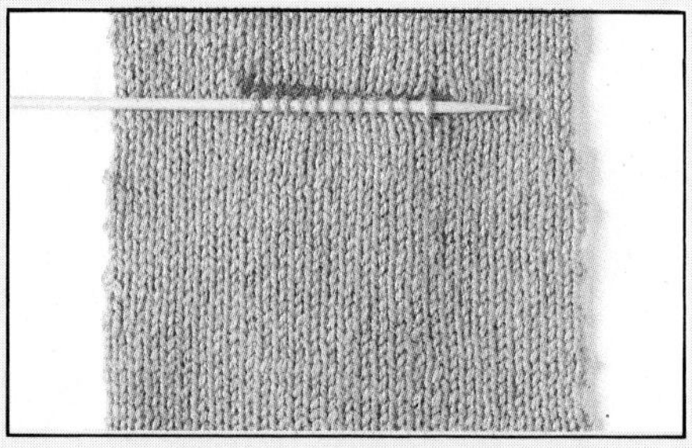

7 After the section of garment you are working on is complete, finish stitches left on holder with a ribbed border—called the "pocket top." This is normally worked on needles two sizes smaller. With RS of work facing, slip stitches from holder onto left-hand needle.

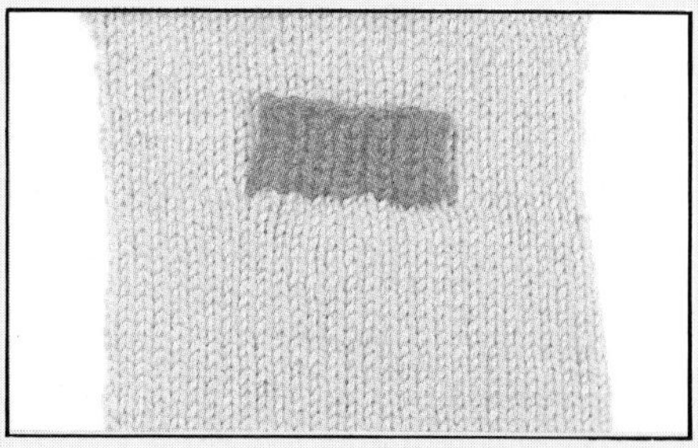

8 Join on yarn and make a border about $1\frac{1}{4}$in (3cm) deep. Here it is worked in K1, P1 ribbing, but you can use other combinations of ribbing or a different kind of stitch. Bind off in ribbing.

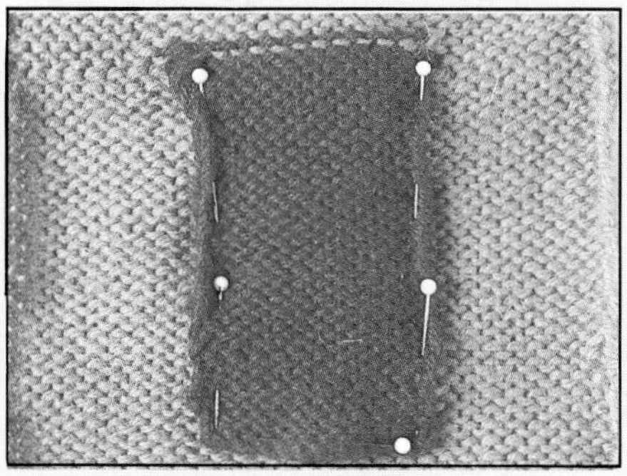

9 To finish the pocket, pin the lining in position on the wrong side of the work. If the main fabric is in stockinette stitch, try to match the lining to the correct number of rows and stitches: this prevents it from pulling the main fabric out of shape.

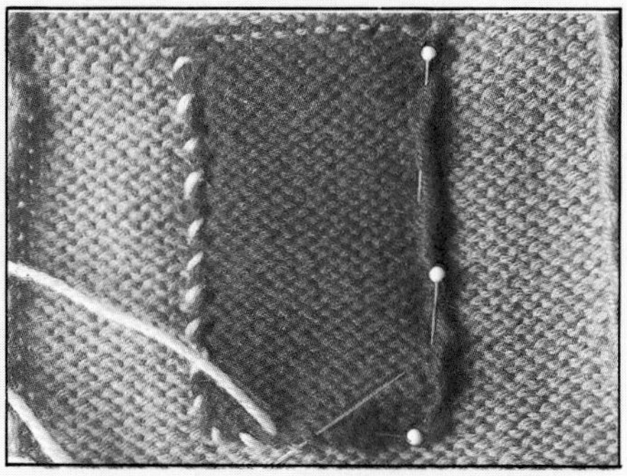

10 Using a blunt-ended yarn needle and matching yarn—here it is contrasting for clarity—slip stitch around the three sides of the lining flap.

11 To complete the pocket on the right side of the work, sew down the short ends of the border; slip stitch them neatly in position using a matching colored yarn.

Making an inserted vertical pocket

This pocket is similar in type to the horizontal one except that the opening lies vertically on the garment. The opening goes across rows rather than a group of stitches as in the horizontal version.

For a vertical pocket there is no need to work the lining separately; when you divide the work for the opening, you cast on extra stitches and work the lining in one with the main fabric.

The lining of a vertical pocket always lies toward the center front of a garment. If you adapt a cardigan pattern to include this type of pocket, you must make sure that it doesn't extend beyond the front edge.

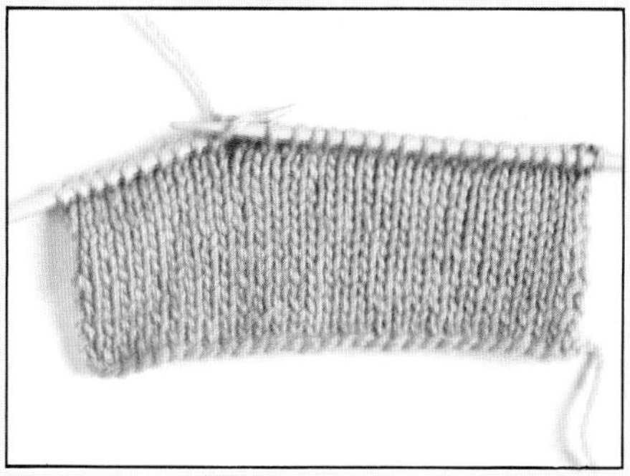

1 Work the main fabric—here it is stockinette stitch—until you reach the position for the pocket. On a wrong-side row, purl to where the fabric is to be divided for the opening. Turn and continue on the first set of stitches for one side of the opening.

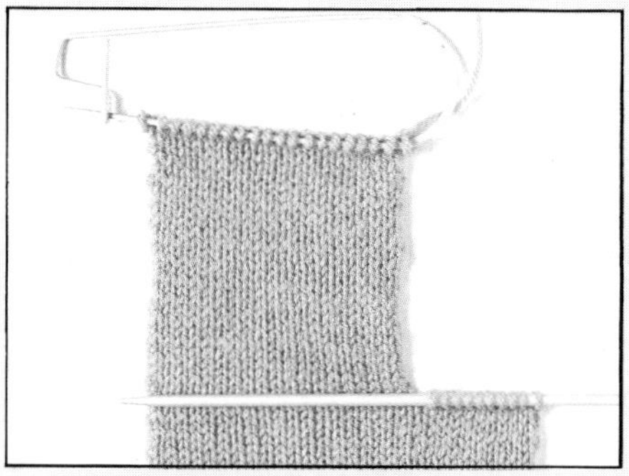

2 Patterns give detailed directions of the number of rows you must work on the first set of stitches to give the necessary depth for the opening. For our sample you must work an even number of rows—26—so ending with a wrong-side row. Cut off the yarn and leave these stitches on a holder.

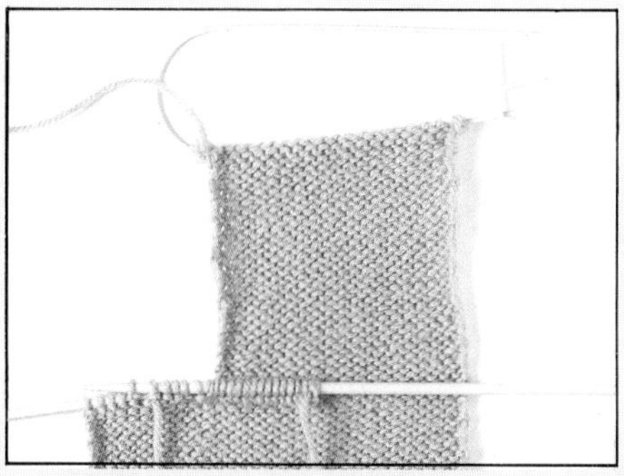

3 Using the same ball of yarn, cast the pocket lining stitches onto the free needle. For our sample, cast on 16 stitches; the pattern you are using will specify the precise number. Take the needle with the cast-on stitches in your right hand; then, with the wrong side of the work facing, purl across the stitches on the left-hand needle that were left at the base of the opening.

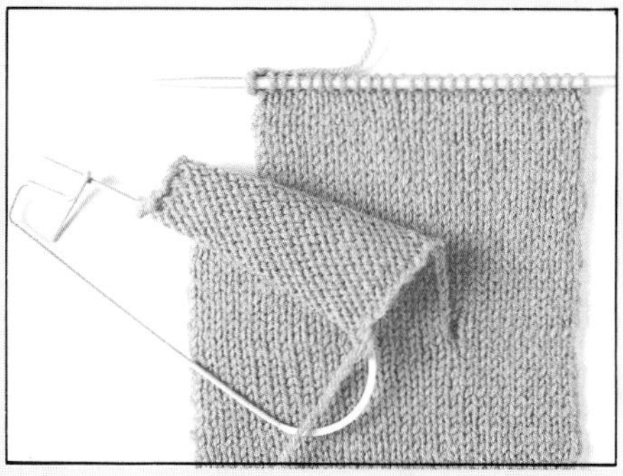

4 Continue in stockinette stitch for the second side of the opening and the lining. Work one less row than for the previous side—25 in this case—so ending with a right-side row.

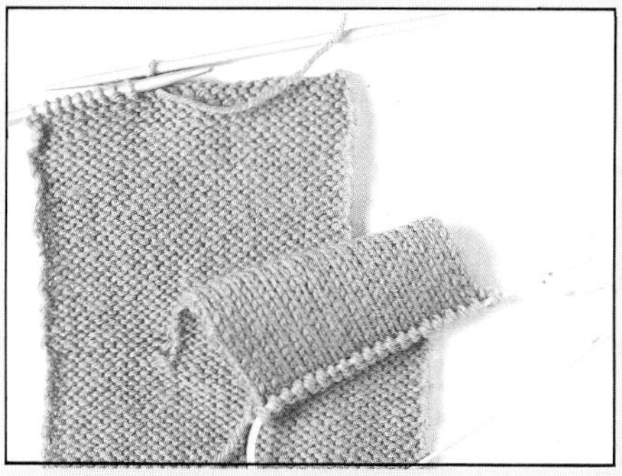

5 The lining is now complete. At the beginning of the next (purl) row, bind off the same number of stitches that you cast on previously for the pocket lining. After binding off the stitches, purl to the end of the row.

Fred Mancini

continued

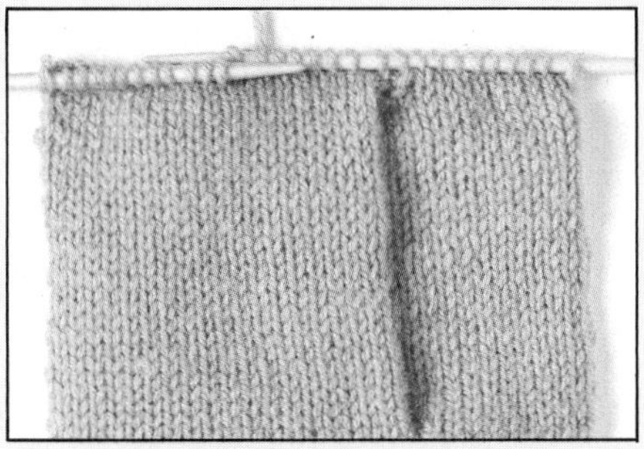

6 Both sides of the opening are now complete. Join the two separate sections on the next row. Knit across side just completed; transfer stitches from first side from holder onto left-hand needle and knit across them.

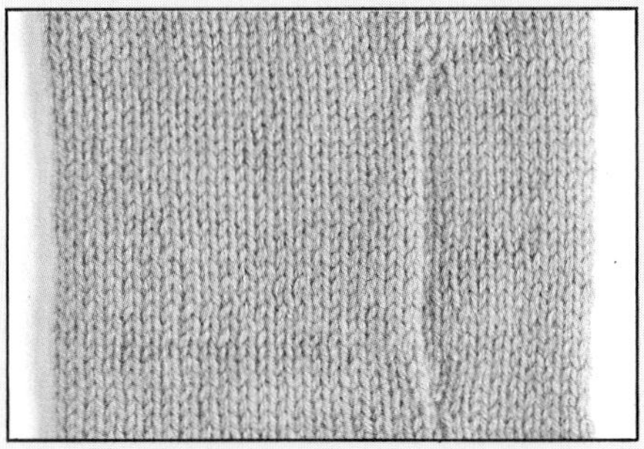

7 Beginning with a purl row, continue working the main fabric across all the stitches. You now have a vertical slit in the fabric for the pocket opening.

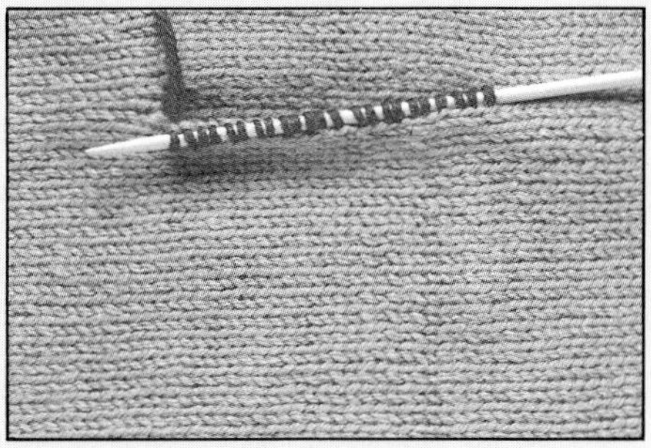

8 After the section of the garment you are working on is complete, finish one edge of the pocket with a ribbed border. With the right side of the work facing, pick up the required number of stitches along the pocket edge.

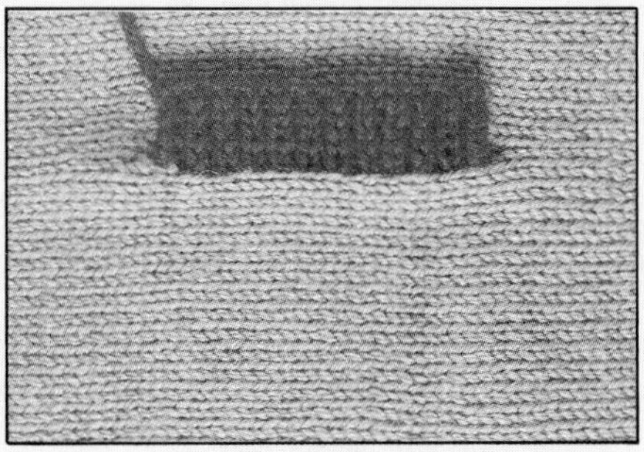

9 The border for our sample is $1\frac{1}{4}$in (3cm) deep, worked in K1, P1 ribbing. You can, of course, use a different ribbing pattern. Note opening lies horizontally as you work border. Bind off in ribbing.

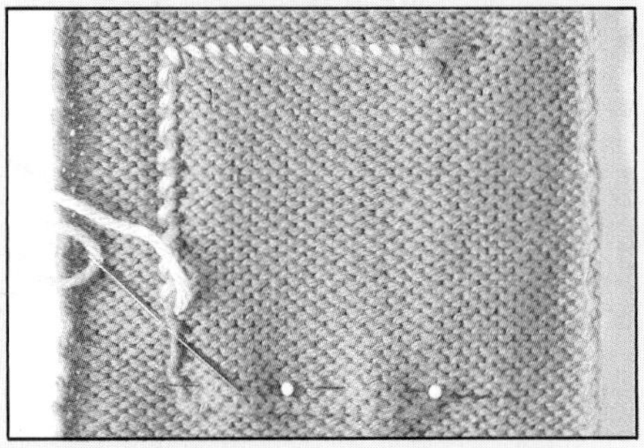

10 Pin the lining in position on the wrong side of the work. Using a blunt-ended yarn needle and matching yarn—here it is contrasting for clarity—slip stitch around three sides of lining.

11 To complete the pocket on the right side of the work, sew down the short ends of the border. Slip stitch them neatly in position using a matching colored yarn.

Fred Mancini

Pick-a-pocket

Four pockets—two vertical and two horizontal—give extra style to this casual jacket in toning shades of blue. Textural interest is achieved by alternating the yarns that are used, for a fun, sporty look.

Sizes
To fit 32[34:36:38]in (83[87:92:97]cm) bust.
Length, 26[26:$26\frac{1}{2}$:27]in (66[66:67:68.5]cm).
Sleeve seam, 18in (45cm).

Note Directions for larger sizes are in [] brackets; where there is only one set of figures it applies to all sizes.

Materials
22[22:25:25]oz (600[600:700:700]g) of a knitting worsted (A)
11[13:13:15]oz (300[350:350:400]g) of a medium-weight mohair (B)
1 pair each Nos. 8 and 10 ($5\frac{1}{2}$ and $6\frac{1}{2}$mm) knitting needles
1 x 22in (56cm) open-ended zipper

Gauge
13 sts and 22 rows to 4in (10cm) in seed stitch (sd st) using yarn A on No. 10 ($6\frac{1}{2}$mm) needles; 13 sts and 16 rows to 4in (10cm) in rev stockinette st using yarn B on No. 10 ($6\frac{1}{2}$mm) needles.

Back
Using No. 8 ($5\frac{1}{2}$mm) needles and A, cast on 58[62:66:70] sts.
1st row P2, *K2, P2, rep from * to end.
2nd row K2, *P2, K2, rep from * to end.
Rep these 2 rows until work measures $3\frac{1}{4}$in (8cm); end with WS row. Change to No. 10 ($6\frac{1}{2}$mm) needles.
Joining on and cutting off colors as required, beg patt.
1st row With B, K to end.
2nd to 12th rows With B, beg K row, work in rev stockinette st.
13th row With A, K to end.
14th to 28th rows With A, K1, (P1, K1) to end.
These 28 rows form the patt. Rep the last 28 rows once more, then the first 12 rows again.

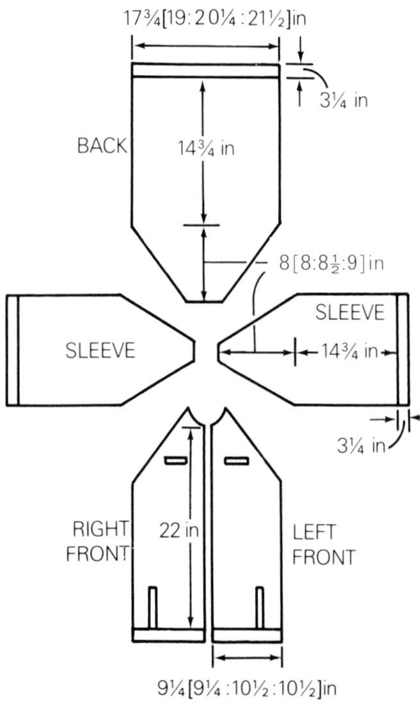

John Hutchinson

Shape raglan
Cont working in patt, dec one st at each end of next and every other row until 18[20:22:24] sts rem; end with WS row. Bind off.

Pocket linings (make 2)
Using No. 10 ($6\frac{1}{2}$mm) needles and A cast on 12 sts and work in stockinette st for $3\frac{1}{4}$in (8cm); end with P row. Cut off yarn and leave these 12 sts on holder.

Left front
Using No. 8 ($5\frac{1}{2}$mm) needles and A, cast on 30[30:34:34] sts and work 2 ribbing rows of back for $3\frac{1}{4}$in (8cm); end with WS row and inc 2 sts on last row for 2nd and 4th sizes only. 30[32:34:36] sts. Change to No. 10 ($6\frac{1}{2}$mm) needles and join on B.
Next row K to end.
Next row K20[21:22:23] sts, turn and leave rem sts on a holder.
Working 2 sts at inner edge in garter st, cont in patt for 26 rows in all; end with WS row. Cut off yarn and leave these sts on holder. Using No. 10 ($6\frac{1}{2}$mm) needles and B, cast on 16 sts, K 1 row, then with WS facing K 10[11:12:13] sts from holder. Cont on these sts, work 24 rows in all; end with RS row.
Next row Bind off 16 sts, patt to end.
Next row Patt across 10[11:12:13] sts, then patt 20[21:22:23] sts from holder. 30[32:34:36] sts. Cont on these sts until front measures same as back, up to beg of raglan shaping; end at armhole edge.
Shape raglan
Dec one stitch at beg of next and foll 7 alternate rows; end with WS row. 22[24:26:28] sts.
Next row Using B, K2 tog, P2[3:4:5], slip next 12 sts onto holder, P across 12 sts of pocket lining, P to last 2 sts, K2. Cont in patt, dec one st at armhole edge on every alternate row until 16[18:20:22] sts rem; end with RS row.
Shape neck
Bind off 4 sts at beg of next row. Dec one st at each end of next and foll 3[4:5:6] alternate rows. Dec at armhole edge only on next 2 alternate rows. Bind off rem 2 sts.

Right front
Work as for left front reversing shaping and position of both pockets.

Sleeves
Using No. 8 ($5\frac{1}{2}$mm) needles and A, cast on 26[26:30:30] sts and work 2 ribbing rows of back for $3\frac{1}{4}$in (8cm); end with WS row and inc one st at each end of last row on 2nd and 4th sizes only. 26[28:30:32] sts.
Change to No. 10 ($6\frac{1}{2}$mm) needles. Join on B. Cont in patt as for back, inc one st at each end of 3rd and every foll 6th row until there are 46[48:50:52] sts. Cont without shaping on these sts until 68 rows have been worked from top of cuff.
Shape top
Cont in patt, dec one st at each end of next and every other row until 6 sts rem; end with WS row. Bind off.

Gary Warren

Collar
Using No. 8 ($5\frac{1}{2}$mm) needles and A, cast on 26[26:30:30] sts and work one row in ribbing as for back. Cont in ribbing, cast on 4 sts at beg of next 10 rows. 66[66:70:70] sts. Working 2 sts at each end of row in garter st cont in ribbing for $3\frac{1}{4}$in (8cm). Bind off loosely in ribbing.

Pocket edges (lower pockets)
Using No. 8 ($5\frac{1}{2}$mm) needles and A, with RS facing, pick up and P into front and back of first st, (K2, P2), to last 3 sts, K2, P into front and back of last st. 14 sts. Cont in ribbing until it measures $1\frac{1}{4}$in (3cm). Bind off loosely in ribbing.

Pocket tops (top pockets)
Place 12 sts from holder onto a No. 8 ($5\frac{1}{2}$mm) needle, with RS facing join on A and P into the front and back of first st, (K2, P2), to last 3 sts, K2, P into front and back of last st. 14 sts. Cont in ribbing until work measures $1\frac{1}{4}$in (3cm). Bind off loosely in ribbing.

To finish
Press lightly with a cool iron over a dry cloth. Join raglan seams. Join side and sleeve seams. Sew down pocket tops and edges and pocket linings. Sew on collar. Sew in zipper. Press seams.

Shoestring

Teddy Bear Apron

Cover and protect your children's clothes from splashes and spills with this brightly decorated vinyl apron.

Size
To fit a 6- to 7-year-old child.

Materials

Piece of vinyl 24×20in (60×50cm)
2¼yds (2m) of 1in (2.5cm)-wide cotton twill tape
Contrasting thread
Three ⅝in (1.5cm)-diameter buttons
20in (50cm) of 1½in (3.5cm)-wide contrasting ribbon
Masking tape
Grease pencil or soft crayon

1 Lay the vinyl fabric on a flat surface, wrong side up. Measure and mark 6in (15cm) in from each corner along one short side. Measure and mark 8in (20cm) down the long edges from the same corners. Using a soft pencil draw a gentle curve between each pair of corner points, forming underarm curves. Cut along these lines to form the shape of the apron.
2 Turn under a ⅜in (1cm) margin along the straight side and top edges. On wrong side, hold in place with masking tape.
3 Turn curved edges under ⅜in (1cm). Clip seam allowance at regular intervals, so that vinyl lies flat. Tape in place.
4 Turn under bottom hem edge and tape in place as in step 2.
5 Zig-zag around the entire outer edge in contrasting-colored thread. Remove masking tape "basting."
6 For apron ties, cut twill tape in half. Turn under one raw end on one piece of tape. Sew this end to one top corner of apron bib. Knot the remaining raw end of tape, to prevent raveling.
7 Repeat step 6 with second piece of twill tape for other side of apron.
8 Make a thread loop at the top of each side edge, just below underarm curve, to hold the apron ties.
9 Using a grease pencil, draw two teddy bear ears and a mouth in the center of apron bib. Zig-zag around outlines of ears and mouth in contrasting thread.
10 For nose and eyes, hand-sew buttons in place.
11 Tie ribbon in a bow. Sew bow to apron under mouth.
12 To tie apron, criss-cross the cotton twill tapes, thread through loops and tie in a bow at the back.

Knitting/COURSE 22

*Decorative increasing
*Introduction to simple lace patterns
*Stitch Wise: more lacy patterns
*Pattern for a lacy bedjacket

Decorative increasing

This method of increasing involves winding the yard over or around the needle to create an extra stitch. The combination of stitches immediately before and after the increased stitch determines whether you must bring the yarn forward, or bring it over the needle or wind it around the needle (all abbreviated–yo). You can use these techniques for shaping a garment; but more commonly they form the basis of lace patterns, as they make a small eyelet hole in the fabric–hence the name "decorative increasing."
In the section entitled "Stitch Wise" we give you two lace stitch patterns that incorporate decorative increasing techniques. The bedjacket on page 51 also uses these techniques.

Increasing between two knit stitches

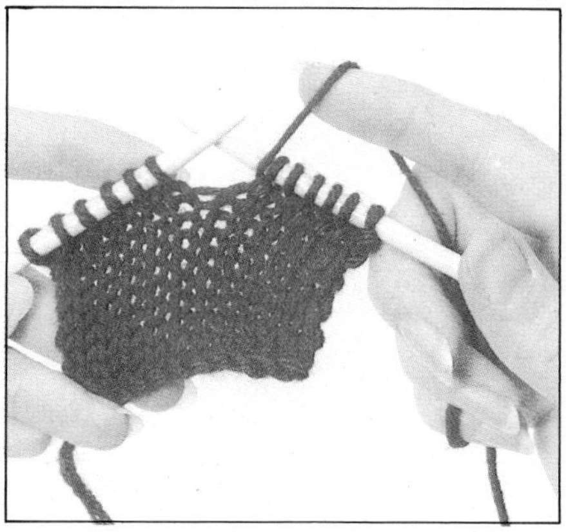

1 To make a stitch between two knit stitches, bring the yarn forward to the front of the work between the two needles.

2 Knit the next stitch in the usual way. Notice that the yarn makes an extra loop on the right-hand needle as you take it back to wind it over the needle point.

3 On the following–in this case, purl–row, work as usual into each stitch including the extra loop. This makes a hole in the fabric.

Increasing between a purl and a knit stitch

1 To make a stitch between a purl and a knit stitch–for example, in a ribbed fabric–proceed as follows: note that as you begin the increase the yarn is already at the front of the work from purling the previous stitch.

2 Instead of taking the yarn to the back, as you would normally do before knitting the next stitch, simply proceed to knit the stitch. As you do so, you automatically bring the yarn over the needle so creating an extra loop.

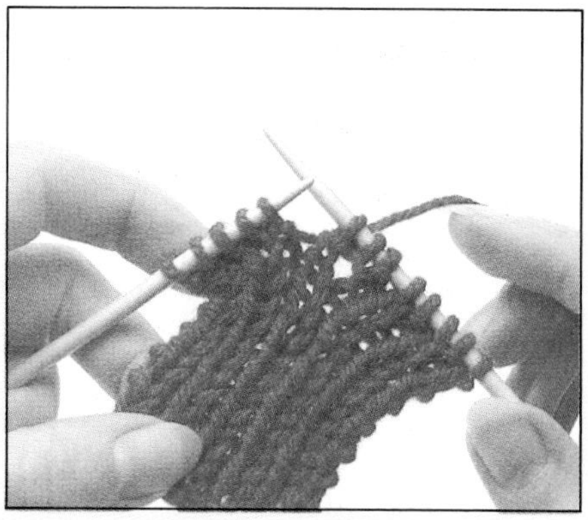

3 On the next row, work into the extra loop as directed in the pattern; if you are making eyelet holes in ribbing you may have to purl the extra loop together with the stitch before it to keep the number of stitches and pattern correct.

Mike Berend

continued

Increasing between two purl stitches

1 To make a stitch between two purl stitches take the yarn completely around the right-hand needle point and to the front again between the two needles.

2 Purl the next stitch in the usual way. The yarn previously wound around the right-hand needle forms an extra loop.

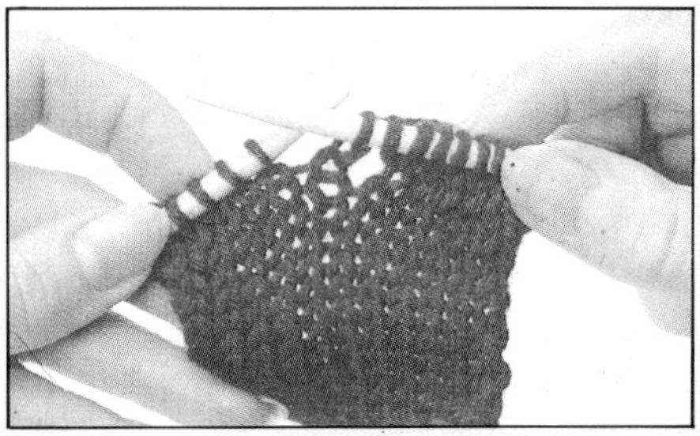

3 On the following – in this case, knitted – row work into the extra loop in the usual way, so making a hole in the fabric.

Increasing between a knit and a purl stitch

1 To make a stitch between a knit and purl stitch bring the yarn forward to the front between the two needles.

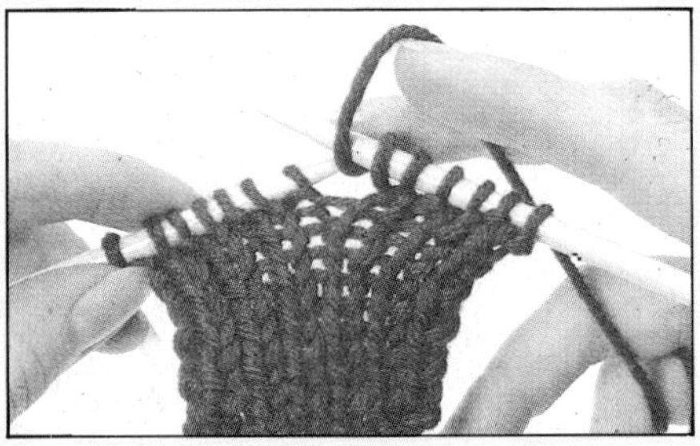

2 Now take the yarn over the top of the right-hand needle point and around to the front again between the two needles.

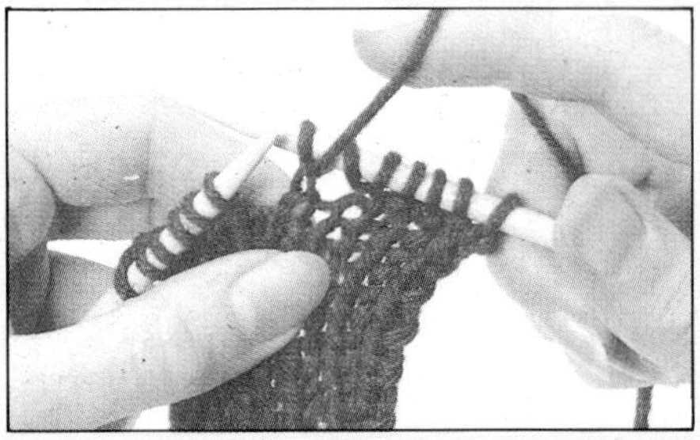

3 Purl the next stitch in the usual way. The new loop leaves a characteristic hole in the fabric when the following row has been worked.

Introduction to simple lace patterns

A lacy knitted fabric usually consists of a small pattern that repeats across a row: any decorative increase within a pattern repeat must be counterbalanced by a decrease to keep the number of stitches within a row constant. The combination of holes, stitches and decreases forms a lacy pattern.

The correct balance of yarn and needles is important in lace knitting. It is pointless using thick yarn, as the holes produced will be indistinct; using needles which are too small will also create this effect. When you make practice samples, try using a sport – or finer – yarn with needles one or two sizes larger than those you would normally use for that particular quality of yarn.

The following step-by-step pictures show various stages of making the "falling leaf" pattern used in the bedjacket on page 51. Detailed instructions for working the "falling leaf" pattern appear in the directions for the bedjacket.

Mike Berend

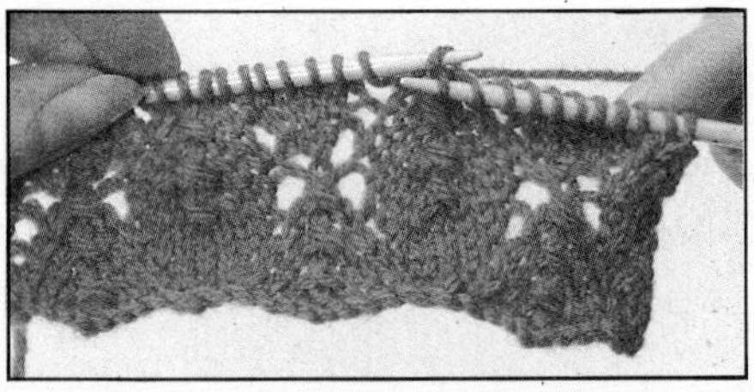

1 Many lace patterns include the direction "sl 1, K2 tog, psso"; it occurs in all the right-side rows in the "falling leaf" pattern. Here, the slipped stitch is being lifted over the knitted-together stitches. Besides shaping the "falling leaf," this action makes an interesting design when it is repeated in a line up the center.

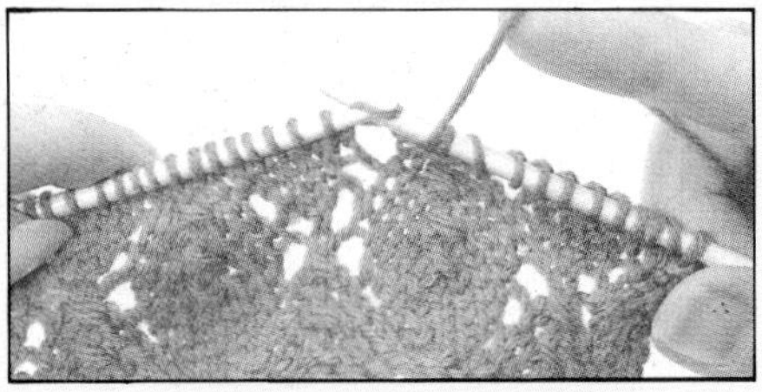

2 Here the pattern instructions say "yo, K7" (see the 15th row). In this case the yarn has been put forward before knitting the *first* of the seven stitches, so increasing one stitch. Don't put the yarn forward before each of the seven stitches individually.

3 The leaves in this pattern are staggered, so that during the course of one row of knitting you are decreasing to shape the top of some leaves and increasing to form the base of others. Here, alternate leaves have been completed – as in the first and 8th pattern rows: the other leaves are half formed at this stage.

Stitch Wise

Cat's paw pattern

Cast on a multiple of 12 sts plus 1 extra.
1st row (RS) K5, *yo, sl 1, K2 tog, psso, yo, K9, rep from * to last 8 sts, yo, sl 1, K2 tog, psso, yo, K5.
2nd and all WS rows P to end.
3rd row K3, *K2 tog, yo, K3, yo, sl 1, K1, psso, K5, rep from * to last 10 sts, K2 tog, yo, K3, yo, sl 1, K1, psso, K3.
5th row As first.
7th row K to end.
9th row K2 tog, *yo, K9, yo, sl 1, K2 tog, psso, rep from * to last 11 sts, yo, K9, yo, sl 1, K1, psso.
11th row K2, *yo, sl 1, K1, psso, K5, K2 tog, yo, K3, rep from * to last 11 sts, yo, sl 1, K1, psso, K5, K2 tog, yo, K2.
13th row As 9th.
15th row As 7th.
16th row As 2nd.
These 16 rows form the pattern.

Checked mesh pattern

Cast on a multiple of 10 sts plus 4 extra.
1st and all WS rows P to end.
2nd row K4, *yo, sl 1, K1, psso, K1, (K2 tog, yo) twice, K4, rep from * to end.
4th row *K3, (yo, sl 1, K1, psso) twice, K1, K2 tog, yo, rep from * ending with K4.
6th row K2, *(yo, sl 1, K1, psso) 3 times, K4, rep from * ending with yo, sl 1, K1, psso.
8th row K1, *(yo, sl 1, K1, psso) 4 times, K2, rep from * ending with yo, sl 1, K1, psso, K1.
10th row As 6th.
12th row As 4th.
14th row As 2nd.
16th row K2 tog, yo, *K4, (K2 tog, yo) 3 times, rep from * ending with K2.
18th row K1, K2 tog, yo, *K2, (K2 tog, yo) 4 times, rep from * ending with K1.
20th row As 16th row.
These 20 rows form the pattern.

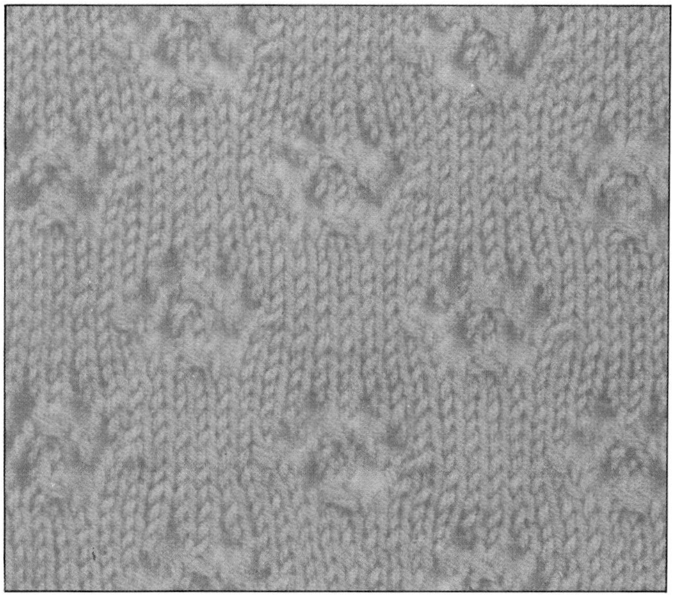

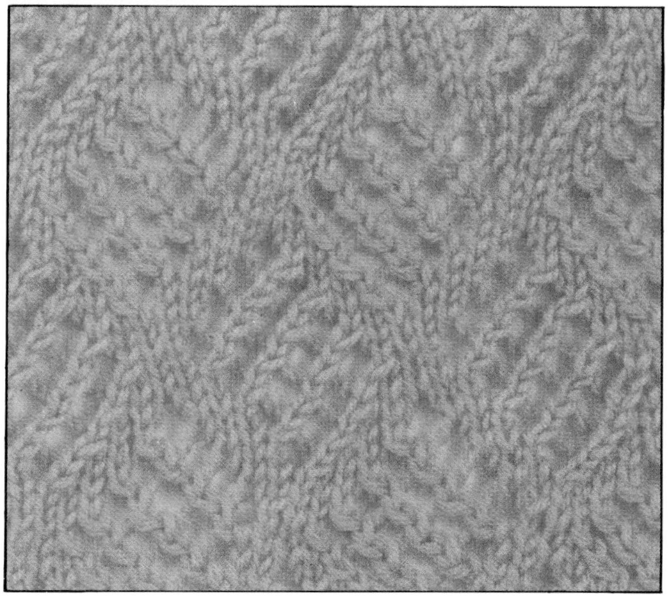

Lace for lounging

Now you have learned some of the basic techniques of knitting lacy patterns, why not try knitting a comfortable bedjacket? It is just the thing to wear for extra warmth when you are reading—or being served breakfast—in bed.

Sizes

To fit, 32-34[36-38]in (83-87[92-97] cm) bust.
Length, 19$\frac{1}{2}$[20$\frac{1}{2}$]in (49[51]cm).
Sleeve seam, 16$\frac{1}{2}$in (41cm).
Note Directions for larger sizes are in brackets [ ]; where there is only one set of figures it applies to both sizes.

Materials

9[10]oz (240[280]g) of a sport yarn
1 pair each Nos. 4 and 5 (3$\frac{3}{4}$ and 4mm) needles
No. 4 (3$\frac{3}{4}$mm) circular needle
4 buttons
1$\frac{3}{4}$yd (1.50m) of ribbon

Gauge

20 sts and 28 rows to 4in (10cm) in patt using No. 5 (4mm) needles.
22 sts and 44 rows to 4in (10cm) in garter stitch using No. 4 (3$\frac{3}{4}$mm) needles.

Back

Using No. 5 (4mm) needles cast on 121 [141] sts. **Beg with a K row, work 3 rows stockinette st.
Picot row K1, *yo, K2 tog, rep from * to end.
Beg with a K row, work 4 rows stockinette st. Beg patt.
1st row K1, *yo, K3, sl 1, K2 tog, psso, K3, yo, K1, rep from * to end.
2nd and all WS rows P to end.
3rd row K2, *yo, K2, sl 1, K2 tog, psso, K2, yo, K3, rep from * to end, ending last rep K2 instead of K3.
5th row K3, *yo, K1, sl 1, K2 tog, psso, K1, yo, K5, rep from * to end, ending last rep K3 instead of K5.
7th row K4, *yo, sl 1, K2 tog, psso, yo,

K7, rep from * to end, ending last rep K4.
9th row K2 tog, *K3, yo, K1, yo, K3, sl 1, K2 tog, psso, rep from * to end, ending last rep sl 1, K1, psso.
11th row K2 tog, *K2, yo, K3, yo, K2, sl 1, K2 tog, psso, rep from * to end, ending last rep sl 1, K1, psso.
13th row K2 tog, *K1, yo, K5, yo, K1, sl 1, K2 tog, psso, rep from * to end, ending last rep sl 1, K1, psso.
15th row K2 tog, *yo, K7, yo, sl 1, K2 tog, psso, rep from * to end, ending last rep sl 1, K1, psso.
16th row As 2nd row.
These 16 rows form the patt. Rep them 3 times more.**

Shape armholes
Dec one st at each end of next and foll 3 alternate rows by omitting yo at beg and end of rows. 113[133] sts. P1 row. Cut off yarn and leave sts on holder.

Left front
Using No. 5 (4mm) needles cast on 61[71] sts. Work as for back from ** to **

Shape armhole
Dec one st at beg of next and foll 3 alternate rows by omitting yo at beg of rows. 57[67] sts. P 1 row. Cut off yarn and leave sts on holder.

Right front
Work as left front, but reverse shaping at armhole by decreasing at the end of each alternate row.

Sleeves
Using No. 5 (4mm) needles cast on 61[71] sts and work as for back from ** to **. Cont in patt, work 48 more rows.

Shape top
Dec one st at each end of next and foll 3 alternate rows by omitting yo at beg and end of rows. 53[63] sts. P 1 row. Cut off yarn and leave sts on holder.

Yoke
Using No. 4 (3¾mm) circular needle and with RS facing, knitting 2 sts tog at each seam, K sts of right front 57[67] sts, right sleeve 53[63] sts, back 113[133] sts, left sleeve 53[63] sts and left front 57[67] sts. 329[389] sts.
Next row K4[1], *K2 tog, K3[2], rep from * to end. 264[292] sts.
1st buttonhole row K2, bind off 2 sts, K to end.
2nd buttonhole row K to end, casting on 2 sts over sts that were bound-off on previous row.
K14 rows.
Next row K5, *K2 tog, K5, rep from * to end. 227[251] sts.
K15[17] rows, working a buttonhole over 6th and 7th[8th and 9th] rows.
Next row K5, *K2 tog, K4, rep from * to end. 190[210] sts.
K15[17] rows, working buttonhole over 12th and 13th[14th and 15th] rows.
Next row K2, *K2 tog, K3, rep from * to last 3 sts, K2 tog, K1. 152[168] sts.
K15[17] rows.
Next row K1, *K2 tog, K2, rep from * to last 3 sts, K2 tog, K1. 114[126] sts.
K15[17] rows, working buttonhole over 2nd and 3rd rows.
Next row K1, *K2 tog, K3, rep from * to last 3[5] sts, K2 tog, K1[3]. 91[101] sts.
K4 rows.
Eyelet-hole row (WS) K1, *yo, K2 tog, rep from * to end.
K7 rows.
Picot row K1, *yo, K2 tog, rep from * to end.
K4 rows. Bind off.

Front borders
Using No. 4 (3¾mm) needles and with

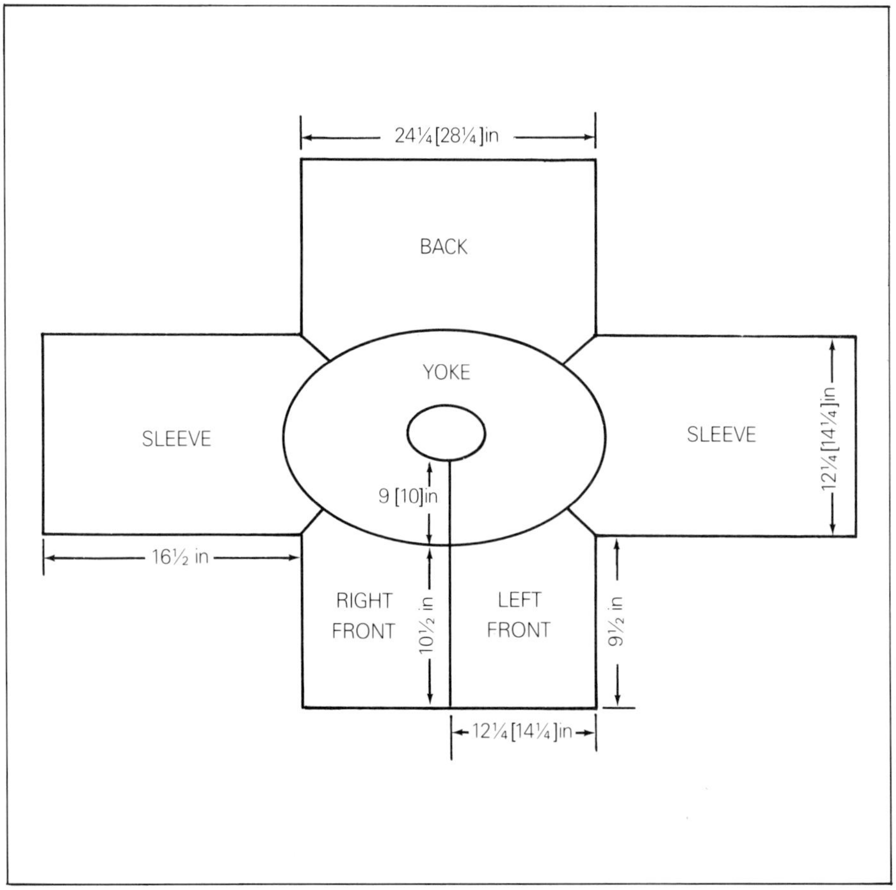

John Hutchinson

RS facing, beg at picot row on right front, pick up and K 105[109] sts along front edge. Beg with P row, work 2 rows stockinette st.

Next row (hemline) K1, *yo, K2 tog, rep from * to end. Beg with K row, work 4 rows in stockinette st. Bind off knitwise. Work along left front in same way.

To finish

Do not press. Sew in sleeves. Join side and sleeve seams.

Turn in all edges along picot row and slip stitch in place.

Sew on buttons. Thread ribbon through eyelet holes at neck.

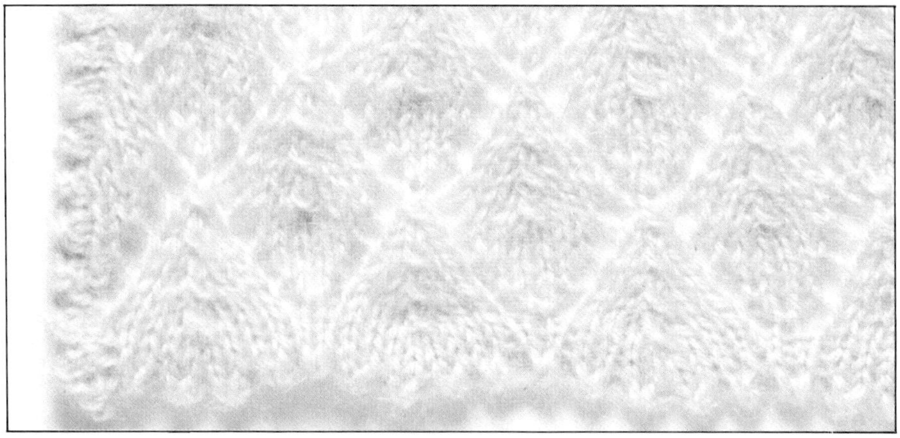

Fred Mancini

Knitting/COURSE 23

- *Twisting stitches to the left
- *Twisting stitches to the right
- *Working a mock cable
- *Stitch Wise: two twisted stitch patterns
- *Pattern for a man's sweater

Twisting stitches

The technique of twisting stitches—though a simple one—forms the basis of a number of interesting and varied patterns. You can use twisted stitches as a substitute for cables—or in conjunction with them—in Aran designs, either as an allover pattern or in panels. Twisted stitches can also be used to form "traveling lines" across the surface of a fabric, making diagonal and check patterns. One of these—double diagonal pattern—is used in the man's sweater at the end of this course.

Twisted stitches are usually worked over a small number of stitches—either two or three. They work well with most weights of yarn as long as the needles are the correct size for the yarn. Over-large needles open up the pattern and make it too sloppy.

The following sequences of step-by-step photographs show you how to work stitches twisting either to the left or to the right.

Twisting stitches to the left

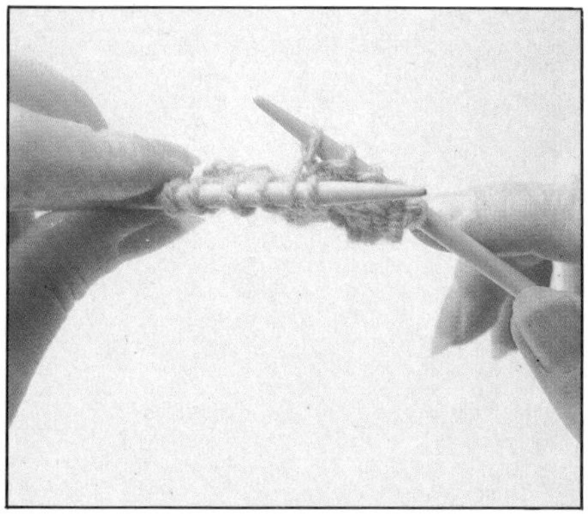

1 Work the twist over two knitted stitches. To work a twist that lies to the left, knit the *second* stitch on the left-hand needle through the back of the loop. At this stage the original stitch remains on the needle.

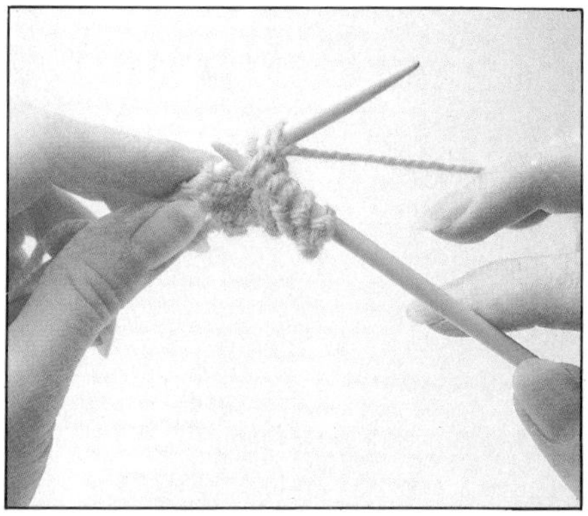

2 Now, with the new stitch on the right-hand needle, knit the first stitch (the one that you skipped) on the left-hand needle in the usual way.

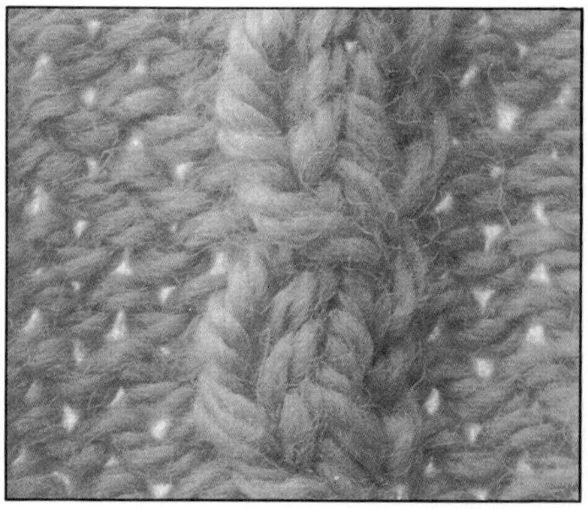

3 Slip both stitches off the left-hand needle and continue in pattern. This is called "twist two left (T2L)." Here a series of left twists has been worked on every 4th row to create a miniature cable effect.

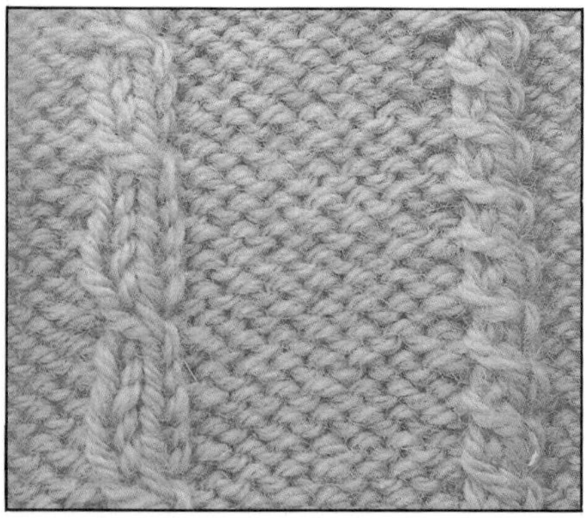

4 You can vary the number of rows between twists to give a tighter or looser "cable." On one side of this sample, left twists have been worked on every 6th row: the other side is twisted on every other row.

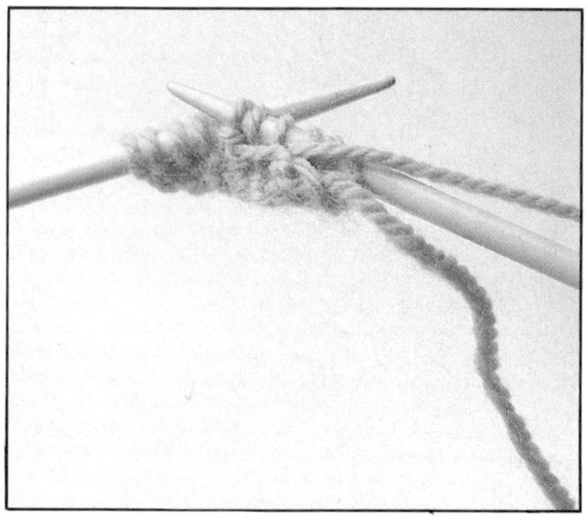

5 In some cases you may need to work a left twist on wrong-side rows to produce a tight twist. Purl the *second* stitch on the left-hand needle through the back of the loop, then purl the first stitch (the one that you skipped) on the left-hand needle in the usual way.

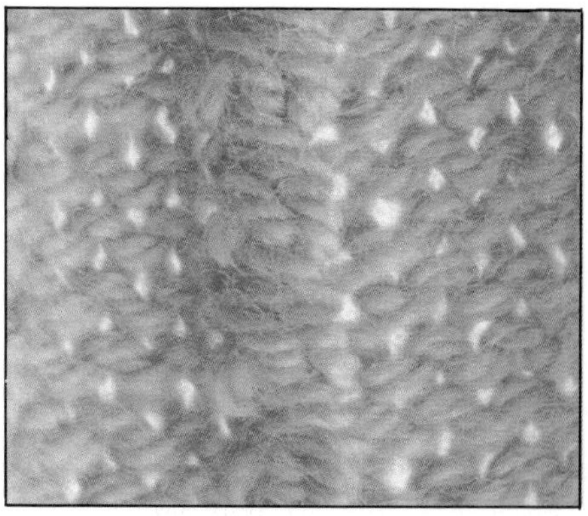

6 Slip both stitches off the left-hand needle and continue in pattern. This is called "twist two left back (T2LB)." Here a series of left twists has been worked on every row to give a tightly twisted cable effect.

Paul Williams

Twisting stitches to the right

1 To work a twist that lies to the right, knit *second* stitch on left-hand needle through front of loop in the usual way. At this stage the original stitch remains on the left-hand needle.

2 Now, with the new stitch on the right-hand needle, knit the first stitch (the one that you skipped) on the left-hand needle in the usual way.

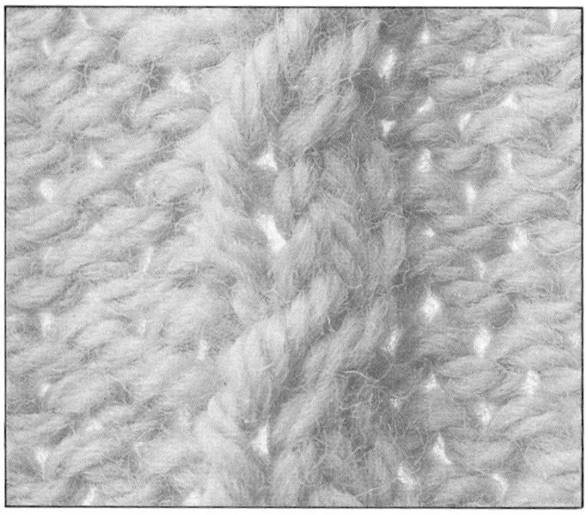

3 Slip both stitches off the left-hand needle and continue in pattern. This is called "twist two right (T2R)." Here two right twists have been worked on every 4th row to create a miniature cable effect.

4 To produce a right twist on the right side of the fabric when you are working a wrong-side row, purl the *second* stitch on the left-hand needle through the front of the loop in the usual way.

5 Now, with the new stitch on the right-hand needle, purl the first stitch on the left-hand needle in the usual way. Take care to keep remaining loop of second stitch on left of first stitch while you are working into it.

6 Slip both stitches off the left-hand needle together and continue in pattern. This is called "twist two right back (T2RB)." Here a series of right twists has been worked on every row.

Working a mock cable

Twisted stitches are an ideal way of producing a very realistic cable pattern without the use of a cable needle: the mock cable pattern in Stitch Wise is an example of this. The cable here is worked over four stitches and the method of twisting them is slightly complicated: it involves twisting two pairs of stitches left, but working the second pair before the first; the step-by-step sequence here describes this clearly. When worked in a vertical line, as in mock cable patterns, twisted stitches tend to pull the work together in the same way as ribbing does. Most patterns will compensate for this by instructing you to cast on more stitches than would be normally required.

1 The 5th pattern row of mock cable pattern in Stitch Wise describes how to twist the four cable stitches to make a mock cable. Start to work first T2L by knitting 4th stitch on left-hand needle through the back of the loop.

2 To complete the first T2L, bring the right-hand needle completely around to the front of the fabric and knit the third stitch on the left-hand needle in the usual way.

continued

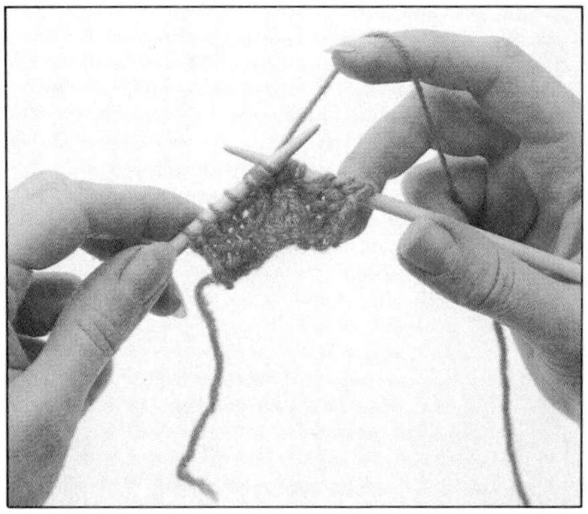

3 With original stitches still on left-hand needle and two new loops on right-hand needle, start to work second T2L by knitting 2nd stitch on left-hand needle through back of loop.

4 Complete the second T2L by knitting the first stitch on the left-hand needle in the usual way. Note that the original four stitches still remain on the left-hand needle.

5 Here the "double twist" is complete with the four cable stitches on the right-hand needle: the four loops that were left on the left-hand needle are dropped simultaneously.

Stitch Wise

Twisted rib

Cast on a multiple of 5 sts plus 3 extra.
1st row (RS) P3, *K2, P3 rep from * to end.
2nd row K3, *P2, K3, rep from * to end.
3rd row As first row.
4th row As 2nd row.
5th row P3, *T2L, P3, rep from * to end.
6th row As 2nd. 6 rows form pattern.

Mock cable pattern

Cast on a multiple of 14 sts plus 2 extra.
1st row (RS) P2, *T2L, P2, K4, P2, T2L, P2, rep from * to end.
2nd row K2, *P2, K2, P4, K2, P2, K2, rep from * to end.
3rd row As first row.
4th row As 2nd row.
5th row P2, *T2L, P2, work T2L into 4th and 3rd sts on left-hand needle leaving sts on needle, then work T2L into 2nd and first sts and slip all 4 sts off needle tog, P2, T2L, P2, rep from * to end.
6th row As 2nd. 6 rows form pattern.

Latticed warmth

This casual and comfortable sweater has a patterned back and front and a turtleneck collar and is certain to please any man.

Sizes
To fit 38[40:42]in (97[102:107]cm) chest.
Length, $26\frac{1}{2}$in (67cm).
Sleeve seam, $20\frac{3}{4}$in (53cm), with cuff.
Note Directions for larger sizes are in brackets []; where there is only one set of figures it applies to all sizes.

Materials
24[25:26]oz (675[700:725]g) of a knitting worsted
1 pair each Nos. 4, 5 and 7 ($3\frac{3}{4}$, 4 and 5mm) needles

Gauge
22 sts and 28 rows to 4in (10cm) in stockinette st on No. 5 (4mm) needles.
26 sts and 27 rows to 4in (10cm) in patt st on No. 7 (5mm) needles.

Front
Using No. 4 ($3\frac{3}{4}$mm) needles, cast on 136[142:148] sts and work in K1, P1 ribbing for 4in (10cm).
Change to No. 7 (5mm) needles. Beg patt.
1st row *K 2nd st on left-hand needle tbl, then K first st, let both sts drop from left-hand needle—called twist 2 left or T2L—, (K 2nd st on left-hand needle, then K first st, let sts drop from left-hand needle—called twist 2 right or T2R) twice, rep from * to last 4 sts, T2L, T2R.
2nd and alternate rows P to end.
3rd row K1, T2L, *T2R, (T2L) twice, rep from * to last st, K1.
5th row (T2L) twice, *K2, (T2L) twice, rep from * to end.
7th row K1, *(T2L) twice, T2R, rep from

Gary Warren

* to last 3 sts, T2L, K1.
9th row T2R, T2L, *(T2R) twice, T2L, rep from * to end.
11th row K3, *(T2R) twice, K2, rep from * to last st, K1.
12th row P to end.
These 12 rows form patt. Cont in patt until work measures 22½in (57cm) from beg; end with WS row.

Shape neck
Next row Patt 54[56:58], turn and leave rem sts on spare needle. Complete this side of neck first.
Dec one st at neck edge on next and foll alternate rows until 47[49:51] sts rem, ending at side edge.

Shape shoulders
Bind off 5[7:9] sts at beg of next row and 7 sts at beg of foll 5 alternate rows. Work 1 row.
Bind off.
Return to sts on spare needle. Place next 28[30:32] sts on holder, join yarn to next st and patt to end of row. Complete to match first side.

Back
Work as for front, omitting neck shaping, until the back is the same length as the front to beg of shoulder shaping; end with WS row.

Shape shoulders
Bind off 5[7:9] sts at beg of next 2 rows and 7 sts at beg of foll 12 rows. Cut off

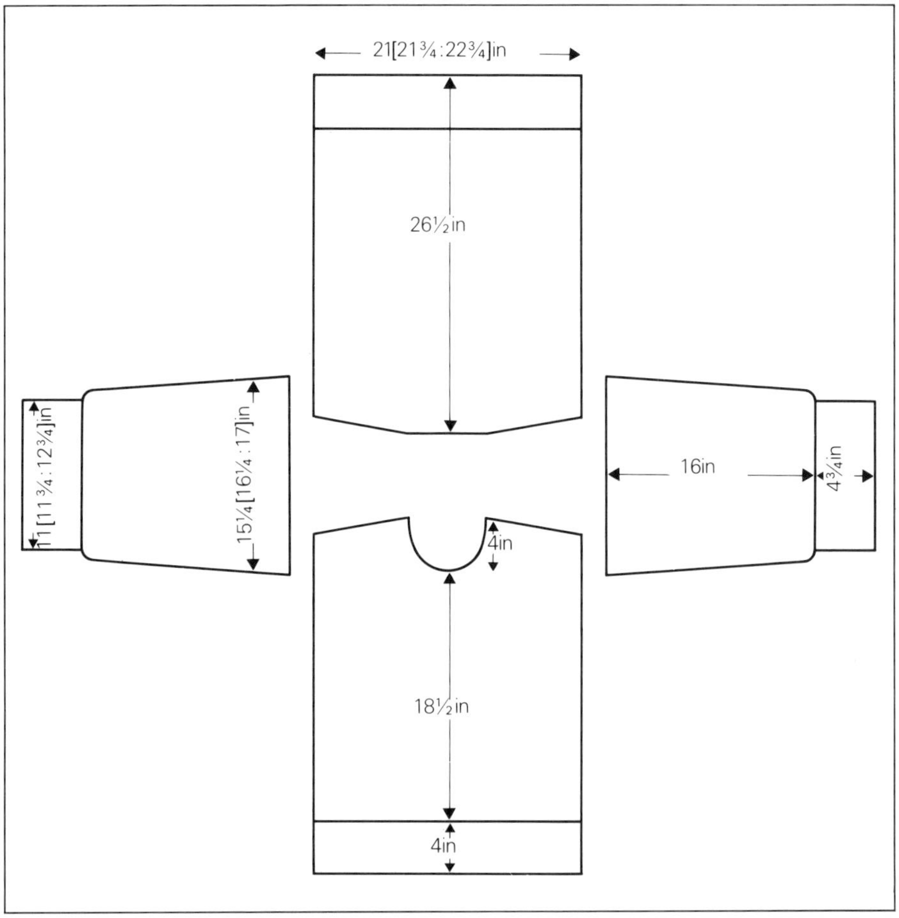

yarn and leave rem 42[44:46] sts on holder.

Sleeves
Using No. 4 (3¾mm) needles cast on 48[52:56] sts and work in K1, P1 ribbing for 4¾in (12cm).
Inc row (Rib 3, inc in next st) to end. 60[65:70] sts.
Change to No. 5 (4mm) needles. Cont in stockinette st inc one st at each end of 7th and every foll 8th row until there are 84[89:94] sts. Cont without shaping until work measures 20¾in (53cm) from beg. Bind off loosely.

Turtleneck collar
Join right shoulder seam. With RS facing and using No. 4 (3¾mm) needles pick up and K 27 sts from left front neck, K sts from holder, pick up and K 27 sts from right front neck, then K back neck sts from holder. 124[128:132] sts. Working in K1, P1 ribbing, work 22 rows, change to No. 7 (5mm) needles and work 28 more rows. Bind off.

To finish
Press stockinette st sections only. Join left shoulder and collar seam. Mark center of bound-off edge of sleeves with a pin, match pin to shoulder seams, then sew sleeves to back and front. Join side and sleeve seams reversing seam on cuffs. Turn back cuffs. Press seams lightly.

Sewing/COURSE 20

*Fitting problems at the shoulder
*Front placket opening
*Shirt collar and collar band
*Shirt: directions for making (1)

Fitting problems at the shoulder

A good fit at the shoulder is an important part of achieving a professional look on a garment. In this course we show you how to alter a pattern to fit narrow and broad shoulders. The pattern used is the shirt pattern from the Pattern Pack, for which we provide directions at the end of the course.
This pattern has a yoke, which means that you must join the yoke pieces to the front and back bodice pieces before making the alterations. On patterns without yokes, the alterations are made in essentially the same way.
If there is a shoulder dart, it must be re-drawn to the same size after the alteration is made, and located the same distance from the neck edge as before.

Narrow shoulders

Narrow shoulders will make the shoulder seam on a shirt or dress extend over the top of the arm, and the sleeve seam will drop. For a perfect fit, the shoulder width on the pattern must be decreased.

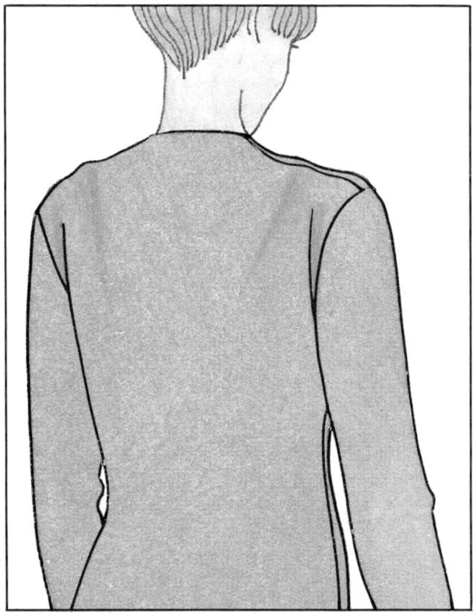

Terry Evans

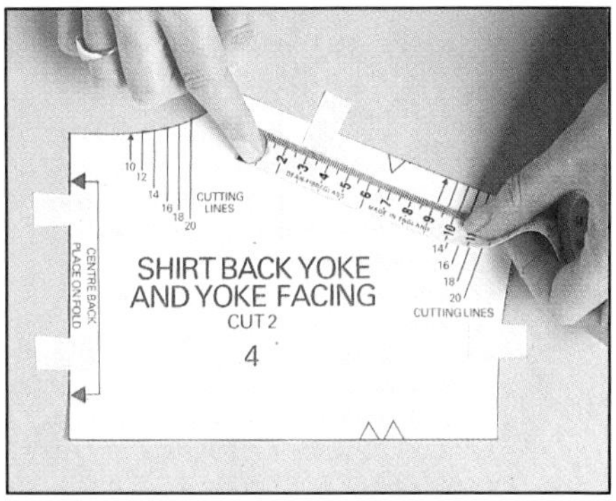

1 To determine the amount of decrease necessary, get someone to measure across your shoulder from the neck edge to the top of the arm. Subtract this measurement from the finished shoulder width on the pattern. The resulting figure is the amount of decrease.

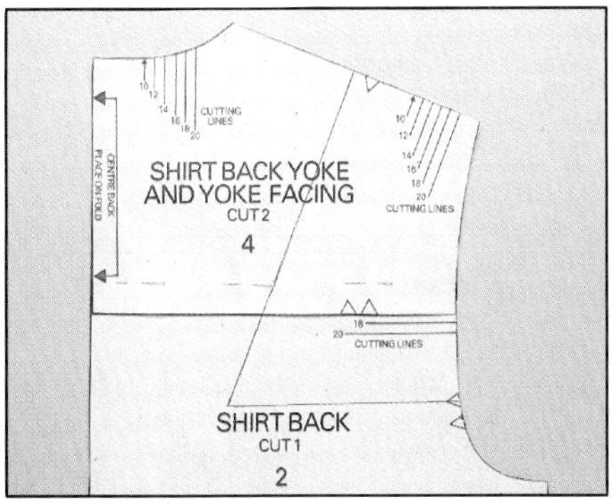

2 Pin the yoke and lower bodice pattern pieces together for both back and front. On both the front and back pieces draw a line diagonally inward from the center of the shoulder seam to a point level with the armhole notch. Draw a horizontal line joining the first line to the notch on the armhole.

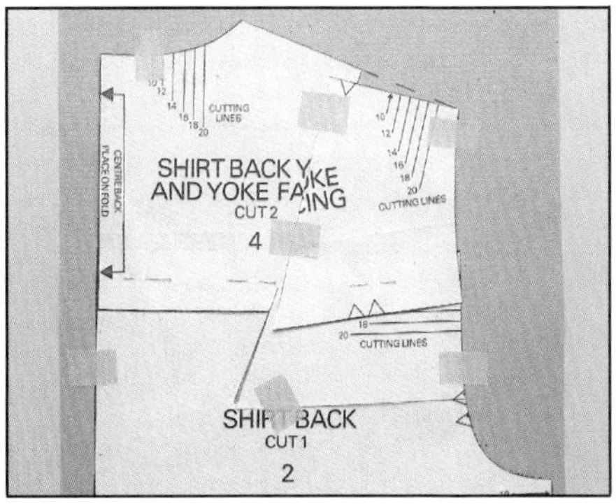

3 Cut down the line from the shoulder and across the horizontal line just to the armhole seamline. Place a piece of paper under the pattern. Lap the shoulder seam edges by the amount you need to decrease and tape in place.

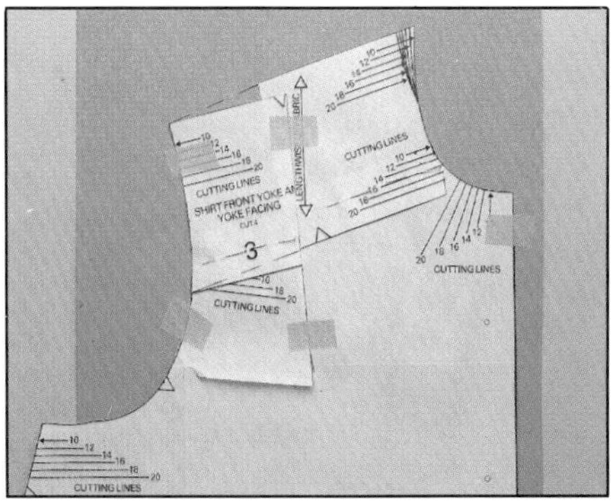

Paul Williams

4 Re-draw the shoulder line straight to the top of the armhole and re-draw the yoke line from the center back to the armhole.
Cut across the lower edge of the yoke piece, as indicated by the broken line, to obtain a straight edge. Separate the yoke pattern pieces from the lower bodice pieces. Tape some paper under the bodice and re-draw the upper edge. Re-mark the notches on the shoulder seamlines.

Broad shoulders

Broad shoulders will pull the armhole seamline out of position, causing the sleeve cap to ride up over the shoulder. For a perfect fit, the width of the shoulder on the pattern must be increased.

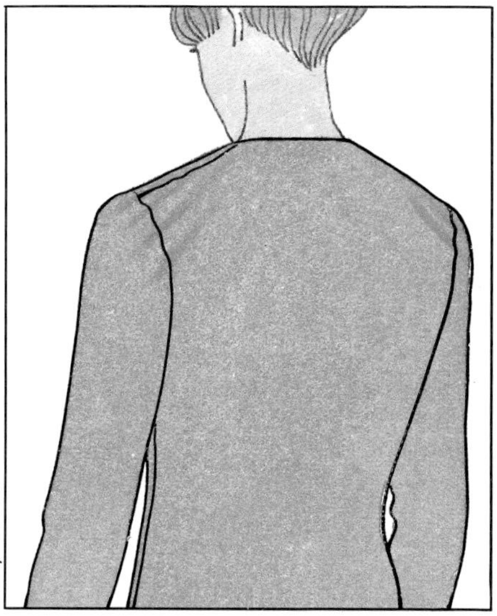

Terry Evans

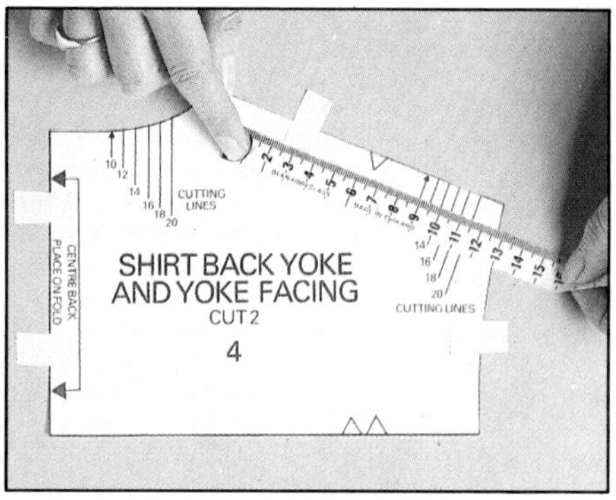

1 Compare the length of the finished shoulder seam on the pattern with the measurement across your shoulders from the neck edge to the top of the arm. The difference will be the amount of increase necessary on the pattern.

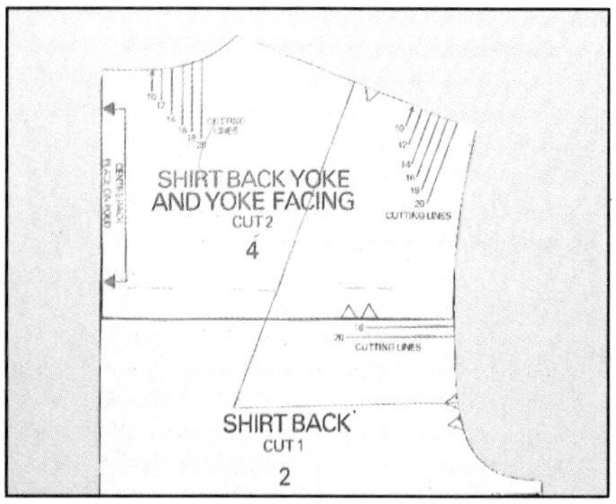

2 Following step 2 for narrow shoulders, draw in the vertical and horizontal lines on the back and front pattern pieces.

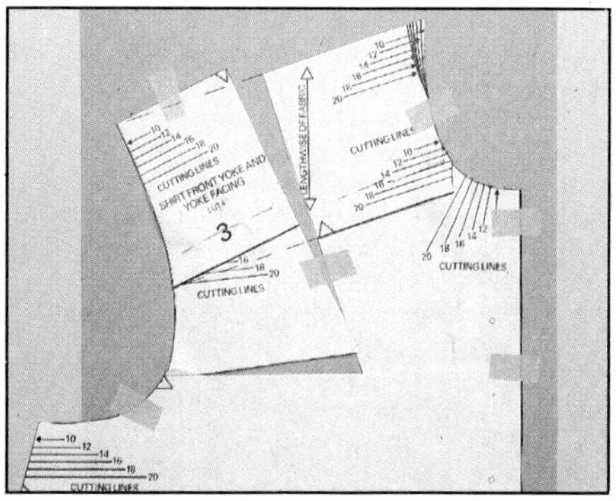

3 On both pieces, cut down the line from the shoulder and across the horizontal line—just to the armhole seamline. Spread out the shoulder edges until the shoulder seam is the correct length. Tape the pattern in place over paper and re-draw the shoulder line from the neck edge to the armhole. Re-draw the yoke line from the slash to the armhole.

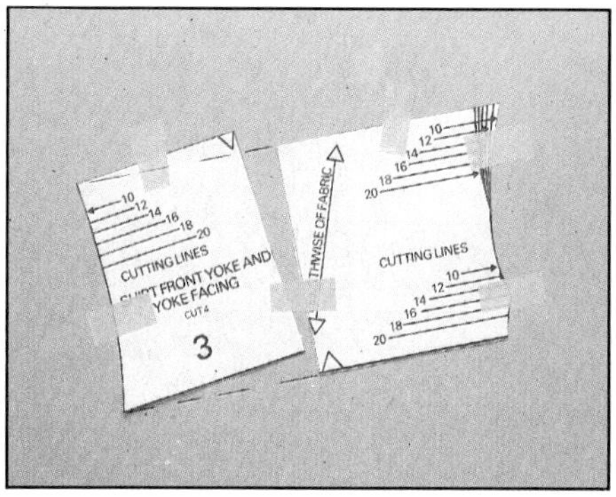

4 Separate the yoke pieces from the bodice pieces adding to the yoke the small pieces of bodice pattern included above the broken line. Where the bodice has been trimmed away at the top, add paper to make up the necessary depth. Re-draw the notches at the shoulder seam.

Front placket opening

The directions that follow are for making the kind of placket used on the shirt on page 61.
Careful stitching and pressing are essential in order to achieve a placket that lies smoothly on the garment.

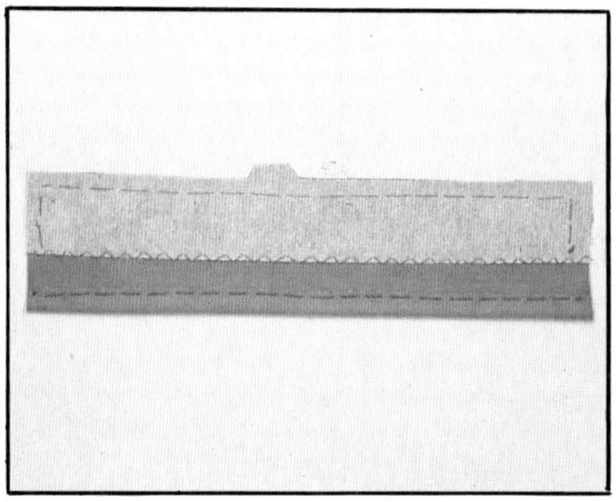

1 Baste interfacing to the wrong side of the two front bands, and catch-stitch the inner edge of the interfacing to the foldline. On the un-notched edge of each band, turn under and baste the seam allowance. Press flat.

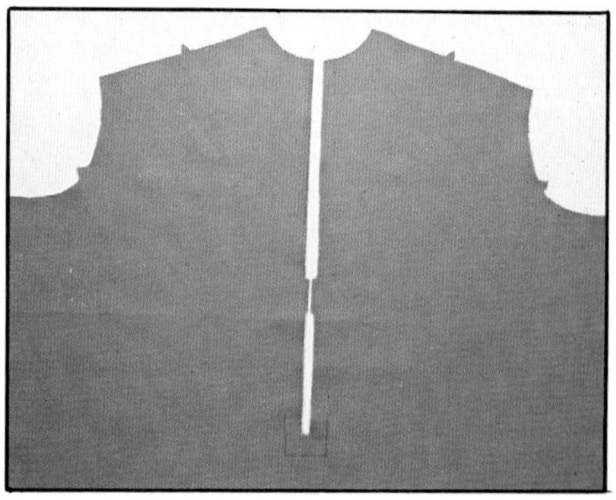

2 On the front opening of the shirt front, staystitch around the bottom corners, marked by the lower circles on the pattern. Cut down the center foldline to within ⅝in (1.5cm) of the stitching. Reposition the pattern piece and cut out the notches on the shirt center front.

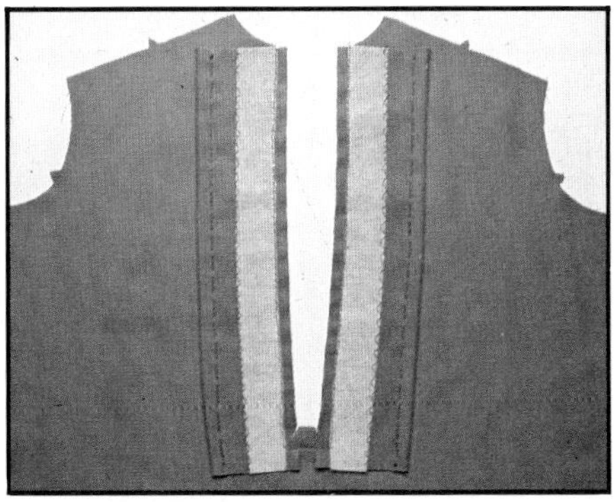

3 Baste a front band to each side of the front opening, matching notches and circles and taking $\frac{5}{8}$in (1.5cm) seams. Trim the interfacing close to the stitching and trim the seam allowance to $\frac{3}{8}$in (1cm). Clip diagonally to the circles at the bottom of the opening.

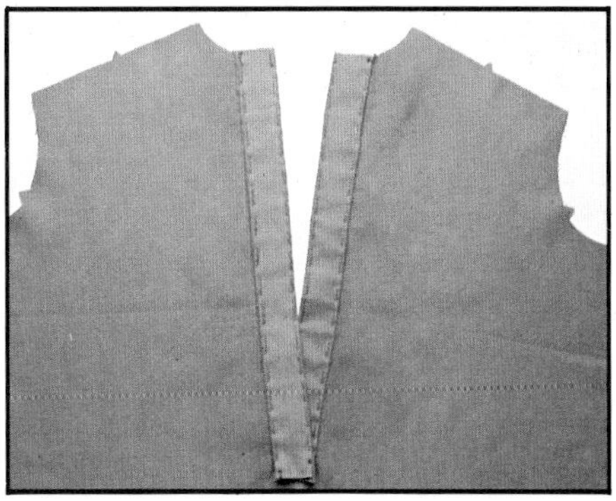

4 Fold the bands to the inside and baste along the foldline. Turn under the long raw edge on each band and baste in place to the stitching line.

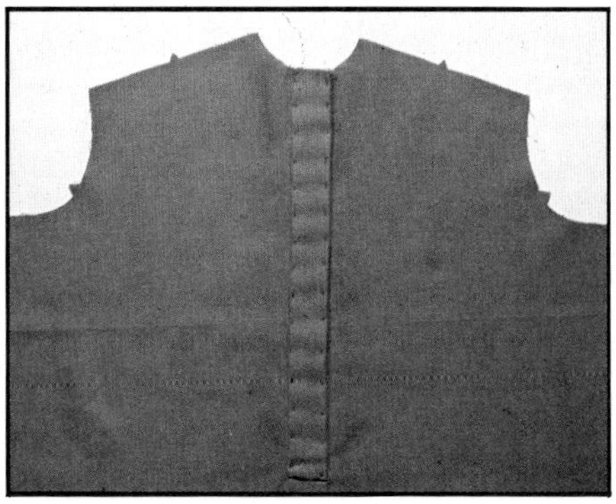

5 On the right side of the shirt, lap the right band over the left band and tuck the short raw ends into the bottom of the opening.

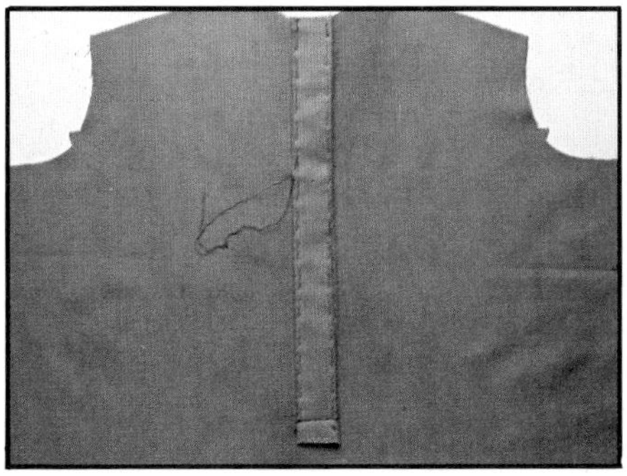

6 Working from the wrong side, baste and stitch the shirt bands to the small turning at the bottom of the opening on the shirt front, being careful not to catch in the fabric on either side of the placket. Finish the seam together by overcasting, and slip stitch the bands to the stitching lines on the inside. Press. On the right side, topstitch both long edges of each band $\frac{1}{4}$in (6mm) from the edge.

7 Stitch across the lower edge of the right band through all layers $\frac{1}{4}$in (6mm) from the bottom edge of opening and diagonally upward to a point 1in (2.5cm) from the lower edge.

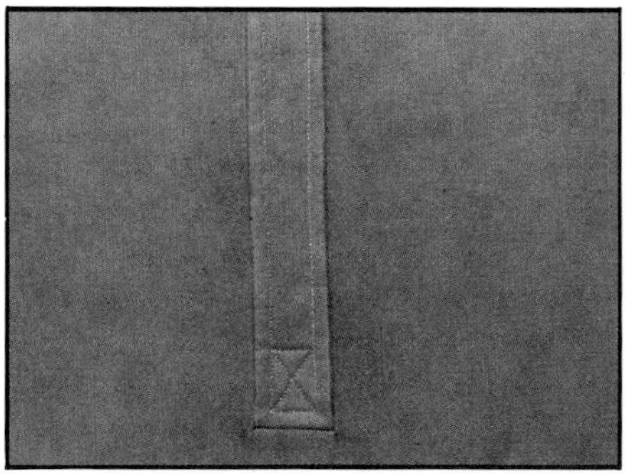

8 Stitch across the band horizontally and then diagonally down to the other corner. The topstitching will hold the bands in place and prevent strain at the corners of the opening.

Shirt collar and collar band

These directions are for attaching a regular shirt collar, like the one used in the pattern at the end of this course.

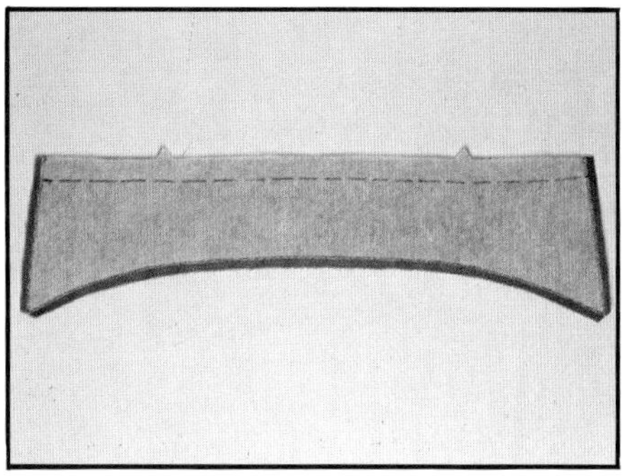

1 Baste or iron interfacing to the wrong side of one collar piece. Baste the right sides of the two collar pieces together with notches matching. Stitch around the outer edges. Trim interfacing close to stitching. Trim the seam allowances; trim across the corners.

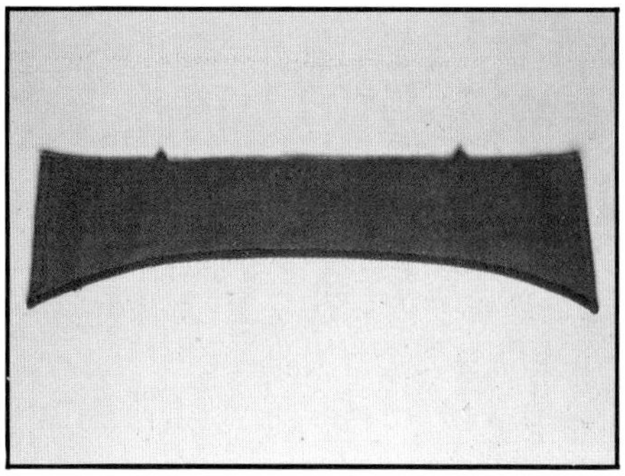

2 Turn the collar right side out. Baste close to the stitched edges and press flat. Topstitch around the seam $\frac{1}{4}$in (6mm) from the edge.

Paul Williams

continued

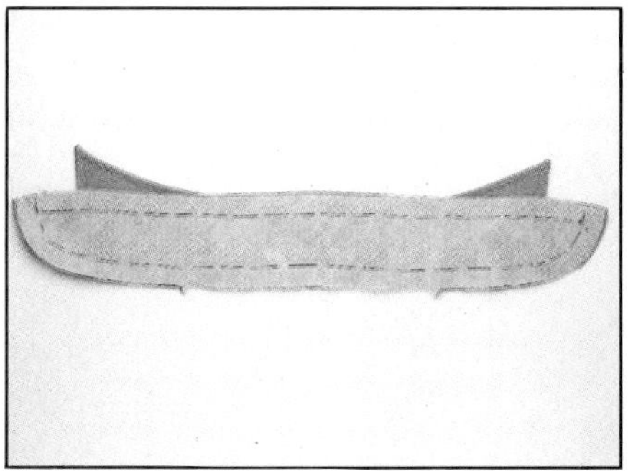

3 Baste or iron interfacing to the wrong side of one collar band piece. Place the collar between the two collar band pieces as shown, right sides together and notches matching. Pin and baste in place.

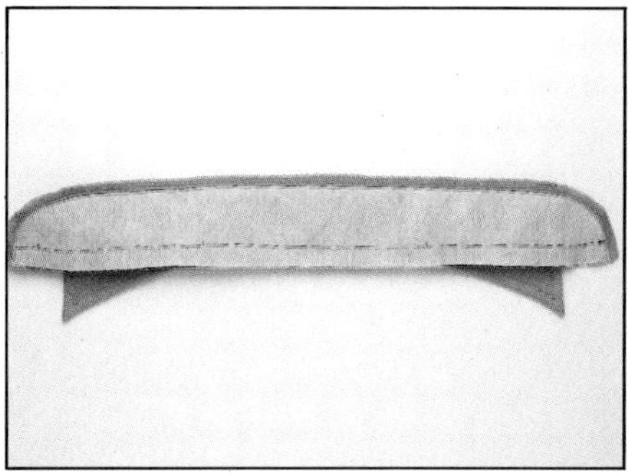

4 Stitch the collar band seam to secure the collar. Trim interfacing close to the stitching, grade the seam allowance and clip into the curves.

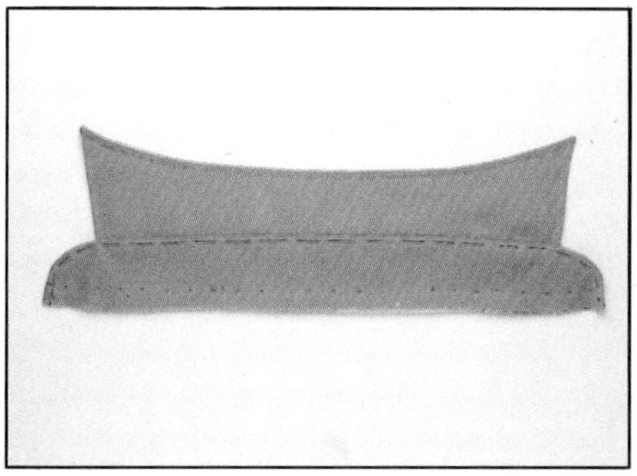

5 Turn the band right side out and baste close to the seamed edge. Press flat.

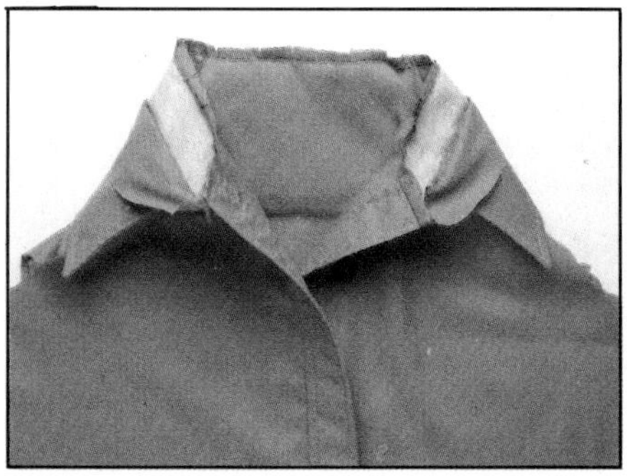

6 Baste and stitch the interfaced side of the collar band to the neck edge of the shirt with right sides together and the circles at shoulder seams and center fronts matched to those on the collar. Be careful not to catch the other side of the collar band into the seam. Grade the seams, trimming the interfacing close to the stitching. Clip curves and press the seam allowance toward the collar band.

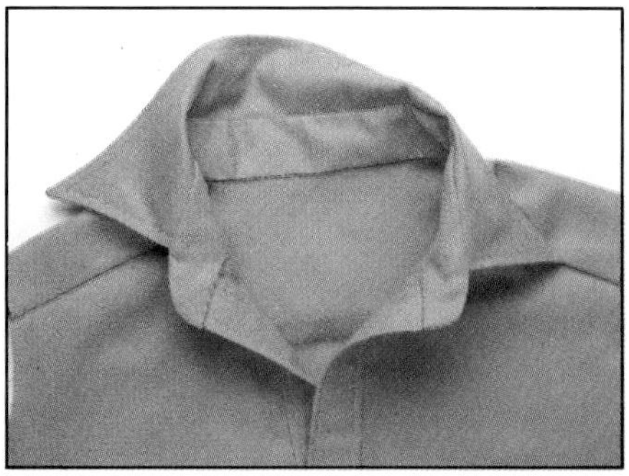

7 Turn under the seam allowance on the inside collar band. Baste and slip stitch it to the stitching line. Press flat.

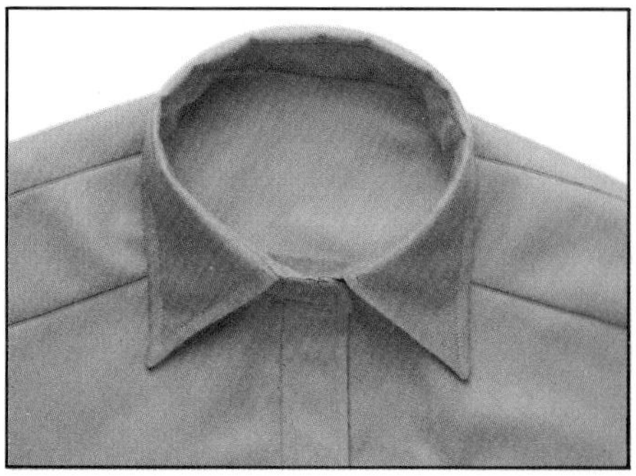

8 On the right side, topstitch the collar band around the upper seam line $\frac{1}{4}$in (6mm) from the edge and topstitch $\frac{1}{8}$in (3mm) above the neck seamline.

Paul Williams

Shirt: directions for making (1)

This classic shirt is one that you'll probably want to make in several kinds of fabric for different seasons and occasions. We chose a soft cotton and wool mixture, which is especially comfortable.

The pattern is from the Stitch by Stitch Pattern Pack. The directions will be completed on page 64.

Measurements

The pattern is given in sizes 10, 12, 14, 16, 18 and 20. $\frac{5}{8}$in (1.5cm) seam allowances are included throughout.

Suggested fabrics

Cottons, cotton mixtures, Viyella®, lightweight woolens and denim. More advanced dressmakers could use silk.

Materials

36in (90cm)-wide fabric with or without nap:
Sizes 10, 12 and 14: $3\frac{1}{4}$yd (2.90m)
Sizes 16, 18 and 20: $3\frac{1}{3}$yd (3.00m)
45in (115cm)-wide fabric with or without nap:
Sizes 10, 12 and 14: $2\frac{2}{3}$yd (2.40m)
Sizes 16 and 18: $2\frac{5}{8}$yd (2.60m)
Size 20: 3yd (2.70m)
54in (140cm)-wide fabric with or without nap:
Sizes 10 and 12: $1\frac{3}{4}$yd (1.60m)
Sizes 14, 16, 18 and 20: 2yd (1.80m)
36in (90cm)-wide interfacing for all sizes: $\frac{5}{8}$yd (50cm)
Matching thread
Six $\frac{1}{2}$in (1.3cm) buttons

1 Cut out the pattern pieces from the pattern sheet.
2 Prepare fabric and cut out pattern pieces following layout overleaf.
3 Transfer all the pattern marks.

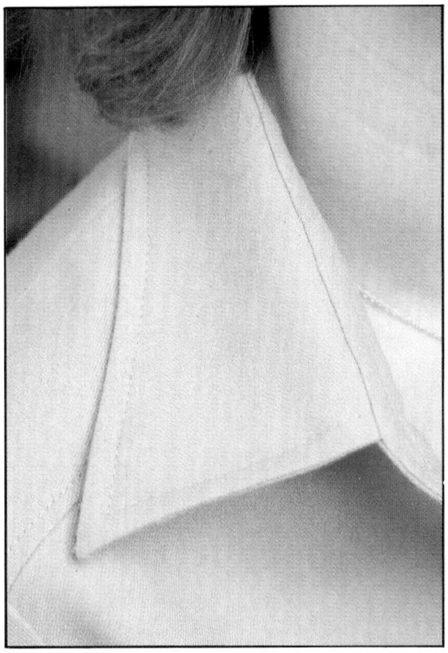

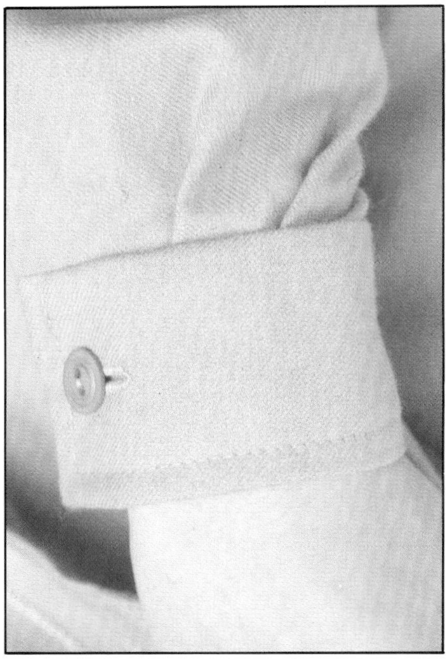

Gary Warren

4 Baste and stitch the bust darts and press them downward.

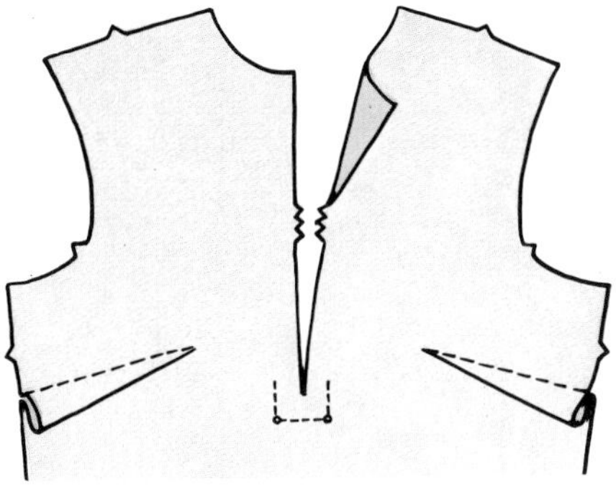

5 Prepare and slash front opening as described on page 58.

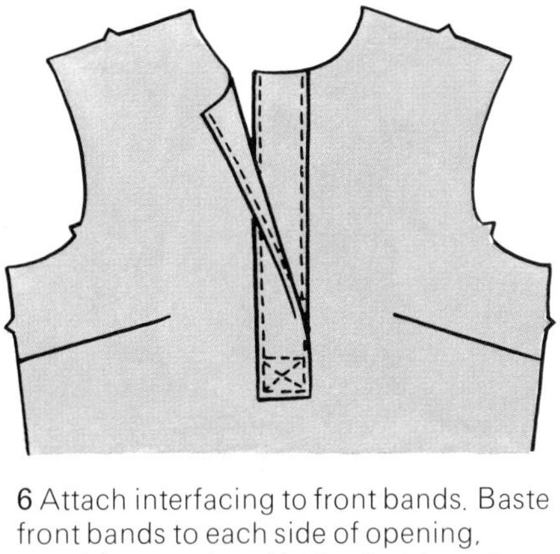

6 Attach interfacing to front bands. Baste front bands to each side of opening, matching notches. Fold to inside and turn under raw edges. Finish the bands and topstitch in place as described on page 59.

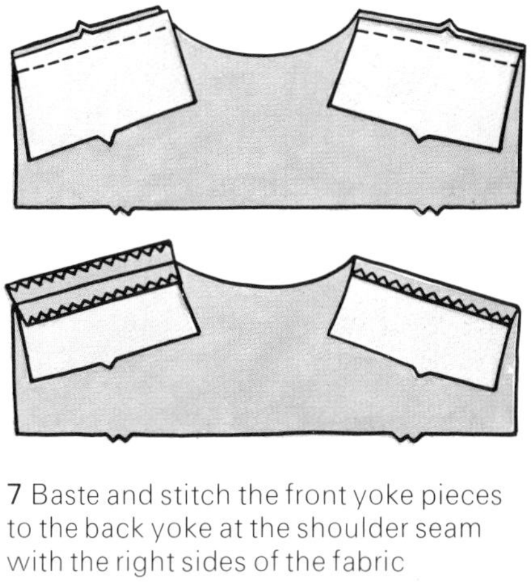

Terry Evans

7 Baste and stitch the front yoke pieces to the back yoke at the shoulder seam with the right sides of the fabric together and notches matching. Repeat for the yoke facing. Finish the seams and press open.

36in–wide fabric with or without nap

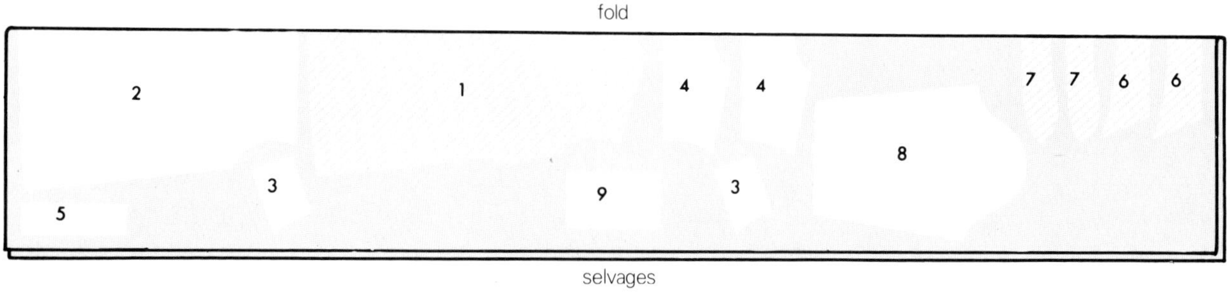

45in–wide fabric with or without nap

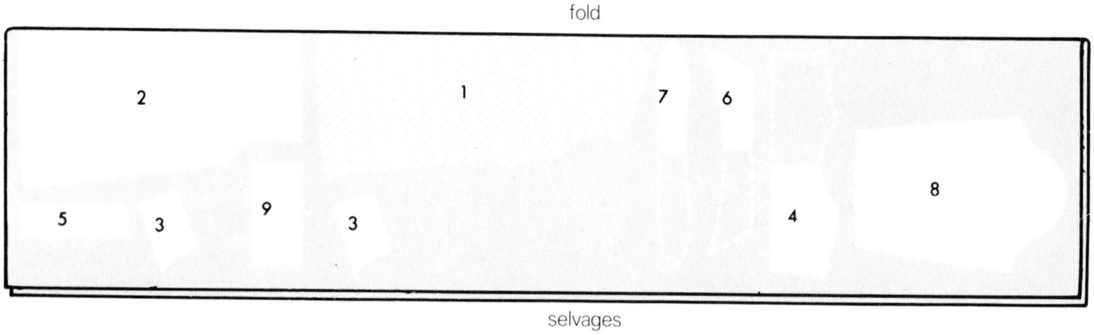

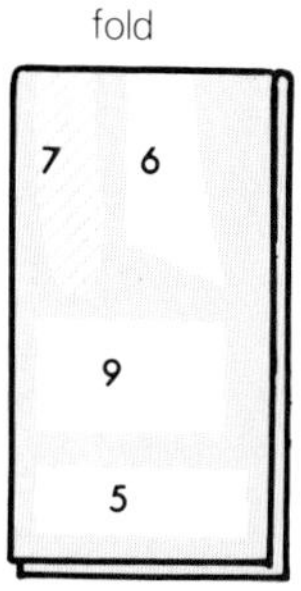

Interfacing 36in–wide fabric

54in–wide fabric with or without nap

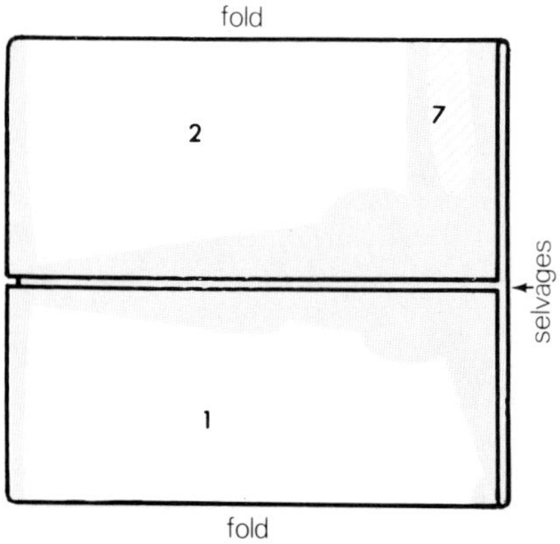

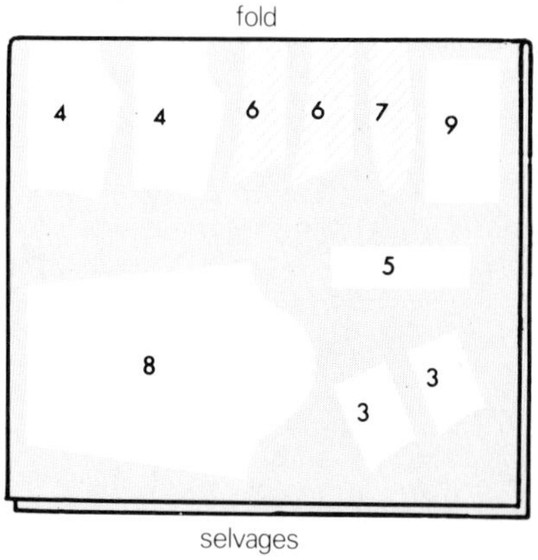

Key to pattern pieces

1	Shirt front	Cut 1 on fold
2	Shirt back	Cut 1 on fold
3	Front yoke and yoke facing	Cut 4
4	Back yoke and yoke facing	Cut 2 on fold
5	Front band	Cut 2
6	Collar	Cut 2 on fold
7	Collar band	Cut 2 on fold
8	Sleeve	Cut 2
9	Cuff	Cut 2

Interfacing: use pieces 5, 6, 7 and 9

John Hutchinson

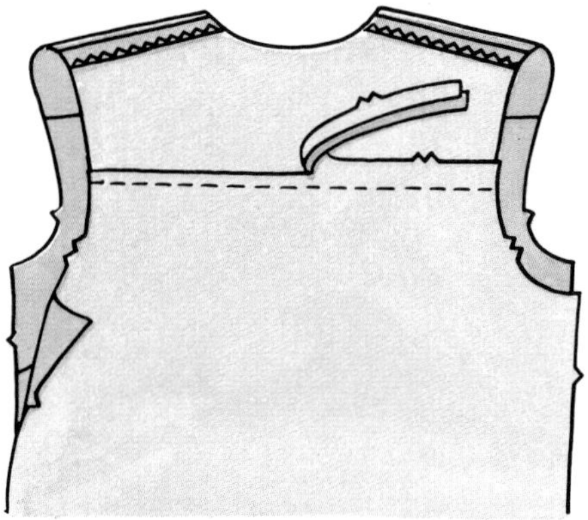

8 Baste and stitch the front yokes to the front of the shirt with right sides together and notches matching. Baste and stitch the back yoke to the back of the shirt in the same way. Trim the seam allowances and press them toward the yokes.

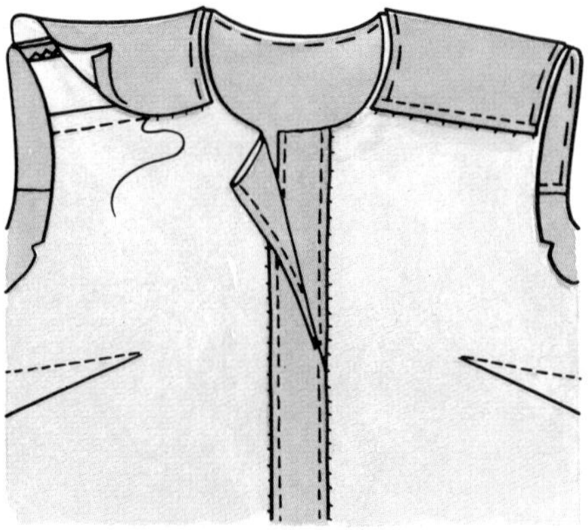

9 Baste the yoke facings to the yokes around neck and armhole edges with wrong sides together and shoulder seams matching. Fold the seam allowance on the yoke facings to the wrong side and slip stitch the folded edges to the stitching line. Press. On the right side, topstitch $\frac{1}{4}$in (6mm) in from the yoke seam line on back and front yokes.

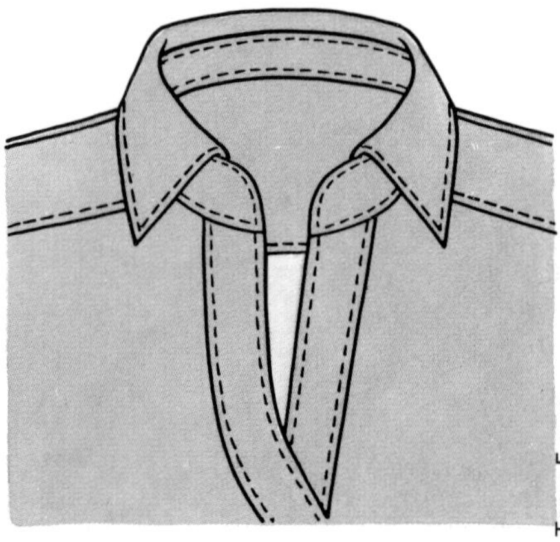

Terry Evans

10 Assemble the collar, attach it to the neck of the shirt and topstitch as shown on page 60.

*Continuous lap sleeve opening
*Lapped cuff
*Shirt: directions for making (2)

Continuous lap sleeve opening

This type of opening is made at the cuff of the sleeve before the underarm seam is stitched. The facing of the opening does not show when the cuff is closed.
This type of facing is only suitable on light- and medium-weight fabrics. On thick fabrics the extra bulk will cause the opening to gape when the cuff is closed.

1 On the wrong side of the sleeve, mark the center line of the opening with basting stitches or tailor's chalk. Reinforce the opening by staystitching along both sides of this line, starting $\frac{1}{4}$in (6mm) from the line at the lower edge, tapering to a point at the top, and back to $\frac{1}{4}$in (6mm) at the other side.

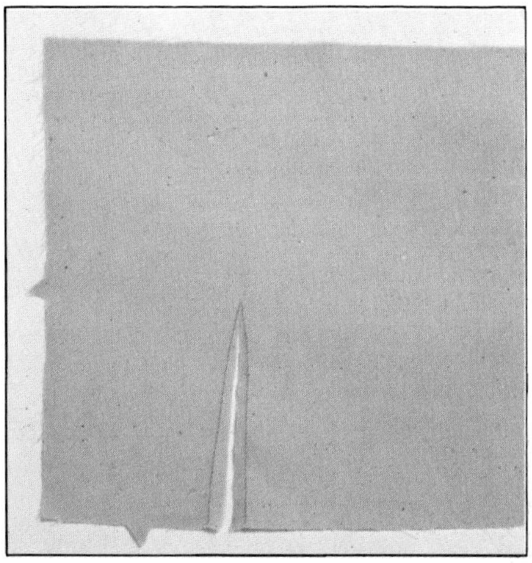

2 Cut along the center line almost to the stitching at the point.

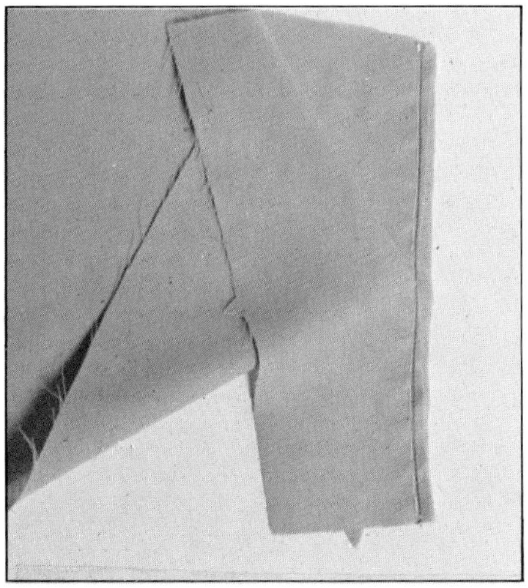

3 Cut a bias strip of fabric, twice the length of the opening and 1 in (2.5cm) wide. Spread out the opening in the sleeve until the line of staystitching is straight. Pin and baste the bias strip to the opening with right sides together and the line of staystitching $\frac{1}{4}$in (6mm) from the raw edge of the strip. Stitch the strip to the opening along the line of staystitching.

4 Press the seam allowances toward the strip. Turn $\frac{1}{4}$in (6mm) to the wrong side on the raw edge of the strip and slip stitch the folded edge to the stitching line. Press flat.

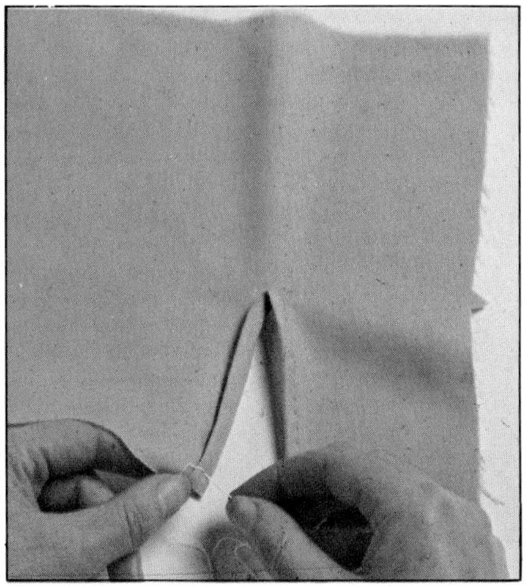

5 Turn the placket strip on the front edge of the sleeve to the inside and baste down on the lower edge. Leave the back placket strip flat.

Fred Mancini

Lapped cuff

A small section of this cuff extends beyond the back sleeve edge so that when the cuff is closed the front of the cuff overlaps it.
The cuff is attached after the sleeve placket and underarm seam have been stitched and after the tucks have been folded and basted in place.

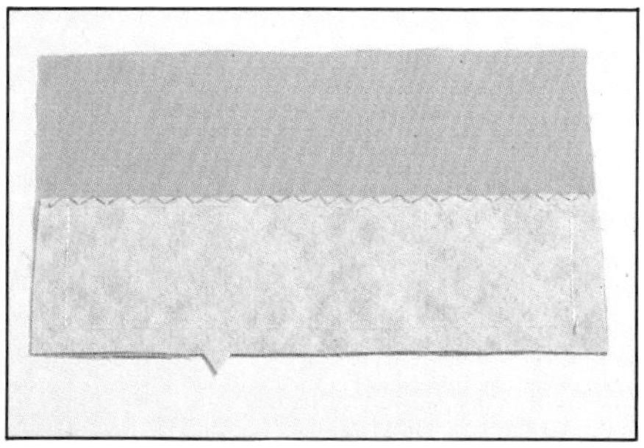

1 Baste the interfacing to the wrong side of the cuff on the notched edge. Catch-stitch the interfacing in place along the cuff fold line.

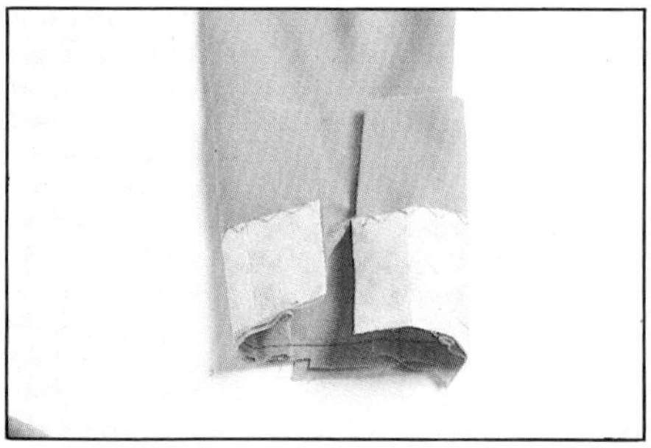

2 Pin and baste the interfaced edge of the cuff to the lower edge of the sleeve, matching notches. Stitch the seam from the edge of the back placket to the front folded placket. Grade the seam allowances, trimming the interfacing close to the stitching. Press the seam down toward the cuff.

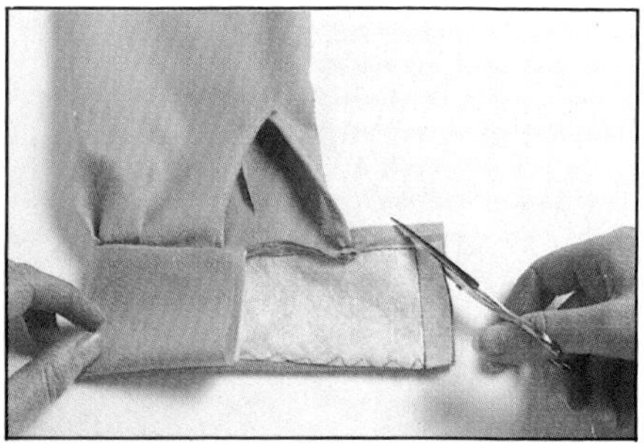

3 Fold the cuff on the foldline with right sides together. Baste and stitch across the straight edge and the small right-angled seam extending beyond the sleeve at the back of the cuff.

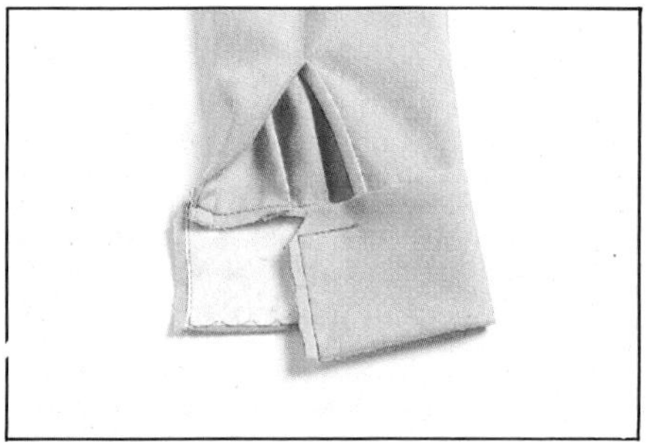

4 Cut across the corner. Baste and stitch the straight seam at the front edge of the cuff. Grade the seam allowances, trimming the interfacing close to the stitching, and trim the second corner.

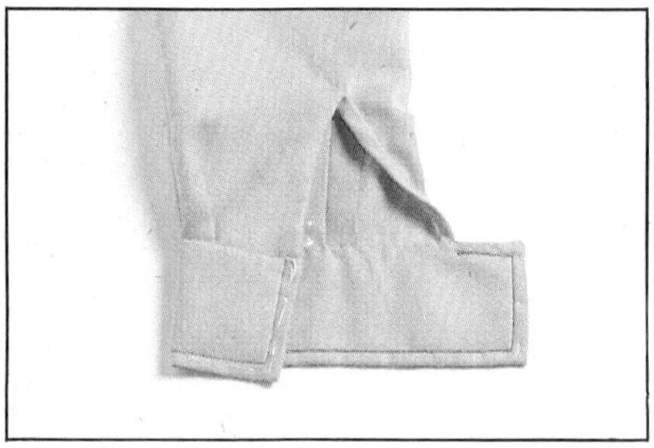

5 Turn the cuff right side out and baste around the outer edge. Press. On the inside of the sleeve, turn in the seam allowance on the free edge of the cuff and slip stitch the folded edge to the stitching line. Press. On the right side, topstitch $\frac{1}{4}$in (6mm) in from outer edges of cuff.

Fred Mancini

Shirt: directions for making (2)

In Sewing course 20, we gave the first set of directions for making the shirt from the Stitch by Stitch Pattern Pack. Now we show you how to finish the sleeves and complete the shirt.

1 The directions on page 60-62 show how to stitch the main seams and fit the collar. The next step is to make the sleeves and fit them to the main part of the shirt.
Make a continuous lap sleeve opening in the lower edge of both sleeves as shown on page 63, cutting bias strips to bind the edges from the remnants of the fabric.
Fold the tucks at the sleeve edge in the direction indicated on the pattern, and baste in place.

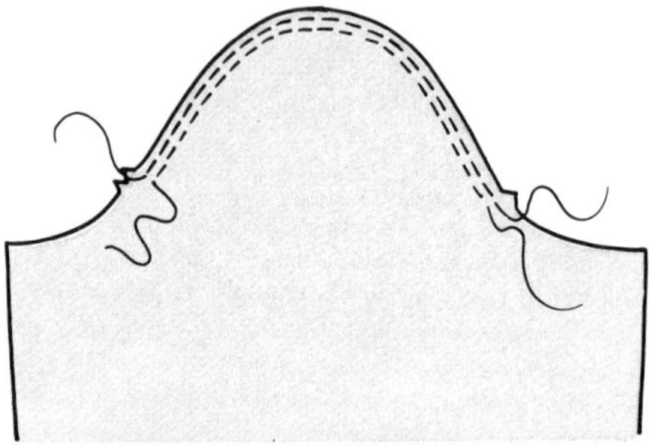

2 Run two rows of gathering stitches between the notches on the sleeve cap.

3 Baste and stitch the sleeve underarm seam. Press open and finish the raw edges.
4 Attach the cuff to the lower sleeve edge and topstitch as shown above.
Make the other sleeve in exactly the same way.

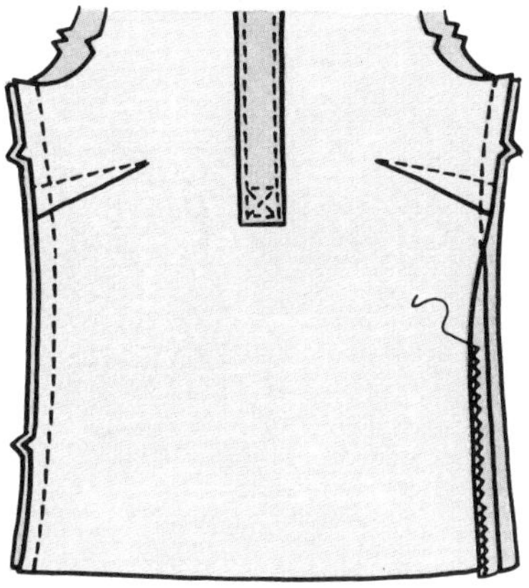

5 Baste and stitch the front and back of the shirt together at the side seams, matching notches. Press the seams open and finish.

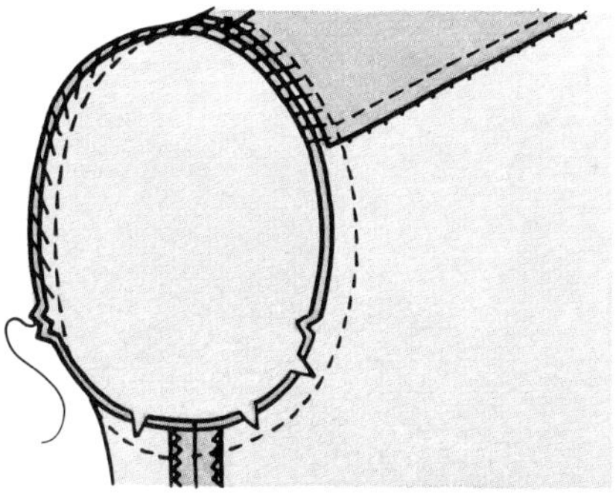

6 Pin the sleeve into the armhole with right sides of fabric facing and notches matching. Match the circle marking on the sleeve cap to the shoulder seam and the underarm seam to the side seam of shirt. Pull up the gathers until the sleeve fits the armhole. Baste in place, making sure the ease is evenly spread. Stitch the seam with the sleeve uppermost on the machine.

7 Trim the seam and clip into the curves. Finish the seam by overcasting the raw edges together and press the seam toward the sleeve.

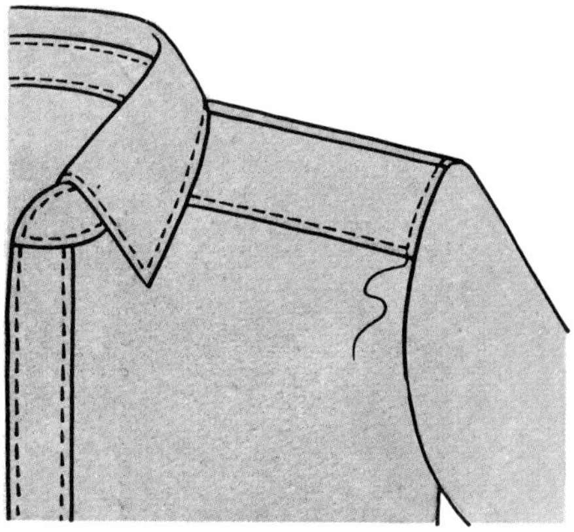

8 On the right side of the shirt yoke, topstitch around the top of the sleeve, $\frac{1}{4}$in (6mm) in from the seamline, working the stitches from the topstitching at the front yoke across to the topstitching on the back yoke.

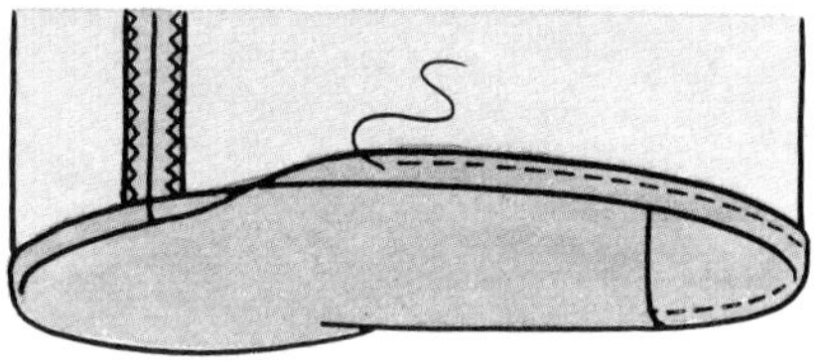

9 Turn $\frac{1}{4}$in (6mm) to the wrong side on the lower edge of the shirt. Make another fold $\frac{3}{8}$in (1cm) deep and baste the hem in place. Stitch the hem $\frac{1}{4}$in (6mm) from the bottom fold. Press.

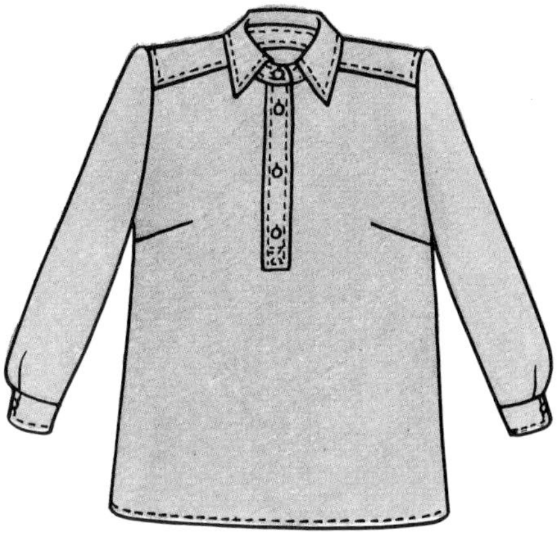

10 Stitch buttonholes by hand or machine (see Volume 4, pages 56-57) down the center front of the right placket band and on the cuffs in the positions indicated on the pattern. Lap the front band over the left band and mark the positions for the buttons directly beneath the buttonholes. Do the same on the cuffs. Sew on the buttons in the positions marked.

Bath mitt

Make this handy mitt from a worn-out hand towel or from a piece of terry cloth.

Kim Sayer

Finished size
About 12½in (32cm) long.

Materials
A worn hand towel or piece of terry cloth 40×20½in (100×52cm)
A package of 1in (2.5cm)-wide bias binding
Matching thread
Paper for pattern

1 Place your hand on the paper and mark around it, allowing about ⅜in (1cm) extra on all edges.
2 At the widest part of the hand, extend the pattern lines straight down for 3¼in (8.5cm). Alter the pattern if necessary for a smooth shape, and cut it out.
3 Using paper pattern, cut out four mitts from towel, adding ¼in (5mm) all around except at the wrist edge.
4 Place the mitt pieces together in two pairs. Pin, baste and stitch across wrist edge ¼in (5mm) from the outer edge. Fold bias binding in half across stitched edges. Pin, baste and topstitch bias binding in place.
5 Place the two pairs together and pin, baste and stitch all around outer edges, ¼in (5mm) from the raw edges, through all four thicknesses.
6 Fold bias binding in half along stitched edges. Pin, baste and topstitch bias binding in place.
7 Fold a 5½in (14cm) piece of bias binding in half lengthwise and then widthwise to form a loop. Turn in raw edges and sew loop to back of mitt. Slip stitch bias binding edges together around loop.

*Unpressed pleats with stay tape
*Skirt with soft pleats: adapting the pattern; directions for making (1)

Unpressed pleats with stay tape

Pleats are folds in the fabric which give fullness and shape to a garment. Unpressed pleats—as their name suggests—are softer than pleats with a definite crease line. Unlike other types of pleat, unpressed pleats are not stitched vertically. Sometimes they simply fall freely from the waistband or bodice. On other garments (such as the skirt on page 69), they are anchored in place with seam binding stitched horizontally across the back of the pleats. Unpressed pleats will hang well only if made of soft, easily draped fabrics. Patterns containing them usually suggest a suitable fabric.

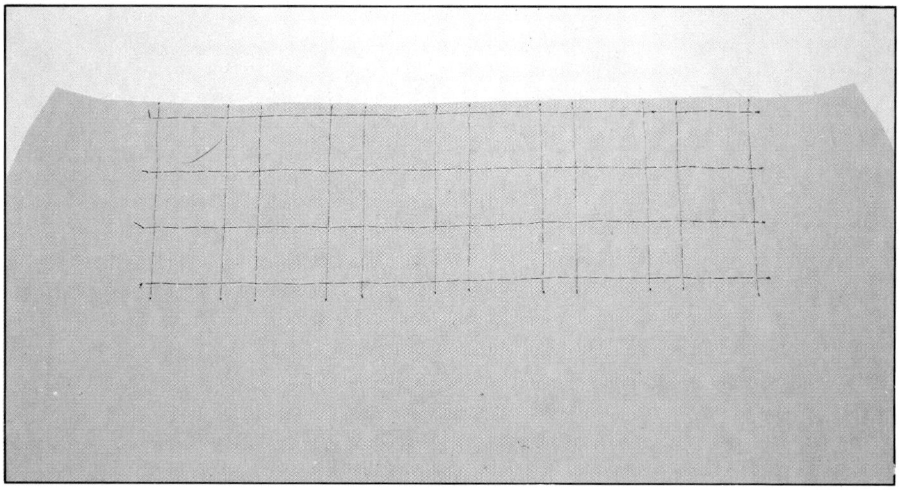

1 Mark each pleat line as indicated on the pattern with a line of stitches. Mark the lines for the seam binding across the pleated section in the same way.

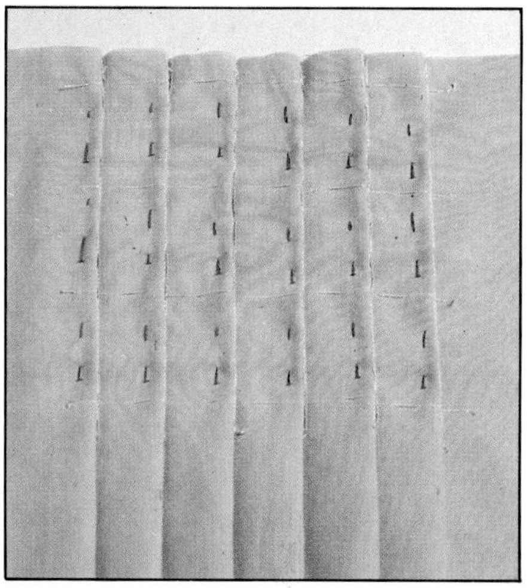

2 Working from the right side, fold the pleats in place by bringing together the two lines of basting for each pleat. Fold each pleat to the right so that the fabric under the pleat lies to the left. Do not press the pleats.

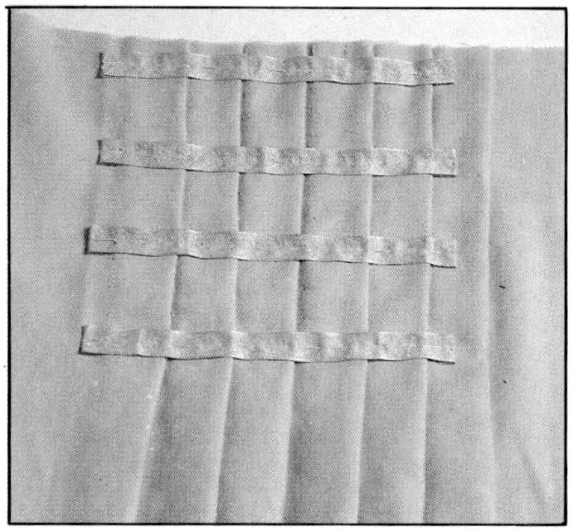

3 Cut a piece of seam binding long enough to overlap the pleated section by $\frac{5}{8}$in (1.5cm) at each end, for every line on the pattern. Baste the seam binding to the wrong side of the pleated section, centering it over the basted lines and turning in the short ends at each side.

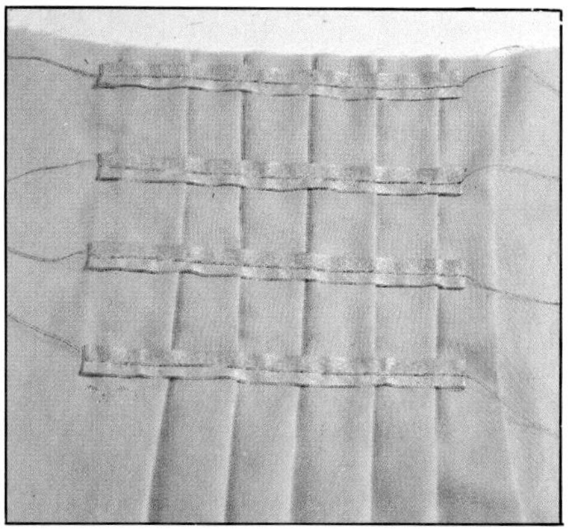

4 Stitch along the center of each piece of seam binding, beginning and ending the stitching $\frac{3}{8}$in (1cm) beyond the folded edge of the last pleat on each side.

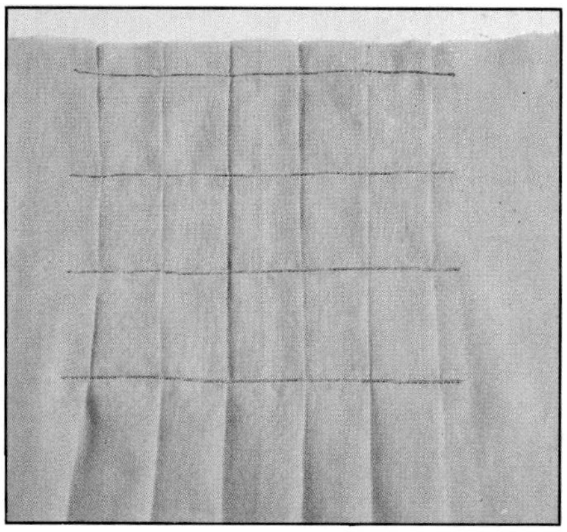

5 Take the threads to the wrong side and secure the ends. Remove the basting but do not press the pleats. The stitching will hold the pleats in place.

Fred Mancini

Skirt with soft pleats

With this elegant three-piece outfit we begin our series of variations on the Pattern Pack. In this course and the next one we show you how to adapt the A-line skirt pattern to make this becoming skirt with unpressed pleats.

Adapting the pattern

Materials

Sheets of tracing paper at least 24 x 34in (60 x 86cm)

A flexible curve

1 Trace the A-line skirt front pattern onto the pattern paper, making sure there is at least an extra 8in (20cm) of paper at the center front.

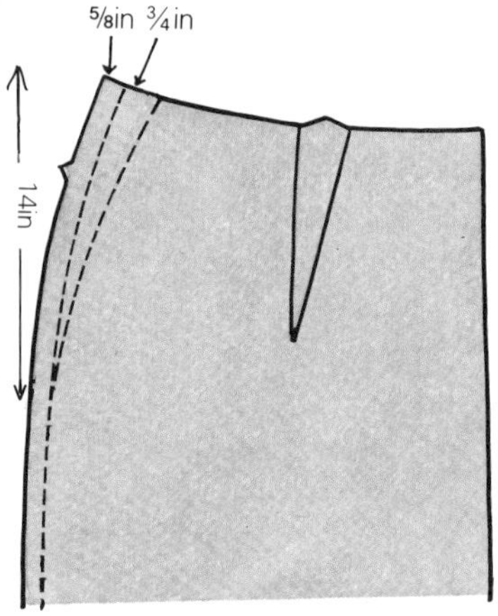

2 As the darts are not needed in this design, the dart allowance is taken off the side edge of the pattern. Measure in and mark a point $\frac{3}{4}$in (2cm) from the seam line on the waist edge. Measure 14in (35.5cm) down from the waist edge and mark this point on the seamline. Join the two points to form the new cutting line, using a flexible curve. Mark the notch on the side seam, $4\frac{1}{4}$in (10.5cm) down from the waist edge.

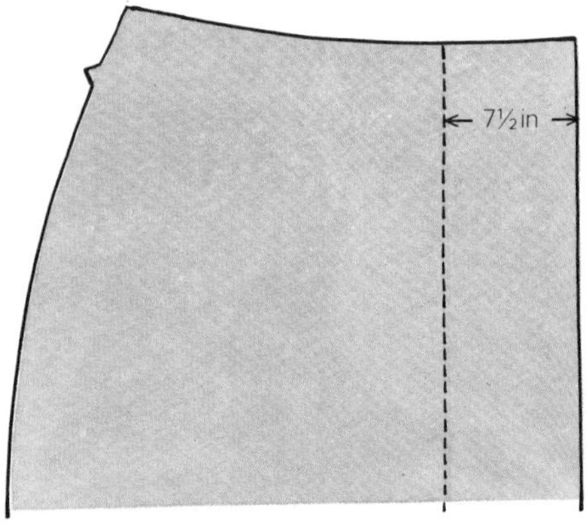

3 Draw a new center front line, $7\frac{1}{2}$in (19cm) outside the original center front line, to allow for the pleats.

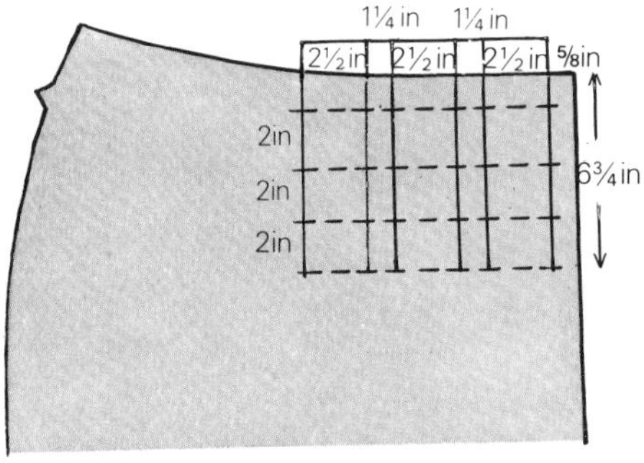

4 Measure in $\frac{5}{8}$in (1.5cm) from the new center front line and mark a vertical line $6\frac{3}{4}$in (17cm) long. Measure in $2\frac{1}{2}$in (6.5cm) from the first line and mark another line $6\frac{3}{4}$in (17cm) long. The space between these two lines forms a pleat. Measure in $1\frac{1}{4}$in (3cm) from the last line for the next pleat. Mark off the pleat $2\frac{1}{2}$in (6.5cm) wide. Measure off and mark the next $1\frac{1}{4}$in (3cm) space and $2\frac{1}{2}$in (6.5cm) wide pleat in the same way

5 Draw the first seam binding stitching line on the waist seamline across the whole of the pleated section. Mark in three other horizontal lines, spacing them at 2in (5cm) intervals below the first.

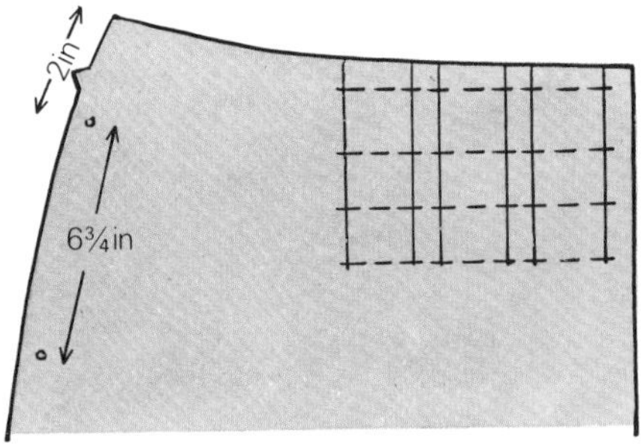

6 Mark the position for the top of the pocket on the side seamline 2in (5cm) below the waist seamline. Mark the position of the bottom of the pocket $6\frac{3}{4}$in (17cm) below the first point, also on the seamline.

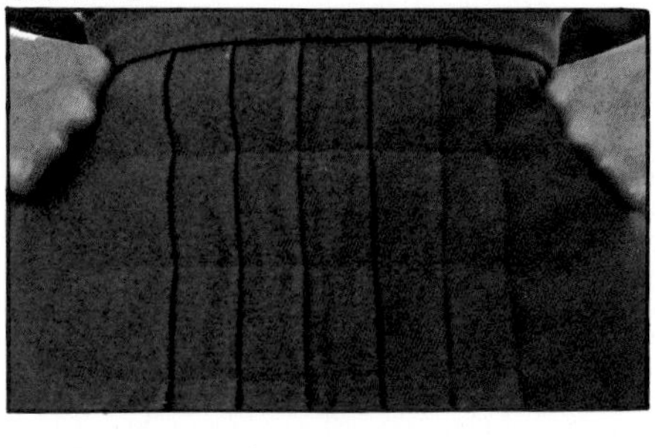

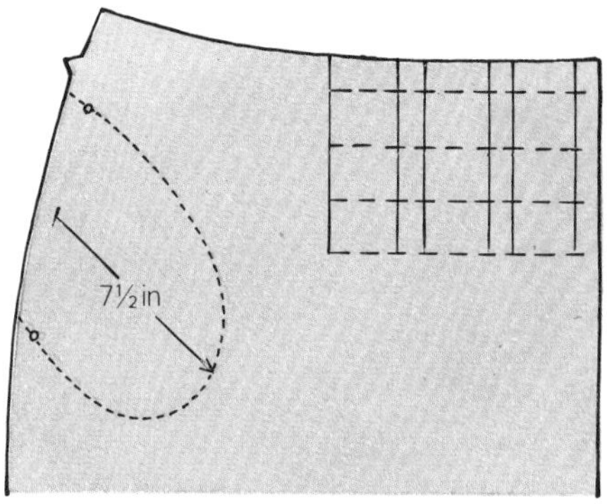

7 Draw in the shape of the pocket between the two marks as shown, using a flexible curve. The pocket should be 7½in (19cm) deep and should slant downward as shown. Mark the grain line for the pocket parallel to the center front of the skirt.

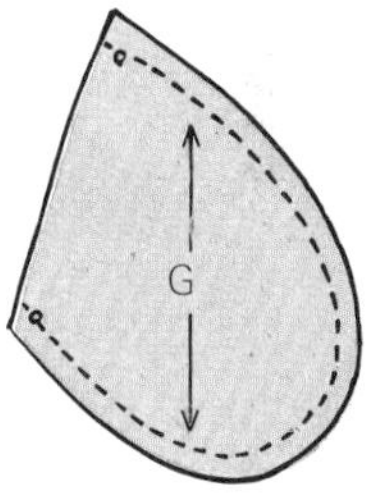

8 Trace the pocket shape, mark in the grain line, and add ⅝in (1.5cm) seam allowance all around the curved edge.

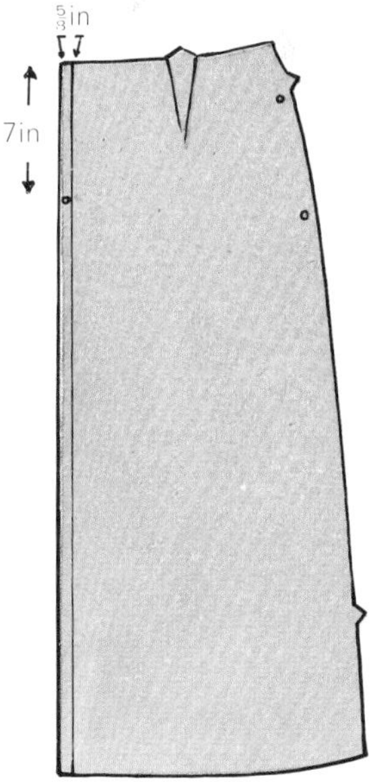

Terry Evans

9 Now trace the A-line skirt back. The adapted design has a center back seam with a zipper, so add a ⅝in (1.5cm)-wide seam allowance to the center back. Mark the position for the base of the zipper, 7in (18cm) below the waistline seam on the foldline, which will now be the stitching line.

10 Lay the new skirt back pattern piece over the new skirt front, matching the side seams. Trace the marks for the top and bottom of the pocket onto the back.

Serge Krouglikoff

Serge Krouglikoff

Directions for making

Measurements

The pattern—based on the A-line skirt—is given in sizes 10, 12, 14, 16, 18 and 20. Finished lengths from natural waistline: $28\frac{1}{2}$in (72.5cm), 29in (73.5cm), $29\frac{1}{2}$in (75cm), $30\frac{1}{8}$in (76.5cm), $30\frac{3}{4}$in (78cm) and 31in (78.5cm).

Suggested fabrics

Soft fabrics such as lightweight wool crepe, challis, single knit jersey, flannel.

Materials

54in (140cm)-wide fabric with or without nap:
Sizes 10-18: $2\frac{1}{4}$yd (2m)
Size 20: $2\frac{3}{8}$yd (2.1m)
36in (90cm)-wide interfacing:
Sizes 10-18: $\frac{1}{4}$yd (.2m)
Size 20: $\frac{3}{8}$yd (.3m)
Matching thread
7in (18cm) skirt zipper
Hooks and eyes
$\frac{7}{8}$yd (.8m) of seam binding

Key to adjusted pattern pieces

1 Skirt front	Cut 1 on fold
2 Skirt back	Cut 2
3 Waistband	Cut 1
A Pocket	Cut 4

Interfacing, use piece 3

1 Alter the pattern pieces for the skirt front and back and make the pocket pattern as instructed on pages 68-69. Use the waistband pattern from the A-line skirt pattern, following the correct line for your size and trimming off the waist seam notch. Cut out the pieces.

2 Prepare the fabric and pin on the pattern pieces, following the layout given. Place the grain lines on the straight grain of the fabric. Cut out each piece.

3 Transfer the markings for the darts and dots to the fabric, using tailor's tacks. Mark the lines for pleats and seam binding with lines of basting.

4 Fold and baste the pleats in position and attach seam binding to the wrong side of the skirt front as illustrated on page 67. Do not press the pleats.

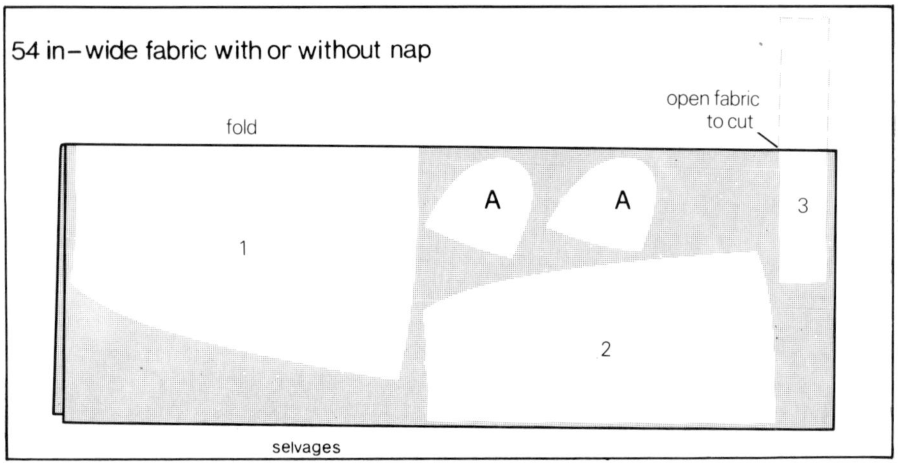

Brian Mayor

Sewing/COURSE 23

*Pockets in side seams—three methods
*Topstitched hem
*Skirt with soft pleats: directions for making (2)

Pockets in side seams

There are three methods for inserting pockets into the side panel seams of a garment and all look inconspicuous from the right side.
The easiest kind is the all-in-one pocket, in which the two pocket pieces are cut in one with the garment front and back.
Separate pockets in seams, as used in the skirt on page 74, are cut out separately from the garment front and back but are attached before sewing the side seams.
An extension pocket is a combination of the two previous pocket types. A small extension is cut in one with the garment front and back and the pocket sections are cut out from strong lining fabric. This method is particularly well suited to garments made of bulky fabrics as extra bulk in the pocket itself is eliminated, but the contrasting lining fabric is invisible, because of the extension.

Reinforcing the pocket

The three types of pockets in seams described in this course can all be strengthened with seam binding to prevent the pocket from pulling out of shape. The tape is attached before the side seams are stitched and—in the case of separate or extension pockets—before the pocket pieces are joined to the main garment sections. This sample shows how an all-in-one pocket is reinforced.

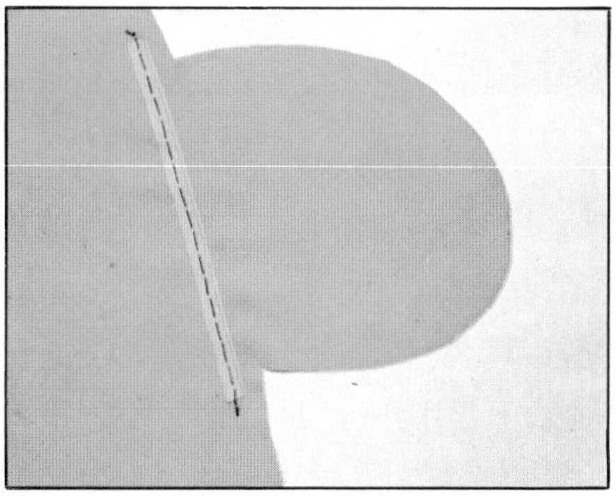

1 Cut a piece of seam binding $1\frac{1}{4}$in (3cm) longer than the pocket opening. Baste it to the wrong side of the garment front so that the inner edge lies over the pocket line (the section of the seam line where the pocket opening will be). Stitch the binding in place close to the inner edge.

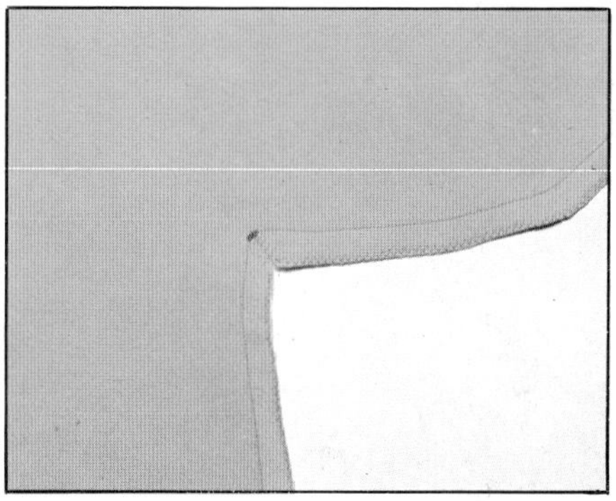

2 When the pocket is completed, clip into seam allowance at top and bottom of pocket. Sew a bar tack (see Volume 2, page 63) at the junction of the side and pocket seams.

All-in-one pockets

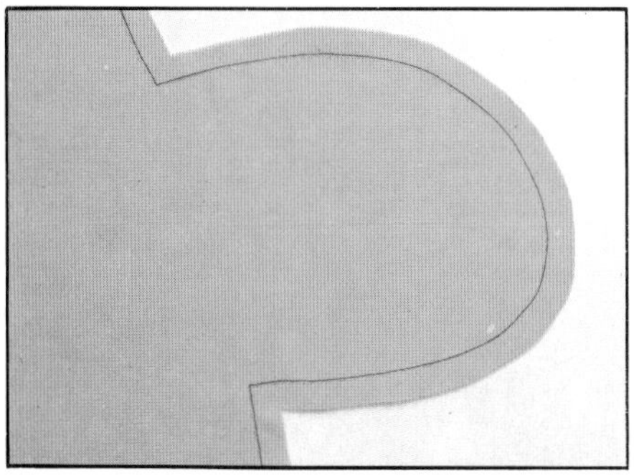

1 Baste the back and front of the garment together with right sides together. Stitch the side seam in one continuous line from the lower edge up around the pocket shape and up to the waist line.

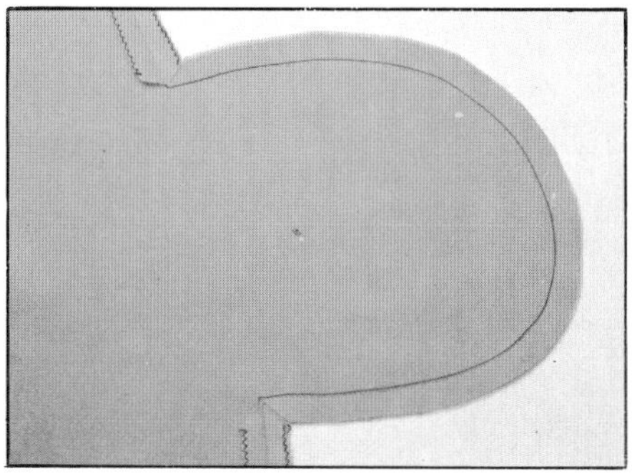

2 Clip into the corner of the pocket and press the side seams open. Finish these edges separately.

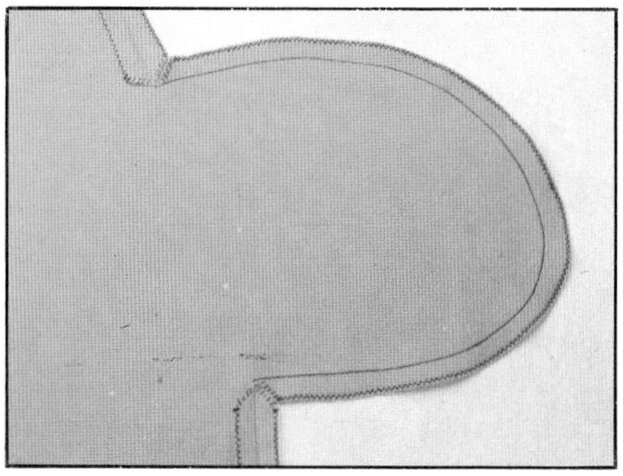

3 Stitch the edges of the pocket together with overcasting or zig-zag stitches. Overcast the short ends of the seam allowances.

Separate pockets in seams

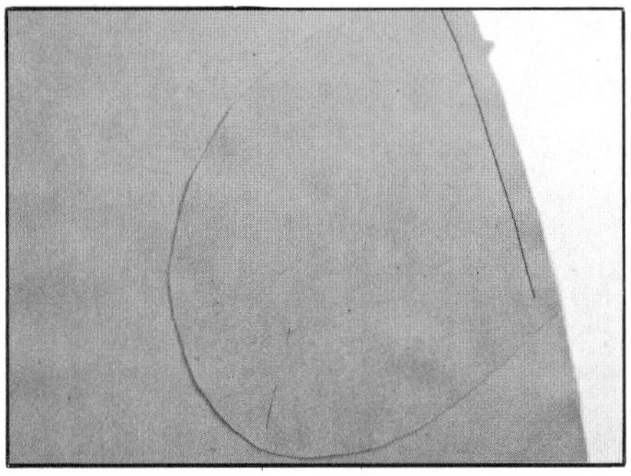

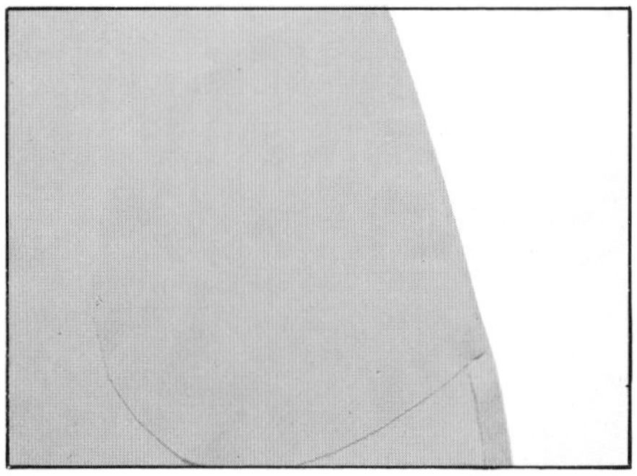

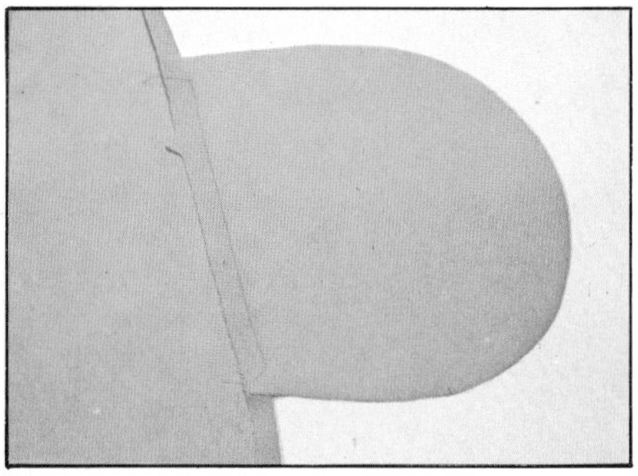

1 Baste a pocket section to the front and back pieces of the garment along the seamline between the dots for the pocket position, making sure that right sides are together. Stitch pocket pieces in place, stitching to within ⅝in (1.5cm) of the top and bottom of the pocket.

2 On the garment back, press the side seam allowances toward the center back and the pocket piece away from it.

3 On the garment front, press seam allowances and pocket piece toward the center front.

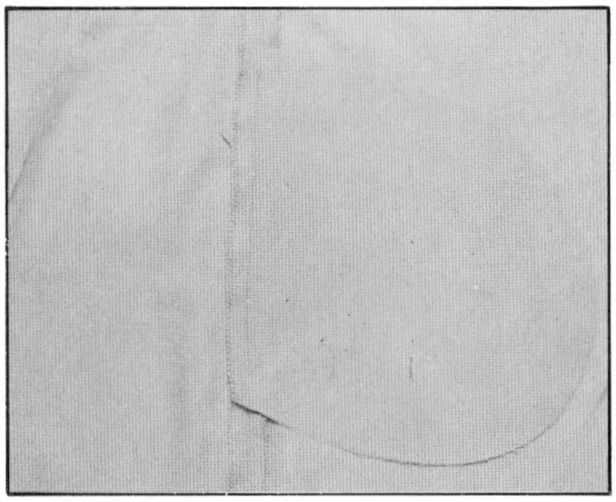

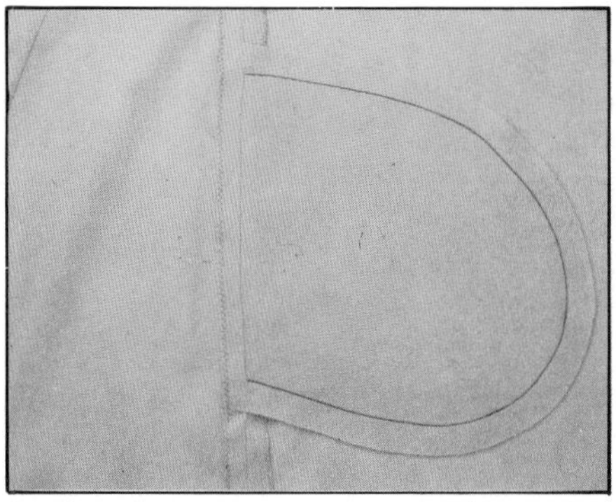

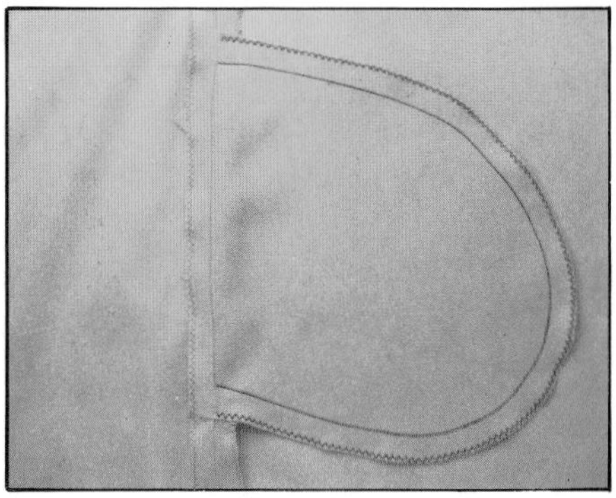

4 Open out the pressed seam allowances. Baste and stitch the side seams of the garment from the hem to the bottom of the stitching at pocket and from the stitching at the top of the pocket upward. Finish the seam allowances and press open.

5 Baste and stitch the pocket pieces together around the outer edge from the side seam at the top to the side seam at the bottom.

6 Trim the seam allowances slightly and finish with overcasting or zig-zag stitches. Press.

Extension pocket

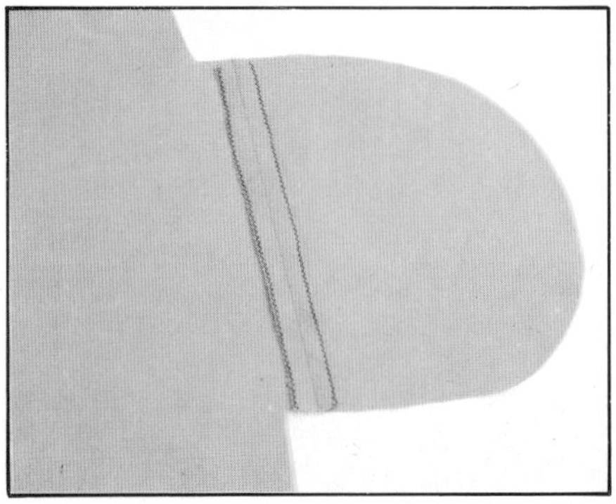

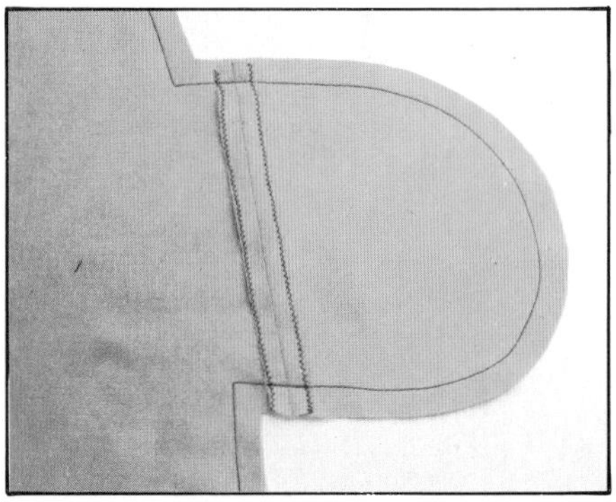

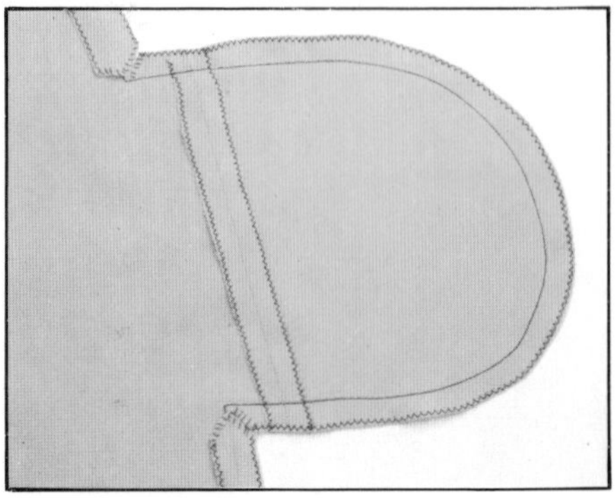

1 Baste the pocket sections to the extensions on the front and back of the garment with right sides together. Stitch the seams, press them open and finish.

2 Baste the front and back of the garment together with right sides together and stitch the side seam in one continuous line including the pocket.

3 Clip into the corner of the pocket, press the side seams open and finish. Overcast the short raw ends of the side seams. Sew the raw edges of the pocket together with overcasting or zig-zag stitches.

Fred Mancini/Paul Williams

Topstitched hem

Topstitching is a decorative and practical method of finishing a hem. The rows of stitching should be parallel and are usually equally spaced. The skirt opposite has eight rows of stitching spaced at $\frac{1}{4}$in (6mm) intervals, but the distance between the rows can be altered if you wish.
Topstitched hems are most successful on straight-sided garments. If a hem is much wider at the raw edge than the part of the skirt to which it will be stitched, small ripples may form on the wrong side when the hem is topstitched.

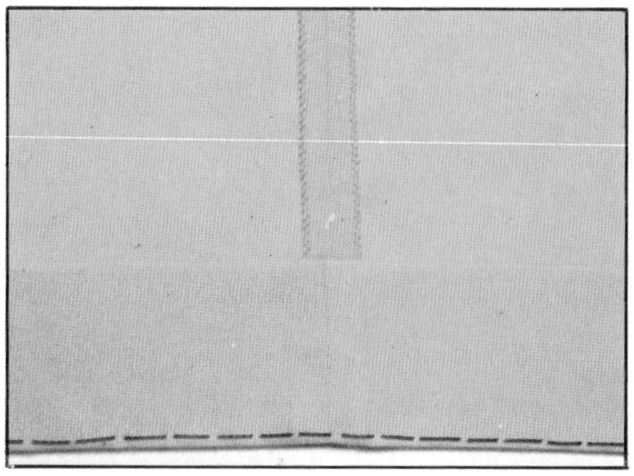

1 Try on the skirt and mark the hemline. Fold up the hem and baste close to the folded edge. Decide how many rows of topstitching you want and how far apart to space the rows. Check that the hem will be deep enough for this many rows plus $\frac{5}{8}$in (1.5cm) hem allowance. Finish the raw edge with zig-zag stitch or overcasting and baste the hem in place close to the finished edge.

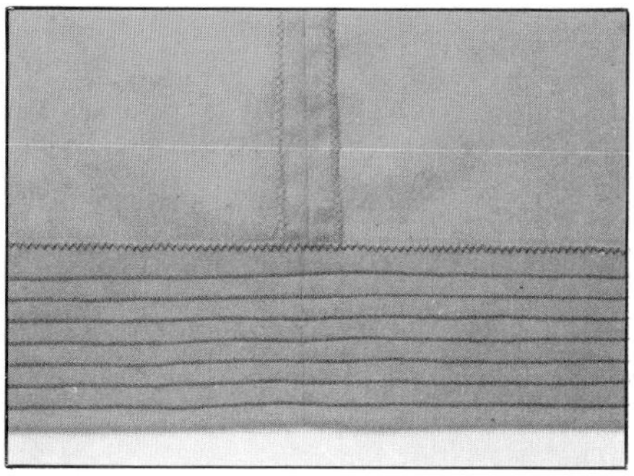

2 On the right side of the garment, make the bottom line of topstitching parallel to the folded edge. Topstitch the remaining rows parallel to, and spaced equally from, the first row. Take the threads through to the wrong side and fasten off the ends securely. Press.

Skirt with soft pleats: directions for making (2)

The directions below show how to finish the skirt with unpressed pleats. Directions for the shirt and vest will be given in later courses.

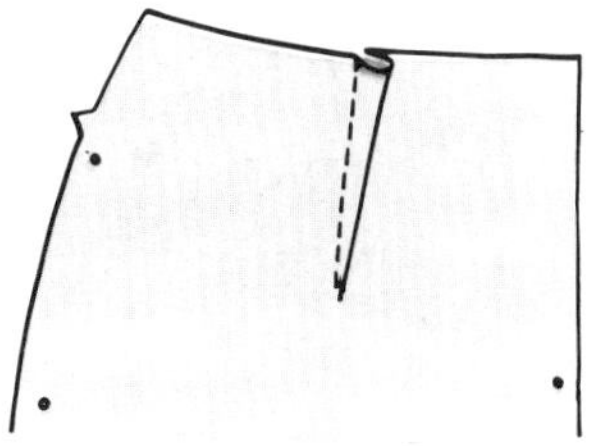

1 Baste and stitch the back waist darts and press them to the center back.

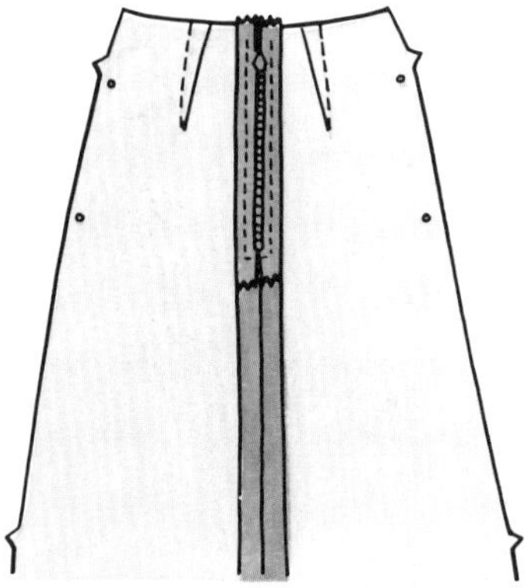

2 Baste and stitch the center back seam from the hem edge to the position for the bottom of the zipper. Finish the seam allowances and press open.
3 Baste and stitch the zipper into the center back opening using the lapped seam method (see Volume 2, page 11).

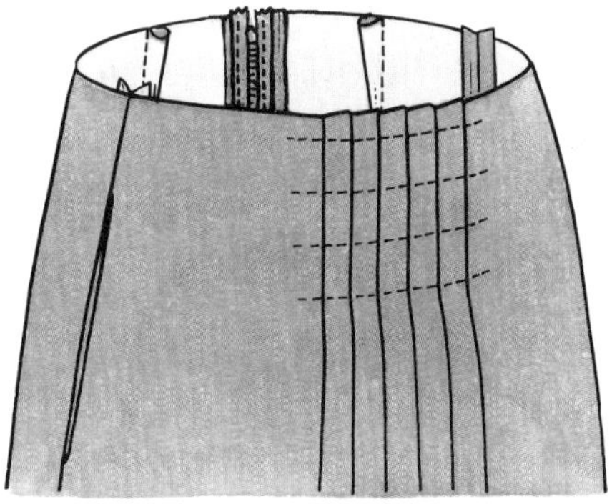

4 Baste and stitch the pocket pieces to the skirt front and back on both side edges. Baste and stitch the front and back together at the side seams above and below the pockets. Finish the seams and press open.
Stitch the outer edges of the pockets, then overcast the raw edges together (see page 72).

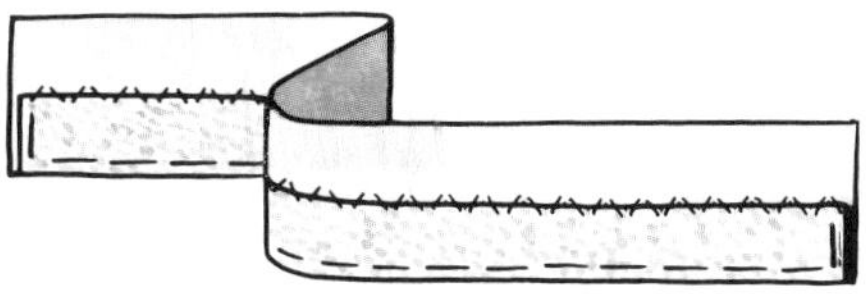

5 Baste the interfacing to the wrong side of the waistband with the edge of the interfacing on the fold. Catch-stitch the interfacing in place along the foldline.

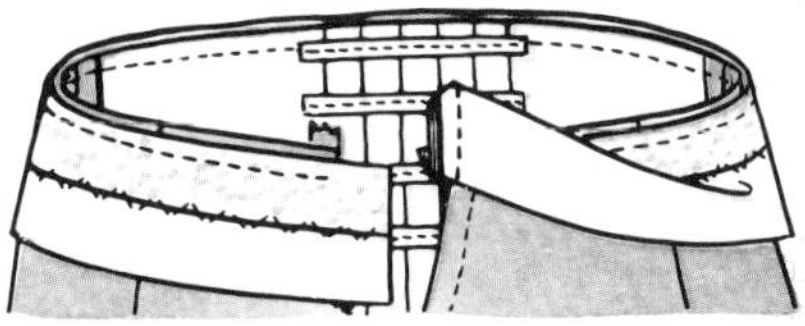

6 Baste and stitch the interfaced side of the waistband to the skirt with right sides together. Grade the seam allowances, trimming the interfacing close to the stitching, and press the seam up.
Fold the waistband in half on the fold line with right sides together. Baste and stitch across the short ends, trim the interfacing close to stitching and clip off the corners.

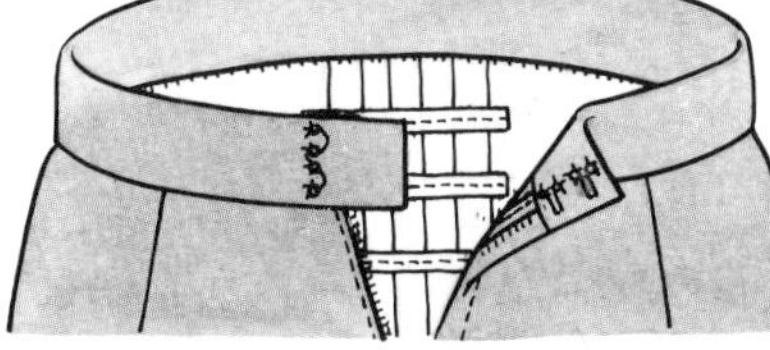

Terry Evans

7 Fold the waistband to the right side and baste along the folded edge. Fold under the seam allowance on the free edge of the waistband and slip stitch to the stitching line. Press.
Stitch a large hook and eye, or two smaller ones, to the inside edges of the waistband above the zipper.
8 Try on the skirt and mark the hemline. Turn up the hem, stitch it in place and add topstitching as shown above, spacing the eight lines of stitching at $\frac{1}{4}$in (6mm) intervals from the folded edge.

Peter Waldman

Needlework/COURSE 7

*Materials
*Backstitch
*Split knot
*French knot
*Designing your own motif
*Embroidered handkerchief

Free embroidery

An ancient art, free embroidery has flourished in almost every culture in every part of the world. It has ranged from simple stitches in yarn on clothing to elaborate wall hangings stitched in gold. Today's embroiderer can choose from a huge range of materials to embroider almost anything made of fabric in simple or complex stitches.

Free embroidery differs from needlepoint and counted thread work such as cross-stitch in that the stitches may be taken anywhere on the background fabric. There is no need to count threads or meshes. For this reason, any fabric from silk to denim is suitable and hundreds of stitches in a wide range of shapes, sizes and textures can be used.

In Needlework course 6 in Volume 4 we introduced crewel, a form of embroidery traditionally worked in crewel wool thread on a coarse linen or cotton background. In this course, we look at some new stitches and other fabrics and threads that can be used in free embroidery. We also encourage you to try designing your own motifs and to experiment with stitches and threads to carry them out.

Fabrics, threads and needles for free embroidery

Fabric	Thread	Needle
Fine		
fine linen	cotton embroidery floss,	crewel 1—10
organdy	1—3 strands	
voile	pearl cotton, No. 8	
lawn	silk embroidery floss	
sheer silk	rayon embroidery floss	
Medium		
medium linen	cotton embroidery floss,	crewel 1—10
cotton	2—5 strands	chenille 23—26
twill	pearl cotton, No. 3, 5,	darning 14—24
rayong	8	
silk	rayon embroidery floss	
lightweight knits	linen embroidery floss	
	crewel wool	
	Persian wool, 1—2 strands	
Heavy		
coarse linen	cotton embroidery floss,	chenille 13—22
terry cloth	6 or more strands	darning 14—18
heavy knits	pearl cotton, doubled	rug yarn needle
burlap	crewel, Persian, or	
felt	tapestry wool	
denim	knitting yarn	
upholstery fabric	rug yarn

Backstitch

The backstitch in embroidery is similar to the backstitch used in sewing to make a strong seam. In embroidery, the backstitch makes a continuous line of stitching with no breaks through which the background fabric shows and is used primarily for straight, curved and jagged lines. It may also be used to outline areas to be filled with other stitches.

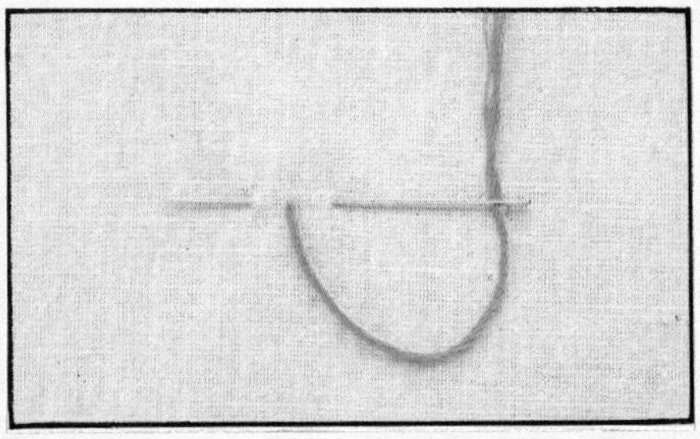

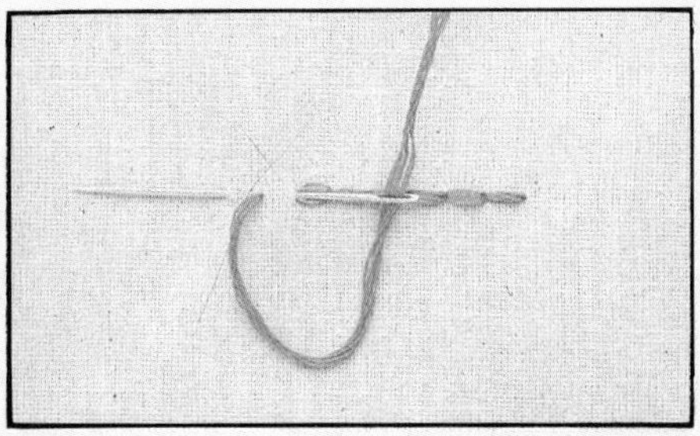

1 Bring needle up at forward end of first stitch. Take it back. Insert it at opposite end of the stitch bringing it up at forward end of second stitch.

2 To complete stitch, insert needle in same hole with the forward end of the previous stitch. Bring it up at forward end of new stitch.

Split stitch

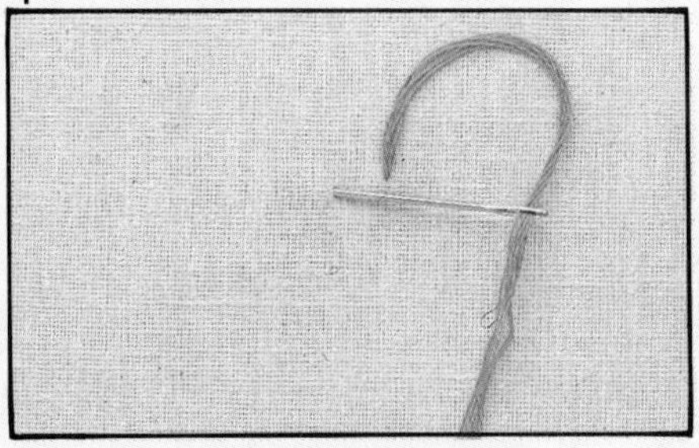

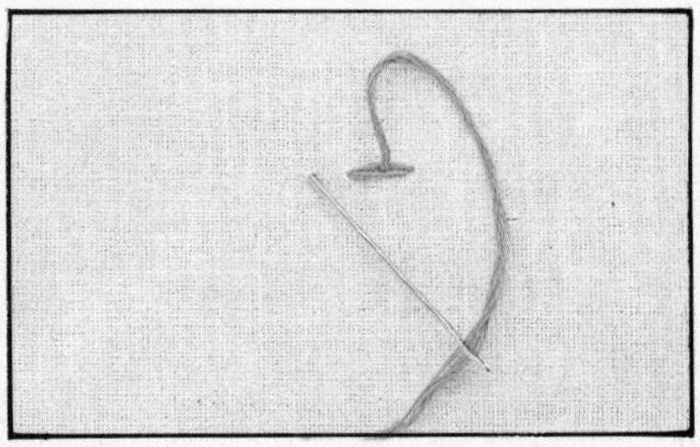

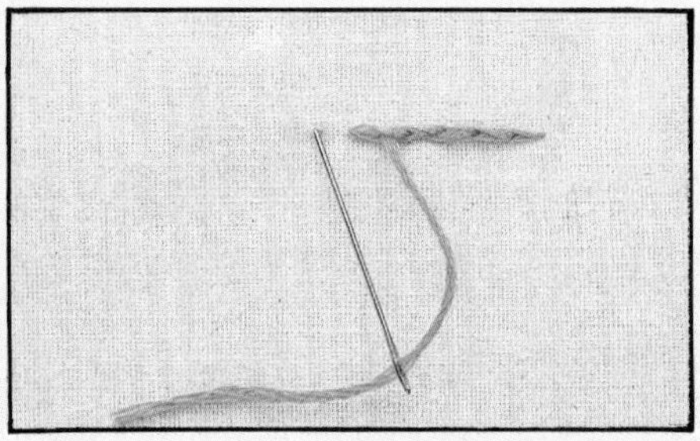

1 The split stitch creates an overlapped line. Like stem stitch (Volume 4, page 75), it can be used for lines and outlining. Rows of split stitch can be placed close together to fill areas. Bring the needle up at the beginning of the first stitch and reinsert it where the stitch is to end.

2 Bring the needle up halfway along and through the thread of the first stitch, splitting it to begin the second stitch. Re-insert it at the end of the second stitch.

3 Begin each succeeding stitch by bringing needle up through hole where the stitch before previous one ended and through the thread of the previous stitch. End it by inserting needle ahead of all previous stitches.

French knot

French knots may be used wherever a dot is needed, such as in the center of a flower or an eye of a bird or animal. They may be scattered at random for a seeded effect. Or they may be used as filling – close together in regular rows for a solid look or farther apart for a more open filling.

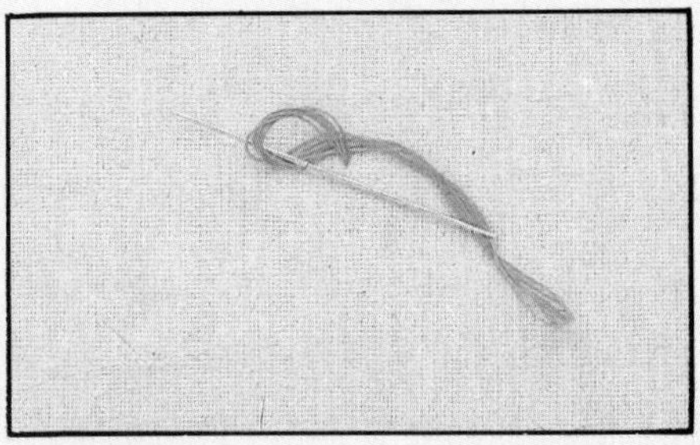

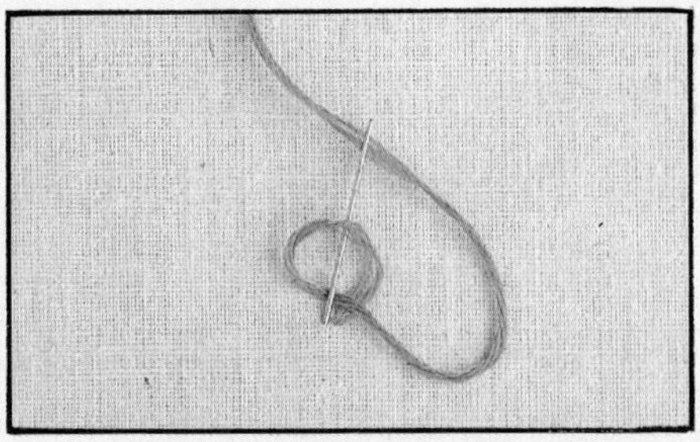

1 Bring needle up at the point where the knot is to be located. Hold the needle in a horizontal position over the hole from which it emerged and, with the left hand, wrap the thread from the hole over the needle toward you and under it away from you.

2 With left hand holding the wrapped thread in place, reinsert the needle into the same hole or as close as possible to the hole from which it has just emerged and pull through gently to form the knot.
To form a French knot on a stalk follow step 1 but reinsert the needle a short distance away from the point where it emerged. The knot will appear where the needle was reinserted.

Simon Butcher

Designing your own motif

Free embroidery can be used to decorate almost anything made of fabric from jeans to wedding dresses and from delicate tablecloths to potholders. In the step-by-step photos below, we show how to create a design for some of the things you wear or use.
The first step in design is to decide what you want to embroider and to accumulate ideas for a motif. Ideas are all around you. Try looking around your house, garden or neighborhood, at plants, birds, favorite objects or landscapes. Or look at fabrics, wallpaper, china or pottery, greeting cards or even ads. At the library, go through books on design, especially historical design in different parts of the world.
Good ideas may also come from your own imagination. If you want to embroider something as a gift, try thinking of the recipient's interests, likes, experiences. For a child, for example, think of favorite toys or stories. For an adult, think of hobbies, favorite vacation spots, pets or flowers. Motifs on household items can be related to the object's use or to the decorating scheme in the room where it will be used. You could even base a motif on a shared family joke.
List ideas as fast as they come to you and sort them out later. Keep working at the list until you come up with something you really like.
The next step is to get your idea on paper in a suitable design scaled to the space you want to fill. If your idea comes from something flat such as wallpaper or a card, trace it and then rework as necessary. If it can't be traced, make rough sketches concentrating on main shapes and lines until you get one you like. Or look through snapshots, magazines, encyclopedias or other books with lots of pictures for something similar to trace or copy and rework into a design you like.

1 Once you have a scale drawing you like, enlarge or reduce is as necessary. You can do this yourself following the procedure in Volume 4, page 76 or have a photostat made. Then trace your correctly-sized motif and color it with crayons or colored pencils in the colors you would like to use.

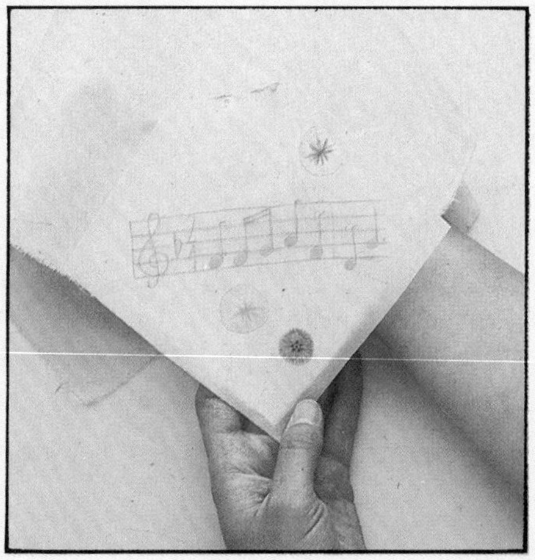

2 Cut out the motif and pin it to the article you plan to embroider or the fabric you intend to use. Look at it carefully. Is it the right size, shape, color? Does it fit the space well? Will it show up in use? If the design does not satisfy you, make another tracing and rework it or start again and draw a new motif.

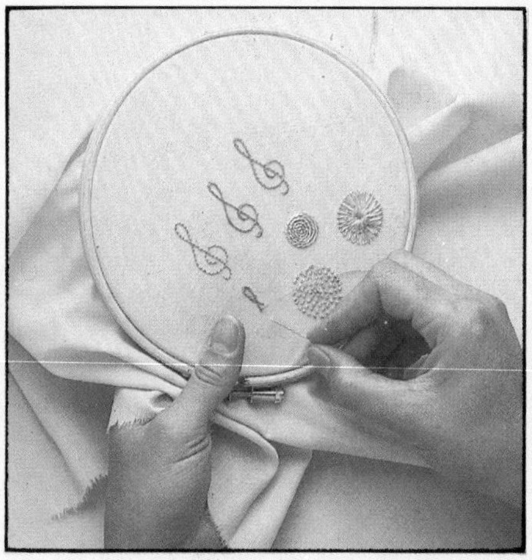

3 Experiment with stitches on the fabric you intend to embroider or something similar. Try the lines and shapes in your design one by one in different stitches and with different thicknesses of thread until you find a combination that pleases you. You can change your mind about stitches, color and even design as the embroidery begins to take shape in your mind.

4 Draw the final design, color it and indicate the stitches to be used for each element.

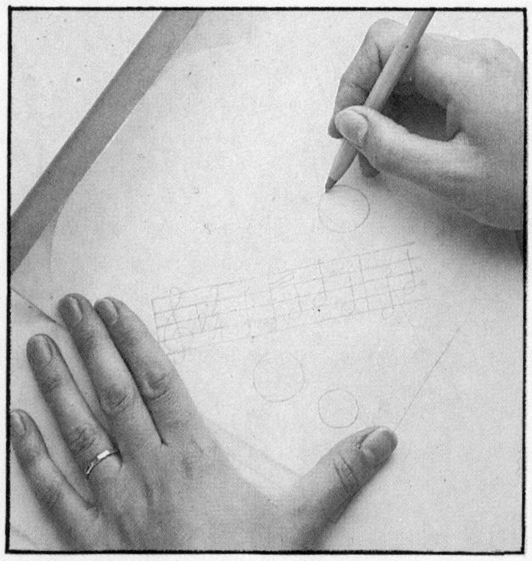

5 Trace the main lines of the design and transfer them to the fabric using dressmaker's carbon paper.

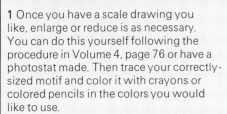

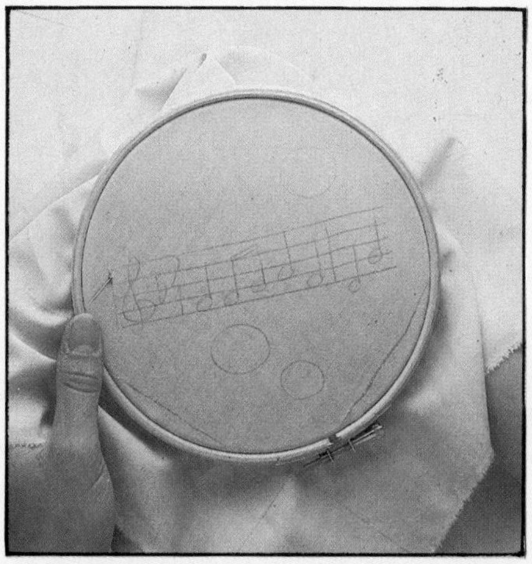

6 Place the fabric in an embroidery hoop and begin to embroider.

Simon Butcher

Motif Musicale

Design a motif for a friend. Then embroider it on a handkerchief in a variety of new stitches.

Simon Butcher

Note: We designed this handkerchief as a gift for a musical friend. It contains the opening phrase from an aria in Mozart's opera *Don Giovanni*. You could use a phrase from a favorite song or symphony.

Size: Our handkerchief is 15$\frac{1}{2}$in (39.5cm) square. Yours could be any size from about 11in (28cm) square up. Our motif is approximately 5×5in (12.5×12.5cm).

Materials

$\frac{5}{8}$yd (.6m) handkerchief linen or fine cotton (any width) or a plain ready-made handkerchief and scraps of similar fabric
cotton embroidery floss (we used 9yd (8m) each of 3 colors–2 shades harmonizing with the background and 1 contrasting)
crewel needle, size 7 or 8
embroidery hoop about 7 or 8in in diameter
sewing thread to match background fabric if making your own handkerchief
drawing paper and pencil
tracing paper, colored pencils, crayons
dressmaker's carbon paper

To make

1 Plan your design as described on page 77. If you wish to follow our design, some of the elements are shown full-size and may be traced.

2 If you are using a ready-made handkerchief, sew strips of material about 3in (7.5cm) wide along two sides to make a larger square so you can center the corner to be embroidered in your hoop; then proceed to Step 5.

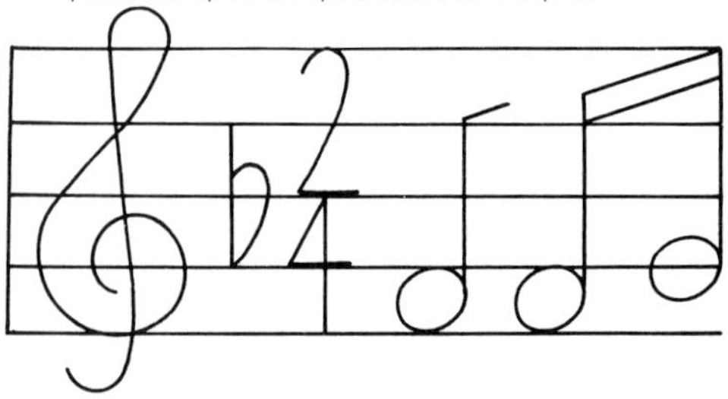

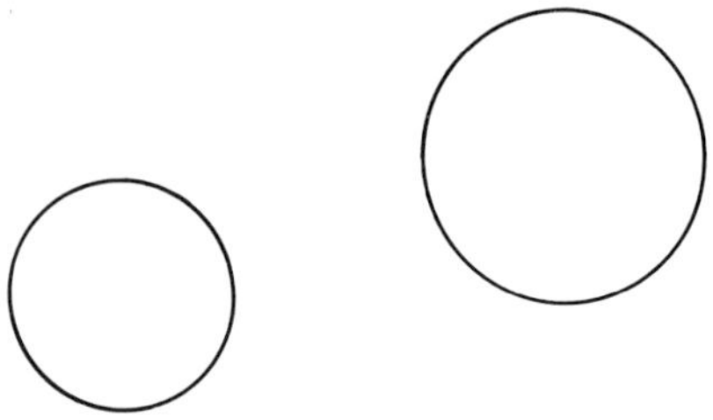

3 If you are making your own handkerchief you will need a square of fabric about 3in (7.5cm) larger all around than the finished handkerchief will be. Cut off the selvedge and then tear crosswise and lengthwise to make a square. Fold diagonally to check that the grain is straight. If the corners do not meet, gently pull the square on the bias until they do.

4 Along two adjacent sides, and roughly in the center of each, measure a distance slightly longer than the finished length of one side. Mark the fabric at these four points and pull a thread at each. The gap or the puckering along the line will serve as a guide showing the edges of the unhemmed handkerchief so you can place the design correctly.

5 Transfer your design to the fabric placing it carefully within one corner of the inner square. Transfer the basic shapes and main lines only, as you may want to change details as you work.

6 Place the fabric or handkerchief in the hoop with the area to be embroidered in the center, and begin embroidering. In our design, the staff was embroidered in backstitch, the notes in padded satin stitch, the stems of the notes, the treble clef sign and lines connecting notes in split stitch, tails of notes in 2 parallel straight stitches and the dots beside the notes and scattered around the flowers in French knots–all with 2 strands of floss. The flowers themselves were done in French knots on stalks with 3 strands of floss. To fill an area with padded satin stitch, place 2 or more layers of satin stitches on top of each other with the stitches of one layer running at right angles to the stitches of the next. The final layer should be done carefully to cover all the layers underneath and present neat even edges.

7 Secure each thread neatly at the beginning and end with tiny backstitches into existing stitches if possible (tiny knots if necessary), as back of handkerchief will be visible. On scattered French knots, tie the two ends of each thread and clip closely. Start each section with a new thread rather than carrying threads across the back.

8 Remove fabric from frame. Place the embroidery face down on a folded towel and press with a steam iron.

9 Remove the strips of cloth from the ready-made handkerchief or finish with a rolled hem if you are making your own. To make a rolled hem, stitch about $\frac{1}{8}$in (3mm) inside the lines marking the unhemmed handkerchief. Trim away the excess material beyond the marking lines. Fold the raw edge to the underside so that the stitching is just inside the fold. Hand sew the hem taking one tiny stitch along the fold and one diagonally on the main fabric just under the raw edge. The stitches should be about $\frac{1}{4}$in (5mm) apart along each edge and should take only one or two threads of the fabric. When you have made several stitches, pull the thread to draw the lines of stitches together and form the rolled hem.

EXTRA SPECIAL CROCHET

Young chick

There's no reason why children's clothes can't have a touch of sophistication. To prove the point: three fashionable raglan-sleeved jackets, one with seams picked out in contrasting yarn and another decorated with crab-stitch edging.

Sizes
To fit 20[22:24]in (51[56:61]cm) chest.
Length, 13[15:16¼]in (35[40:43]cm).
Sleeve seam, 7[8:9]in (17[20:23]cm).

Note Directions for larger sizes are in brackets [ ]; if there is only one set of figures it applies to all sizes.

Materials
Sport yarn:
Plain jacket *8[9:9]oz (200[250:250]g)*
Two-color jacket *8[9:9]oz (200[250:250]g) in main color (A) and 2oz (50g) in contrasting color (B)*
Textured jacket *8[9:9]oz (200[250:250]g) in main color (A) and 2oz (50g) in each of 3 contrasting colors (B, C and D)*
Size E (3.50mm) crochet hook

Gauge
20dc and 12 rows to 4in (10cm) worked on size E (3.50mm) hook.

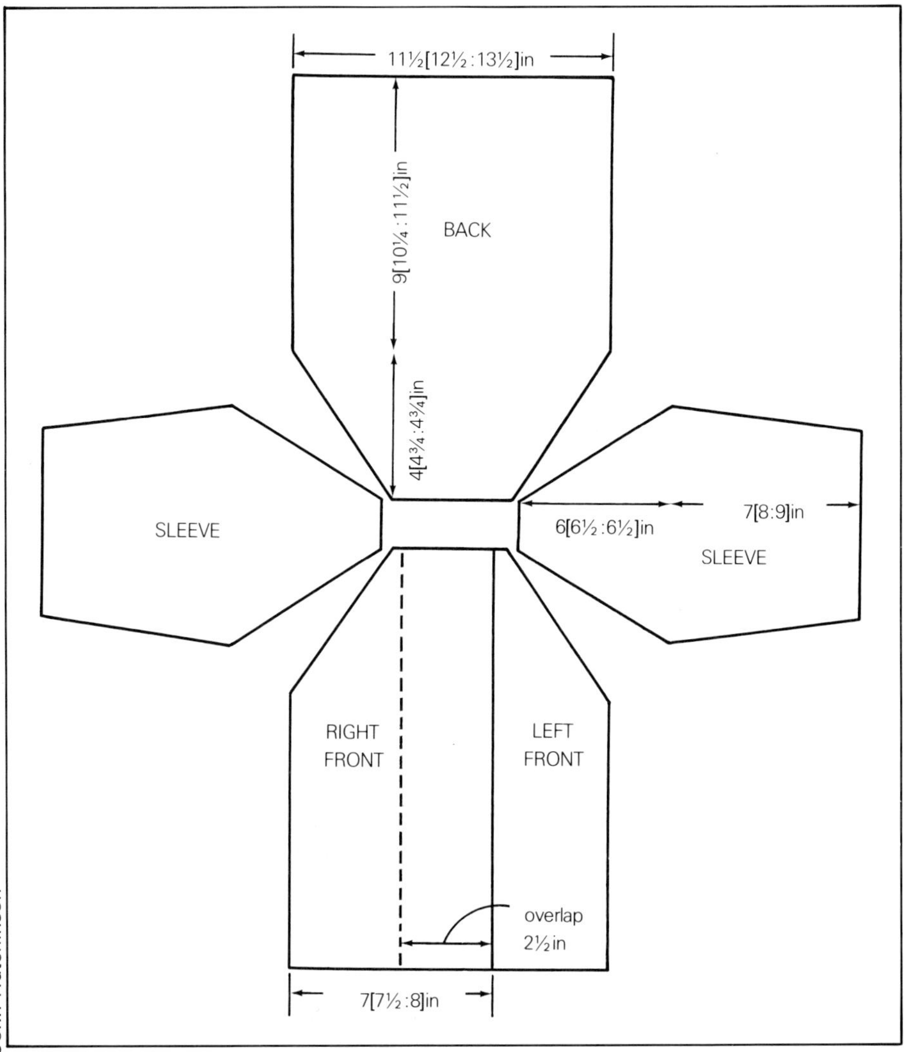

John Hutchinson

Plain jacket

Back
Using size E (3.50mm) hook make 57[62:67]ch.
Base row 1dc into 4th ch from hook, 1dc into each ch to end. Turn. 55[60:65] sts.
***Patt row** 3ch to count as first dc, 1dc into each dc to end, working last dc into turning ch. Turn. This row forms patt.
Cont in patt until work measures 9[10¼:11½]in (23[26:29]cm) from beg.*
Shape raglan armholes
Next row Sl st into first 6[6:7]dc, 3ch, patt to within last 5[5:6]dc, turn. 45[50:53]dc.
Next row Patt to end. Turn.
Next row 3ch, 1dc into next dc, work next 3dc tog to decrease 2dc, 1dc into each dc to within last 5dc, dec 2dc, 1dc into each of last 2dc. Turn.
Rep last 2 rows until 21[22:25]dc rem.

Technique tip

Working the textured effect

To work the textured effect on this pattern you need to leave the front loop of stitches free when working the background fabric. The texture is formed by working crab stitch into the free loops. The stitches that are not to be edged with crab stitch are worked into in the normal way, through both loops.

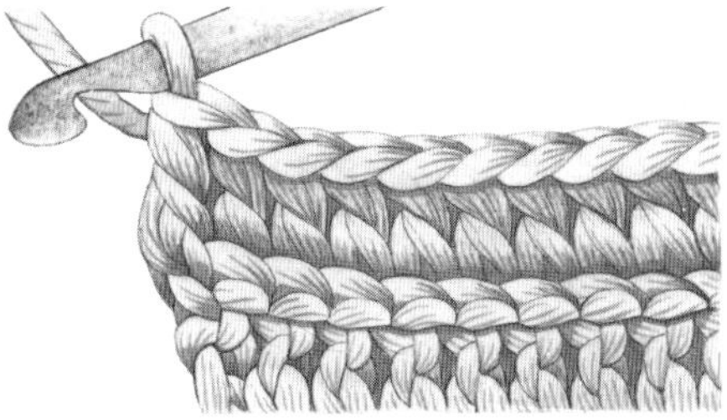

Following the charts for the position of texture, work a double crochet into back loop only of each double crochet shown in one of the contrasting colors.

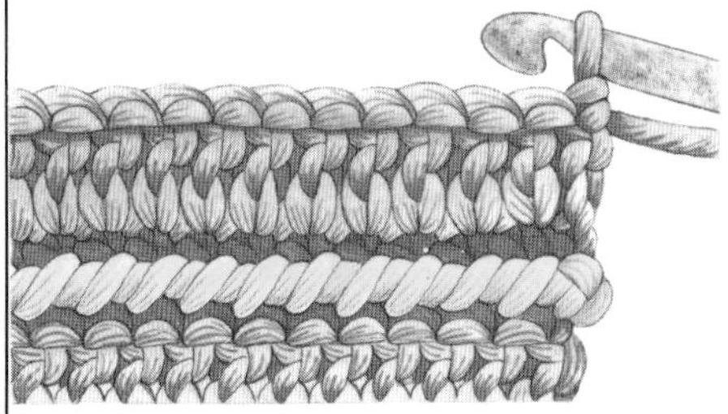

The crab stitch can be worked either after completing every few rows or after completing each piece of the garment. Join the contrasting yarn to the first loop at the left and work crab stitch into each loop to end. Fasten off. Darn in all ends on the wrong side of the fabric.

Coral Mula

Patt 1 row. Fasten off.

Left front
Using size E (3.50mm) hook make 37[40:42]ch. Work base row as for back 35[38:40] sts. Work as for back from * to *

Shape raglan armhole
Next row Sl st into first 6[6:7]dc, 3ch, 1dc into each dc to end. Turn.
Next row Patt to end. Turn.
Next row 3ch, 1dc into next dc, dec 2dc, patt to end. Turn.
Rep last 2 rows until 18[19:20]dc rem. Patt 1 row. Fasten off.

Right front
Work as for left front, reversing raglan shaping.

Sleeves
Using size E (3.50mm) hook make 34[36:38]ch. Work base row and patt row as for back. 32[34:36] sts. Cont in patt, but inc 1dc at each end of next row (by working 2dc into first and last dc) and every foll 4th[3rd:3rd] row until there are 42[46:50]dc. Cont straight until work measures 7[8:9]in (17[20:23]cm) from beg.

Shape raglan armholes
Work back raglan shaping rows until 8[8:10]dc rem. Patt 1 row. Fasten off.

Tony Boase

Belt
Using size E (3.50mm) hook make 8[10:10]ch. Work base row and patt row as for back, then cont in patt for 38[40:42]in (95[100:105]cm). Fasten off.

To finish
All seams are joined by working sc on RS of fabric. Work 1sc into each st and 2sc into each row end. Join raglan, side and sleeve seams. With RS facing join yarn to right front at lower edge and work row of sc evenly along right front, around neck and along left front, do not turn but work row of crab st (sc worked from left to right). Fasten off. Fold back lapels and catch-stitch in place. Make a belt loop on each side seam at waist level. Thread belt through loops.

Ray Duns

Two-color jacket

Work as for plain jacket but work seams and front edging in contrasting color.

Textured jacket

Follow directions for plain jacket but work into back loop only of each st to be bound with crab st, as indicated on charts.

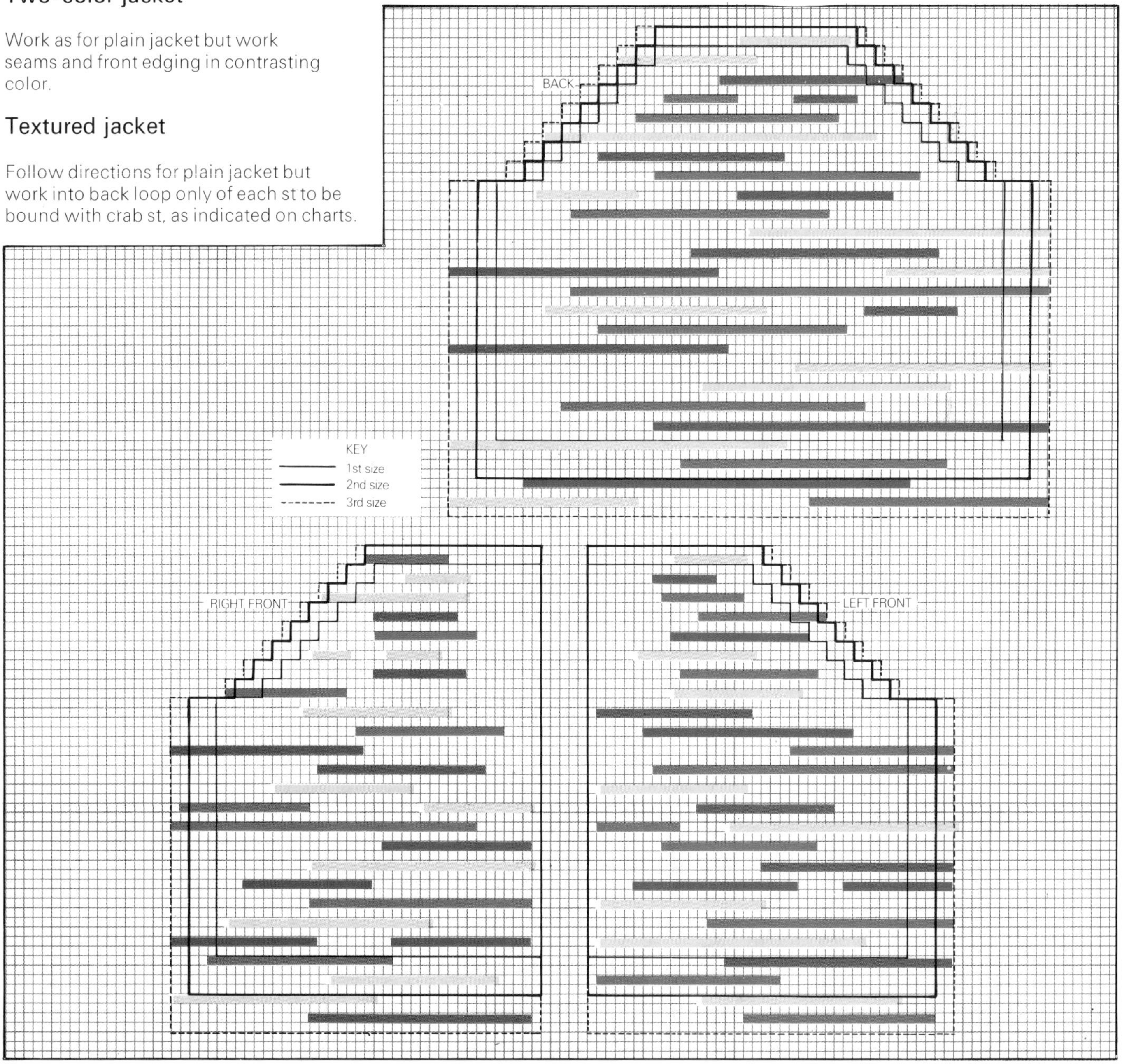

John Hutchinson

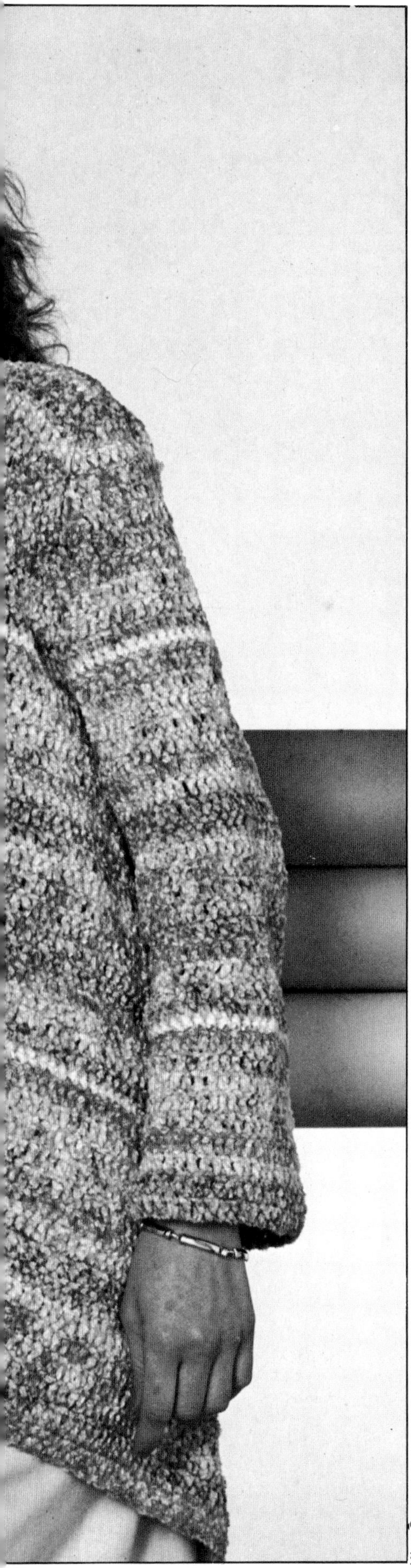

Kim Sayer

EXTRA SPECIAL CROCHET

Ice cool chevrons

A tempting treat for the more experienced . . . this chevron-patterned jacket is made in mouth-watering sherbet shades.

Sizes
To fit 34-36in (87-92cm) bust.
Length to shoulder, 33in (84cm).
Sleeve seam, 17in (43cm).

Materials
8oz (200g) of a medium-weight chenille yarn in main shade (A)
6oz (160g) each of contrasting colors (B, C and D)
1oz (25g) of contrasting color (E)
Size H (5.50mm) crochet hook
Shoulder pads

Gauge
7 sts to 2in (5cm) and 5 rows to 2¼in (6cm) in dc worked on size H (5.50mm) hook.

Notes
It is important to work the pattern in the order given here, starting with the sleeves first.
When changing color, work the last stage of the last st in the new color.
While working the 2-color patt, bring yarn not in use to the front of the work on WS rows.

Left sleeve
Using B, make 49ch.
Base row 1dc into 4th ch from hook, 1dc into each ch to end. Turn. 47 dc.
Beg patt and stripes.
1st row 3ch to count as first dc, 1dc into each dc to end, join in D. Turn.
Work 1 row in dc using D and 1 row in A.
4th row Work in dc, 5 C, *1 D, 5 C, rep from * to end. Turn.
5th row Work in dc, 1 D, 3 C, *3 D, 3 C, rep from * to last st, 1 D. Turn.
6th row Work in dc, 2 D, 1 C, *5 D, 1 C, rep from * to last 2 sts, 2 C. Turn.
Work 1 row in dc using C, 1 row A, 1 row in sc using E, 1 row in dc using B.
11th row Work in dc, 1 D, 3 C, *3 D, 3 C, rep from * to last st, 1 D. Turn.
12th row As 11th.
Work 1 row in dc using A and 1 row using B.
15th row Work in dc, 2 A, 3 C, *3 A, 3 C, rep from * to end. Turn.
16th row Work in dc, 1 A, 3 C, *3 A, 3 C, rep from * to last st, 1 A. Turn.
17th row Work in dc, 3 C, *3 A, 3 C, rep from * to last 2 sts, 2 A. Turn.
Work 1 row in dc using D and 1 row in B.
The last 19 rows form patt for left sleeve.
Cont in patt until sleeve measures 17in (43cm) from beg. Fasten off.

Shape top
Next row Keeping patt correct, rejoin appropriate color to 5th st, 3ch (dec over next 2 sts) twice, patt to last 9 sts, (dec over next 2 sts) twice, 1 st into next st, turn.
Next row 3ch, dec over next 2 sts, patt to last 3 sts, dec over next 2 sts, 1 st into last st. Turn.
Rep last row 8 times more.
Next row 3ch, (dec over next 2 sts) twice, patt to last 5 sts, (dec over next 2 sts) twice, 1 st into last st. Fasten off.

Right sleeve
Work as left sleeve up to 15th patt row.
15th row Work in dc, 3 C, *3 A, 3 C, rep from * to last 2 sts, 2 A.
16th row Work in dc, 1 A, 3 C, *3 A, 3 C, rep from * to last st, 1 A.
17th row Work in dc, 2 A, 3 C, *3 A, 3 C, rep from * to end.
Work 1 row in dc using D and 1 row using B.
The last 19 rows form patt for right sleeve.
Complete as for left sleeve.

Left front
Using B, make 38ch.
Base row Dec 1dc over 4th and 5th ch, 1dc into each ch to last ch, inc 1dc into last ch. Turn. 36 sts.
Beg patt and stripes.
Shape chevron by inc one st at front edge and dec one st at side edge on every row.
1st row Work in dc, 2 C, *3 A, 3 C, rep from * ending last rep with 1 C instead of 3 C. Turn.
2nd row Work in dc, 2 A, (3 C, 3 A) 5 times, 4 C. Turn.
3rd row Work in dc, *3 A, 3 C, rep from * to end. Turn.

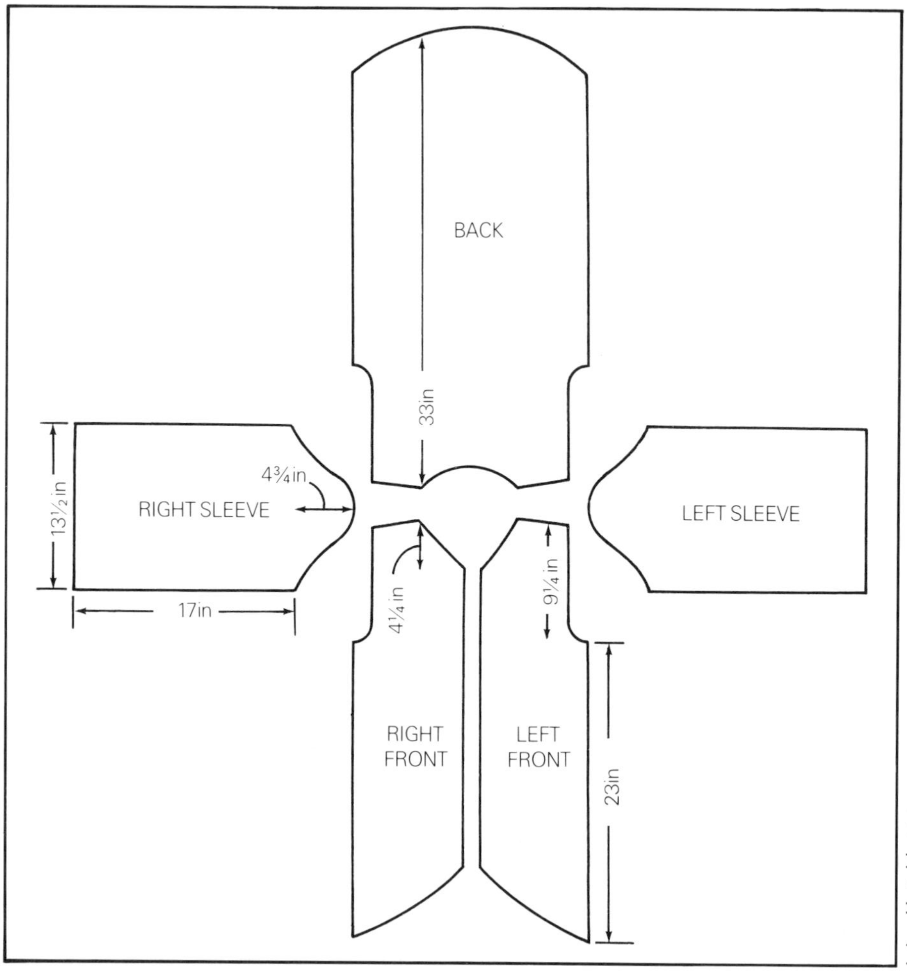

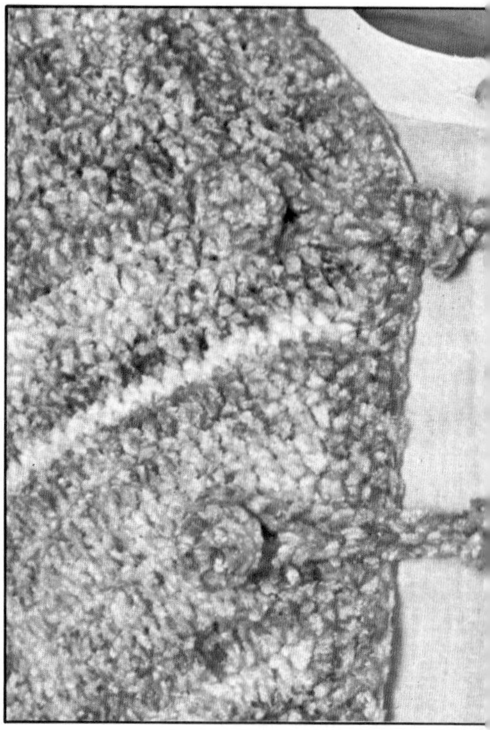

John Hutchinson

Work 1 row in dc using D, 2 rows using B, 1 row using D and 1 row using A.
9th row Work in dc, *1 D, 5 C, rep from * to end. Turn.
10th row Work in dc, *3 C, 3 D, rep from * to end. Turn.
11th row Work in dc, *5 D, 1 C, rep from * to end. Turn.
Work 1 row in dc using C, 1 row using A, 1 row in sc using E and 1 row in dc using B.
16th row Work in dc, 1 D, *3 C, 3 D, rep from * ending last rep with 2 D. Turn.
17th row Work in dc, *3 D, 3 C, rep from * to end. Turn.
Work 1 row in dc using A and 1 row in B. These 19 rows form patt. Note that when working the 2-color patt rows on next repeat, read the rows from back to front. Cont in patt until work measures 23in (58.5cm) along side edge, ending with same patt row as sleeve at underarm. Fasten off.

Shape armhole
Next row Keeping patt correct, rejoin appropriate color to 5th st, 3ch, (dec over next 2 sts) twice, patt to last st, 2 sts into last st. Turn.
Next row 3ch, 1 st into st at base of 3ch, patt to last 5 sts, (dec over next 2 sts) twice, 1 st into last st. Turn.
Next row 3ch, (dec over next 2 sts) twice, patt to last st, 2 sts into last st. Turn.

**Shape neck
Next row 3ch, dec over next 2 sts, patt to last 3 sts, dec over next 2 sts, 1 st into last st. Turn.
Rep last row 6 times more. **15 sts.
Next row 3ch, dec over next 2 sts, patt to end. Turn.
Next row 3ch, 1 st into st at base of 3ch, patt to last 3 sts, dec over next 2 sts, 1 st into last st. Turn.
Next row 3ch, 1dc into each of next 6 sts, 1sc into each st to end. Fasten off.

Right front
Using B, make 38ch.
Base row 1dc into 4th ch from hook, 1dc into each ch to last 3ch, dec 1dc over next 2ch, 1dc into last ch. Turn.
Beg patt and stripes.
Shape chevron by inc one st at front edge and dec one st at side edge on every row.
1st row Work in dc, 1 C, *3 A, 3 C, rep from * ending last rep with 2 C. Turn.
2nd row Work in dc, 4 C, 3 A, *3 C, 3 A, rep from * ending last rep with 2 A. Turn.
3rd row Work in dc, *3 C, 3 A, rep from * to end. Turn.
Work 1 row in dc using D, 2 rows using B, 1 row using D and 1 row using A.
9th row Work in dc, *5 C, 1 D, rep from * to end. Turn.
10th row Work in dc, *3 D, 3 C, rep from * to end. Turn.
11th row Work in dc, *1 C, 5 D, rep from * to end. Turn.
Work 1 row in dc using C, 1 row using A, 1 row in sc using E and 1 row in dc using B.
16th row Work in dc, 2 D, *3 C, 3 D, rep from * ending last rep with 1 D. Turn.
17th row Work in dc, *3 C, 3 D, rep from * to end. Turn.
Work 1 row in dc using A and 1 row in B. These 19 rows form patt. Note that when working the 2-color patt rows on next repeat, read rows from back to front. Cont in patt until work measures 23in (58.5cm) along side edge, ending with same patt row as sleeve at underarm.

Shape armhole
Next row Keeping patt correct, 3ch, 1st into st at base of 3ch, patt to last 9 sts, (dec over next 2 sts) twice, 1 st into next st, turn.
Next row 3ch, (dec over next 2 sts) twice, patt to last st, 2 sts into last st. Turn.
Next row 3ch, 1 st into st at base of 3ch, patt to last 5 sts, (dec over next 2 sts) twice, 1 st into last st. Turn.
Rep from ** to ** as for left front.
Next row 3ch, patt to last 3 sts, dec over next 2 sts, 1 st into last st. Turn.
Next row 3ch, dec over next 2 sts, patt to last st, 2 sts into last st. Turn.
Next row 1 ch, 1sc into each of next 5sts, 1dc into each st to end. Fasten off.

Back
Using D, make 4ch and beg at center back.
Base row 1dc into 3rd ch from hook, 1sc into last ch, join in A. Turn.
Next row Using A, 3ch, 2dc into sc at base of 3ch, 3dc into next dc, 3dc into 2nd

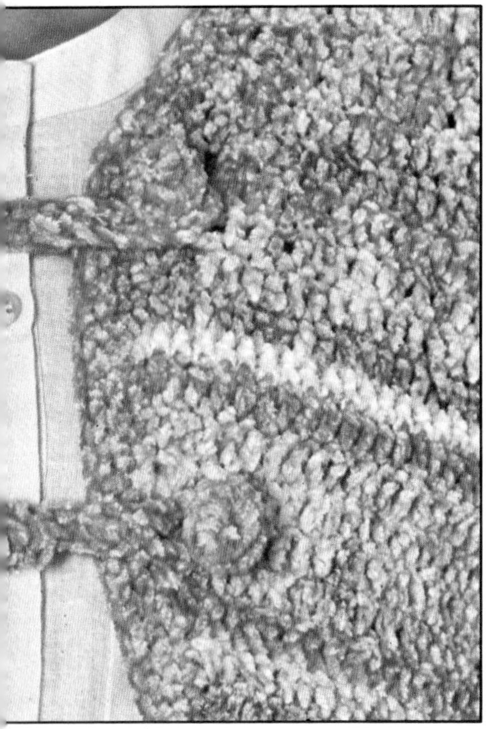

of 2ch, join in C.
Turn.
Beg patt and stripes.
Cont to shape chevron and lower edge by inc 2 sts in first and last sts and inc 2 sts in center st on every row.
1st row Work in dc, 1 C, 1 D, (5 C, 1 D) twice, 1 C. Turn.
2nd row Work in dc, 2 C, 3 D, 3, C, 5 D, 3 C, 3 D, 2 C. Turn.
3rd row Work in dc, 2 D, 1 C, 5 D, 1 C, 9 D, 1 C, 5 D, 1 C, 2 D. Turn.
Work 1 row in dc using D, 1 row using A, 1 row in sc using E and 1 row in dc using B.
8th row Work in dc, 3 C, *3 D, 3 C, rep from * to end. Turn.
9th row Work in dc, 2 D, 3 C, (3 D, 3 C) 4 times, 5 D, (3 C, 3 D) 4 times, 3 C, 2 D. Turn.
Work 1 row in dc using A. The lower edge is now complete. Cont to shape chevron, inc in center st as before.
Shape sides by dec one st inside the first and last st in each row, while cont patt as foll:
1st row Using B, 3ch, dec 1 dc over 2nd and 3rd dc, 1dc into each dc to center dc, 3dc into center dc, 1dc into each dc to last 3dc, dec 1dc over next 2dc, 1dc into last dc. Turn.
2nd row Work in dc, 1 C, *3 A, 3 C, rep from * ending last rep with 1 C. Turn.
3rd row Work in dc, 2 A, (3 C, 3 A) 5 times, 7 C, (3 A, 3 C) 5 times, 2 A. Turn.
4th row Work in dc, 3 C, (3 A, 3 C) 5 times, 5 A, (3 C, 3 A) 5 times, 3 C. Turn.
Work 1 row in dc using D, 2 rows using B, 1 row using D and 1 row using A.
10th row Work in dc, 5 C, *1 D, 5 C, rep from * to end. Turn.
11th row Work in dc, 3 C, (3 D, 3 C) 5 times, 5 D, (3 C, 3 D) 5 times, 3 C. Turn.
12th row Work in dc, 1 C, (5 D, 1 C) 5 times, 9 D, (1 C, 5 D) 5 times, 1 C. Turn.
Work 1 row in dc using C, 1 row using A, 1 row in sc using E, and 1 row in dc using B.
17th row Work in dc, 1 D, *3 C, 3 D, rep from * ending last rep with 1 D. Turn.
18th row Work in dc, 3 C, (3 D, 3 C) 5 times, 5 D, (3 C, 3 D) 5 times, 3 C. Turn.
Work 1 row in dc using A.
The last 19 rows form the patt. Cont in patt until back measures 23in (58.5cm) along side edge, ending with same patt row as sleeves at underarm. Fasten off.

Shape armhole
Next row Keeping patt correct, rejoin appropriate color to 5th st, 3ch, (dec over next 2 sts) twice, patt to center st, 3 sts into center st, patt to last 9 sts, (dec over next 2 sts) twice, 1 st into next st, turn.
Next row 3ch, (dec over next 2 sts) twice, patt to center st, 3 sts into center st, patt to last 5 sts, (dec over next 2 sts) twice, 1 st into last st. Turn.
Rep last row once more. Cont in patt until armhole measures 5in (12.5cm), measured at side edge. Complete first armhole and shape back neck and shoulder as foll:
Next row 3ch, dec over 2nd and 3rd sts, 1 st into each of next 19 sts, (dec over next 2 sts) twice, 1 st into next st, turn.
Next row 3ch, (dec over next 2 sts) twice, patt to last 3 sts, dec over next 2 sts, 1 st into last st. Turn.
Next row 3ch, dec over next 2 sts, patt to last 5 sts, (dec over next 2 sts) twice, 1 st into last st. Turn.
Rep last 2 rows twice more.
Next row 3ch, 1 sc into each of next 5 sts, 1dc into each st to end. Fasten off.
Complete second armhole and shape back neck as foll:
Next row Skip center st, rejoin appropriate color to next st, 3ch, (dec over next 2 sts) twice, patt to last 3 sts, dec over next 2 sts, 1 st into last st. Turn.
Next row 3ch, dec over next 2 sts, patt to last 5 sts, (dec over next 2 sts) twice, 1 st into last st. Turn.
Next row 3ch, (dec over next 2 sts) twice, patt to last 3 sts, dec over next 2 sts, 1 st into last st. Turn.
Rep last 2 rows twice more.
Next row 3ch, 1dc into each of next 5 sts, 1 sc into each st to end. Fasten off.

To finish
Press lightly on WS of work using a cool iron over a dry cloth. Join shoulder, side and sleeve seams, matching patt and stripes. Sew sleeves into armholes, matching patt as far as possible. Sew shoulder pads in position.
Edging With RS of work facing, join A to lower edge of left side seam and work a row of sc evenly all around edge. Join with sl st to first st. Turn.
Next round 1ch, 1 sc into each sc to end. Join with sl st to first ch. Turn.
Rep last round once more. Fasten off.
Frog fastener Make two, following the Technique tip.
Sew fasteners in position on right front.
Buttons Using A, make 4ch. Join with a sl st into first ch to form a ring. Work 6sc into ring, cont in rounds.
Next round (2sc into next sc, 1sc into next sc) 3 times.
Next round (Dec 1sc over next 2sc) 4 times, 1 sc into next sc.
Stuff with cotton. Cut off yarn about 8in (20cm) from button, thread around edge and gather up.
Make 3 more buttons in the same way.
Sew in position. Press seams and edging.

Technique tip

Frog fasteners

Frog fasteners are a very simple and secure way of fastening a garment. This type of fastener is usually used on an overgarment such as a coat or jacket.
To make the center of our fasteners more effective we have tied a loose knot, but the loop can be sewn at the center for a simpler fastener.

To make the frog fastener, first make 51 chain in color A using the yarn double (this produces a rounder chain), then slip stitch into the first chain to form a ring. Fasten off and sew in the ends.

Tie the ring into a loose knot at center and secure the knot with a few stitches.
Sew the two loops together at each side of the knot for approximately $1\frac{1}{4}$in (3cm), leaving the remainder of loop to fit over buttons.
To complete the fastener you will need two buttons. The buttons are sewn to each front and the loops are slipped over them.

Coral Mula

EXTRA SPECIAL CROCHET

The soft pastel colors in these tops look pretty on mother or child. The vertical stripes emphasize the flattering shape.

Ice-cream colors

Kim Sayer

Sizes

Child's version to fit 24[26:28:30]in (61[66:71:76]cm) chest.
Length from shoulder, 19[21:23:25]in (48[53:58:63]cm).
Sleeve seam, 10[12:14:16]in (25.5[30.5:40.5]cm), excluding cuff.
Mother's version to fit 32[34:36:38]in (83[87:92:97]cm) bust.
Length from shoulder, 27[28:28:29]in (68.5[71:71:73]cm).
Sleeve seam, 17½[18:18½:19]in (44.5[45.5:47:48.5]cm), excluding cuff.
Note Directions for larger sizes are in brackets []; where there is only one set of figures it applies to all sizes.

Materials

Sport yarn
Child's version *2 x 2oz (50g) balls in main color (A)*
1[2:2:2] balls each in contrasting colors (B and C)
1 ball in contrasting color (D)
Mother's version *3 x 2oz (50g) balls in main color (A)*
2[2:3:3] balls each in contrasting colors (B and C)
2[3:3:3] balls in contrasting color (D)
Sizes E and F (3.50 and 4.00mm) crochet hooks

Gauge

8 V sts and 14 rows to 4in (10cm) in patt worked on size F(4.00mm) hook.

Child's version

Back

Using size F(4.00mm) hook and A, make 119[131:143:155]ch for side seam.
Base row Into 5th ch from hook work (1hdc, 1ch, 1hdc–called V st), *skip 2ch, V st into next ch, rep from * to last 3ch, skip 2ch, 1hdc into last ch. Turn. 38[42:46:50] V sts.
Patt row 2ch to count as first hdc, *V st into 1 ch sp of V in previous row, rep from * ending with 1 hdc into top of turning ch. Turn.
Cont in patt, work in stripe sequence of 1 row A, 3 rows B, 1 row each C, D and C, 3 rows each A and D, 1 row each C, B and C, 3 rows each A and B, 1 row C[4 rows C:2 rows C, 1 row D, 2 rows C:2 rows C, 1 row D, 2 rows C, 1 row A, 2 rows C, 1 row D, 2 rows C]. Rep first 24 rows in reverse order, beg with 3 rows B. Fasten off.

Front

Work as given for back.

Sleeves

Using size F (4.00mm) hook and A, make 65[77:89:101]ch. Work base row as for back. Work in stripe sequence of 2 more rows A, **3 rows B, 1 row each C, D and C, 3 rows each A, D, A and B**, 3 rows each C, A and C[3 rows each C and A, 1 row D, 3 rows each A and C:4 rows each C and A, 2 rows D, 4 rows each A and C:4 rows each C and A, 2 rows D, 4 rows each A and C].
Rep 18 rows from ** to ** in reverse order. Work 3 rows A. Fasten off.

To finish

Join shoulder seams, leaving 5[5½:6:6¼]in (13[14:15:16]cm) open for neck.
Fold sleeve in half lengthwise and, matching center top of sleeve to shoulder seam, sew sleeve in position. Join side and sleeve seams.
Cuffs Using size E (3.50mm) hook, B and with RS facing, work 1 sc into alternate row ends at sleeve edge. Turn.
Next row 1 ch, sc to end. Turn.
Rep last row until cuff measures 1½in (4cm).
Fasten off. Join cuff seam.
Neck edge Using size E (3.50mm) hook, B and with RS facing, work *1 sc into next row end, 2 sc into next row end, rep from * all around neck edge. Turn.
Work 1 sc into each sc to end. Fasten off. Join neck seam.
Lower edge Using size E (3.50mm) hook, B and with RS facing, work 1 sc into each row end all around lower edge. Turn.
Next row 3 ch, skip first sc, 1 dc into each sc to end. Fasten off.
Tie Using size E (3.50mm) hook, and 2 strands of B, make a chain approx 55in (140cm) long. Thread through row of dc at lower edge.
Bobbles (make 2) Using size E (3.50mm) hook and B, make 3ch. Join with sl st to first ch to form circle. 3ch, work 11dc into circle. Join with sl st to first ch. Fasten off. Attach a bobble to each end of tie.

Mother's version

Back

**Using size F (4.00mm) hook and A, make 167[173:173:179]ch for side seam.
Base row Into 5th ch from hook work (1hdc, 1ch, 1hdc–called V st), *skip 2ch, V st into next ch, rep from * to last 3ch, skip 2ch, 1hdc into last ch. Turn. 54[56:56:58] V sts.
Patt row 2ch to count as first hdc, *V st into 1ch sp of V in previous row, rep from * ending with 1hdc into top of turning ch. Turn.
Cont in patt, work in stripe sequence of 1 more row A, 3 rows B, 1 row each C, B and C, 3 rows each A and D, 1 row each C, B and C, 6 rows each D and A, 1 row C**, 1 row B[2 rows B, 1 row A, 2 rows B:4 rows B, 1 row A, 4 rows B:6 rows B, 1 row A, 6 rows B]. Rep 31

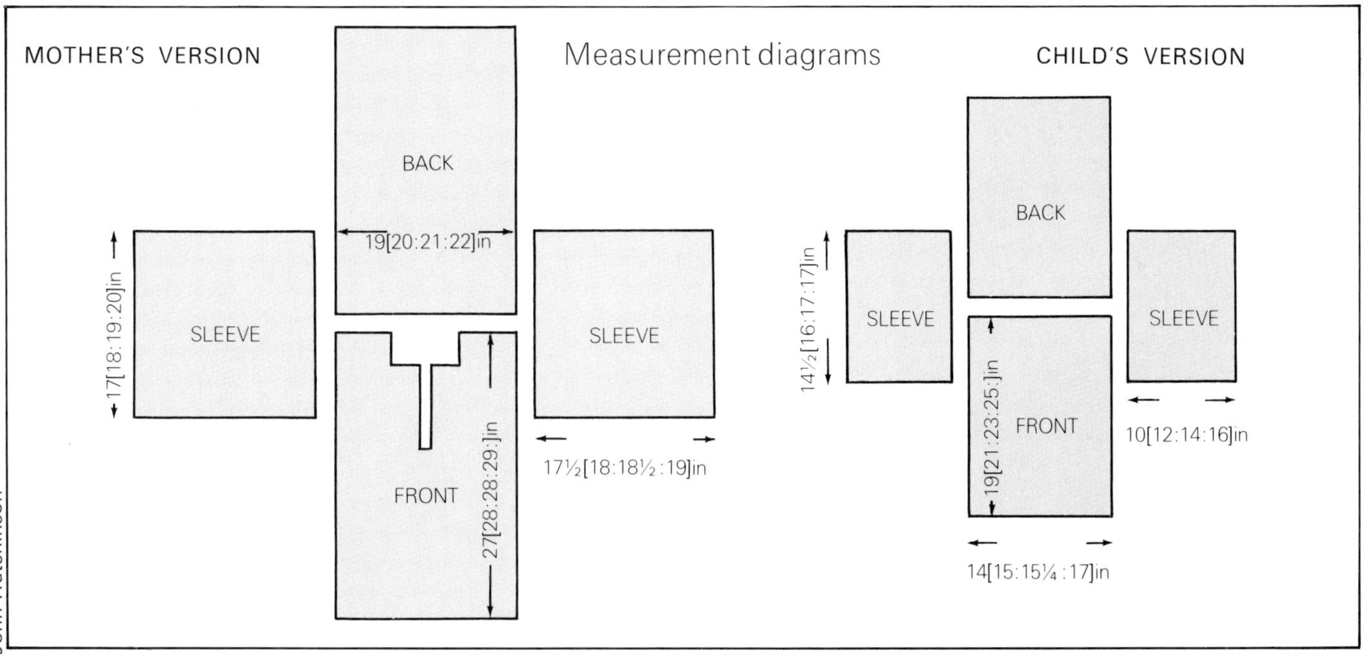

John Hutchinson

rows from ** to ** in reverse order. Fasten off.

Front
Work as for back until 21[22:23:24] rows have been completed from beg.
1st and 3rd sizes only
Shape neck
Next row Keeping stripe sequence same as back, patt across first 49[51] V sts, 1hdc into first hdc of next V, turn. Cont until 31[35] rows have been worked from beg; end at lower edge.
Divide for front opening
Next row Patt to last 16 V sts, 1hdc into first hdc of next V st. Fasten off.
Make 53ch and work base row across these ch until there are 16 V sts, then cont in patt down front.
Cont without shaping until 41[47] rows have been worked from beg. Fasten off.
Next row Make 19 ch in correct color, patt to end. Turn.
Next row Patt to 19ch, (skip 2ch, V st into next ch) 4 times, skip 2 ch, 1hdc into last ch. Turn. Finish to match back.
2nd and 4th sizes only
Shape neck
Next row Keeping stripe sequence same as back, sl st across first hdc and next 4 V sts, sl st into first hdc of next V, 2ch, patt to end. Cont straight until 33[37] rows have been worked from beg; end at lower edge.
Divide for front opening
Next row Patt to last 16 V sts, 1 hdc into first hdc of next V st. Fasten off.
Make 50ch and work base row across these ch, then cont in patt down front.
Cont without shaping until 44[48] rows have been worked from beg. Fasten off.
Next row Make 17ch in correct color, patt to end. Turn. Finish to match back.

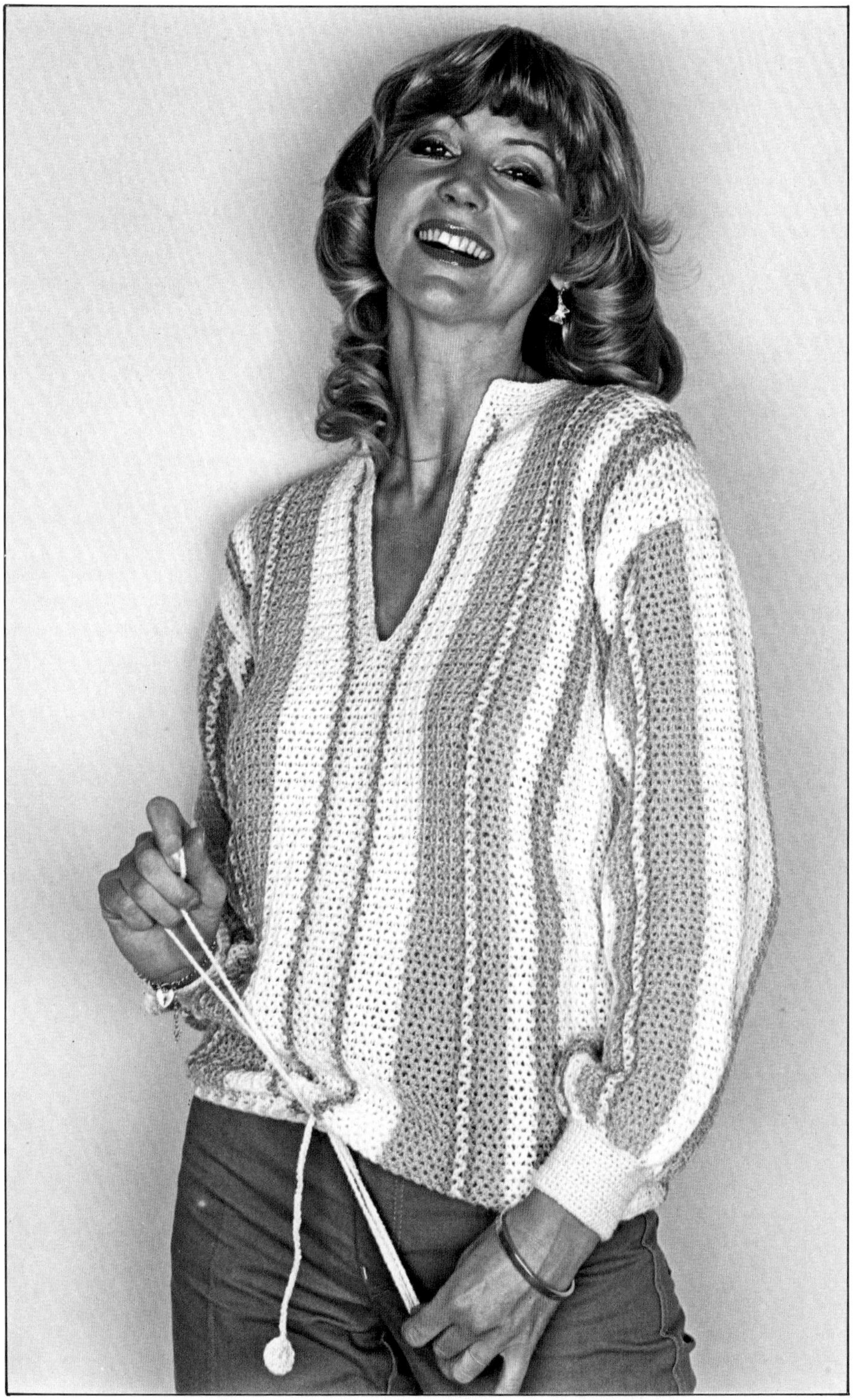
Kim Sayer

Sleeves
Using size F (4.00mm) hook and A, make 110[113:116:119]ch. Work base row as for back. Cont in patt, work stripe sequence as for first 29[31:31:31] rows of back, then 1[1:4:8] rows A. Rep first 29[31:31:31] rows in reverse order. Fasten off.
Cuff
Using size E (3.50mm) hook, B and with RS facing, work along row ends on one edge, *1sc into each of next 2 row ends, skip 1 row end, rep from * to end. Turn.
Next row 1ch, 1sc into each sc to end. Turn.
Rep last row until cuff measures 2¼in (6cm). Fasten off.

To finish
Join shoulder seams.
Neck edge Using size E (3.50mm) hook, B and with RS facing, work in sc around neck edge, 1sc into each row end along straight part of front neck, 1sc into each sp along side neck, 1sc into each row end along back neck, 1sc into each sp along side neck, then 1sc into each row end along left front neck. Turn.
Next row 1ch, sc to end. Turn.
Rep last row 5 times more. Fasten off.
Front opening Using size E (3.50mm) hook, B and with RS facing, work a row of sc up front opening, around neck and down other side of front opening. Fasten off.
Fold sleeve in half lengthwise and, matching center top of sleeve to shoulder seam, sew sleeve in position. Join side and sleeve seams.
Lower edge Using size E (3.50mm) hook, B and with RS facing, work 1sc into each sc all around lower edge. Turn.
Next row 3ch, 1dc into each sc to end. Fasten off.
Tie Using size E (3.50mm) hook and 2 strands of B, make a chain approx 83in (210cm) long. Thread through row of dc at lower edge.
Bobbles (make 2) Using size E (3.50mm) hook and B, make 3ch. Join with sl st to first ch to form circle. 3ch, 11dc into circle. Join with sl st to first ch. Fasten off. Attach one bobble to each end of tie.
Press front neck very lightly.

EXTRA SPECIAL KNITTING

Slim-line cardigan

Lightweight sport yarn makes the kind of easy cardigan a man will enjoy wearing when he needs just a little extra warmth—perfect for early fall, when there's a slight nip in the air.

Sizes
To fit 38[40:42]in (97[102:107]cm) chest.
Length, $26\frac{1}{2}$[27:$27\frac{1}{2}$]in (67[68:70]cm).
Sleeve seam, $20\frac{3}{4}$[$21\frac{1}{4}$:22]in (53[54:56]cm).

Note Directions for larger sizes are in brackets [ ]; where there is only one set of figures it applies to all sizes.

Materials
18[20:22]oz (500[550:600]g) of a sport yarn
1 pair each Nos. 4 and 6 ($3\frac{3}{4}$ and $4\frac{1}{2}$mm) knitting needles
7 buttons

Gauge
20 sts and 36 rows to 4in (10cm) in patt worked on No. 6 ($4\frac{1}{2}$mm) knitting needles.

Back
Using No. 4 ($3\frac{3}{4}$mm) needles cast on 99[103:107] sts.
1st row (RS) K2, *P1, K1, rep from * to last st, K1.
2nd row K1, *P1, K1, rep from * to end.
Rep these 2 rows for $2\frac{3}{4}$in (7cm); end with 2nd row. Change to No. 6 ($4\frac{1}{2}$mm) needles. Beg patt.
1st row K3, *sl 1 purlwise, K3, rep from * to end.
2nd row K3, *P1, K3, rep from * to end.
These 2 rows form patt. Cont in patt until work measures $18\frac{1}{4}$in (46cm) from beg; end with WS row. Place marker at each end of last row to mark beg of armholes. Cont in patt until work measures $26\frac{1}{2}$[27:$27\frac{1}{2}$]in (67[68:70]cm) from beg; end with WS row.
Shape shoulders
Bind off 3 sts at beg of next 8 rows, 4 sts at beg of next 4 rows, 4[5:6] sts at beg of next 4 rows and 5 sts at beg of foll 2 rows. Cut off yarn and leave rem 33 sts on a holder.

Pocket linings (make 2)
Using No. 6 ($4\frac{1}{2}$mm) needles cast on 24 sts. Beg with K row, work $5\frac{1}{2}$in (14cm) stockinette st; end with P row. Bind off.

Left front
Using No. 4 ($3\frac{3}{4}$mm) needles cast on 47[51:51] sts. Work 2 ribbing rows of back for $2\frac{3}{4}$in (7cm); end with 2nd row. Change to No. 6 ($4\frac{1}{2}$mm) needles. Cont in patt as for back until work measures $5\frac{1}{4}$in (13cm) from beg; end with WS row.
Divide for pocket
Next row Patt 21[23:23], turn and leave rem sts on a spare needle.
Cont in patt on these sts until work measures $5\frac{1}{2}$in (14cm) from division of pocket; end with RS row. Cut off yarn and leave sts on holder. With RS of work facing rejoin yarn to inner end of sts on spare needle and cont in patt on these 26[28:28] sts until work measures $5\frac{1}{2}$in (14cm) from division of pocket; end with RS row.
Next row Patt to end, then onto same needle patt sts from holder.
47[51:51] sts. This completes pocket opening.
Cont in patt until work measures same as back to armholes; end with WS row. Place marker at end of last row to mark beg of armhole. Cont in patt until work measures $6\frac{3}{4}$[7:$7\frac{1}{2}$]in (17[18:19]cm) from marker; end with WS row.
Shape neck
Next row Patt to last 11 sts, K2 tog, turn and leave rem sts on holder. Dec one st at neck edge on every foll alternate row until 33[35:37] sts rem. Cont straight until work measures same as back to beg of shoulder shaping; end at armhole edge.
Shape shoulder
Bind off 3 sts at beg of next and foll 3 alternate rows, 4 sts at beg of foll 2 alternate rows and 4[5:6] sts at beg of foll 2 alternate rows. Work 1 row. Bind off.

Right front
Work as for left front reversing shaping and position for pocket opening so that pocket row will read thus:
Next row Patt 26[28:28], turn and leave rem sts on a spare needle.

Sleeves
Using No. 4 ($3\frac{3}{4}$mm) needles cast on 63[63:67] sts. Work 2 ribbing rows of

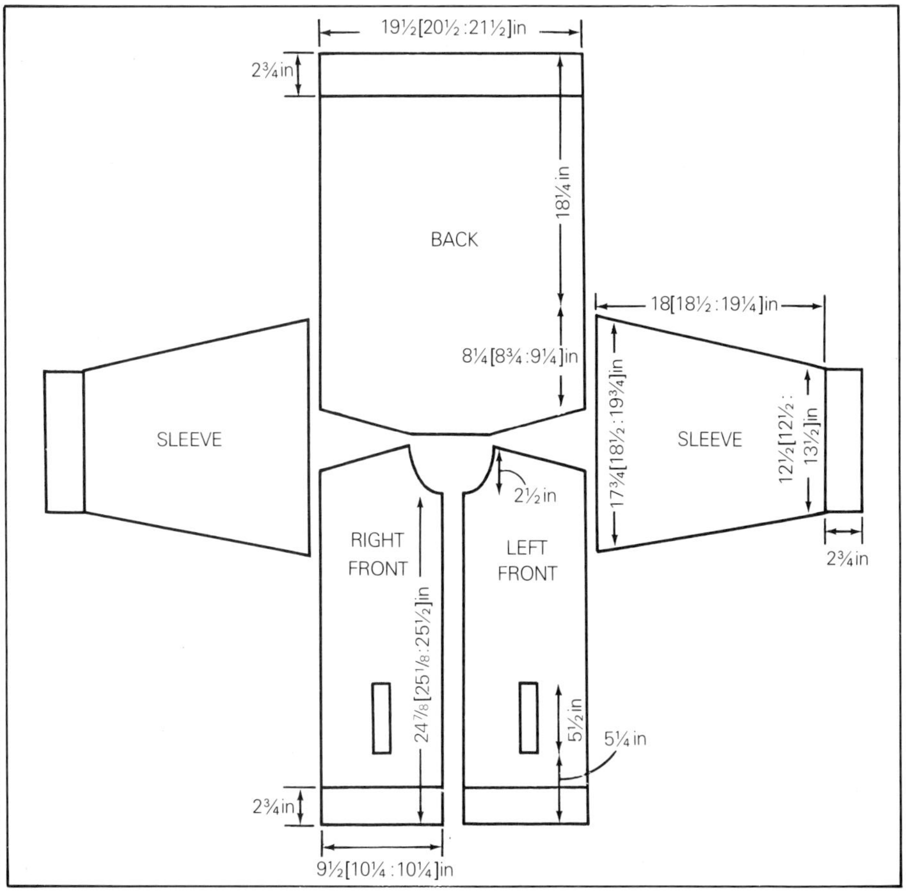

Rod Delroy

back for $2\frac{3}{4}$in (7cm); end with 2nd row. Change to No. 6 ($4\frac{1}{2}$mm) needles and cont in patt as for back but inc one st at each end of 5th and every foll 6th row until there are 89[93:99] sts. Cont straight until work measures $20\frac{3}{4}$[$21\frac{1}{4}$:22]in (53[54:56]cm) from beg; end with WS row. Bind off.

Collar

Join shoulder seams. With RS of work facing and using No. 4 ($3\frac{3}{4}$mm) needles K right front neck sts from holder but inc one st at center, pick up and K 20 sts from right front neck, K sts from holder, inc 5 sts evenly, pick up and K 20 sts from left front neck, then K left front neck sts from holder but inc one st at center. 98 sts.
K 6 rows.
Next row K7, (pick up loop lying between needles and K tbl—called make 1 or M1—, K7) 13 times. 111 sts.
Change to No. 6 ($4\frac{1}{2}$mm) needles. P 1 row.

Shape collar

Cont in ribbing as for back, work 2 rows.
Next row Rib to last 4 sts, turn.
Next row Sl 1, rib to last 4 sts, turn.
Next 2 rows Sl 1, rib to last 8 sts, turn.
Next 2 rows Sl 1, rib to last 12 sts, turn.
Cont in ribbing working 4 sts less on every row until you have worked 2 rows of Sl 1, rib to last 40 sts, turn.
Next row Sl 1, rib to end of row.
Cont in ribbing working across all sts until collar measures 9in (23cm) from neck edge measured at center. Bind off loosely in ribbing.

Button border

Using No. 4 ($3\frac{3}{4}$mm) needles cast on 9 sts. Work in garter st until border, slightly stretched, fits along front edge and collar. Bind off. Mark 7 button positions on this border, the first $\frac{1}{2}$in (1cm) from lower edge, the last level with marker at armhole and others evenly spaced between.

Buttonhole border

Work as for button border but make buttonholes to match markers:
1st buttonhole row K3, bind off 3, K to end.
2nd buttonhole row K3, cast on 3, K to end.

Pocket borders (alike)

Using No. 4 ($3\frac{3}{4}$mm) needles cast on 7 sts. Work in garter st until border, slightly stretched, fits along pocket. Bind off.

To finish

Do not press. Mark center of bound-off edge of sleeves with pin, and match to shoulder seam, then sew on sleeves. Join side and sleeve seams. Sew each pocket lining to back, sew pocket borders to front. Sew borders and buttons in position.

EXTRA SPECIAL KNITTING

Seaside special

Treat the whole family to a tunic-style sweater with a knitted-in motif—just the thing to brighten up a gray day when you're on vacation.

Serge Krouglikoff

Sizes

To fit 26[28:30:32:34:36:38:40]in (66[71:76:83:87:92:97:102]cm) chest/bust.
Length, 20$\frac{3}{4}$[23:24$\frac{3}{4}$:26:27$\frac{1}{4}$:27$\frac{1}{4}$:28:28]in (53[58:63:66:69:69:71:71]cm).
Sleeve seam, 13[15:16:17:17$\frac{1}{4}$:17$\frac{1}{4}$:18:18]in (33[38:41:43:44:44:46:46]cm).
Note Directions for larger sizes are in brackets [ ]; where there is only one set of figures it applies to all sizes.

Materials

Knitting worsted
11[11:13:13:13:15:15:15]oz (300[300:350:350:350:400:400:400]g) in white (A)
8[8:9:9:9:11:11:11]oz (200[200:250:250:250:300:300:300]g) in yellow (B)
6[6:8:8:8:9:9:9]oz (150[150:200:200:200:250:250:250]g) in blue (C)
2oz (50g) each in rust (D) for boat motif and in dark blue (E) for island motif
1 pair each Nos. 5 and 7 (4 and 5mm) knitting needles

Gauge

18 sts and 26 rows to 4in (10cm) in stockinette st on No. 7 (5mm) needles.

Back

**Using No. 5 (4mm) needles and C, cast on 72[78:84:90:96:102:108:114] sts. K10 rows. Change to No. 7 (5mm) needles. Cut off C and join on B. Cont in stockinette st until work measures 6in (15cm); end with P row. Cast on 4 sts at beg of next 2 rows for top of slits. 80[86:92:98:104:110:116:122] sts. Cont in stockinette st until work measures 7$\frac{1}{2}$[8$\frac{1}{2}$:9$\frac{1}{2}$:10$\frac{1}{4}$:10$\frac{1}{2}$:11:11:11]in (19[21.5:24:26:26.5:28:28:28]cm) from beg; end with P row. Cut off B. Joining on and cutting off colors as required beg wave patt.

1st row With A, K1, *K2 tog, (K into front and back of next st) twice, K2 tog, rep from * to last st, K1.
2nd row With A, K to end.
3rd row With C, as first row.
4th row With C, P to end.
These 4 rows from patt. Rep them 7 times more. Cut off C. ** Cont in stockinette st with A only, until work measures 14$\frac{1}{2}$[16$\frac{1}{4}$:17$\frac{1}{2}$:18$\frac{1}{2}$:19:19:19$\frac{1}{2}$:19$\frac{1}{2}$]in (37[41:44.5:47:48:48:49.5:49.5]cm) from beg; end with P row.

Shape armholes
Bind off 3[3:4:4:4:5:5:5] sts at beg of next 2 rows. Dec one st at each end of next and every foll alternate row until 64[68:72:76:80:84:88:92] sts rem. Cont straight until work measures 6$\frac{1}{4}$[6$\frac{3}{4}$:7$\frac{1}{4}$:7$\frac{1}{2}$:8$\frac{1}{4}$:8$\frac{1}{4}$:8$\frac{1}{2}$:8$\frac{1}{2}$]in (16[17:18.5:19:21:21:21.5:21.5]cm) from beg of armhole; end with P row.

Shape shoulders
Bind off 7[7:8:8:9:9:10:10] sts at beg of next 4 rows and 6[8:7:9:8:10:9:11] sts at beg of foll 2 rows. Change to No. 5 (4mm) needles and K 10 rows for neckband. Bind off.

Front

Work as for back from ** to **. Beg motif. Note that for 4th size you can choose either boat or sun motif and for 6th size you can choose either sun or island motif. For 1st, 2nd, 3rd and 4th sizes, K10[13:15:18] A, 24 D (as row 1 of boat chart), with A, K to end.
For 4th, 5th and 6th sizes, K50[53:55] A, 30 B (as row 1 of sun chart), with A, K to end.
For 6th, 7th and 8th sizes, K28[34:40] A, 80 E (as row 1 of island chart), with A, K to end.
Foll chart for design you are making, cont in stockinette st twisting yarns when changing color to avoid a hole, until work measures same as back to armhole;

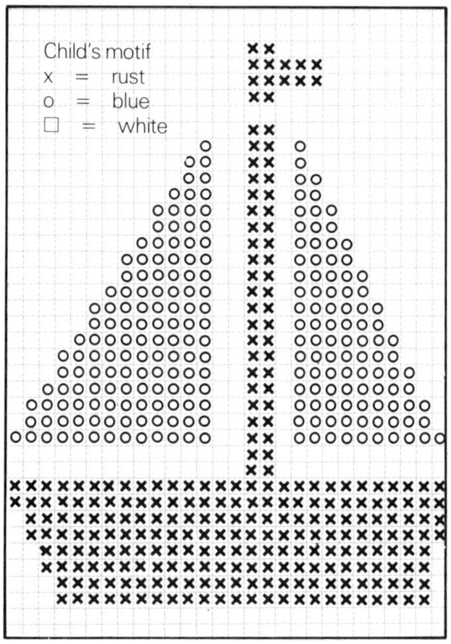

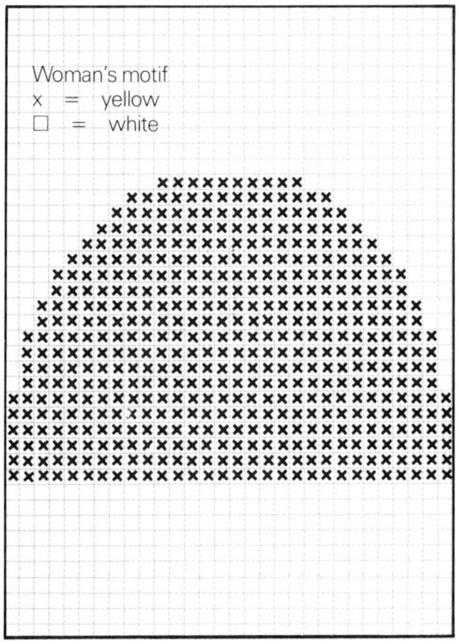

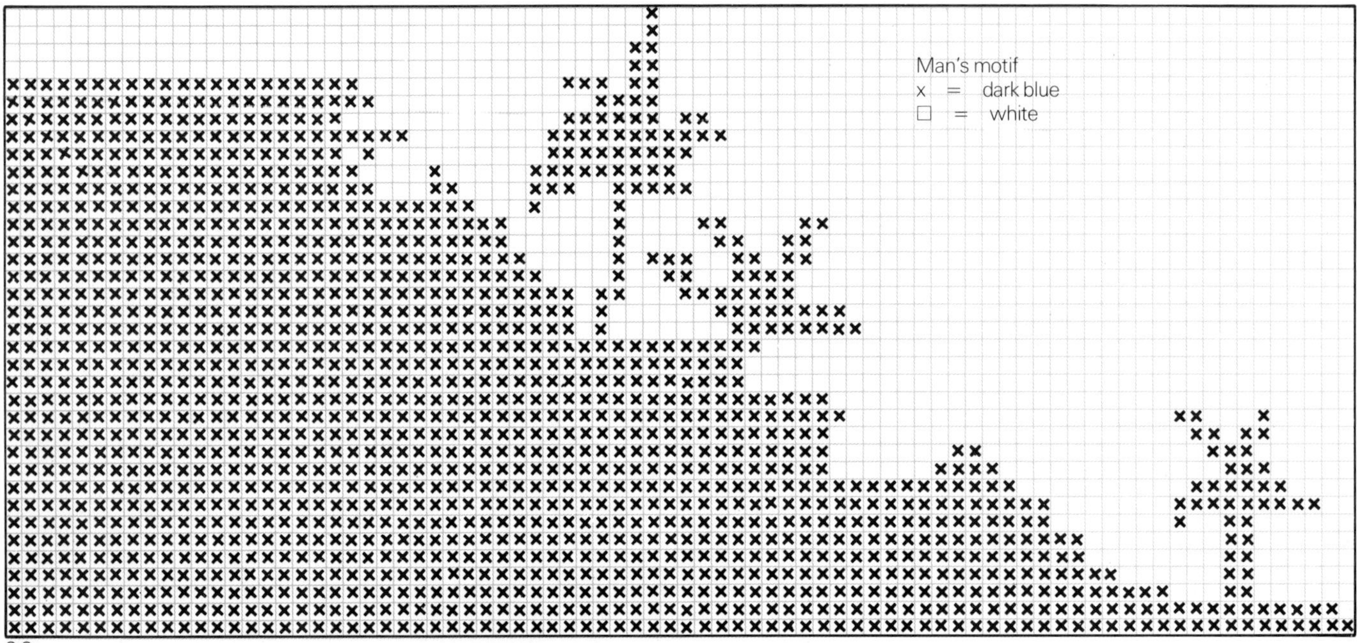

John Hutchinson

end with P row.

Shape armhole and divide for neck

Next row Cont to foll chart, bind off 3[3:4:4:4:5:5:5], K until there are 37[40:42:45:48:50:53:56] sts on right-hand needle, turn and leave rem sts on spare needle. Complete left side of neck first. Work 1 row. Dec one st at armhole edge on next and every foll alternate row and at same time dec one st at neck edge on next and every foll 4th row until 29[31:33:34:36:38:39:41] sts rem. Keeping armhole edge straight, cont to dec at front edge on every 4th row until 20[22:23:25:26:28:29:31] sts rem. Cont straight until front measures same as back up to shoulder; end with P row.

Shape shoulder

Bind off 7[7:8:8:9:9:10:10] sts at beg of next and foll alternate row. Work 1 row. Bind off. With RS facing rejoin yarn to inner end of sts on spare needle and K to end. Match first side, reversing shaping and completing motif.

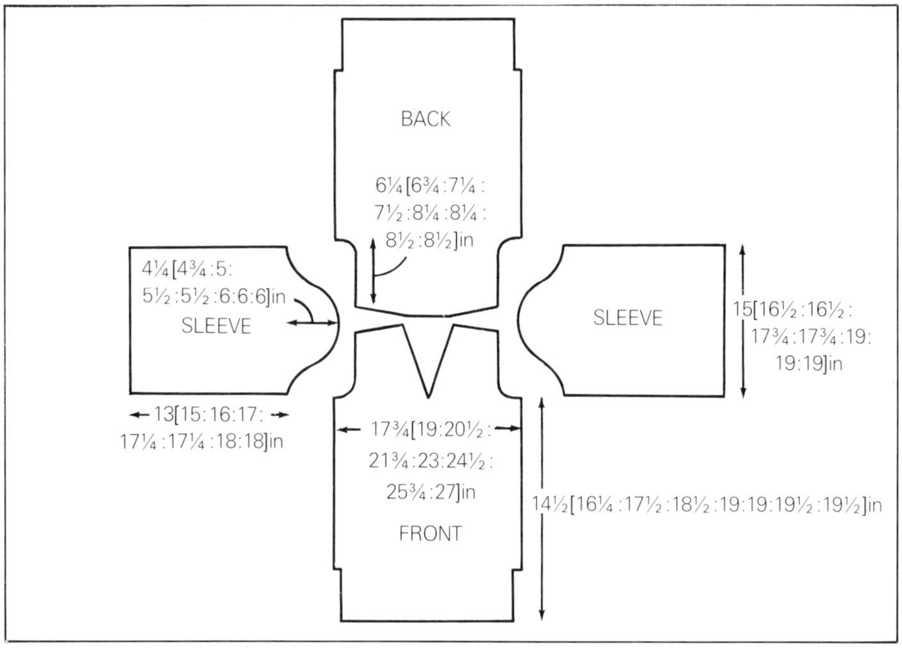

John Hutchinson

Sleeves

Using No. 5 (4mm) needles and C, cast on 68[74:74:80:80:86:86:86] sts. K 10 rows. Change to No. 7 (5mm) needles. Cut off C and join on B. Cont in stockinette st until sleeve measures 6[7½:7¾:9:9½:9½:9½:9½]in (15[19:20:23:24:24:24:24]cm) from beg; end with P row. Joining on and cutting off colors as required work 4 wave patt rows as for back 8 times. Cut off C. Cont in stockinette st with A only until sleeve measures 13[15:16:17:17¼:17¼:18:18]in (33[38:41:43:44:44:46:46]cm) from beg; end with P row.

Shape top

Bind off 3[3:4:4:4:5:5:5] sts at beg of next 2 rows. Dec one st at each end of next and every foll alternate row until 48[48:50:50:52:52:54:54] sts rem, then at each end of every row until 14[16:16:18:18:20:20:20] sts rem. Bind off.

Neckband

With RS facing, using No. 5 (4mm) needles and C, pick up and K 36[38:40:40:42:42:44:44] sts evenly along left side of neck. K 9 rows. Bind off. Work along right neck in same way.

Slit borders (4 alike)

With RS facing, using No. 5 (4mm) needles and C, pick up and K 30 sts along side slit between lower edge and cast-on group. K 9 rows. Bind off.

To finish

Press with warm iron over damp cloth, omitting borders. Join shoulder seams. Set in sleeves. Join side and sleeve seams.
Overlap neckband at front and sew in position.
Embroider sun rays in duplicate stitch.

Technique tip

Side slits

Side slit openings are very popular on longer style sweaters because they allow a bit of extra movement.
Slits usually have a border which sits in, rather than extends beyond, the side seam.
To make a side slit in this way, first calculate the width of the back of the garment, then decide on the depth of the border to be worked. The combined depth of the borders should then be deducted from the width of the garment—for example, if you want your garment to measure 18in (46cm) across the back and each border to measure 1¼in (3cm), you will need to cast on stitches to produce 15½in (40cm) in width. Calculate the number of stitches for this width, cast on the stitches required and knit until the slit depth has been reached. Cast on stitches at beginning of next 2 rows to give an extra 1¼in (3cm) at each end—you will now have the total width of the back on the needles. Complete your knitting, then work the borders.
The slit borders can either be knitted onto the main fabric or knitted separately and sewed on.
To knit onto the main fabric, pick up and knit stitches evenly along side of slit between group of stitches cast onto garment and lower edge. Knit for 1¼in (3cm), then bind off. Sew the top edge to cast-on group of stitches.

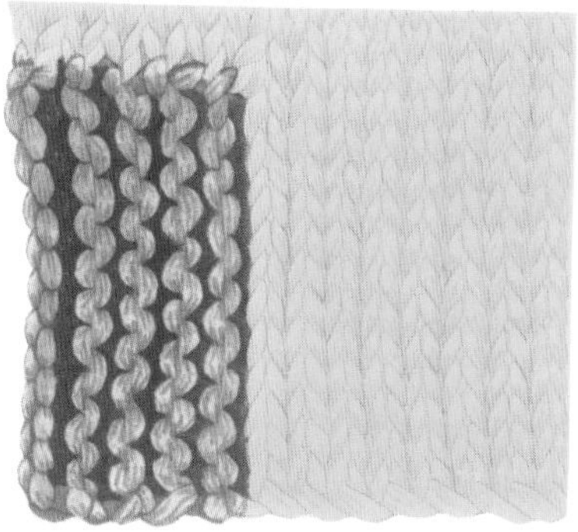

To knit separately, cast on stitches to produce 1¼in (3cm) in width. Knit for depth of opening, then bind off. Sew border to side and top of slit opening.

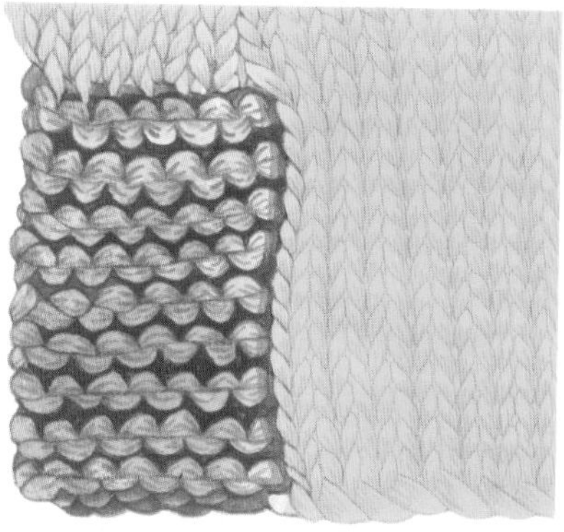

EXTRA SPECIAL KNITTING

Flights of fancy

It's a lacy look to hit the high spots! Worked in a bouclé yarn, this super sweater has just the right kind of flattering shape.

Sizes
To fit 34 to 38in (87 to 97cm) bust.
Length, 19in (48cm).

Materials
23oz (650g) of a medium-weight cotton bouclé yarn
1 pair each Nos. 6 and 10½ (4½ and 7mm) knitting needles

Gauge
14 sts and 16 rows to 4in (10cm) in patt using yarn double on No. 10½ (7mm) needles.

Front
Using No. 10½ (7mm) needles and yarn double throughout, cast on 241 sts loosely. P1 row.
Beg first patt.
1st row K1, *yo, K6, sl 1, K2tog, psso, K6, yo, K1, rep from * to end.
2nd and foll alternate rows P to end.
3rd row K2, *yo, K5, sl 1, K2tog, psso, K5, yo, K3, rep from * to end, but finish last rep K2 instead of K3.
5th row K3, *yo, K4, sl 1, K2tog, psso, K4, yo, K5, rep from * to end, but finish last rep K3 instead of K5.
7th row K4, *yo, K3, sl 1, K2tog, psso, K3, yo, K7, rep from * to end, but finish last rep K4.
9th row K5, *yo, K2, sl 1, K2tog, psso, K2, yo, K9, rep from * to end, but finish last rep K5.
11th row K6, *yo, K1, sl 1, K2tog, psso, K1, yo, K11, rep from * to end, but finish last rep K6.
13th row K7, *yo, sl 1, K2tog, psso, yo, K13, rep from * to end, but finish last rep K7.
14th row P to end.
1st dec row K7, *sl 1, K2tog, psso, K13, rep from * to end, but finish last rep K7. 211 sts. P1 row.
Beg 2nd patt.
1st row K1, *yo, K5, sl 1, K2tog, psso, K5, yo, K1, rep from * to end.
2nd and foll alternate rows P to end.
3rd row K2, *yo, K4, sl 1, K2tog, psso, K4, yo, K3, rep from * to end, but finish last rep K2.
5th row K3, *yo, K3, sl 1, K2tog, psso,

Serge Krouglikoff

K3, yo, K5, rep from * to end, but finish last rep K3.
7th row K4, *yo, K2, sl 1, K2tog, psso, K2, yo, K7, rep from * to end, but finish last rep K4.
9th row K5, *yo, K1, sl 1, K2tog, psso, K1, yo, K9, rep from * to end, but finish last rep K5.
11th row K6, *yo, sl 1, K2tog, psso, yo, K11, rep from * to end, but finish last rep K6.
12th row P to end.
2nd dec row K6, *sl 1, K2tog, psso, K11, rep from * to end, but finish last rep, K6. 181 sts.
P1 row.
Beg 3rd patt.
1st row K1, *yo, K4, sl 1, K2tog, psso, K4, yo, K1, rep from * to end.
2nd and foll alternate rows P to end.
3rd row K2, *yo, K3, sl 1, K2tog, psso, K3, yo, K3, rep from * to end, but finish last rep K2.
5th row K3, *yo, K2, sl 1, K2tog, psso, K2, yo, K5, rep from * to end, but finish last rep K3.
7th row K4, *yo, K1, sl 1, K2tog, psso, K1, yo, K7, rep from * to end, but finish last rep K4.
9th row K5, *yo, sl 1, K2tog, psso, yo, K9, rep from * to end, but finish last rep K5.
10th row P to end.
3rd dec row K5, *sl 1, K2tog, psso, K9, rep from * to end, but finish last rep K5. 151 sts.
P1 row.
Beg 4th patt.
1st row K1, *yo, K3, sl 1, K2tog, psso, K3, yo, K1, rep from * to end.
2nd and foll alternate rows P to end.
3rd row K2, *yo, K2, sl 1, K2tog, psso, K2, yo, K3, rep from * to end, but finish last rep K2.
5th row K3, *yo, K1, sl 1, K2tog, psso, K1, yo, K5, rep from * to end, but finish last rep K3.
7th row K4, *yo, sl 1, K2tog, psso, yo, K7, rep from * to end, but finish last rep K4.
8th row P to end.
4th dec row K4, *sl 1, K2tog, psso, K7, rep from * to end, but finish last rep K4. 121 sts. P1 row.
Beg 5th patt.
1st row K1, *yo, K2, sl 1, K2tog, psso, K2, yo, K1, rep from * to end.
2nd row P to end.
3rd row K2, *yo, K1, sl 1, K2tog, psso, K1, yo, K3, rep from * to end, but finish last rep K2.
4th row P to end.
5th row K3, *yo, sl 1, K2tog, psso, yo, K5, rep from * to end, but finish last rep K3.
6th row P to end.
5th dec row K3, *sl 1, K2tog, psso, K5, rep from * to end, but finish last rep K3. 91 sts.
P1 row.
Beg 6th patt.
1st row K2, *yo, sl 1, K2tog, psso, yo, K3,

Serge Krouglikoff

rep from * to end, but finish last rep K2.
2nd row P to end.
Rep last 2 rows until work measures 17$\frac{3}{4}$in (45cm) from beg; end with 2nd row.
Next row K1, now K2tog to end of row.
Bind off knitwise.

Waistband

Mark 89th st from each side edge on cast-on edge. Using No. 6 (4$\frac{1}{2}$mm) needles and yarn double pick up and K 65 sts between markers.
1st row *K1, P1, rep from * to last st, K1.
2nd row K2, *P1, K1, rep from * to last st, K1.
3rd row As first row.
4th row K1, *yo, K2tog, rep from * to end.
Rep 1st and 2nd rows 4 times more.
Bind off loosely in ribbing.

Back

Work exactly as for front.

To finish

See ball band for pressing details. Join upper sleeve and shoulder seams.
Cuffs (alike)
Place a marker at cast-on edge on the 24th st on each side of seam. Using No. 6 (4$\frac{1}{2}$mm) needles and yarn double, pick up and K 48 sts between markers.
Next row *P1, P2tog, rep from * to end. 32 sts.
Work in K1, P1 ribbing for 3$\frac{1}{4}$in (8cm).
Bind off in ribbing.
Join side seams. Press seams lightly.

Drawstring for waist
Using four 5yd (4.6m) lengths of yarn together, make a twisted cord and thread through holes at waistband.
Drawstring for neck
Using four 4yd (3.8m) lengths of yarn together, make a twisted cord. Thread through last row of holes in pattern at neck.

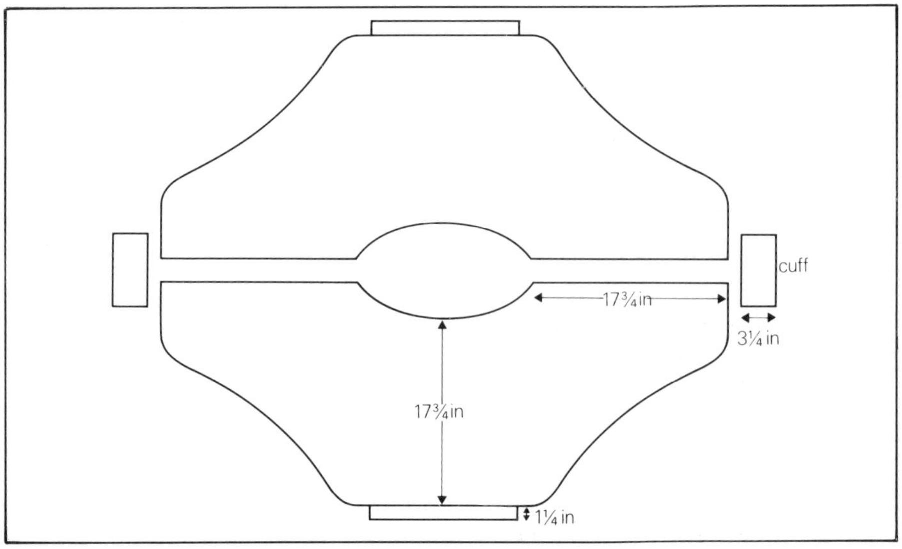

Brian Mayor

EXTRA SPECIAL

KNITTING

Sun time

These dresses, knitted in lightweight yarn, are great for warm days.

Tony Boase

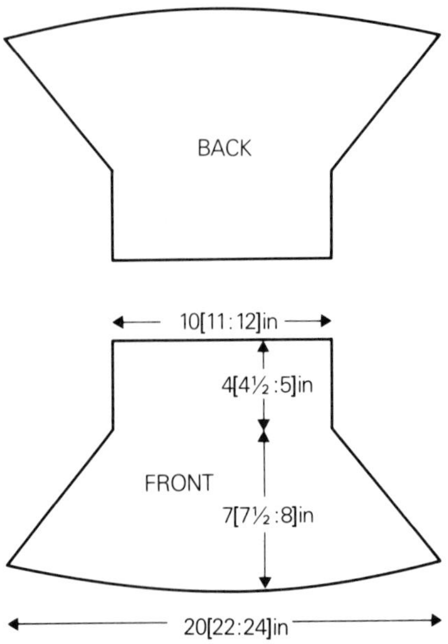

Brian Mayor

Sizes
To fit 20[22:24]in (51[56:61]cm) chest.
Length from top of bodice: 11[12:13]in (28[30:33]cm).
Note Directions for larger sizes are in brackets [ ]; where there is only one set of figures it applies to all sizes.

Materials
Sport yarn
Dress with striped hem *5[5:6] x 1oz (20g) balls in main shade (A)*
2 balls in contrasting color (B)
Dress with pockets *5[5:6] x 1oz (20g) balls in main shade (A)*
2 balls in contrasting color (B)
Striped dress *2[3:3] x 1oz (20g) balls in main shade (A) (at hem)*
1[2:2] balls each in contrasting colors (B, C and D)
1 pair each Nos.2 and 3 (2¾ and 3¼mm) knitting needles
1 pair No. 00 (2mm) knitting needles for dress with striped hem

Gauge
26 sts and 34 rows to 4in (10cm) in stockinette st on No. 3 (3¼mm) needles.

Dress with striped hem

Front
Using No. 2 (2¾mm) needles and A, cast on 130[142:154] sts. Beg with K row, work 7 rows stockinette st; end with K row.
Next row K to end to form hemline.
Change to No. 3 (3¼mm) needles. Beg with a K row, work 6 rows stockinette st.
Next row (hem row) *K one st from needle tog with one loop from cast-on edge, rep from * to end.
Beg with P row, work 3 rows stockinette st. Join in B. Cont in stockinette st, work in stripe sequence of 6 rows B, 6 A, 4 B, 4 A and 2 B. Cut off B. Using A throughout, cont in stockinette st until work measures 7[7½:8]in (18[19:20]cm) from hemline; end with K row.

Shape bodice
Next row *P2 tog, rep from * to end. 65[71:77] sts.
Next row K1, *P1, K1, rep from * to end.
Next row P1, *K1, P1, rep from * to end.
Rep last 2 rows until work measures 11[12:13]in (28[30:33]cm) from hemline. Bind off loosely in ribbing.

Back
Work as for front.

Short strap
Using No. 2 (2¾mm) needles and B, cast on 15 sts.
1st row (RS) K2, *P1, K1, rep from * to last st, K1.
2nd row K1, *P1, K1, rep from * to end.
Rep last 2 rows for 10[11:12]in (26[28:30]cm). Bind off.

Long strap
Using No. 2 (2¾mm) needles and B, cast on 3 sts.
1st row (RS) P1, K1, P1.
2nd row K into front and back of first st—called inc 1, P1, inc1.
3rd row Inc 1, P1, K1, P1, inc 1.
4th row Inc 1, (P1, K1) twice, P1, inc 1.
5th row Inc 1, (P1, K1) 3 times, P1, inc 1.
6th row Inc 1, (P1, K1) 4 times, P1, inc 1.
7th row Inc 1, (P1, K1) 5 times, P1, inc 1. 15 sts.
8th row K1, *P1, K1, rep from * to last st, K1.
9th row K2, *P1, K1, rep from * to last st, K1.
Rep last 2 rows for 14½[16:16½]in (37[40:42]cm) from point. Bind off.

Tony Boase

Flower motif
Using No. 00 (2mm) needles and A, cast on 2 sts.
1st row K1, K into front and back of next st—called inc 1.
2nd row K3.
3rd row K2, inc 1.
4th row K4.
5th row K3, inc 1.
6th–9th rows K5.
10th row Bind off one st, K to end.
11th row K to end.
12th–15th rows Rep 10th and 11th rows twice more.
16th row Bind off one st. Using right-hand needle point, pick up and K one st between first and 2nd picot points, bind off one st and transfer rem st to left-hand needle. Rep 16 rows 4 times, joining each petal in same way. Fasten off. Sew into circle to form flower.

To finish
Press under damp cloth with warm iron. Join sides. Place short strap on left shoulder, sewing ½in (1.2cm) at each end to inside of top. Position long strap, sewing ½in (1.2cm) of straight end to inside of back bodice with point just below waist. Catch long strap in position at top of front bodice and waist. Using B, sew flower motif to strap at waist, making one French knot at base of each petal and one in center. Press seams.

Dress with pocket

Front and back
Work as for front and back of dress with striped hem, omitting stripes and changing to B before shaping bodice.

Pocket
Using No. 3 (3¼mm) needles and B, cast on 15 sts. Beg with K row, work 2in (5.5cm) stockinette st; end with K row.
Change to No. 2 (2¾mm) needles.
Next row K to end to mark foldline.
Beg with K row, work 6 rows stockinette st. Bind off.

To finish
Press under damp cloth with warm iron.

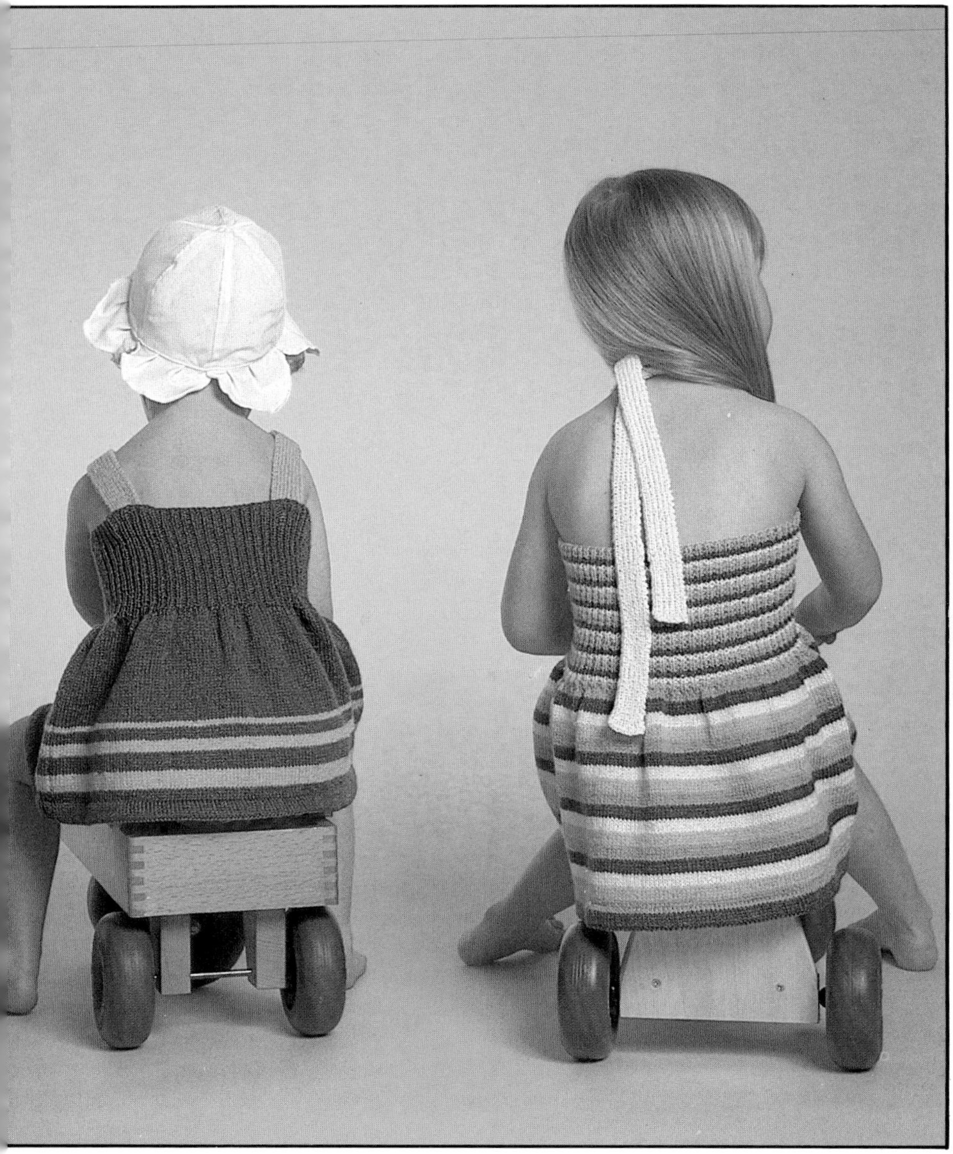

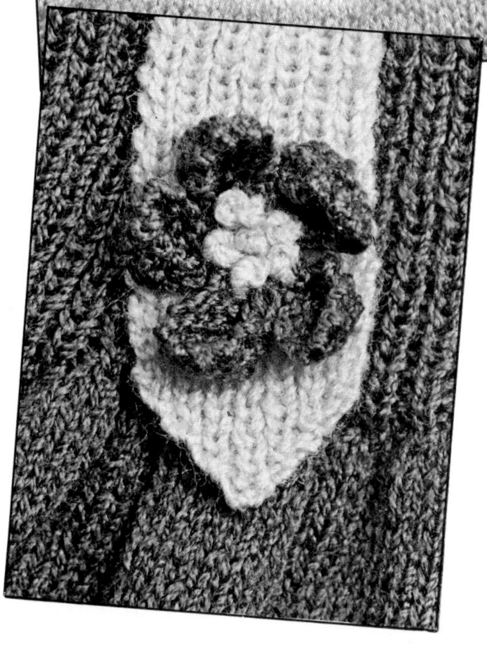

Sew on pockets. Join side seams.
Straps For double straps cut 12 strands of color A, each 20in (50cm) long. Braid tog, using 4 strands in each section. Cut in half, knot ends and sew to outside edge of front and back bodice.

Striped dress

Front
Using No. 2 ($2\frac{3}{4}$mm) needles and A, cast on 130[142:156] sts. Beg with K row, work 7 rows stockinette st; end with K row.
Next row K to end to mark hemline.
Change to No. 3 ($3\frac{1}{4}$mm) needles. Beg with a K row, work 4 rows stockinette st. Join in B and work 2 rows stockinette st.
Next row (hem row) *K one st from needle tog with one loop from cast-on edge, rep from * to end. P1 row using B. Join in C. Cont in stockinette st and stripe sequence of 4 rows each C, D, A and B until work measures 7[$7\frac{1}{2}$:8]in (18[19:20]cm) from hemline, ending with 3rd row of any stripe.

Shape bodice
Next row P0[0:1], *P2 tog, rep from * to last 0[0:1] sts, P0[0:1]. 65[71:79] sts.
Keeping color sequence correct, work 2 rows in each color as foll:
Next row K to end.
Next row P1, *K1, P1, rep from * to end.
Rep last 2 rows until work measures 11[12:13]in (28[30:33]cm) from hemline; end with stripe in C. Bind off loosely in ribbing.

Back
Work as for front.

Straps (make 2)
Using No. 2 ($2\frac{3}{4}$mm) needles and D cast on 9 sts. Rib 20in (50cm) for short strap of dress with striped hem.
Bind off.

To finish
Press under damp cloth with warm iron. Join sides. Position straps on front bodice, sewing $\frac{1}{2}$in (1.2cm) at end to inside of bodice. Press seams.

EXTRA SPECIAL SEWING

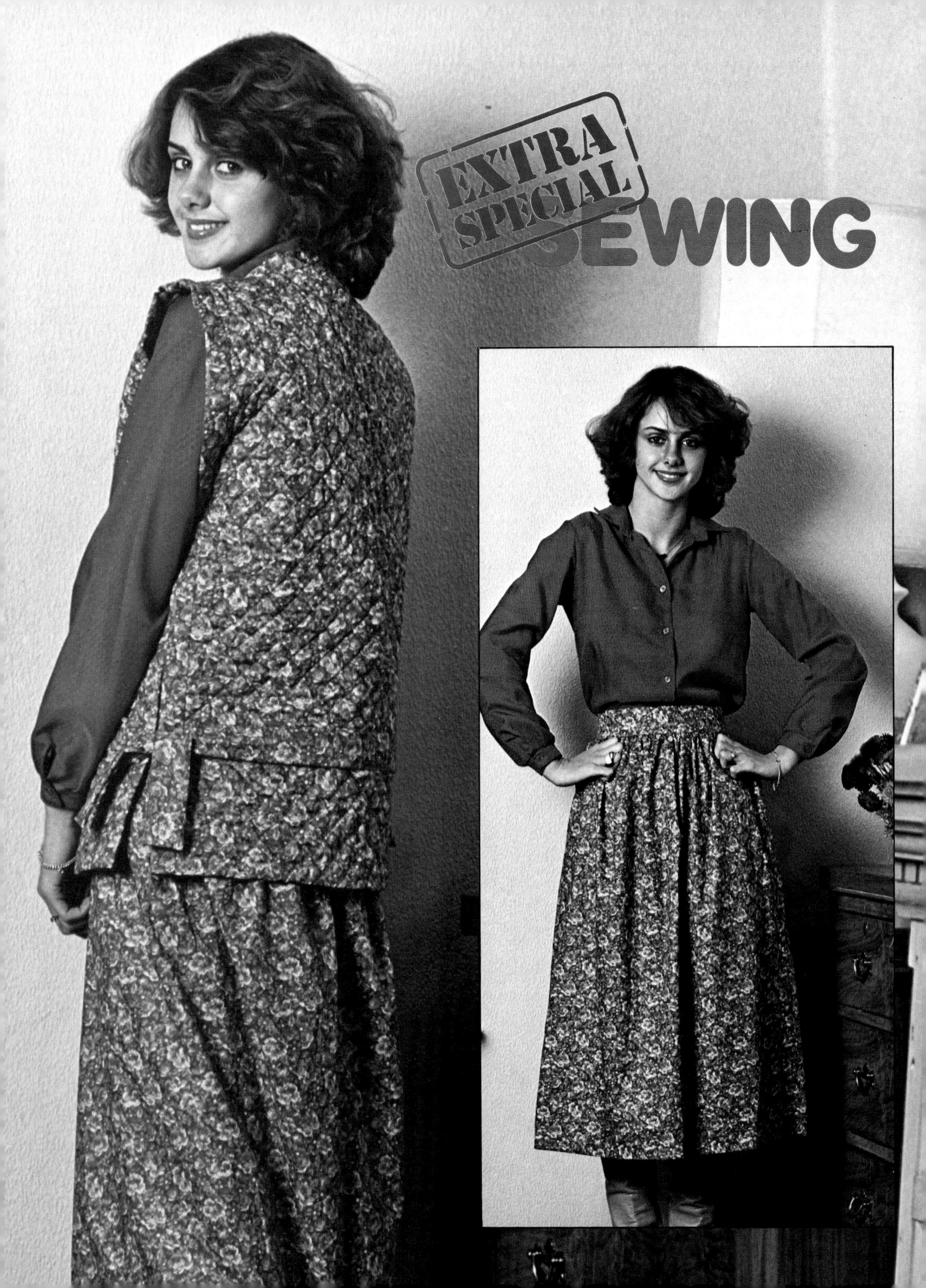

Textured twosome

By using quilted and non-quilted fabric together you can achieve an effective fashion look with little trouble. Choose a pretty print and follow our directions for quilting it yourself. Directions for making the skirt are given in the next Extra Special Sewing course, on page 105.

Measurements
To fit sizes 10, 12, 14 and 16; corresponding to sizes 8-14 in ready-made clothes.
Finished length of vest: $26\frac{3}{8}$in (67cm).
Finished length of skirt: 30in (76cm).
$\frac{5}{8}$in (1.5cm) seam allowances throughout.

Materials
$1\frac{7}{8}$yd (1.7m) of 36in (90cm)-wide fabric
$1\frac{5}{8}$yd (1.5m) of 36in (90cm)-wide fabric
OR $1\frac{1}{4}$yd (1.1m) of 54in (140cm)-wide fabric
$\frac{7}{8}$yd (.8m) of 54in (140cm)-wide backing fabric
$1\frac{5}{8}$yd (1.5m) of 36in (90cm)-wide polyester batting
1 card bias binding
Matching thread
Tailor's chalk
Yardstick
Flexible curve

Note The skirt takes $2\frac{1}{4}$yd (2m) of fabric (either 36in [90cm]- wide or 54in [140cm]- wide) so if you wish to make the skirt too, add this to your fabric.

1 Following the cutting layout, cut two rectangles of fabric 10in (25cm) by $28\frac{1}{2}$in (72.5cm) for the front pieces of the vest and one rectangle $23\frac{1}{2}$in (60cm) by $28\frac{1}{2}$in (72.5cm) for the back.
2 Cut the same shaped pieces from the batting and the backing fabric.
3 From the main fabric, cut four strips each $3\frac{1}{8}$in (8cm) by $27\frac{1}{2}$in (70cm) for the armhole/side bands and two strips $3\frac{1}{8}$in (8cm) by 30in (76cm) for neck/front bands. Cut two strips $4\frac{3}{8}$in (11cm) by 11in (28cm) and one $4\frac{3}{8}$in (11cm) by $31\frac{1}{2}$in (80cm) for belts.
4 Quilt the front and back sections as directed in the Technique tip.
5 Trim the quilted rectangles to the measurements given for your size on the pattern piece diagram. Mark the curved back neck shape and straight shaping lines as indicated on the diagram. Use tailor's chalk and a yardstick to mark the lines on the quilted fabric.

cutting layout 36in-wide fabric

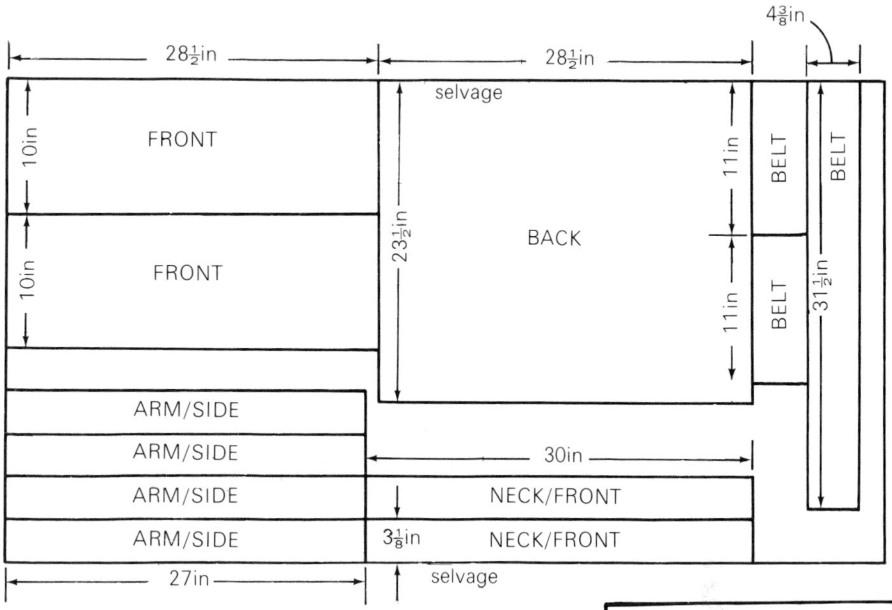

cutting layout 54in-wide fabric

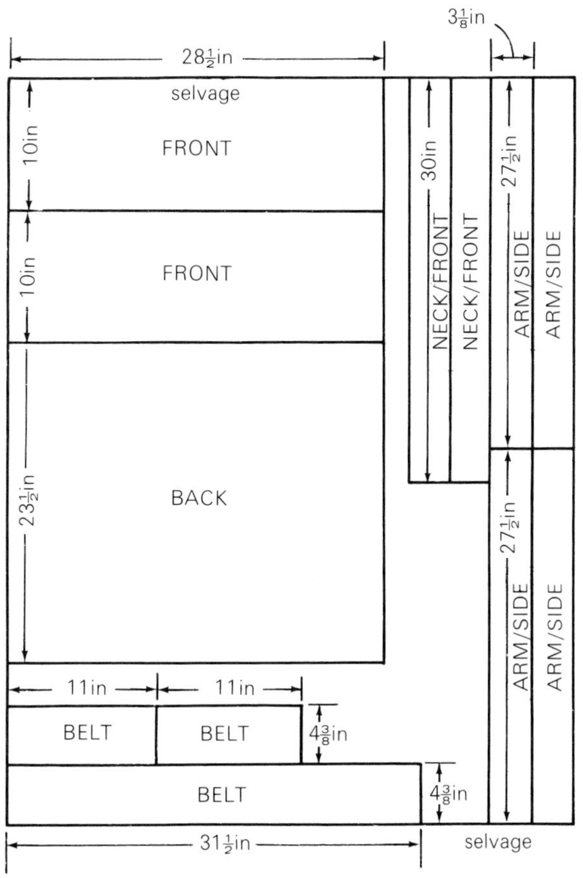

pattern piece diagram

back and 2 front shapes

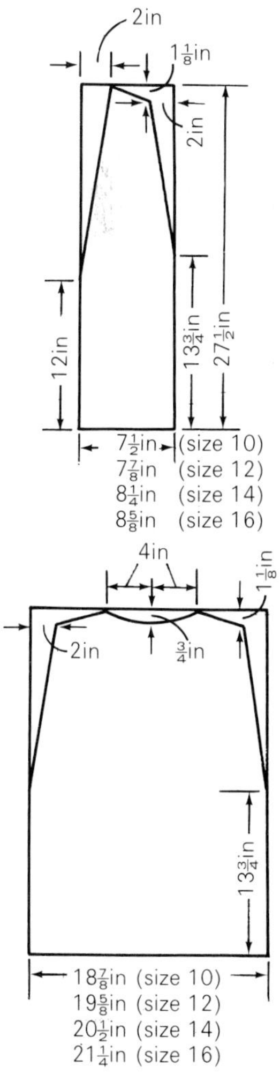

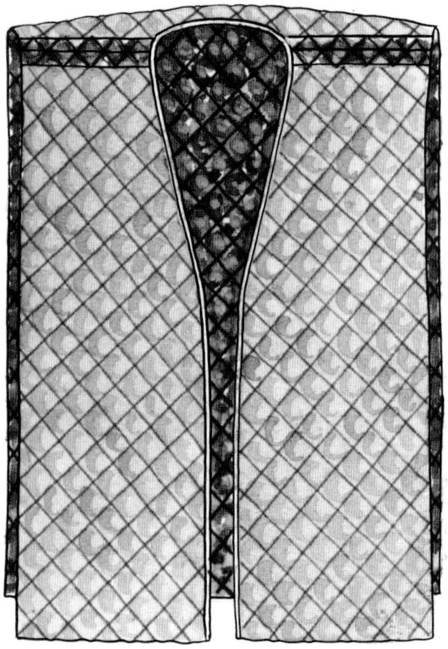

6 Pin, baste and stitch the shoulder seams, raw edges even and right sides together. Press open.

7 Take two of the armhole/side pieces and stitch them together at one short end, right sides together and raw edges even. Repeat for the other two side pieces. Stitch the two neck/front bands in the same way. Press seams open.

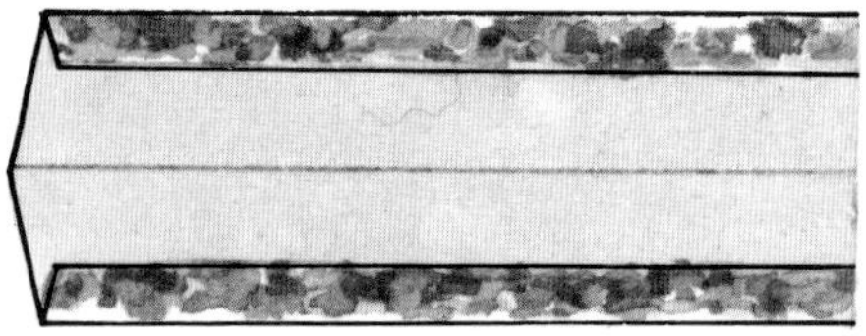

8 Fold each band in half lengthwise, wrong sides together, to form a central crease. Press under the seam allowances on each side of each band.

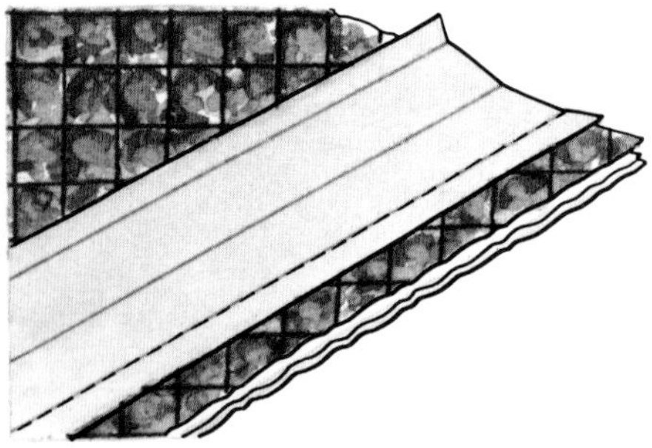

9 Pin and baste the pre-creased front band to the front of the vest, right sides together, positioning the band so that the stitching line is 1in (2.5cm) from the raw edge of the quilted panel. Stitch the neck/front band in place, leaving $\frac{3}{8}$in (1cm) unstitched at each end. Turn to right side and press. Slip stitch free edge to inside backing fabric over the line of machine stitching, leaving $2\frac{3}{4}$in (7cm) unstitched at each end of the strips.

10 Bind the sides of the jacket with the armhole/side bands in the same way.

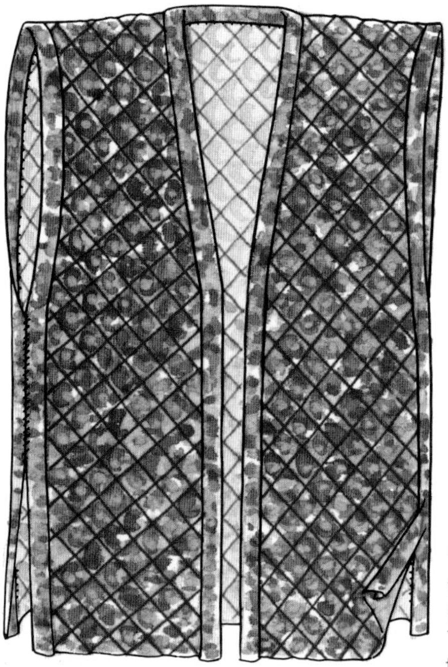

11 Beginning at the shoulder seam, measure 12in (30cm) down the armhole/side bands on the front and back of the vest. Slip stitch the side openings together from this point down for another 4in (10cm).

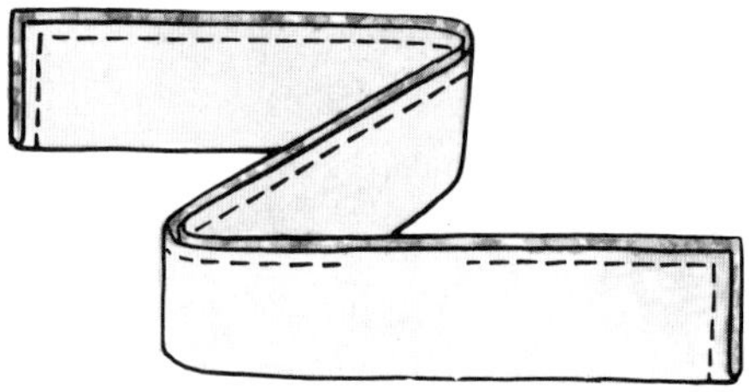

12 Fold one short belt section in half lengthwise, right sides together and raw edges even. Stitch around band, leaving a 4in (10cm) opening in the center of the long edge. Trim corners. Turn band right side out through opening. Press. Slip stitch opening together. Press Repeat for the remaining belt sections.

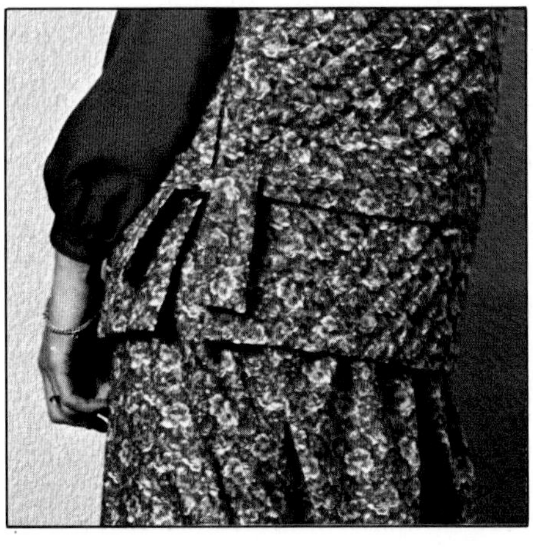

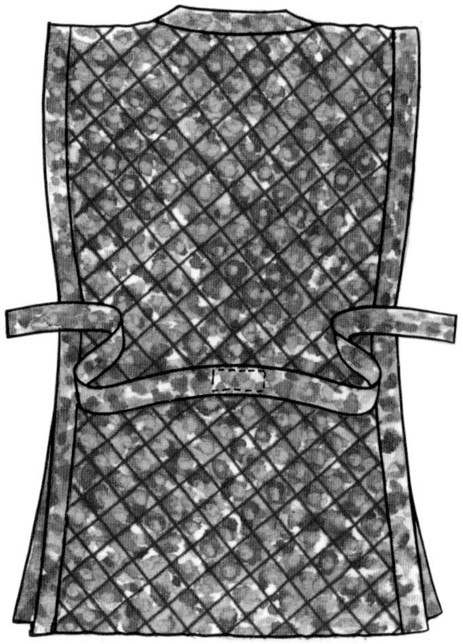

13 Topstitch the longer belt section to the vest at center back as shown, about 6in (16cm) from the lower edge. Topstitch the short belt pieces to the front pieces of the vest 6in (16cm) from lower edges and $4\frac{3}{4}$in (12cm) from the center front edges.

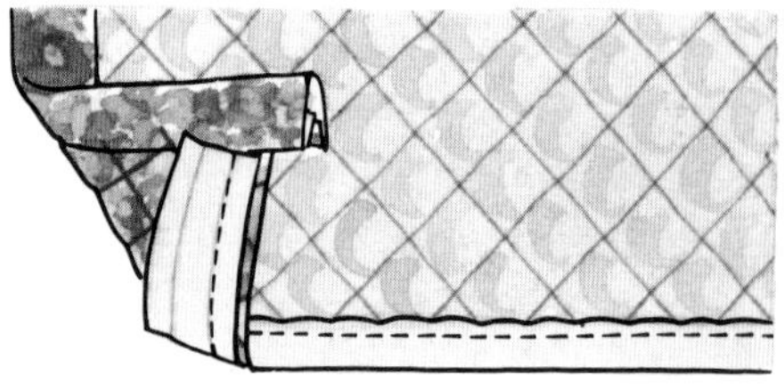

14 Now finish the hem of the vest. Trim away $\frac{3}{8}$in (1cm) of the backing fabric and the batting (you may have to rip out some of the machine quilting stitches at the very edge of the fabric). Pin, baste and stitch the bias binding to the right side of the top layer of quilted fabric, making raw edges even.

15 Turn bias binding to wrong side and press. Hem bias binding to backing fabric along free foldline of binding.

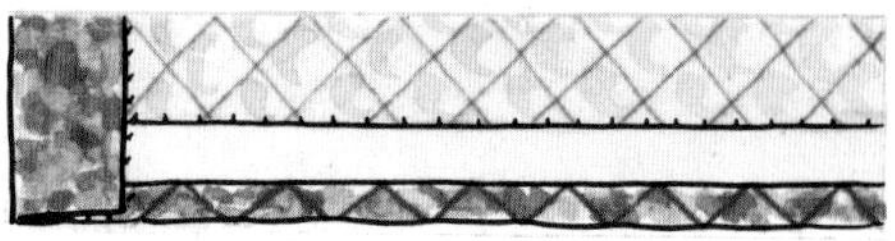

16 Trim binding strips so that only $\frac{5}{8}$in (1.5cm) extends below the lower edge of the vest. Turn under raw edges at the ends of the binding strips. Slip stitch across the lower edges and up the edges of the strips left unstitched in step 9. Press.

Terry Evans

Serge Krouglikoff

Technique tip

Quilting

This is decorative stitching worked through three layers of fabric: a top layer, a backing fabric and a soft filling. The result is both warm and attractive.

The top fabric should be smooth and closely woven. Light- and medium-weight cottons, silk, linen and fine wool are all suitable. The backing fabric should be of similar quality, particularly if it will show when the garment is worn.

There are various weights of polyester batting available for the filling; 2oz- (55gm) weight or 4oz- (110gm) weight are both suitable.

Quilt the fabric before cutting out the pieces and assembling, as a certain amount of width is lost during stitching. It is also much easier to quilt a regular rectangle than a shaped garment piece.

Place the batting on the wrong side of the fabric, then place the backing wrong side down on top of it so that you have a sandwich. Baste the layers together with lines of stitching about 2in (5cm) apart.

The quilting may be done by hand (for small areas) or by machine. You can use regular or irregular designs but a conventional grid of squares or diamonds is the simplest and generally the most effective, particularly on a small-patterned fabric.

Mark guidelines on the right side of the fabric with chalk or basting threads before you start to sew. Work all the lines in one direction and then work in the other direction, crossing all the lines of stitching. It is a good idea to work a test sample first. You may need to adjust the thread tension and reduce the pressure on the presser foot so that the fabric passes under it easily without causing the fullness to pucker in front of the foot.

Your sewing machine may have a quilting attachment. This guide will help you to quilt in straight, evenly spaced lines.

When seaming quilted fabric, first trim away the batting from the seam allowances to prevent unnecessary bulk. To finish quilted fabric, either zig-zag stitch or overcast the two layers of fabric together, keeping the stitching within the seam allowance.

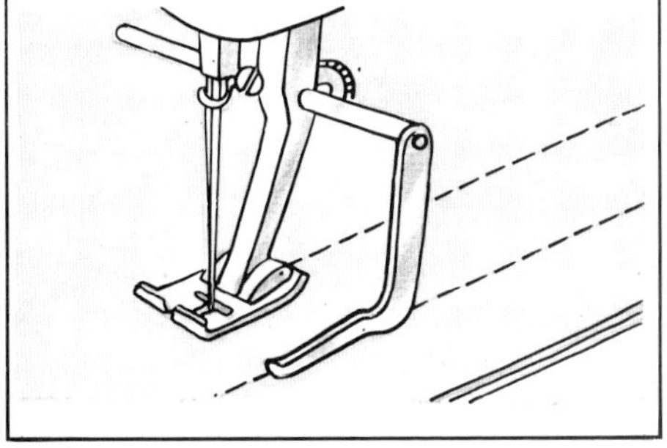

Terry Evans

EXTRA SPECIAL Sewing

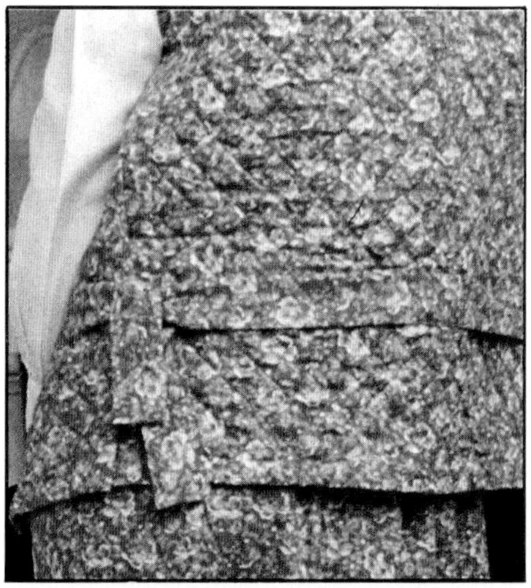

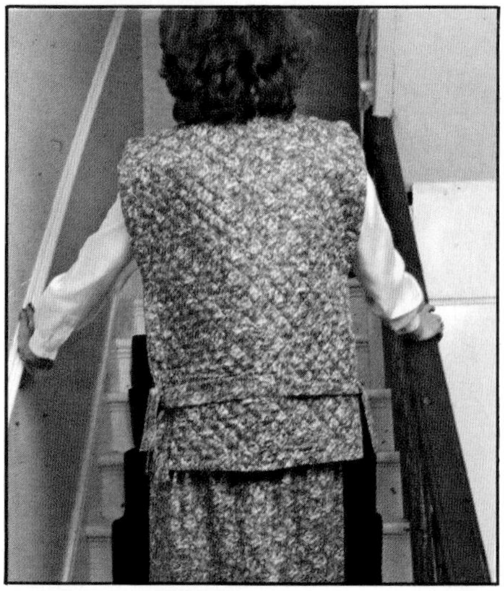

Serge Krouglikoff

Textured twosome (part 2)

This dirndl skirt has a wide, interfaced waistband. It can be worn with its matching vest (shown on page 100) or with any other separates you like, and the beauty of it is that it's always in fashion.

Measurements

To fit sizes 10 to 16, corresponding to sizes 8 to 14 in ready-made clothes. Finished length of skirt 30in (76cm). $\frac{5}{8}$in (1.5cm) seam allowances throughout. Hem allowance is 2in (5cm).

Suggested fabrics

The skirt shown is made in a lightweight cotton, but it could equally well be made from a cotton/polyester mixture or a heavier cotton. A light wool or wool/cotton mixture would also be suitable.

Materials

$2\frac{1}{4}$yd (2m) of either 36in (90cm)-wide or 54in (140cm)-wide fabric
4in (10cm) of 36in (90cm)-wide interfacing
8in (20cm) zipper
Matching thread
4 hooks and eyes
Pencil, yardstick, tailor's chalk

1 Cut out the fabric for the skirt front, back panels and waistband, following the appropriate measurements and the cutting layout overleaf.

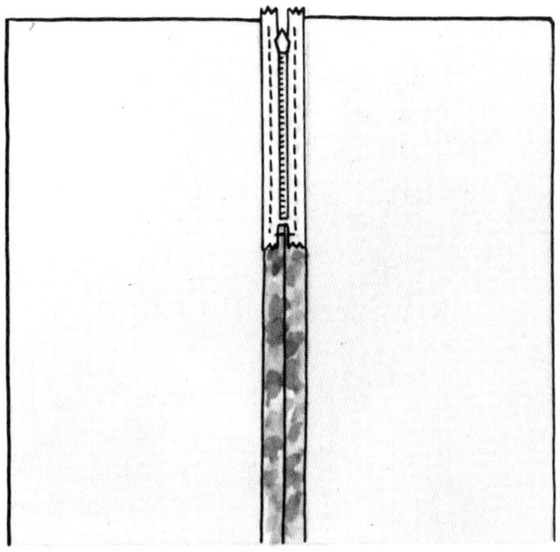

2 Pin, baste and stitch the center back seam, with right sides together and raw edges matching, leaving a 9in (23cm) opening for the zipper.
3 Insert the zipper in the center back seam.
4 Pin, baste and stitch the side seams of the skirt, with right sides together and raw edges matching.
5 Press seams open. Finish raw edges.

Serge Krouglikoff

Cutting layout (all sizes and widths)

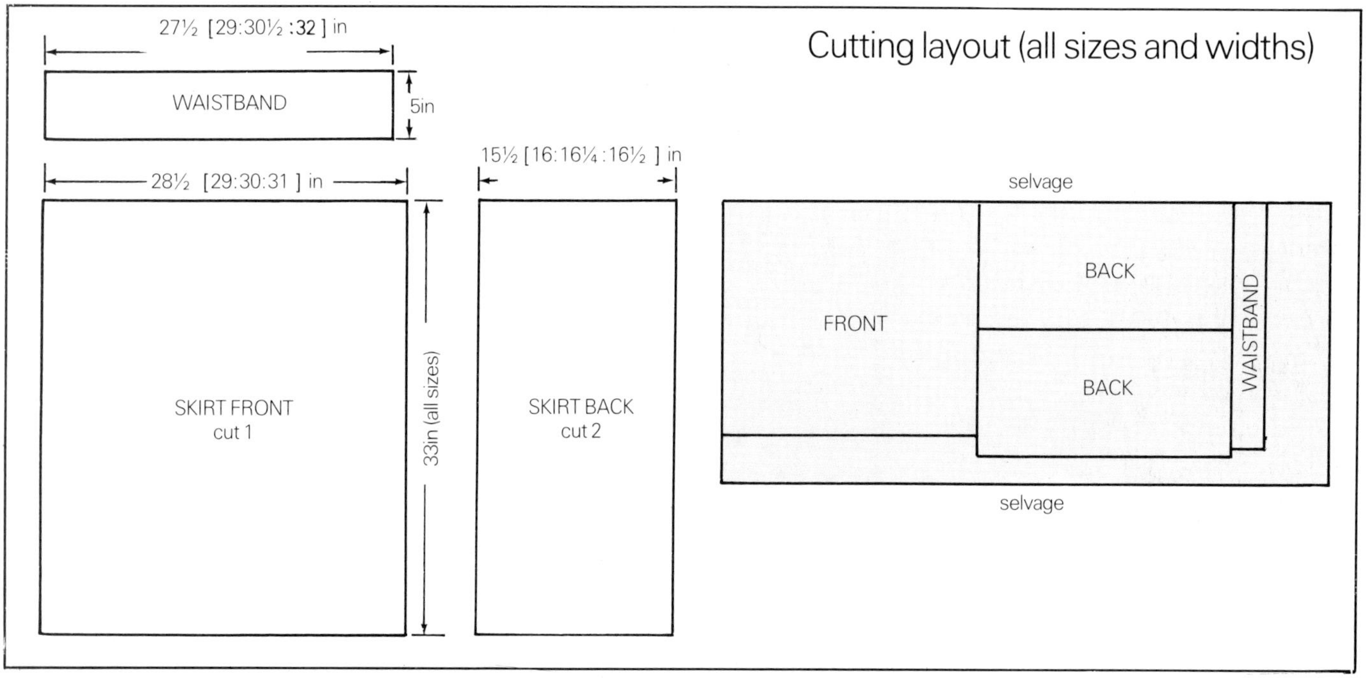

John Hutchinson

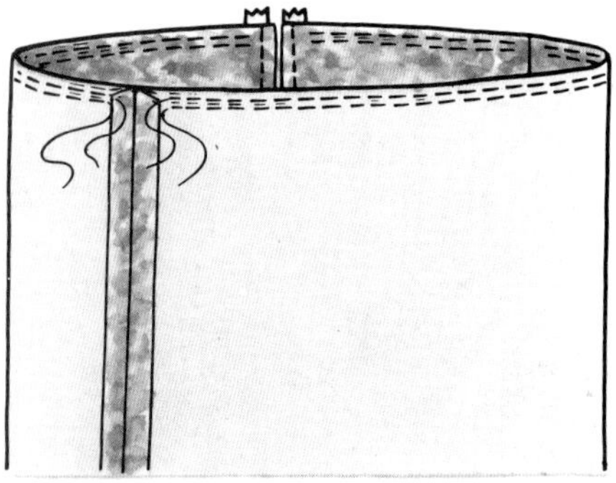

6 Run two lines of gathering stitches around the top of the skirt, one row on each side of the position of the seamline.

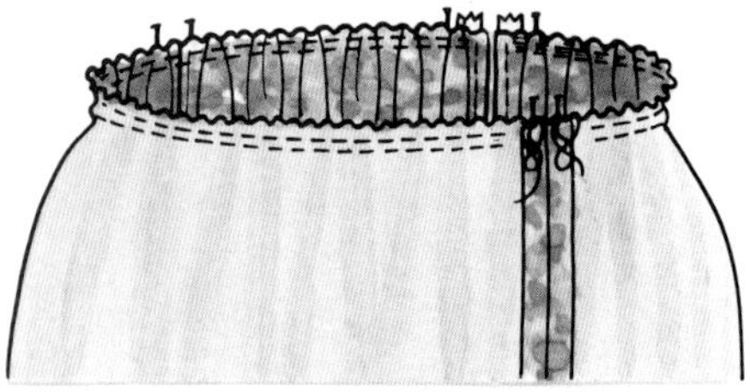

7 Draw up the threads so that the gathered skirt is $2\frac{3}{8}$in (6cm) shorter than the length of the waistband piece. Wind gathering threads around pins to secure them temporarily. Distribute fullness evenly around skirt.

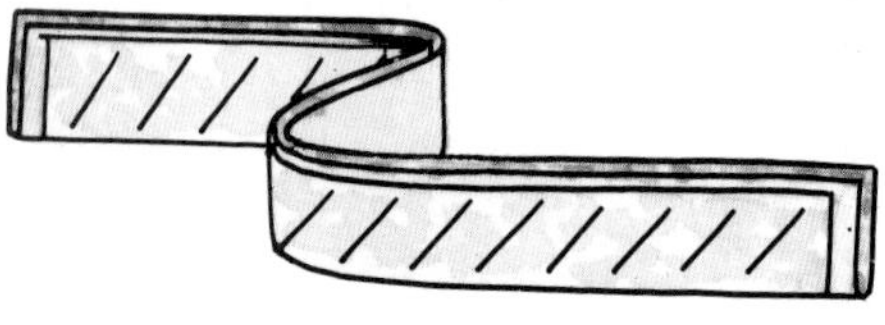

8 Fold the waistband in half lengthwise, right sides together. Press.
9 Cut the interfacing $2\frac{1}{2}$in (6.5cm) wide and 1in (3cm) shorter than the length of the waistband. Baste it to the wrong side of the waistband using diagonal basting stitches and matching one long edge of the interfacing to the center of the waistband.

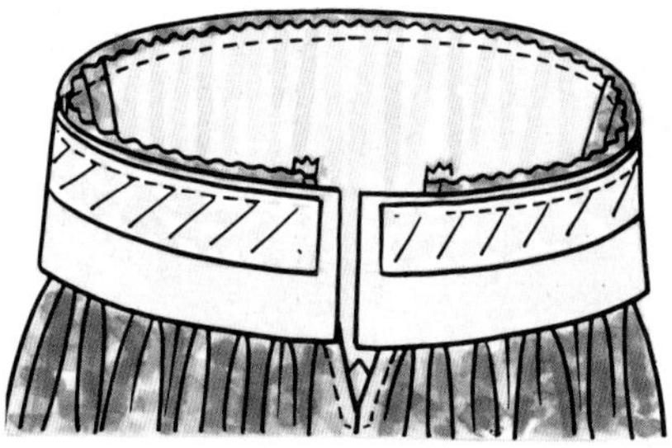

10 Match the raw edge of the interfaced side of the waistband to the raw edge of the top of the skirt, right sides together. Pin in position, leaving a seam allowance of $\frac{5}{8}$in (1.5cm) at the end which will be on the left-hand side of the back and an allowance of $1\frac{3}{4}$in (4.5cm) for the underlap on the right-hand side of the back. Stitch waistband in position. Leave 2in (5cm) unstitched at each end. Trim seam allowance of interfacing. Remove basting holding the interfacing, pins and gathering threads.

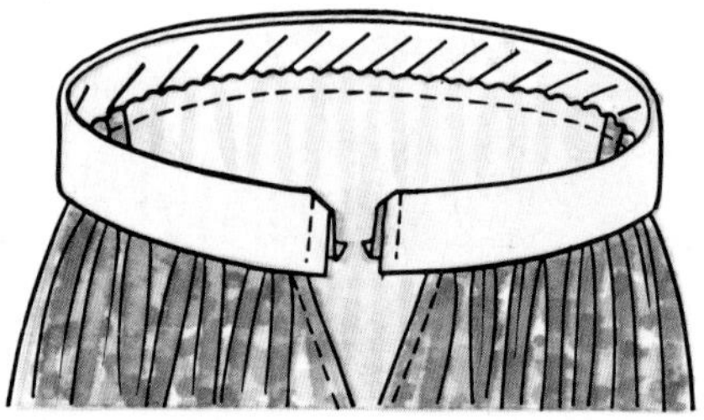

11 Fold waistband back on itself at each end, right sides together, and match raw edges at ends of waistband. Stitch along seamlines at each end. Clip corners. Turn waistband right side out. Press. Press under $\frac{5}{8}$in (1.5cm) along inside of waistband.

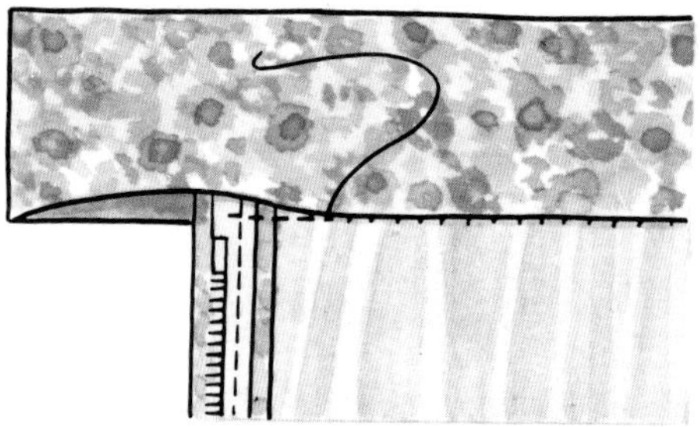

12 Slip stitch unstitched opening on right side of each end of waistband and then slip stitch the underside of the waistband to skirt along the line of machine stitching.

Terry Evans

13 Attach hooks in the positions shown and attach eyes in the corresponding positions at the other end of waistband.
14 Turn under $\frac{1}{4}$in (6mm) along the lower edge of the skirt, then pin up $1\frac{3}{4}$in (4.5cm) for the hem. Try on the skirt for fit and check length. Hem the skirt by hand.

Tony Boase

EXTRA SPECIAL SEWING

Layers of lace

This two-piece evening outfit is perfect for special occasions. It is made of wide lace ruffles, with a simple bodice.

Measurements

To fit sizes 10 to 14. Finished length of skirt 34in (87cm).

Note Measurements are given for size 10. Figures for larger sizes are given in brackets [ ]. If only one figure is given, it applies to all sizes.

To lengthen or shorten dress, add or subtract an equal amount to or from each ruffle to keep correct proportions.

Suggested fabrics

For luxury, cotton lace with silk lining. For economy, synthetic lace and lining.

Materials

Lace: 4yd (3.6m) of 36in (90cm)-wide fabric or $2\frac{7}{8}$yd (2.6m) of 60in (150cm)-wide fabric

Lining: 3yd (2.7m) of 36in (90cm)-wide fabric or $1\frac{5}{8}$yd (1.4m) of 54-60in (140-150cm)-wide fabric

10yd (9m) of $\frac{1}{2}$in (1.2cm)-wide lace edging

$3\frac{1}{4}$yd (3m) of $\frac{1}{2}$in (1.2cm)-wide ribbon for belt

$1\frac{1}{8}$yd (1m) ribbon for shoulder straps

$\frac{5}{8}$yd (.5m) $\frac{1}{4}$in (5mm)-wide elastic

Two snaps, hook and eye

$1\frac{3}{8}$yd (1.2m) matching bias binding

Yardstick, tailor's chalk

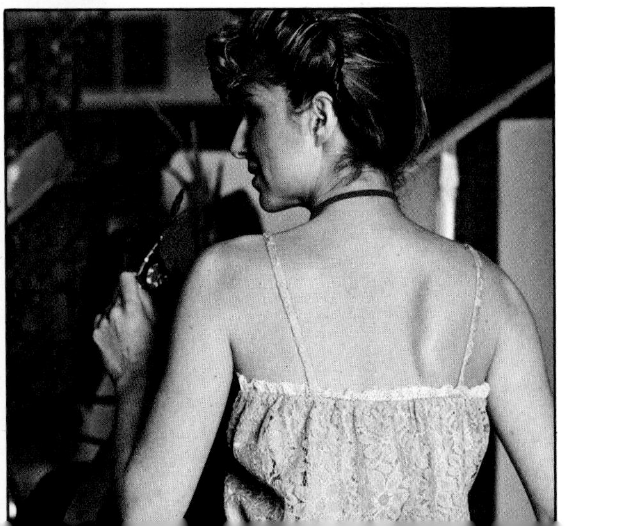

Cutting out

Mark the pattern pieces on the fabric, using tailor's chalk and a yardstick, following the measurement diagram on the right and the cutting layout overleaf. Cut two bodice pieces and nine ruffle pieces from the lace fabric.
Cut two bodice pieces, two skirt pieces and a placket from the lining fabric.
Mark the waistlines and the positions for the ruffles as indicated in the measurement diagrams.

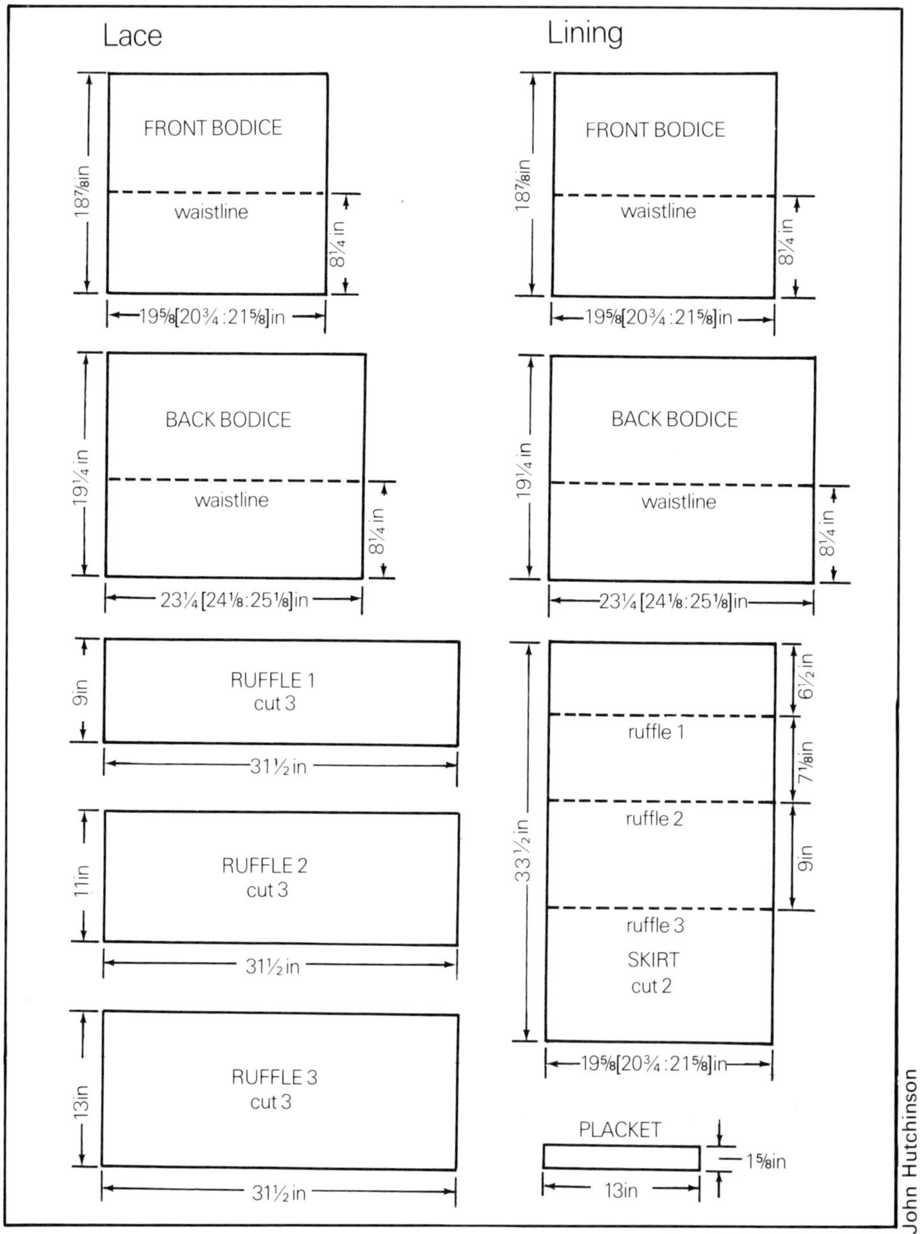

John Hutchinson

Skirt

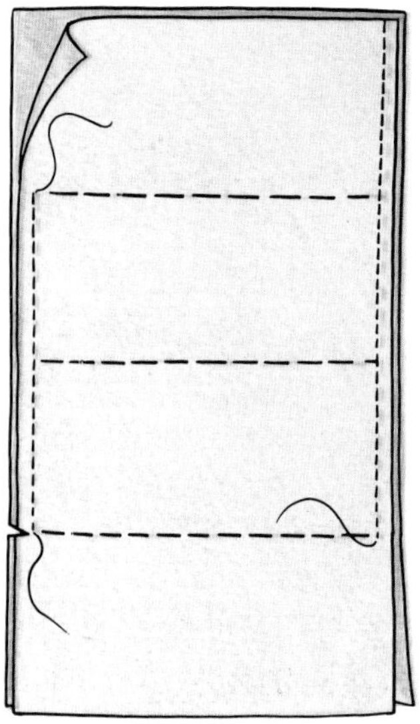

1 Pin and baste the side seams of the skirt lining with right sides together and raw edges even: on the right-hand side, sew as far as the line marked for ruffle 3 and on the left-hand side sew from the line marked for ruffle 1 to the line marked for ruffle 3. Clip into seams at openings and press seams open.

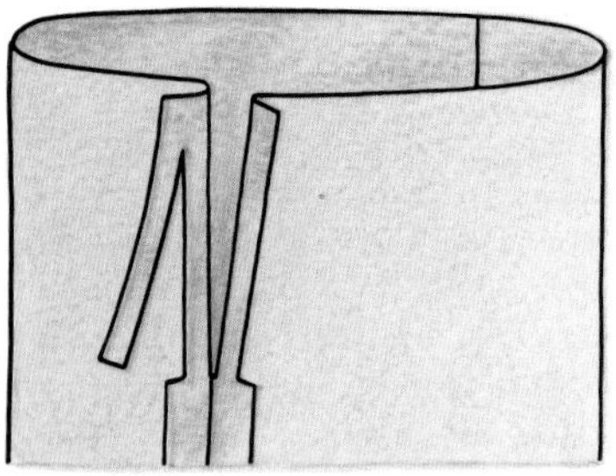

2 Trim the seam allowances to $\frac{1}{4}$in (6mm) on each side of waist opening.

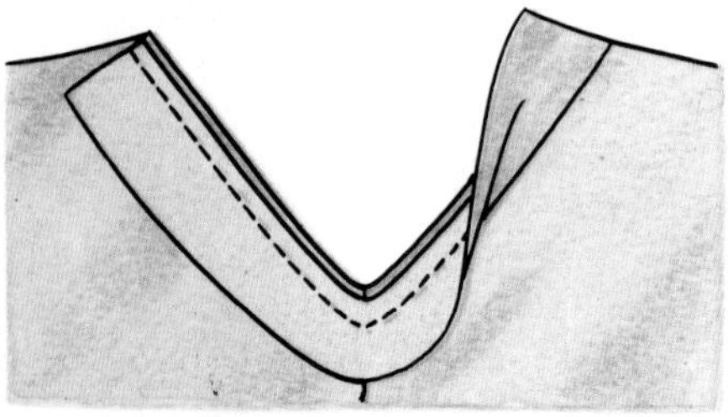

3 Spread opening at waist. Pin, baste and sew placket as shown above.

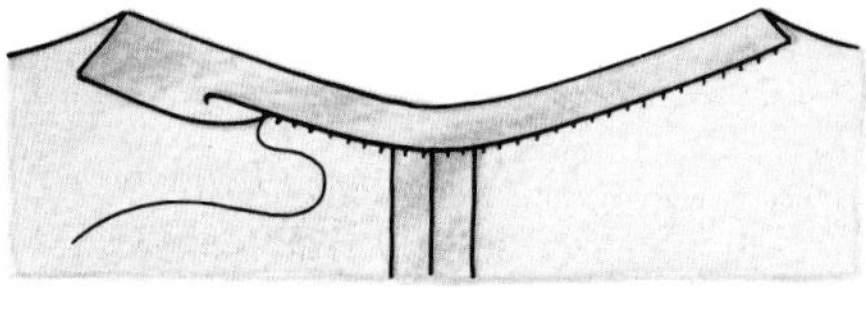

4 Turn under and press $\frac{1}{4}$in (6mm) on free edge of placket. Press up, fold over and turn to wrong side. Slip stitch in place.

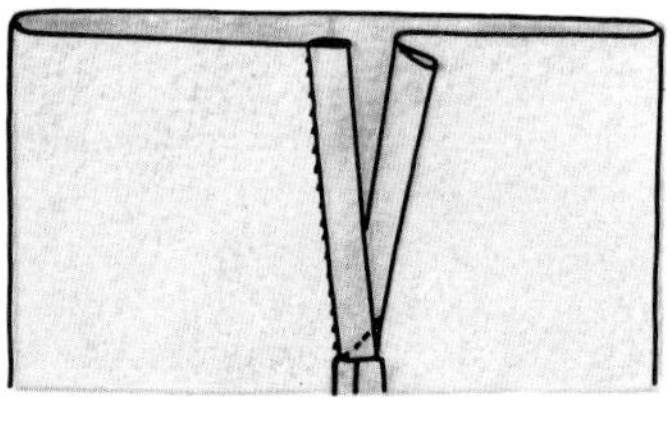

5 Fold the front half of the placket over the back half so that the front is on the outside of the skirt and the back is on the inside. Sew diagonally across the bottom corner of the placket.

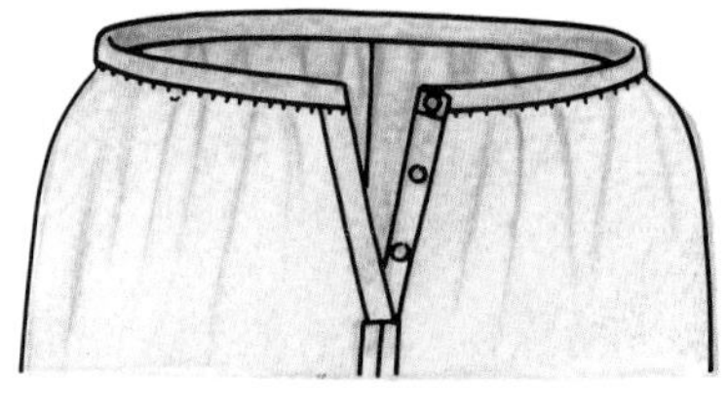

6 Run two lines of gathering around top of skirt, within seam allowance. Draw up gathers to fit waist and fasten ends. Cut a piece of bias binding to fit waistline, adding $\frac{1}{4}$in (6mm) for finishing ends. Pin, baste and sew binding in place around waist, distributing gathers evenly, right sides together and raw edges even. Fold binding to wrong side of lining and slip stitch in place. Sew snaps to fasten placket, and sew a hook and eye to the top of the opening.
7 Finish edges of side openings at hem and slip stitch them in place. Turn up and sew a 2in (5cm) hem.

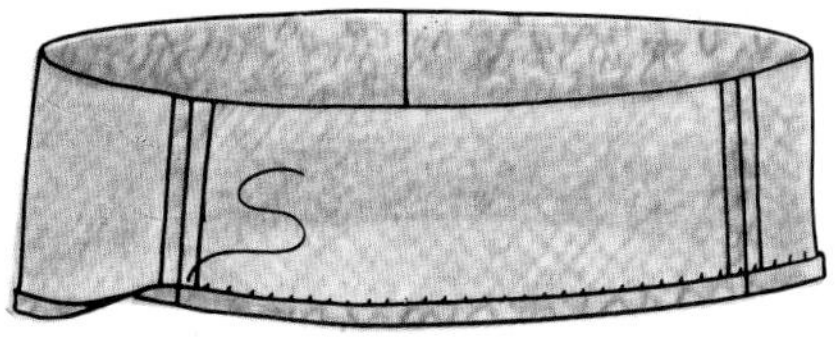

8 For ruffles, join short edges of the three pieces of lace, right sides together and raw edges even. Make sure lace is the right way up. Turn up and machine stitch $\frac{1}{4}$in (6mm) hems around lower edge of each ruffle. Turn up another $\frac{3}{8}$in (1cm) and hem by hand.

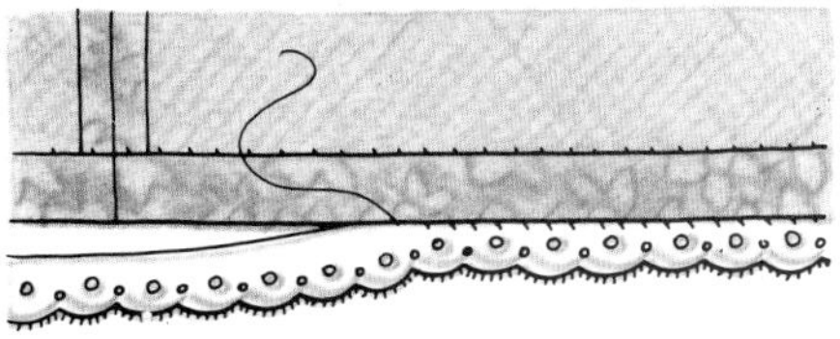

9 Cut lace edging to fit around each ruffle $2\frac{5}{8}$yd (2.4m) plus $1\frac{1}{4}$in (3cm) allowance for finishing seams.
Slip stitch to lower edge of ruffles as shown. Turn under and finish ends.
10 Finish Upper edge of each ruffle with machine zig-zag or hand overcasting.

Cutting layout: lace–60in-wide fabric

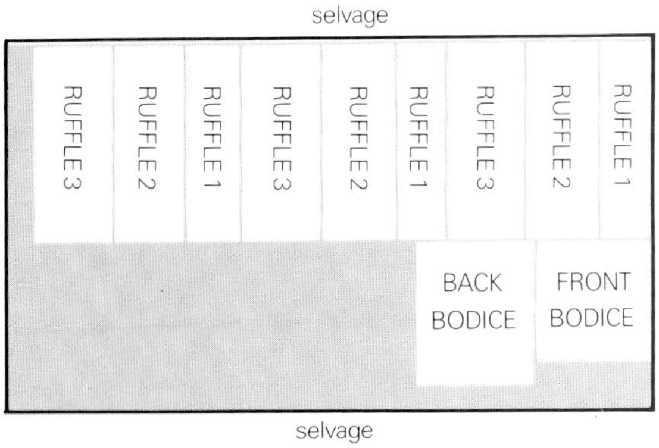

Cutting layout: lace–36in-wide fabric

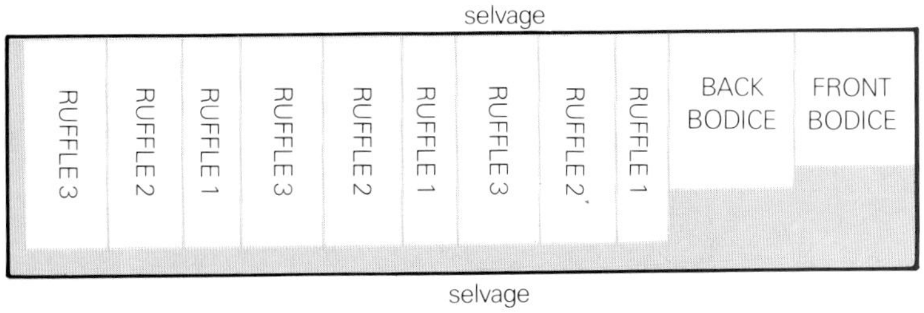

Cutting layout: lining–54in-wide fabric

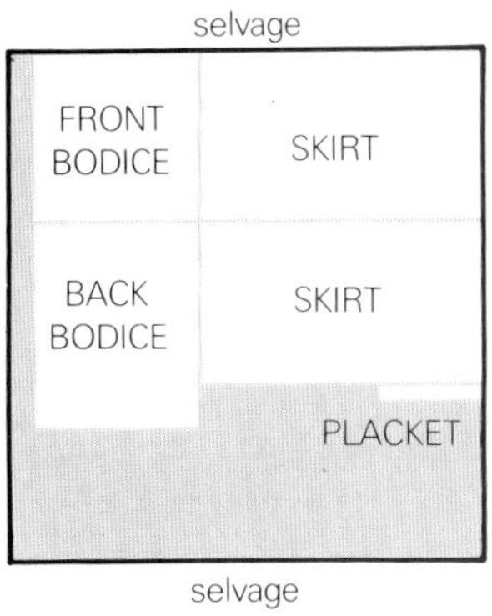

Cutting layout: lining–36in-wide fabric

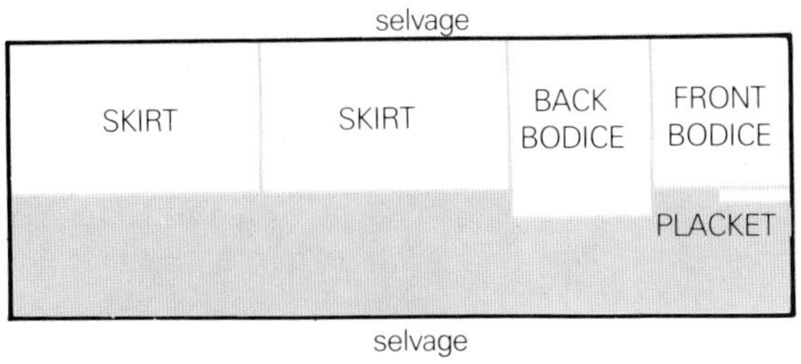

John Hutchinson

Run two lines of gathering along the upper edge of each ruffle within the seam allowance. Draw up threads to fit around the skirt and fasten.

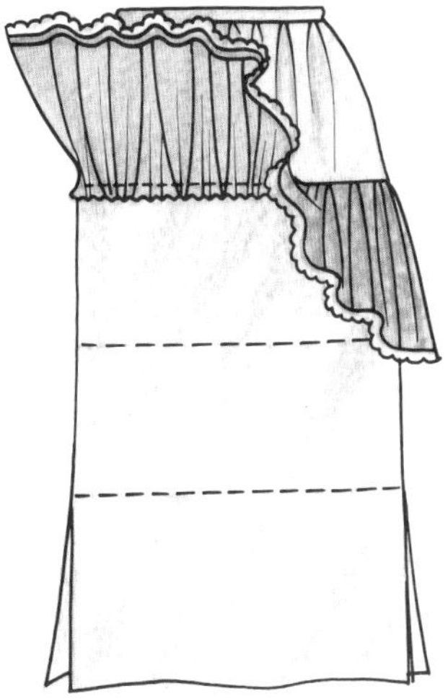

11 With skirt lining right side out and ruffle wrong side out, slip ruffle 1 over lining. Pin, baste and sew in place along marked line on lining and $\frac{5}{8}$in (1.5cm) from upper edge of ruffle. Repeat for second and third ruffles.

Bodice

1 Baste lining pieces to bodice pieces, wrong sides together. Treat as one piece.
2 With right sides together, sew side seams of bodice, matching lower edges so that upper edge of back extends $\frac{3}{8}$in (1cm) above upper edge of front. Turn up and sew $\frac{1}{4}$in (6mm) hems on upper front and lower edges. Turn under another $\frac{3}{8}$in (1cm) and sew by hand.
3 At the upper back edge, turn under and sew $\frac{1}{4}$in (6mm), then make a $\frac{3}{8}$in (1cm) double hem and slip stitch in place to form a casing, leaving ends open.
4 Cut pieces of lace edging to fit around bodice at upper and lower edges, allowing extra for finishing the ends. Slip stitch in place.
5 Thread elastic through casing in the back of the bodice and draw up to fit. Sew ends of elastic firmly into the ends of the casing to anchor it.

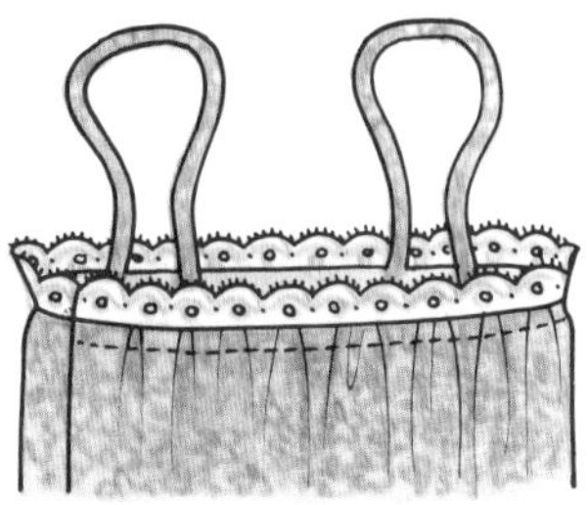

6 Cut two $\frac{5}{8}$yd (.5m) pieces of ribbon for shoulder straps or make tubing straps. Pin in place, try on for fit and adjust. Sew inside dress top.
7 Use the remaining ribbon for a sash.

Homemaker

Curtains, café style

No wonder café curtains are so popular—their cheerful informality gives a room a welcoming aspect—and at a modest cost, too. Here we give you detailed instructions for making café curtains with a scalloped heading, plus tips on making other variations on the café curtain theme.

Café curtains are a good way of hiding an ugly view or obtaining more privacy while still letting in the light, as they usually cover only the bottom half of a window. You can vary the basic style of café curtains in an amazing number of ways. For example, you can make two-tier café curtains and open the upper tier during the day and close it at night. You can add a shallow tier at the upper edge of the window. You can use café curtains along with full-length curtains, with a window shade, or with shutters or with a combination of shades and ordinary curtains or draperies. You can also make the curtains with various kinds of headings: a simple casing, a pinch-pleated heading, a scalloped heading or scallops combined with pleats. Fabric loops make a very stylish heading for café curtains.
Café curtains can be made in most fabrics, though because of their informal style, very formal fabrics are not normally used. Heavier fabrics can be lined with thin cotton if you wish. Café curtains made in sheer fabrics can be particularly charming, as demonstrated by the photograph on page 113.

Measuring for café curtains

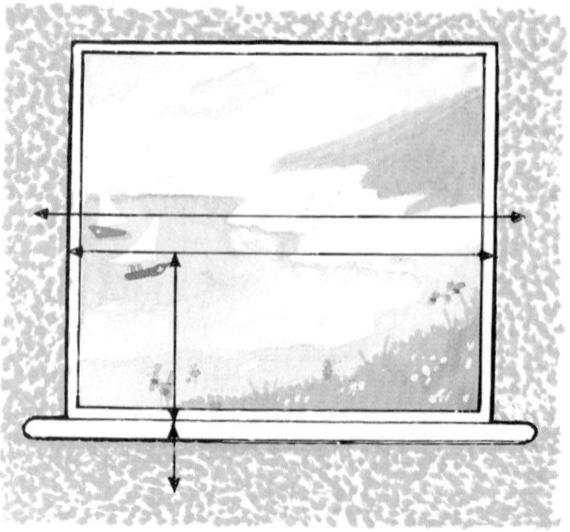

1 First decide on the position of the rod or pole. This can be inside or outside the window recess, and is usually positioned halfway down the frame, although this position can obviously be varied to suit different types of window. To make the window appear larger fix the pole so that the finials are outside the window frame.
2 Decide on the finished pole width, not including finials (decorative ends), that the curtains will cover.
3 Measure the curtain drop—the length from the pole to the finished hem. The hemline may be at sill level, just below the sill or even floor level, if you have full length windows.

Estimating fabric

1 The type of heading you choose will dictate the width of fabric you need for the curtains and the resulting amount of fullness. If you are using heading tape, follow the manufacturer's fabric allowance guide. Shaped headings will need between 2 and $2\frac{1}{2}$ times the rod length, depending on the fabric used. The more delicate the fabric, the more fullness will be required. The instructions below for making curtains with a scalloped heading explain how to estimate fabric for that type of heading.
2 To the finished width add 2in (5cm) for each side hem. Divide this total by the width of your chosen fabric to find the number of fabric widths you will need. If you are using heading tape you may need to trim away some of the width. If not, you may be able to reduce or increase the fullness slightly to use whole widths.
3 Now calculate the length. Add 4in (10cm) to the curtain drop for the bottom hem. The top heading may need between 4in (10cm) and 8in (20cm), depending on whether you use a tape or a shaped heading. If you do use a shaped heading, draw a template first (see page 111) and measure the finished heading depth; then add 2in (5cm) to this measurement to obtain the top heading allowance. The finished length of the curtain, plus the hem and heading allowance, is the cutting length.
4 Calculate how much fabric is needed by multiplying the cutting length of the curtain by the number of widths of fabric. Allow extra fabric to match a large pattern—the salesperson can help you to calculate this.

Making scalloped, hand-pleated café curtains

Made in crisp cotton, these curtains have a scalloped and hand-pleated heading and are hung from the rod on rings. We give instructions for making a pair of curtains, but you can easily make a single panel instead. This type of curtain would also look very pretty in a lacy or a gingham fabric.

1 First plan the size of the scallops. These curtains have 4in (10cm)-wide scallops placed $6\frac{1}{4}$in (16cm) apart. The $6\frac{1}{4}$in (16cm) margin measures only 2in (5cm) when pleated. These measurements may be adjusted if necessary, but do not make the scallops too wide or they will lose their shape when the curtain is pleated. Calculate how many pleats and scallops you will fit across each curtain width and allow 4in (10cm) of fabric per scallop, plus $6\frac{1}{4}$in (16cm) for the pleated sections, plus 2in (5cm) hems at each side. You must have one more pleated section than scallops so there are pleats at both ends.

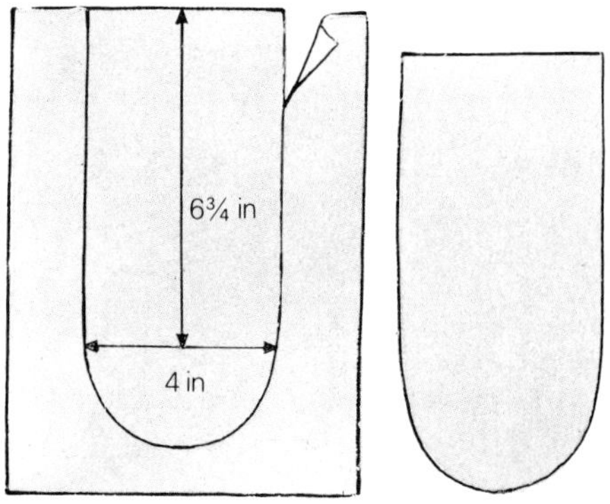

2 Now make a template for the scallops. On thin cardboard draw a circle with a 4in (10cm) diameter. Draw a line horizontally across the diameter and draw lines vertically upward from each end of this line to a depth of $6\frac{3}{4}$in (17cm). Join the two lines at the top, and cut out.

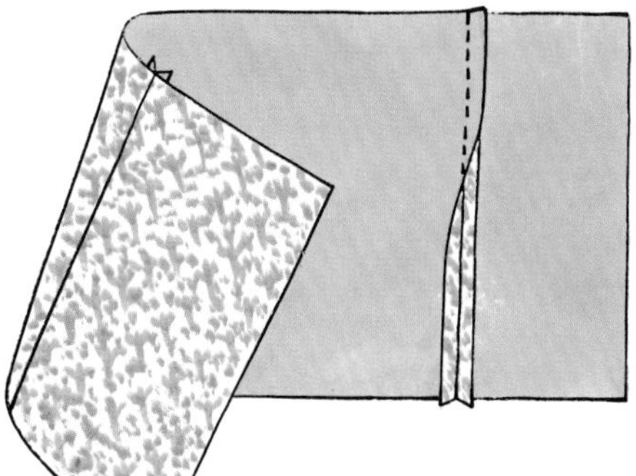

Terry Evans

Gary Warren

3 Join the widths of fabric, matching the pattern if necessary, and finish the seams. Press open.

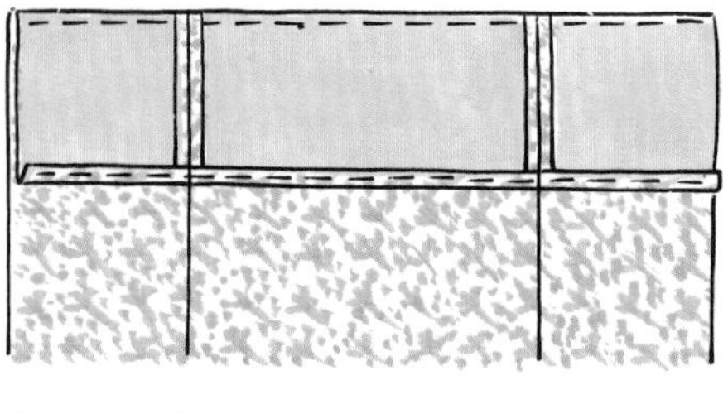

4 Press a $\frac{3}{8}$in (1cm) hem to the wrong side at the top edge of the curtain. Fold the top edge to the right side to a depth of 8in (20cm). Baste along the top and bottom edges of the hem.

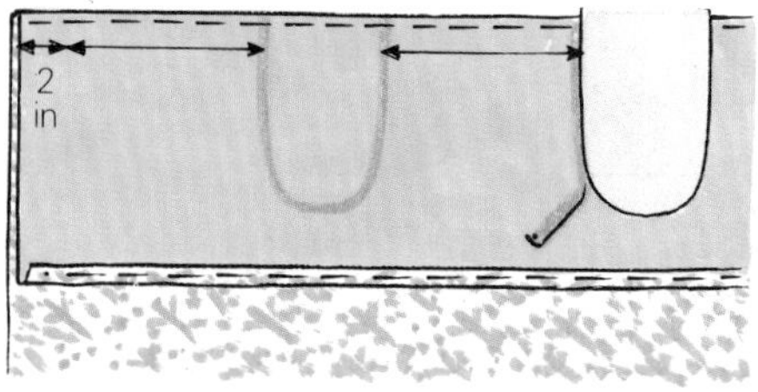

5 Starting at the left-hand edge of the curtain, allow 2in (5cm) for a side hem, and then mark the top fold $6\frac{1}{4}$in (16cm) in from that point. This is the allowance for the first pleated section. Lay the template on the fabric, matching the top edge of the cardboard to the top fold and the side edge to the $6\frac{1}{4}$in (16cm) mark. Draw around the template with tailor's chalk or soft pencil. Mark off the next $6\frac{1}{4}$in (16cm) pleat allowance and draw in the next scallop. Continue in this way across the whole width of each curtain.

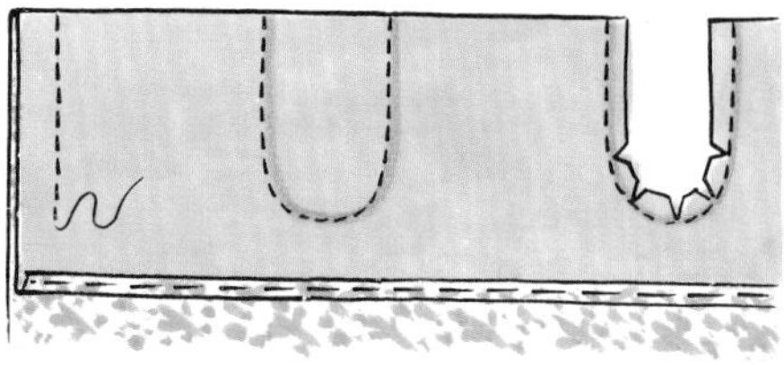

6 Stitch down the side edges of the curtain heading almost to the bottom fold of the heading, 2in (5cm) from the side edge. Stitch around each scallop on the marked line. Trim the scallop seam allowances and clip into the curves. Trim away the side seam allowance $\frac{1}{4}$in (6mm) from the stitching to eliminate unnecessary bulk.

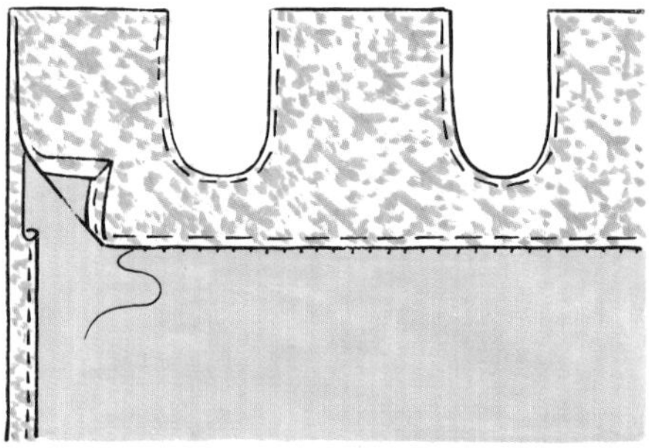

7 Turn the scallops right side out and baste around each scallop close to the edge. Turn under a double 1in (2.5cm)-wide hem down both sides of the curtain. The tops of both hems will be enclosed by the top heading. Catch-stitch the heading to the hem on each side.

Gary Warren

Kirsch Company

8 Mark the finished curtain length by measuring from the top of the pleat allowances down the curtain. Turn up and stitch a 1in (2.5cm) double hem.

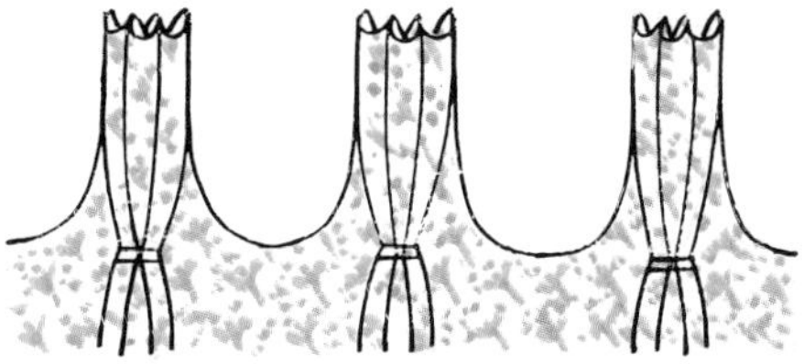

9 Fold the pleat allowance between each scallop into three equal pleats and sew the three folds together on the right side, $4\frac{1}{4}$in (11cm) down from the top edge.

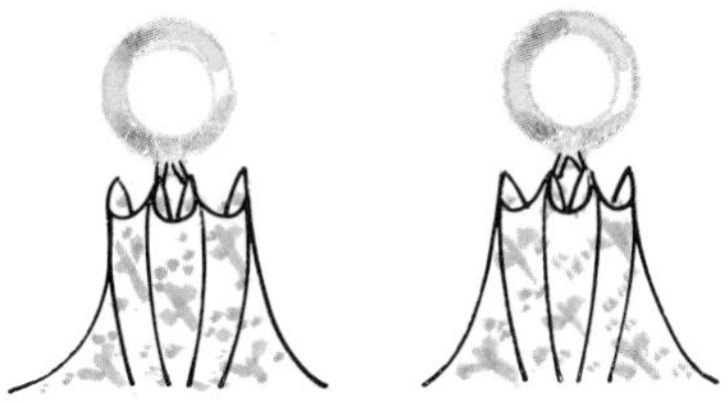

10 Attach a ring to the center pleat in each group. Slip the rings onto the curtain rod, positioning the end ring on each side between the finial and the bracket supporting the rod, to provide some anchorage for the curtains.

On the left: following the same method, curtains can be made up in totally different fabrics to suit any setting. Here we show bright curtains in a workroom and more delicate, printed curtains for a breakfast room.
Top: for a completely different effect, café curtains may be combined with full-length curtains and shades.

Different café curtain headings

Curtains attached to the pole with fabric loops

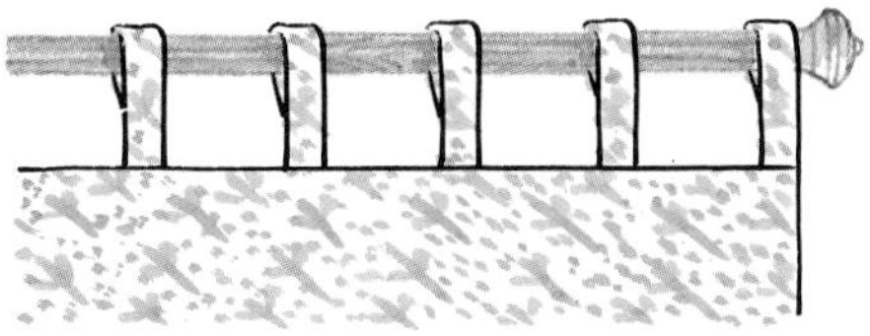

Flat loops are made separately and attached to the top of the curtain. You can use either matching or contrasting fabric.

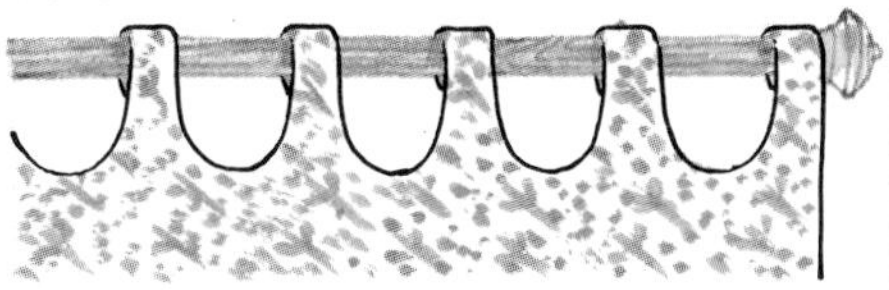

Fabric loops and shaped headings are cut in one with the main curtain and are faced on the wrong side. The loops are sewn in place as shown.

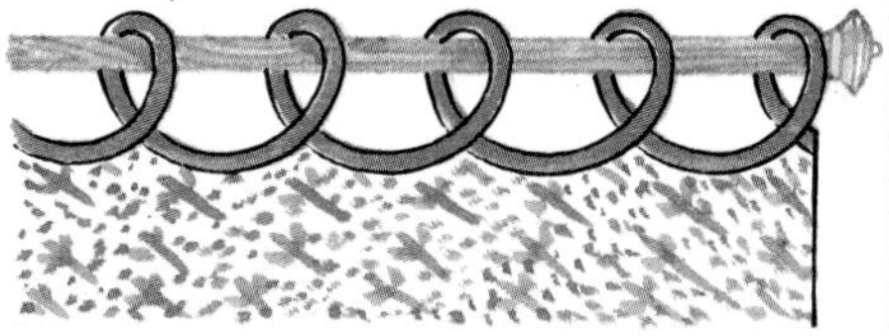

Narrow loops can be made from a bias-cut strip of fabric which can be continued along the top curtain edge as a binding.

Curtains attached with rings

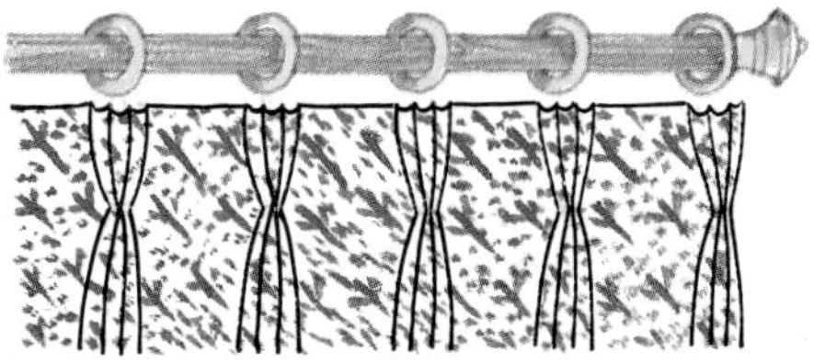

Curtains pleated with heading tape are usually attached to the rings with hooks. There are several kinds of tapes and hooks available. Alternatively, the rings can be stitched to the center pleat in each of the groups.

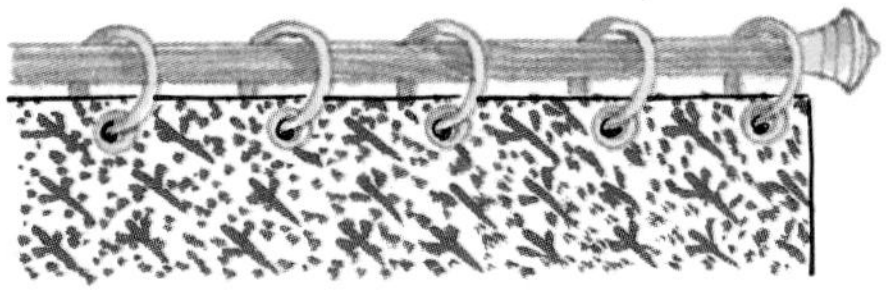

Terry Evans

Split rings can be attached to the curtain through eyelets in the top of the curtain. To make the eyelets, you will need a special type of punch.

Homemaker

Continental comfort

Enjoy the luxurious, lightweight warmth of a Continental quilt, and save lots of money by making it yourself. It's easier than you think. And speaking of ease—even the kids won't mind making their beds when it's just a matter of smoothing out a quilt.

Materials
$4\frac{7}{8}$yd (4.4m) of 56in (142cm)-wide downproof cambric
$2\frac{1}{2}$lbs (1.125kilos) of down and feather mixture
$9\frac{3}{4}$yd (8.8m) of 2in (5cm)-wide white cotton tape, cut into 4×87in (220cm) lengths
Matching thread; tailor's chalk

Note The measurements here are for a 53×86in (135×218cm) quilt for a twin bed. To make a double-size quilt, measuring 79×86in (200×218cm), you will need: $9\frac{3}{4}$yd (8.8m) of 56in (142cm)-wide downproof cambric; 4lbs (1.8 kilos) of down and feather mixture; 17yd (15.4m) of 2in (5cm)-wide white cotton tape; matching thread.

Kim Sayer

Cut one length of fabric, 4yds 29in (440cm) long. From the remaining fabric cut a piece 4yds 29in by $27\frac{1}{2}$in (440 by 70cm). Sew second piece to first, down length, with a flat seam. Follow instructions below, adjusting the number and widths of channels.

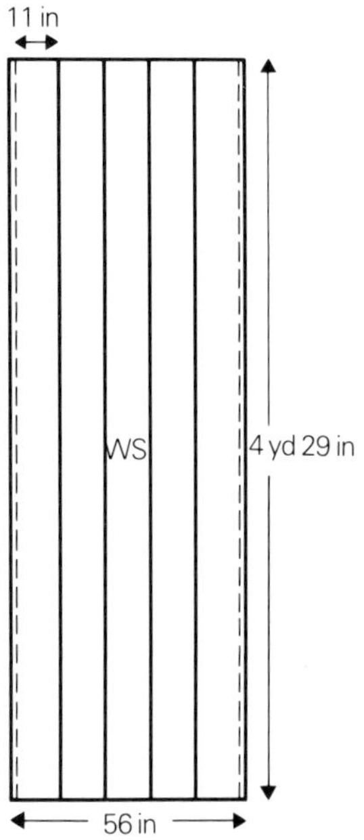

1 On the wrong side of the fabric, mark a $\frac{3}{8}$in (1cm) seam allowance down each long side. At one end, make four marks across the fabric width, at 11in (28cm) intervals. Repeat halfway down the fabric and at the opposite end. Join the marks to form four parallel lines running the length of the fabric.

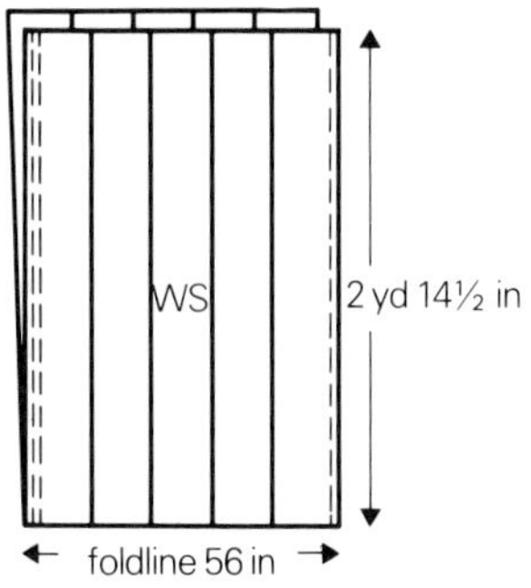

Brian Mayor

2 Fold the fabric in half widthwise, right sides together. Sew one side with two rows of stitching, placed close together, $\frac{3}{8}$in (1cm) from edges. This double row of stitching will prevent the filling from escaping.

3 Turn the bag right side out. Place the bag with the opening toward you and join the two layers to make channels as described below, working from the stitched edge toward the open edge.

Kim Sayer

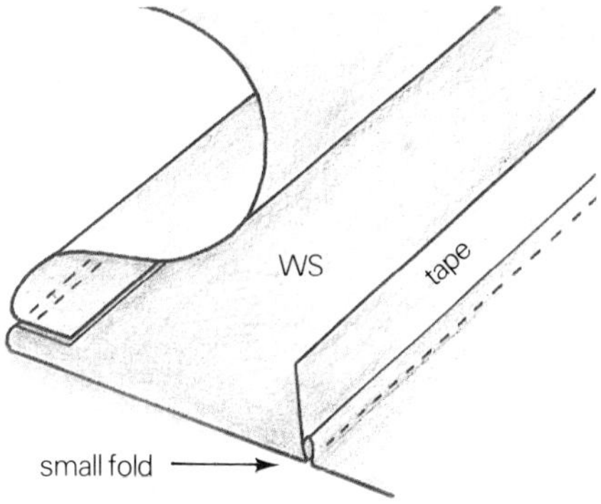

4 At the first line on the bottom layer, pick up a small fold of fabric on the wrong side (inside). Take a piece of tape and pin one long edge of the tape behind this fold. Continue pinning the tape to the fabric in the same way along the first line to the bottom of the quilt. Stitch along the length, $\frac{1}{4}$in (6mm) in from the tape edge close to the folded edge of fabric. This will form a narrow pleat in the bag.

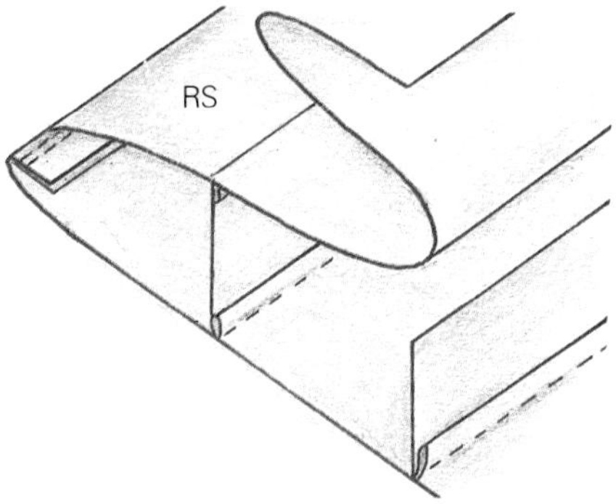

5 Make a similar fold on the marked line on the upper layer. Pin the free edge of the tape behind this fold, lapping the edge of the tape over the fold in the fabric. Stitch in place, stitching as far into the fold at the bottom as possible. The first channel is now completed.

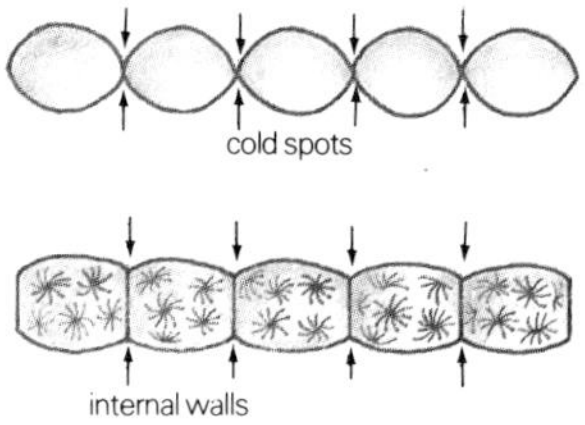

6 Continue in this way across the fabric width, joining each pair of marked lines with a length of tape until the first four channels have been formed. The reason for joining the layers with tape, instead of simply stitching them together, is to prevent cold areas along the seams.

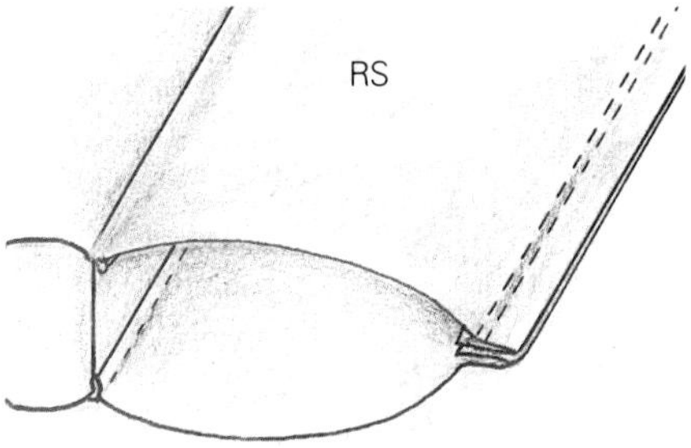

Chris Legee

7 Turn in $\frac{3}{8}$in (1cm) along the two remaining outside edges and stitch together with two rows of stitching.

8 Hang the quilt, with the openings upward, on a clothesline.

10 Working from one side to the other, push a handful of filling into the first channel, shake it down and close the opening with a clothespin. Repeat this for the next channel and so on across the quilt. Return to the first channel and insert another handful. Continue this process until you have filled each channel evenly.

11 Remove the quilt from the line. Turn under $\frac{3}{8}$in (1cm) along the upper edges and join the folded edges with two rows of stitching, placed close together.

Note: Instructions for making a patchwork cover for a Continental quilt are given in Volume 1, pages 120-122.

Homemaker

Three's a crowd . . .

But our penguins will make very pleasant company for someone! If they are for a small child do not use sequins for eyes, and stitch, rather than glue, the features in place.

Gary Warren

Materials

Large penguin:

3oz (60g) of a black sport yarn
2oz (40g) of a white sport yarn
1 spool each of yellow and orange sewing thread
Scrap of black felt 4 x 8in (10 x 20 cm)
Orange felt 4in (10cm) square
Small piece of white felt for eyes
9oz (250g) of white synthetic stuffing
2 sequins or two small circles of felt for eyes
One pair No. 6 (4½mm) knitting needles

Small Penguin:

1oz (20g) of a black sport yarn
1oz (20g) of a white sport yarn
Scrap of orange felt 4 x 8in (10 x 20 cm)
2 sequins or two small circles of felt for eyes
4oz (100g) of white synthetic stuffing
One pair No. 2 (3mm) knitting needles

Chick:

One ball of gray fluffy or variegated sport yarn
Small amount of charcoal gray sport yarn
Small scraps of pink and white and yellow felt
2 sequins or 2 circles of white felt
2oz (50g) of white synthetic stuffing
One pair size No. 2 (3mm) needles

For finishing:

Tracing paper, pencil
Matching thread
Fabric glue (optional)

The large and small penguin are knitted from the same directions. Use the yarn double for the large penguin and single for the small penguin. The shading on the penguin front may be omitted on the small penguin. Separate directions are given for the chick.

Back

*Using No. 6 (4½mm) needles and black yarn, cast on 7 sts for base. Working in stockinette st inc one st at end of next 12 rows; end with P row. 19 sts. * Cut off yarn and leave sts on holder. Repeat from * to *.
Next row K to end, then K across sts of first piece. 38 sts. Work 11 rows stockinette st across both sets of sts. Dec one st at each end of next and every foll 6th row until 22 sts rem. Work 5 rows without shaping.
Next row K9, (K2 tog) twice, K9. 20 sts.
Next row P8, (P2 tog) twice, P8. 18 sts.
Next row K7, (K2 tog) twice, K7. 16 sts.
Next row P6, (P2 tog) twice, P6. 14 sts.
Work 2 rows stockinette st over 14 sts. Bind off.

Front

** Using No. 6 (4½mm) needles and white yarn cast on 7 sts for base. Working in stockinette st inc one st at end of next 12 rows; end with P row. 19 sts. ** Cut off yarn and leave sts on holder. Repeat from ** to **.
Next row K to end, then K across sts of first piece. 38 sts.
Work 3 rows across both sets of sts. Dec one st at each end of next and every foll 6th row until 28 sts rem, work 1 row; end with P row.

Shading

Next row K9, strand in both colors of sewing thread over next 10 sts by knitting them tog with the white yarn, K9.
Next row P9, strand next 10 sts, P9.
Cont stranding in this way but work 1 more st of stranding at each side on every K row and *at same time* cont shaping by dec one st at each end of every 6th row as before until 24 sts rem.
P 1 row.
Next row Cont to strand (K1, K2 tog) to end. 16 sts.
Cut off all yarns. Change to black yarn.
P8, turn and leave rem sts on holder.
Inc one st at beg of next row and at this same edge on foll 5 rows. 14 sts. Work 7 rows in stockinette st. Dec one st at beg on next row and at this same edge on foll 7 rows. 6 sts. Work 1 row and then bind off.
Rejoin yarn to rem sts and work to match the first side, reversing the shaping.

Tail

Using No. 6 (4½mm) needles and black yarn, cast on 18 sts. Work 3 rows stockinette st. Dec one st at each end of next 6 rows.
Bind off.
Make another piece in same way.

Wings (alike)

Using No. 6 (4½mm) needles and black yarn, cast on 8 sts for outside and work 6 rows stockinette st. Inc one st at each end of next row. 10 sts. Work 5 rows stockinette st. Inc one st at each end of next row. 12 sts. Work 9 rows stockinette st.
Dec one st at each end of next and every foll 3rd row until 4 sts rem. Work 1 row stockinette st.
Bind off.
Make one more wing piece in black yarn and make two wing pieces in white yarn.

Finishing

Stitch seam at top of head and stitch side seams. Stuff penguin evenly and stitch base seam. Stitch a white wing piece to inside of a black wing piece and attach finished wing to side seam of body, 1in (2.5cm) below join of yarn at neck. Repeat for other wing.
Join together the side seams of the tail, leaving the cast-on edges open, and stuff tail evenly. Stitch cast-on edges of tail to back of penguin. Work loop of double yarn through outer seam of tail. Take 4 ends of yarn back through loop

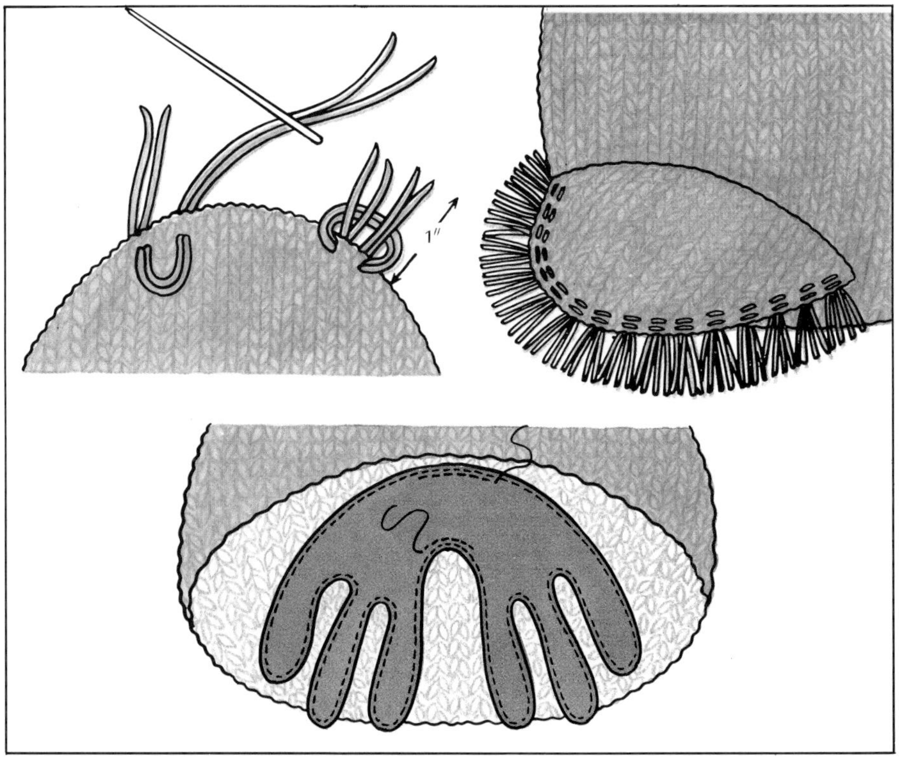

Terry Evans

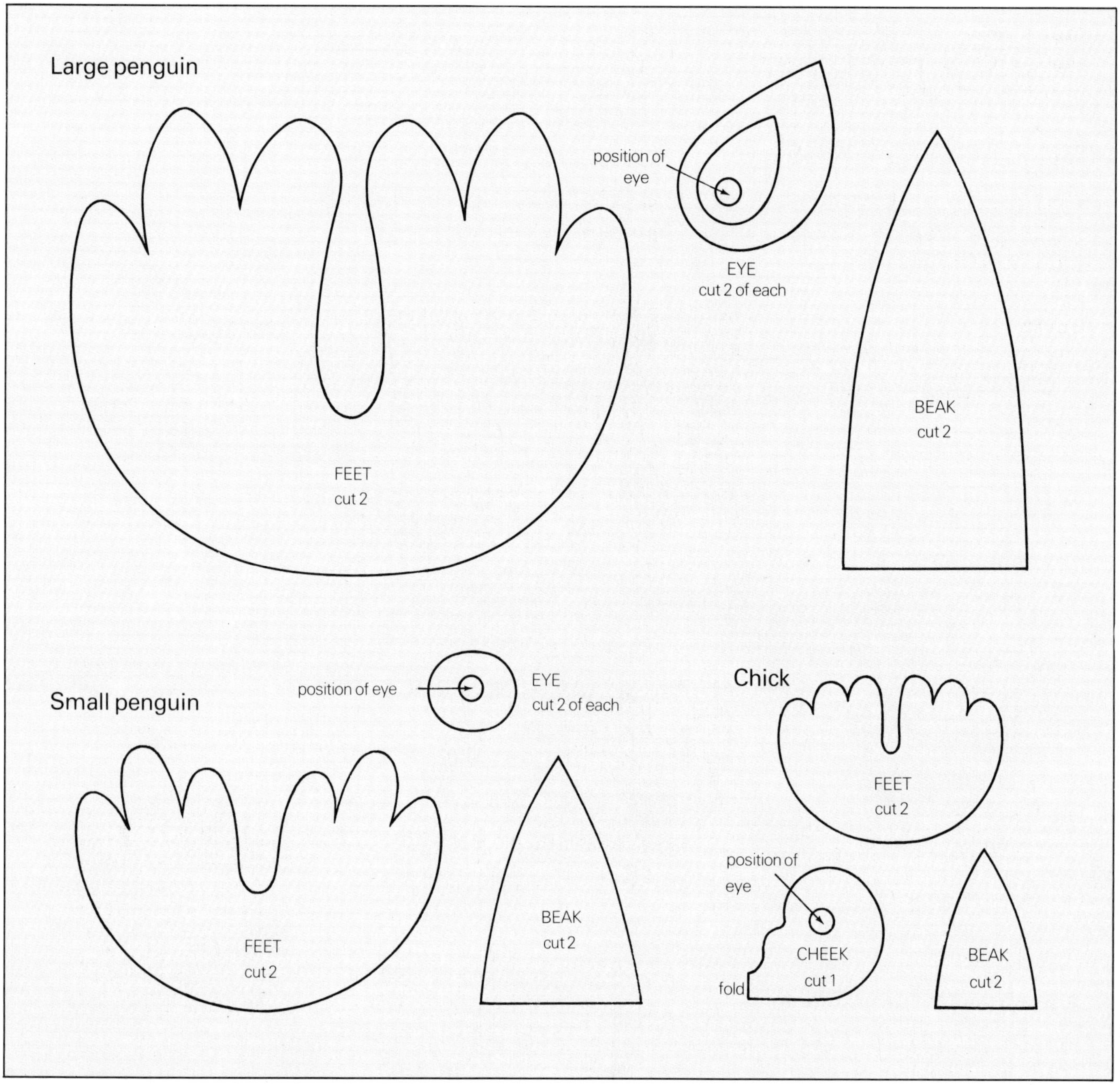

John Hutchinson

and pull firmly to secure. Work in same way around seam. Trim ends to 1in (2.5cm).
Trace off the patterns for the feet, beak and eye pieces. Cut out each piece twice from appropriate colored felt. Stitch two beak pieces tog down long edges using stab stitch. Stuff carefully and attach to body at front of head. Stitch the two pieces for the feet together all around, using stab stitches, and attach carefully to base of body with back edge to body seam. Stitch or glue eye pieces and sequins (if used) in position on head.

Chick
Body
Using No. 2 (3mm) needles and gray yarn, cast on 38 sts for neck edge. Work 21 rows rev stockinette st; end with P row.
Next row K 1 * (K2 tog) twice, K5, rep from * to last st, K1.
Next row P to end.
Next row K1, (K2 tog) 14 times, K1. Bind off.
Using charcoal yarn and with wrong side facing, pick up and K 26 sts evenly along cast-on edge of body. Work 14 rows rev stockinette st.
Next row P1, * (P2 tog) twice, P2, rep from * to last st, P1. 18 sts. K 1 row.
Next row (P2 tog) 9 times. Bind off.

Wings
Using No. 2 (3mm) needles and gray yarn used double, cast on 4 sts. Work 12 rows in garter st.
Next row K2 tog, K2.
Next row K2 tog, K1.
Next row K2 tog and bind off.
Make another wing in same way.

Finishing
Stitch back seam with right sides facing but leave a small opening at base. Stuff body evenly and stitch up opening.
Trace pieces for feet, cheeks and back and cut them out from appropriate colored felt.
Stitch the two pieces for the feet tog with stab stitches and attach them firmly to base of body. Stitch 2 pieces for beak tog around outside edge and stuff firmly. Stitch beak firmly to front of head.
Glue or stitch cheek pieces to face below beak and glue or stitch felt eye pieces (or sequins if used) in position. Stitch wings to each side of body $\frac{1}{2}$in (1.3cm) from join of yarn at neck.

Homemaker

Denim placemats

Hard-wearing and attractive, these simple placemats look great in a relaxed setting for lunch or a snack. They take only a few hours to make.

Materials

1yd (90cm) checked fabric, 36in (90cm) wide, for napkins
$1\frac{1}{8}$yd (1m) denim, 36in (90cm)-wide for mats
Blue thread
White buttonhole twist

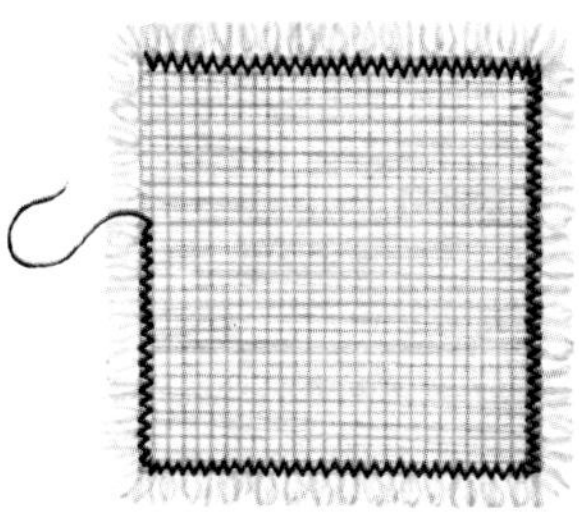

1 Cut out four napkins, measuring 14in (35.5cm) square, from the checked fabric. Machine-stitch a border 1in (2.5cm) in from the edges, preferably using zig-zag. Pull away the threads to form a 1in (2.5cm) fringe all around. Press.

2 Cut out four mats measuring $13\frac{1}{4}$in (33.5cm) by 19in (48.5cm) from the denim. Finish the raw edges by machine zig-zag stitch or by hand, using blue thread.

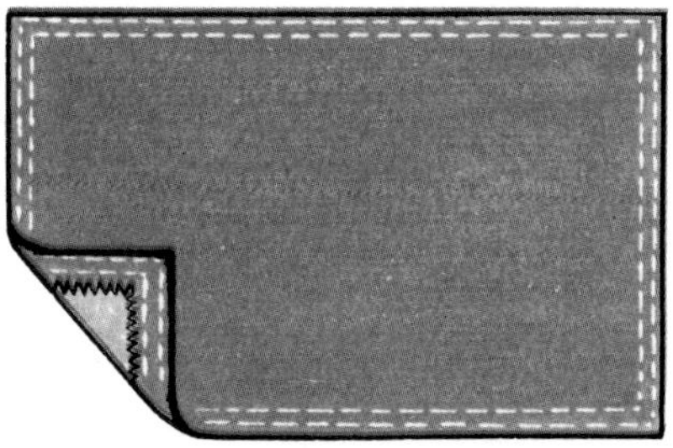

3 Fold over a $\frac{1}{2}$in (1.3cm) hem on the mats and press. Thread the top of the machine with buttonhole twist and adjust the top tension to take the thicker thread. Using the longest stitch on your machine, top-stitch a double border, approximately $\frac{1}{4}$in (6mm) apart, around edges.

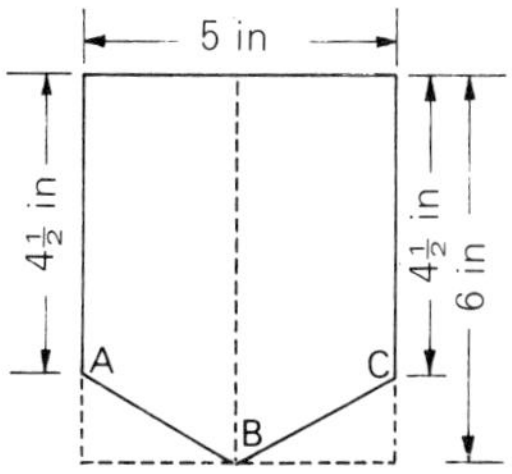

4 Cut out four denim rectangles for pockets – 5 x 6in (12.5 x 15cm). Mark points A and C $4\frac{1}{2}$in (11.5cm) from top and mark point B by folding piece in half lengthwise. Join A to B and C to B. Cut off corners.

5 Finish the raw edges of the pockets by machine stitch or by hand. Fold over a $\frac{1}{2}$in (1.3cm) hem and press. Using the buttonhole twist again, top-stitch a double border, approximately $\frac{1}{4}$in (6mm) apart around edges and across the center in desired pattern.

Steve Bicknell

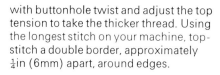

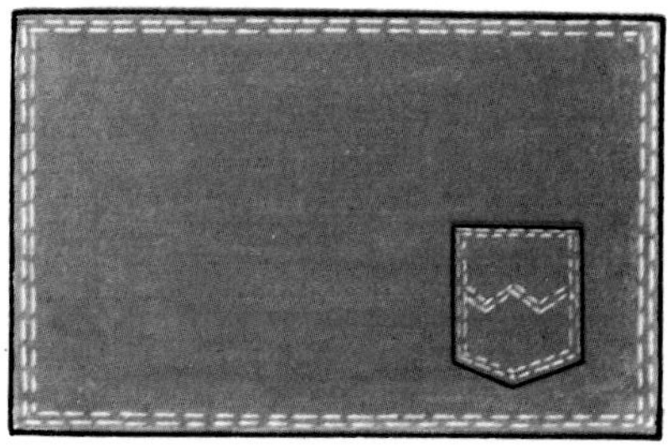

John Hutchinson

6 Press pocket and mat. Position the pocket on the right-hand bottom corner of each mat, pin in place, then machine stitch in place using blue thread.

Homemaker

Decorative trimmings

Make your own distinctive trimmings to match your décor; they're as easy as braiding! Apply them to pillows, lampshades, placemats—whatever needs brightening up.

Gathered ribbon

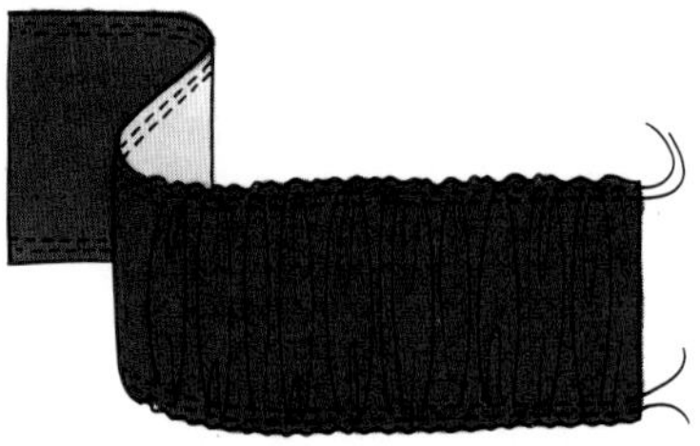

1 Run one or two rows of gathering stitches along a piece of ribbon. Draw up the threads to fit the article to which ribbon is to be attached. Slip stitch ribbon in place just under gathered edge.
2 For a variation, gather up both edges.

Ruched ribbon

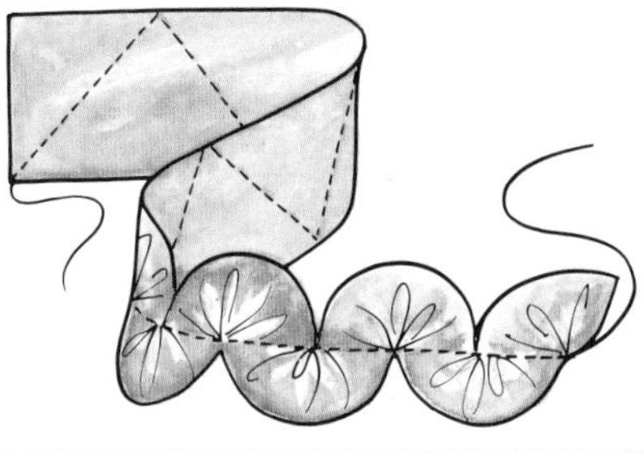

1 Measure and mark 1in (2.5cm) intervals along the ribbon length. For best results, use a fairly wide ribbon. The ribbon used here was $1\frac{1}{8}$in (3cm) wide.
2 Work diagonal lines of stitching from point to point.
3 Draw up threads and secure ends.

Finger cord

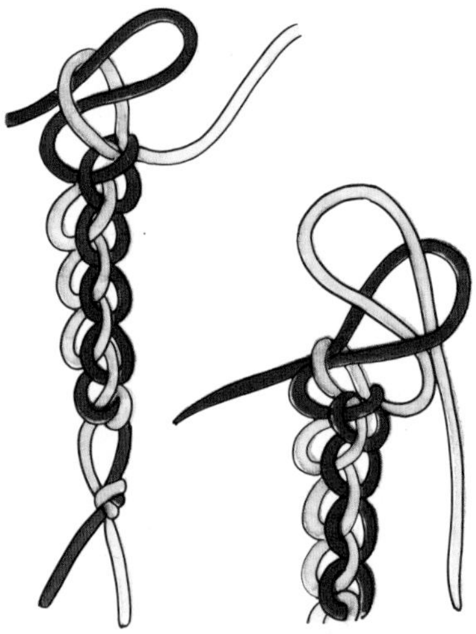

1 We used a decorative cord about $\frac{1}{8}$in (3mm) in diameter for this trimming. Begin by knotting two strands together.
2 Working upward, make a 2in (5cm) loop with the first cord and hold it in one hand. Make a similar loop with the second cord and hold it in the other hand.
3 Thread the first loop through the second loop. Pull the second loop tight around the neck of the first loop, as shown.
4 Make another loop the same size with the second cord and thread it through the first loop. Pull the first loop tight, as shown.
5 Continue making loops with each cord in turn, threading each through the opposite loop, up the length of the cord.

Plain braid

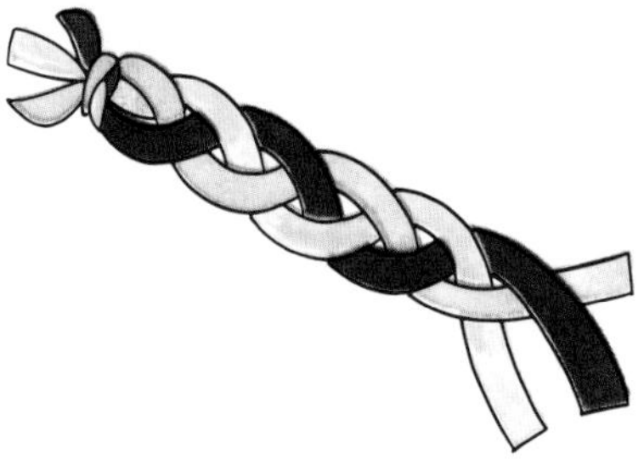

1 Work with three strands, each strand worked over the next. It is easier to get an even tension on the braid if you anchor the end to a board or ask someone to hold it.
2 You can also use six strands, using each length double.

From top to bottom: gathered ribbon, ruched ribbon, finger cord, plain braid, Greek braid, knotted-in fringe, tassel.

Greek braid

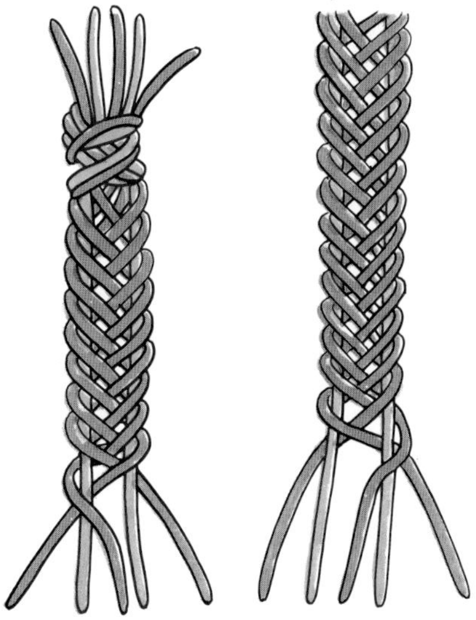

1 This braid is made from five strands; two strands form the foundation, on which the remaining three strands are braided. In the sample on the right, two blue cords are used as the foundation.
2 Knot all five strands together at one end and anchor the ends to a fixed object, such as an old board. Arrange the cords so that the "braiding" cords alternate with the foundation cords.
3 Bring the right-hand strand over two others into the middle.
4 Now one of the foundation strands will be on the outside; bring this back to the middle again over one strand.
5 Work these two movements first on the right and then on the left, to form a braid.

Knotted-in fringe

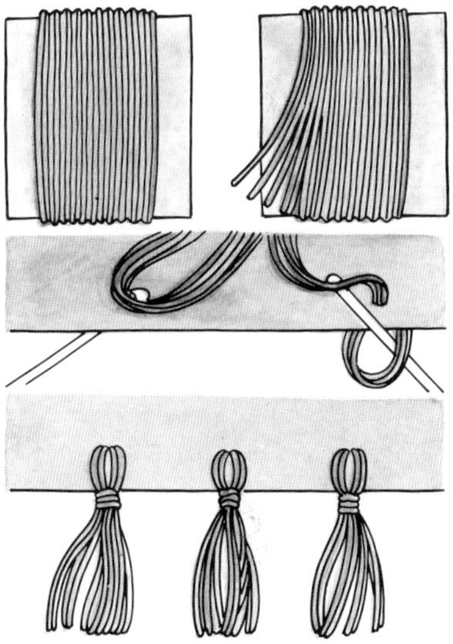

1 Cut a piece of cardboard the depth of the fringe and wind thread around it several times.
2 Cut threads along one edge, producing threads of equal length for fringing.
3 Push crochet hook through edge of loosely-woven fabric from WS to RS. Loop a few folded threads around the hook so that the ends of thread are even in length.
4 Draw the hook, and the folded threads, back through the fabric. Loop the free ends of the thread through the loop on the WS of the fabric. Pull the ends through and adjust the knot at the edge of the fabric.
5 Continue along the fabric edge, at equal distances.

Tassel

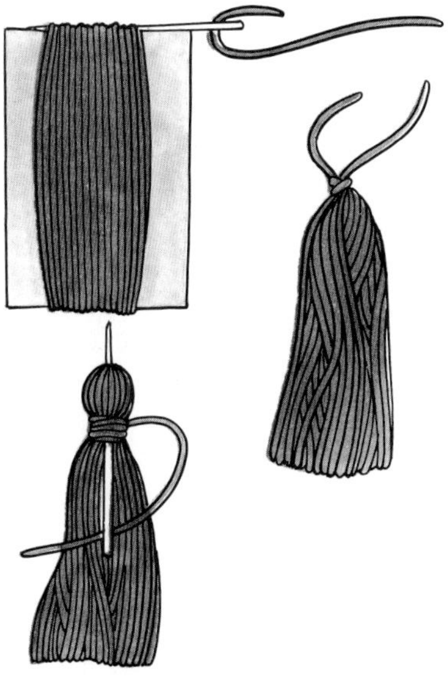

1 Cut a piece of cardboard the required length of the tassel. Wind the thread around the card many times.
2 Thread a needle and slide the thread through the loops at one end of the card; pull it up and tie it.
3 Cut the threads along the opposite side and remove the card.
4 Fold the group of threads to the other side of the tied thread, over the knot to hide it.
5 Place a tiny ball of absorbent cotton inside the tassel top to give it shape. Arrange the threads around the cotton to hide it.
6 Bind the bottom of the cotton ball with a piece of thread and pull it through the top of the tassel so it can be used to tie the tassel in place.

Paul Williams

Terry Evans

Homemaker

Adorable Annabelle

Our old-fashioned doll will tug at the heartstrings of every little girl. She's a model of perfection from her beautifully embroidered face to her neat buttoned shoes.

Gary Warren

Size
Height approximately 18in (45cm).
$\frac{3}{8}$in (1cm) seams are included throughout.

Materials
$\frac{5}{8}$yd (.5m) of 36in (90cm)-wide soft, closely-woven fabric in pale pink
$\frac{5}{8}$yd (.5m) of 36in (90cm)-wide floral print cotton fabric
$\frac{5}{8}$yd (.5m) of 45in (115cm)-wide white lawn
Stranded embroidery floss in pink, peach, brown, blue, black, white
Five small pearl buttons
Mohair-type yarn in light brown
1yd (1m) of $\frac{3}{8}$in (1cm)-wide velvet ribbon
$\frac{1}{2}$yd (.5m) of $\frac{1}{4}$in (6mm)-wide pink satin ribbon
$2\frac{3}{4}$yd (2.5m) of $\frac{5}{8}$in (1.5cm)-wide lace edging
$\frac{3}{4}$yd (.7m) of 3in (7.5cm)-wide eyelet lace edging
5in (12.5cm) of narrow white tape
$\frac{7}{8}$yd (.8m) of $\frac{1}{4}$in (6mm)-wide elastic
Artificial flowers, stuffing
Scraps of black leather
Matching thread, tracing paper
Dressmaker's carbon paper
6in (15cm) diameter embroidery hoop

Cutting out

1 Trace pattern pieces shown on pages 124-127 and, using dressmaker's carbon paper, mark them on the wrong side of the fabrics. Cut out all pieces. Cut one head piece only, for the back of the head.
2 For the head front, cut two pieces of pink fabric, each 10×10in (25×25cm). (The shape is cut later.)
3 From white lawn cut two 5in (12.5cm) diameter circles for bonnet; two pieces, each $10\frac{1}{2}$×10in (27×25cm) for the bloomers; one piece, $39\frac{1}{2}$×$8\frac{1}{2}$in (100×22cm) for the petticoat and one 3in (7.5cm) square for the handkerchief.
4 For skirt of dress cut one piece of floral print fabric, $35\frac{1}{2}$×8in (100×20cm); cut two pieces, each 9×6in (23×15cm), for sleeves.

Face and body

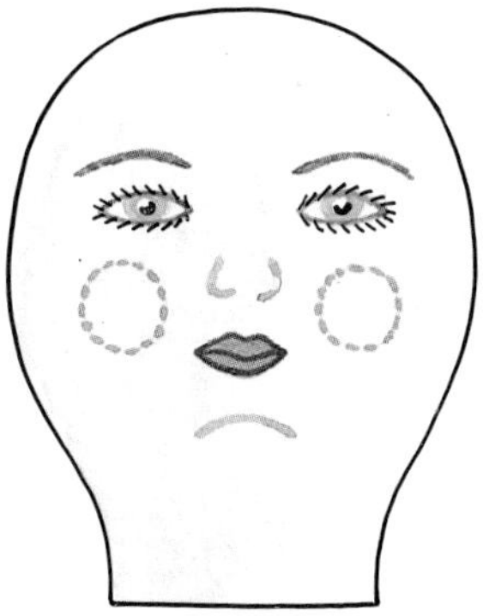

1 Trace the features from the pattern and transfer them to one of the pieces of front head fabric, using dressmaker's carbon paper. (To keep the fabric smooth, pin it to an ironing board or other working surface.) Lay the marked square of fabric over the plain square and stretch both in the embroidery hoop.
2 Using two strands of embroidery floss, work the features. When you have completed the embroidery remove from hoop and press it on the wrong side.
3 Place head pattern piece over embroidered fabric, making sure the features are correctly positioned. Cut away excess fabric to make front head.
4 Place back and front heads with right sides together; pin, baste and stitch, leaving neck open. Turn right side out; fill it firmly and pin neck closed.
5 Place the two body pieces with right sides together; pin, baste and stitch around body, starting at one side of the neck and working around to the other side of the neck. Carefully clip the seam allowance at curves and corners, using a pair of sharp-pointed scissors. Turn body right side out. Fill body firmly, starting with feet and hands and ending with the trunk. Pin neck edge closed.

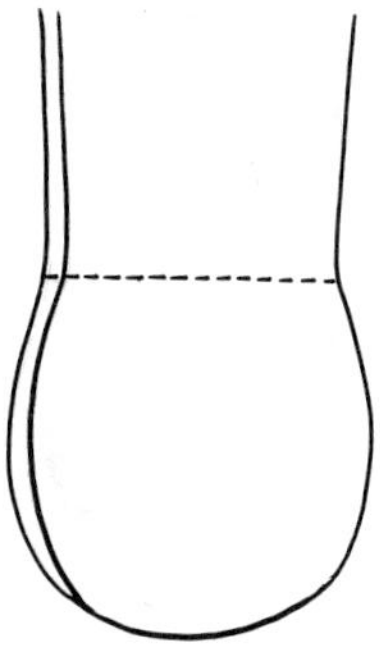

6 At ankles, knees, tops of legs, wrists and elbows, hand sew a line of running stitches across the limbs, squeezing the filling to form a joint, as shown.

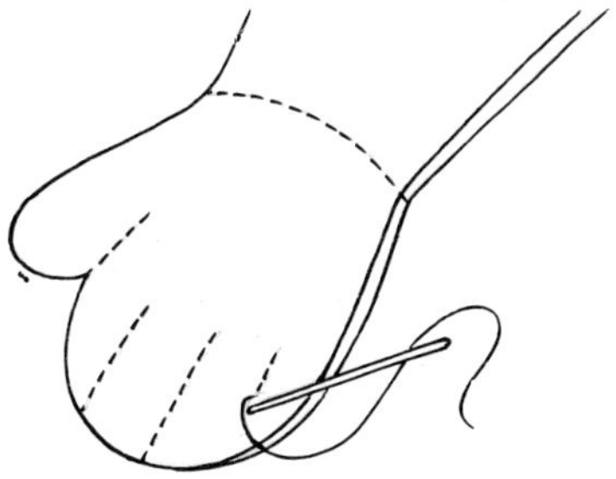

7 Hand sew neat lines of stitching on hands to give the appearance of fingers and thumbs, as shown. Gently bend the hands into a realistic-looking shape, as on the doll in the photographs.
8 Unpin the neck edges and firmly insert the neck down into the neck opening of the body; pin. Turn under raw edge of neck opening and carefully hand sew around this, firmly attaching the head to the body.
9 For the hair, cut pieces of yarn, about 20in (50cm) long. Place the yarn over the strip of white tape at right angles. Carefully stitch the yarn to the tape, using matching thread.

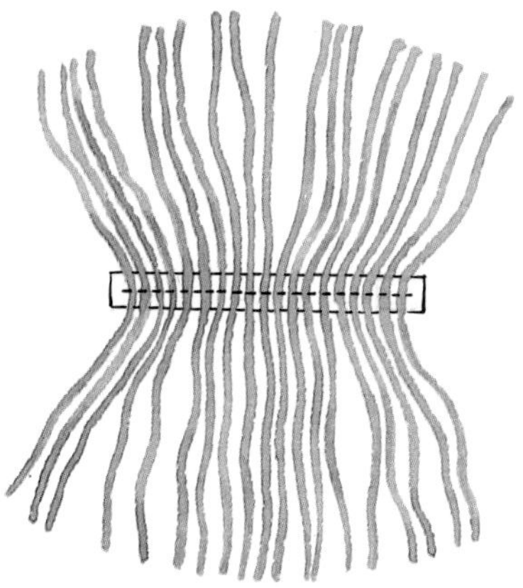

10 Place the hair piece on the head with the stitching running down the center to suggest a parting. Tuck under raw ends of tape and sew the hair to the head along the previous line of stitching.
11 Cut the satin ribbon in half and tie a small bunch of hair at each side of the face. Sew the bunches to the head with small invisible stitches. Decorate each bunch with a small sprig of flowers slipped into the hair immediately above each bow.

Choker and bonnet

1 Cut a piece of velvet ribbon to fit around the neck; turn in raw ends and sew them together at the back to form a choker, to hide the neck seamline.

Terry Evans

2 Stitch the ends of the eyelet lace together. Run a line of gathering stitches around the raw edge. Draw up gathering stitches to fit around the bonnet circle. Pin, baste and stitch the eyelet lace to the bonnet circle, with right sides together. Run another line of gathering stitches around the bonnet circle and draw them up to give the effect of a puffy cap. Pin and sew the bonnet to the doll's head around the seamline so that the stitches are not noticeable.

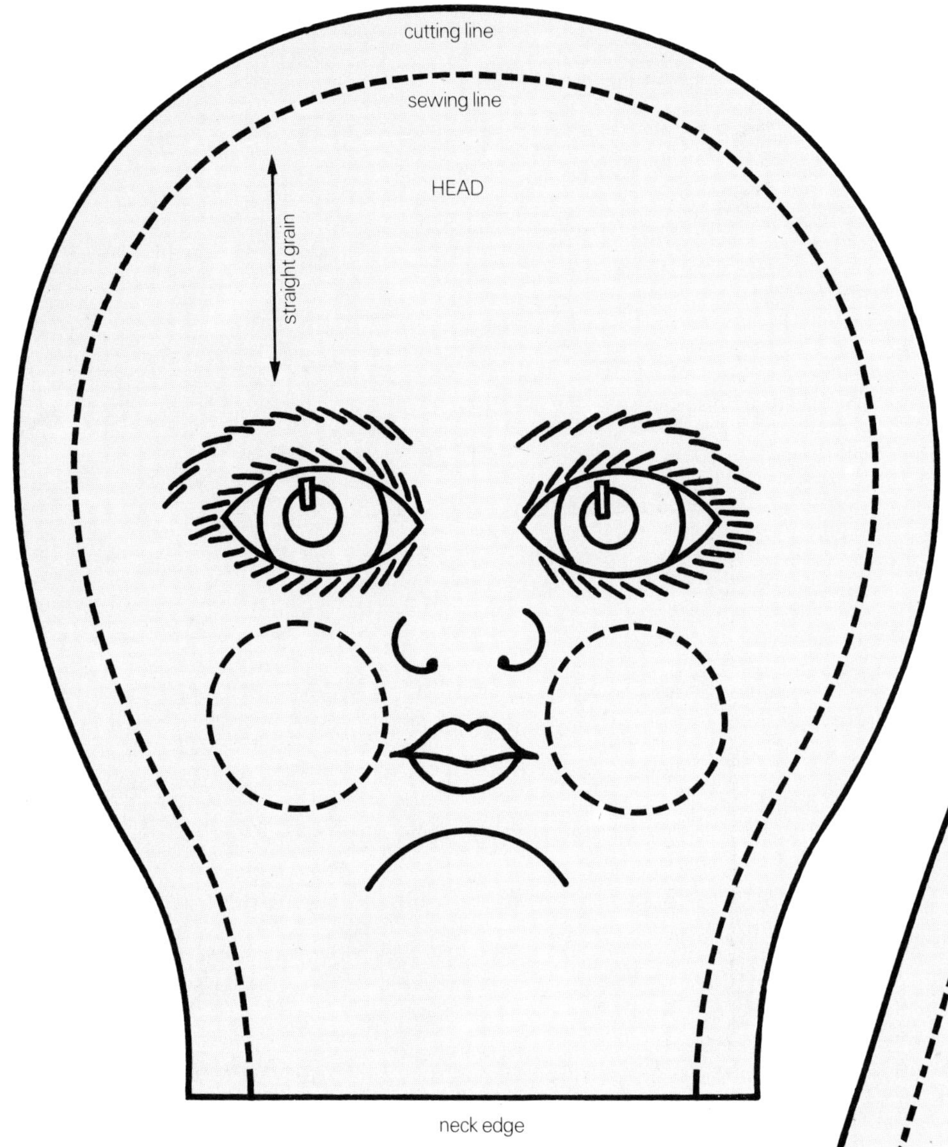
cutting line
sewing line
HEAD
straight grain
neck edge

cutting line
sewing line

SHOE BACK
cut 2 black leather
top stitch line

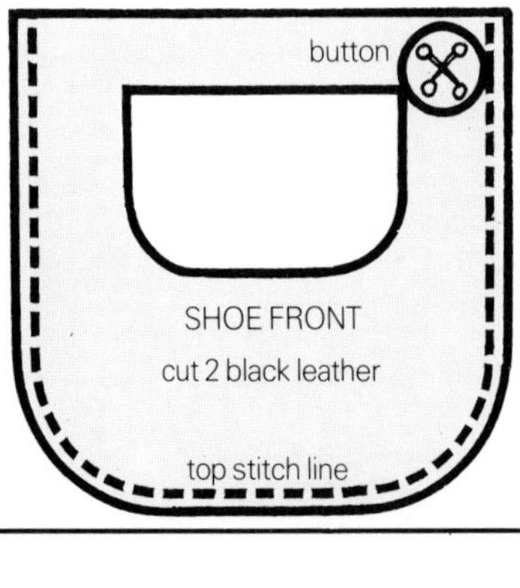
button
SHOE FRONT
cut 2 black leather
top stitch line

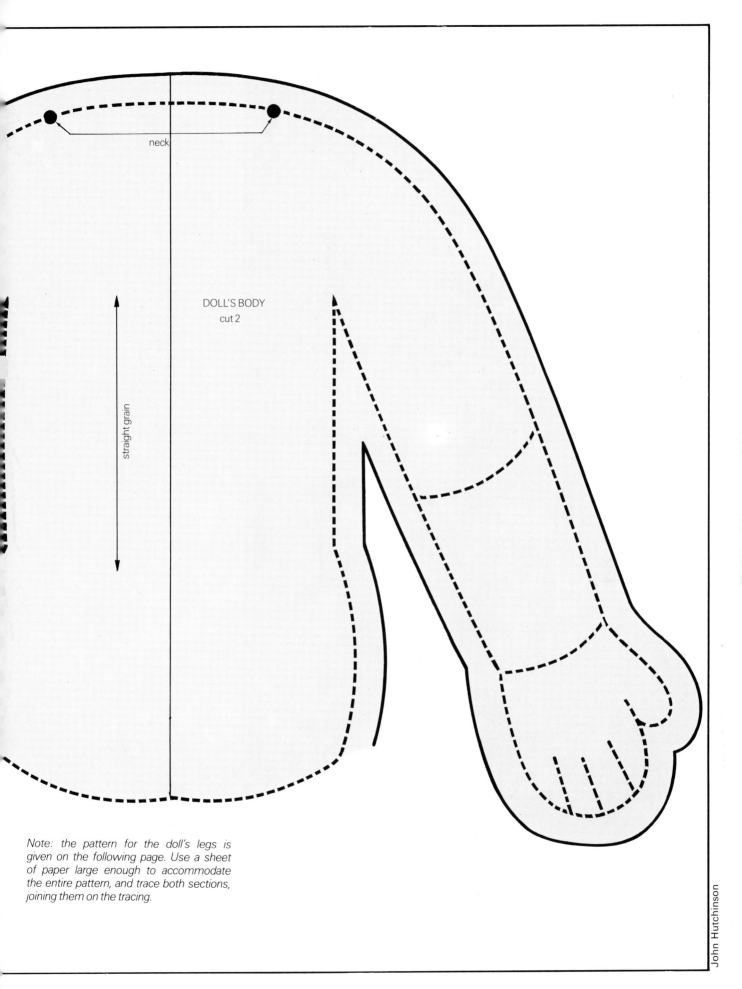

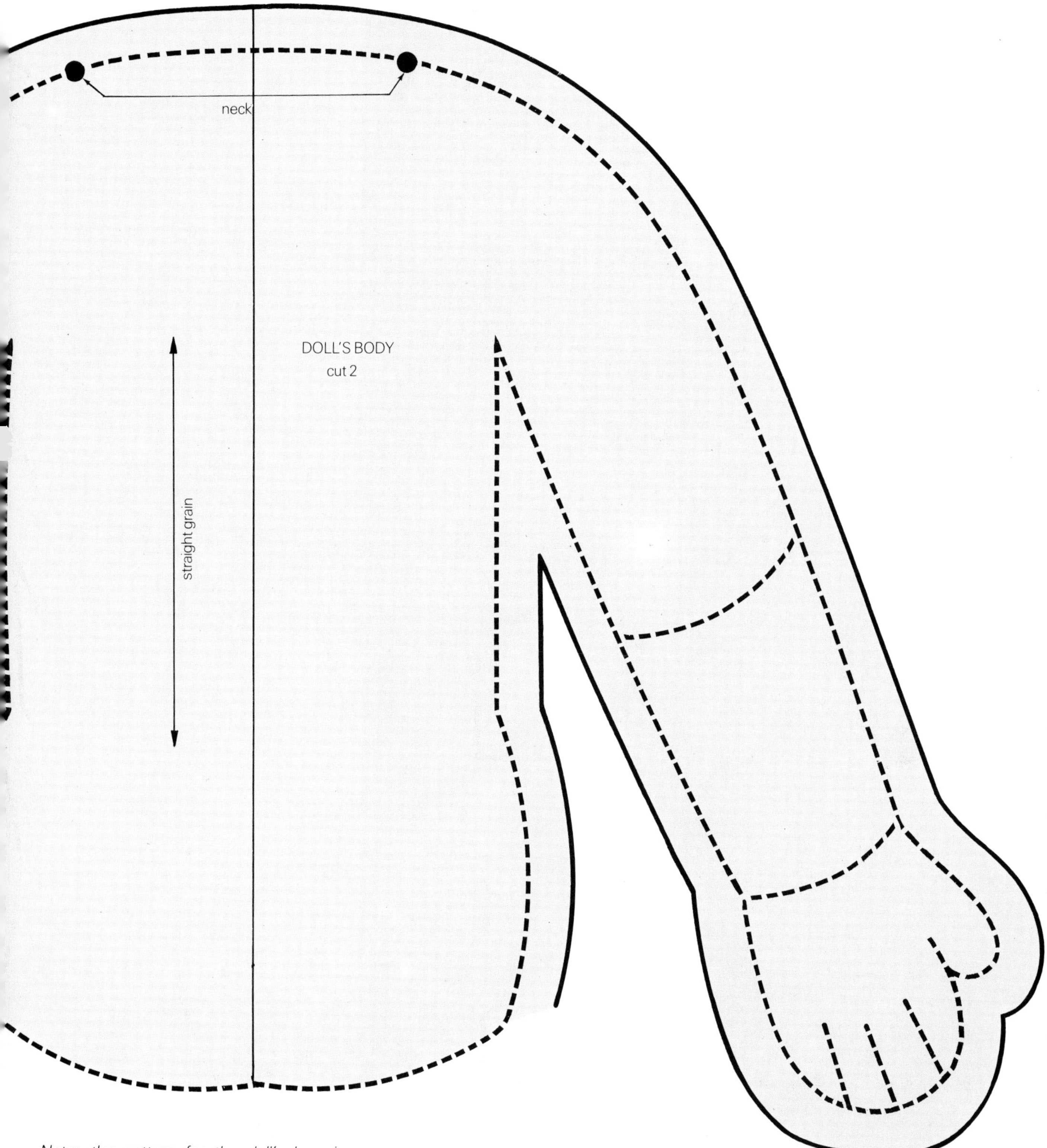

Note: the pattern for the doll's legs is given on the following page. Use a sheet of paper large enough to accommodate the entire pattern, and trace both sections, joining them on the tracing.

John Hutchinson

Note: the pattern for the doll's torso is given on the preceding page. Follow the instructions on that page for tracing the patterns.

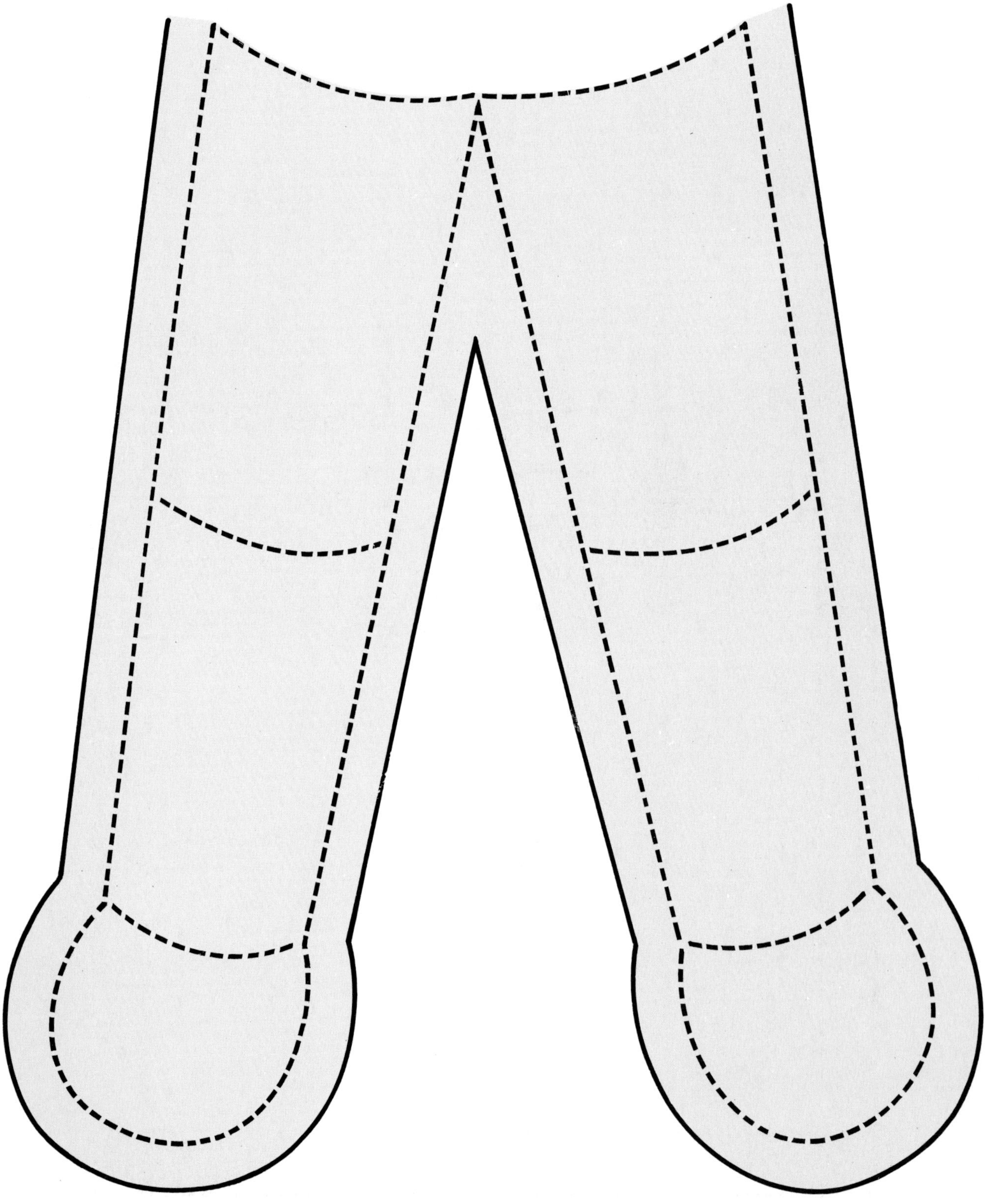

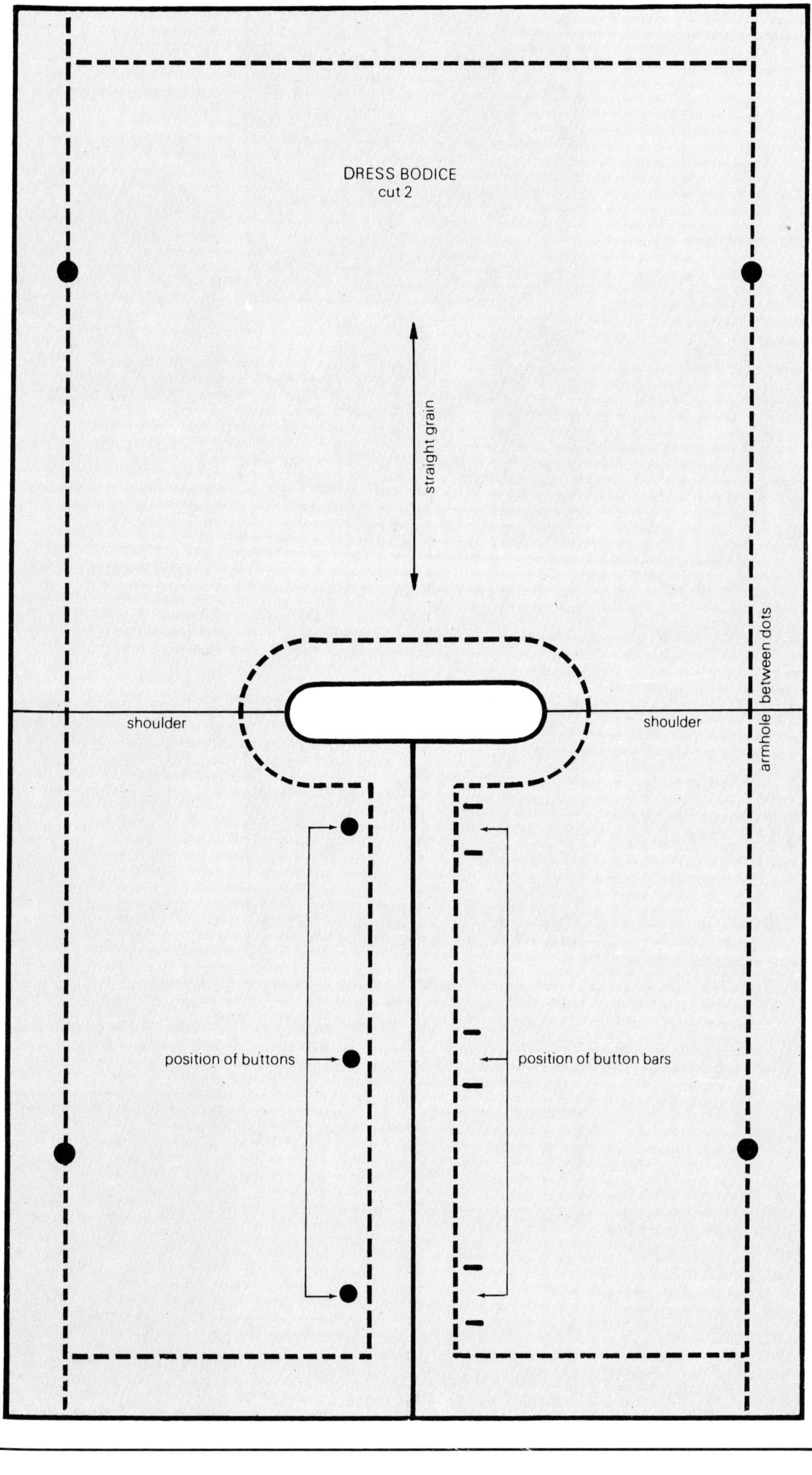

John Hutchinson